W9-BVT-077

Roadside History of
TEXAS

Leon C. Metz

Mountain Press Publishing Company
Missoula, Montana
1994

Copyright © 1994
Leon C. Metz

Third Printing, August 1995

Cover art © 1994 by Dick Gravender
Maps by Trudi Peek and Anna Breuninger

Library of Congress Cataloging-in-Publication Data

Metz, Leon Claire.
Roadside history of Texas / Leon C. Metz.
    p.   cm. — (Roadside history series)
Includes bibliographical references (p.   ) and index.
ISBN 0-87842-293-5 : $30.00 — ISBN 0-87842-294-3 : $18.00
1. Historic sites—Texas—History, Local.
3. Texas—Guidebooks.   4. automobile travel—Texas—Guidebooks.
I. Title.   II. Series.
F387.M47   1994   93-49677
917.6404'63—dc20   CIP

Printed in the U.S.A.

Mountain Press Publishing Company
P.O. Box 2399
Missoula, Montana 59801

*To my brother Will,
the Texas Twister*

Contents

Leon C. Metz. —Steve Lucas

About the Author

Leon C. Metz was born in Parkersburg, West Virginia, and has resided in El Paso since 1952.

He is past president of Western Writers of America, which honored him in 1985 with the prestigious Saddleman Award for his overall contributions to western writing and research. Before dedicating himself to writing full-time, Leon's experience ranged from working in an oil refinery to serving as a public affairs officer for MBank El Paso; in between, he held positions as a university archivist, as an executive assistant to former El Paso Mayor Tom Westfall, and as an assistant to a UT El Paso president.

Author of eleven other books and numerous articles, Metz is a lecturer on gunfighters, military lore, and the Mexican-United States border.

Also by Leon Metz

John Selman: Gunfighter

Dallas Stoudenmire El Paso Marshal

Pat Garrett: The Story of a Western Lawman

The Shooters

City at the Pass

Fort Bliss: An Illustrated History

Turning Points of El Paso, Texas

Desert Army: Fort Bliss on the Texas Border

Border: The U.S.-Mexico Line

Southern New Mexico Empire

El Paso Chronicles: A Record of Historical Events in El Paso, Texas

Facts About Texas

Area: Texas encompasses 275,416 square miles. It is large enough to hold fifteen smaller American states with 1,000 square miles left over. At its extremes, Texas spans 801 north-south miles and 773 east-west miles. Of the state's 254 counties, Brewster, which surrounds Big Bend National Park, is largest; at 5,935 square miles, it is nearly 20 percent larger than Connecticut. Rockwall County, just east of Dallas, is smallest at 154 square miles.

Boundary: The circumference of Texas runs 3,816 miles. Along its southeastern border is 624 miles of coastline where the land gives way to the Gulf of Mexico. Louisiana and Arkansas comprise the state's eastern border, while Oklahoma contains it on the north. New Mexico lies to the west of Texas, and the Mexican states of Chihuahua, Coahuila, Nuevo Leon, and Tamaulipas border Texas along its southwestern curves.

Weather: Texas summers average 78 degrees Fahrenheit in the panhandle and 84 in the lower Rio Grande Valley. Winter temperatures average 40 degrees in the panhandle and 61 along the lower Rio Grande. Nearly sixty inches of rain falls annually where the Sabine River separates Texas from Louisiana, while parts of Far West Texas average less than eight.

Mountains: Texas has ninety-one mountains over a mile in elevation, all in the trans-Pecos (Far West) region. Guadalupe Peak is the state's highest at 8,749 feet.

Forests: Woodlands cover more than 23 million Texas acres in forty-three counties. There are four national forests—Angelina, Davy Crockett, Sabine, and Sam Houston—in the eastern part of the state, north of Houston and Beaumont but south of Nacogdoches. Of the trees harvested, 83 percent are pine.

Rivers: All Texas rivers empty into the Gulf of Mexico (although the Canadian and the Red flow into the Mississippi River first). The Rio Grande separates Texas from Mexico for 1,270 miles. The Red River flows 726 miles between Texas and Oklahoma. The Brazos is wholly within Texas, beginning near Lubbock and meandering diagonally across the state until it reaches the gulf south of Houston. Other major streams include the Colorado, Trinity, Sabine, Nueces, Neches, Pecos, and Guadalupe.

Lakes: Texas has 5,175 square miles of lakes and streams and is second only to Alaska in volume of inland water. Toledo Bend Reservoir, between Texas and Louisiana, is the largest lake in or bordering Texas; its surface covers 185,000 acres. Lake Sam Rayburn, a reservoir on the Angelina River, is the largest body of water within the state. Other large reservoirs include Lake Livingston on the Trinity River, Lake Texoma on the Red River, and Falcon and Amistad international reservoirs on the Rio Grande. There are many other natural and man-made lakes as well.

Indian Reservations: The Tigua Indians have the smallest of the three Indian reservations in Texas; their 66 acres are in Ysleta, a suburb of El Paso. The 4,600-acre Alabama-Coushatta Reservation is in the Big Thicket country of East Texas between Livingston and Woodville. The Kickapoos occupy a 125-acre reservation near Eagle Pass on the Rio Grande.

- *Name:*
  From *tejas,* or "friendly"
- *Motto:*
  Friendship
- *Nickname:*
  Lone Star State
- *Bird:*
  Mockingbird
- *Tree:*
  Pecan
- *Flower:*
  Bluebonnet
- *Grass:*
  Sideoats Grama

- *Gem:*
  Texas Blue Topaz
- *Stone:*
  Petrified Palmwood
- *Dish:*
  Chili
- *Shell:*
  Lightning Whelk
- *Song:*
  "Texas, Our Texas"
- *Capital:*
  Austin

Texas Highway System

Highways: Texas has 77,552 miles of designated highways, of which 41,787 miles are paved.

Shortest Highway: Loop 168 in downtown Teṇaha in Shelby County is .074 miles long, or 391 feet.

Longest Highway: I-10 runs east-west across 878.7 miles of Texas countryside.

Number of Bridges in the Highway System: 30,000.

Longest Bridge: The Queen Isabella Causeway, connecting Port Isabel and South Padre Island, is 2.37 miles long.

Only Tunnel in the Highway System: At the lower end of the Houston Ship Channel, along Highway 146, is a 4,110-foot tunnel connecting Baytown and La Porte. The Washburn Tunnel, which runs between Pasadena and Galena Park near the upper end of the Houston Ship Channel, is not part of the state highway system.

(Portions of the preceding information came from *Texas Facts*, published by the Texas State Department of Highways and Public Transportation, Travel and Information Division, Austin.)

Texas Chronology

Various groups of paleo-Americans inhabited Texas for many centuries before recorded history. Their cultures are known as Clovis, Folsom, and Plainview. These people were ancestors of the native tribes who first greeted, then struggled against, European intruders.

1519   Alvar Alvarez de Piñeda mapped the Texas coast. He called it "Amichel."

1528   Alvar Núñez Cabeza de Vaca, a shipwrecked sailor, embarked on a nine-year trek across Texas.

1540   Francisco Vásquez de Coronado led a Spanish expedition across northern Texas in search of wealth in the Seven Cities of Cíbola. He discovered Palo Duro Canyon in 1541.

1542   Hernando de Soto's expedition explored part of northeast Texas.

1581   The Rodríquez-Chamuscado Expedition traveled north from Mexico and passed through what is now El Paso.

1598   Juan de Oñate, a Mexican conquistador, led 500 pilgrims north from Santa Barbara, Chihuahua. On April 30, twenty miles southeast of modern El Paso, the colonists celebrated the first thanksgiving in North America. On May 4, they crossed the Rio Grande at a ford they named El Paso del Rio del Norte, "the Pass Across the River of the North." The ford became "El Paso del Norte" on maps, the namesake of El Paso, Texas.

1680   The Pueblo Indian Revolt in northern New Mexico sent the Tigua and Piro Indians scurrying south with the Spanish into present-day Texas, where they established communities called Ysleta and Socorro. Their towns and missions were the first in Texas.

1685   René Robert Cavelier, Sieur de La Salle, established Fort St. Louis in the Matagorda or Lavaca Bay area between Houston and Corpus Christi.

1691   Domingo Terán de los Ríos blazed the Old San Antonio Road.

1718   Fray Antonio de San Buenaventura Olivares established Mission San Antonio de Valero, later known as the Alamo, on May 1. Four days later Martín de Alarcón, charged with protecting the mission, founded the presidio San Antonio de Bexar and dubbed the nearby village San Antonio.

1749   Spanish governor's palace constructed in San Antonio.

1772   San Antonio becomes the capital of Spanish Texas.

1779   Gil Antonio Ibarvo built Old Stone Fort in Nacogdoches.

1793   Nuestra Señora del Refugio Mission, the last Spanish mission in Texas, is constructed.

1803   The Louisiana Purchase established the northeastern boundary of Texas.

1812   The Gutiérrez-Magee filibustering expedition entered Texas.

1813   *Graceta de Tejas*, the first newspaper in Texas, began publishing.

1821   Mexico expelled Spain and authorized Moses Austin to settle 300 American families in Texas.

1823   Stephen F. Austin organized a band of "rangers" for defense against Indians.

1826   The Republic of Fredonia was proclaimed at Nacogdoches.

1827   Mexico adopted a constitution for Texas and Coahuila.

1835   The Texas Revolution started. Texas Rangers were "formally" organized and stationed in small, scattered detachments along the Indian frontier.

1836   On February 24 Gen. Antonio López de Santa Anna laid siege to the Alamo. On March 6 the Alamo fell. On March 27 the Goliad massacre occurred. Sam Houston's victory on April 21 at San Jacinto resulted in Texas independence. In October, Texas became a republic after being refused admission into the United States.

1837   Houston became capital of the Republic of Texas.

1840   Austin became the Texas capital. Texas Rangers won important victories over Comanches in the Council House and Plum Creek engagements.

1841   The 400-man Texas-Santa Fe Expedition left Austin but was captured in New Mexico.

1842   Mexico invaded Texas and seized San Antonio. The capital moved to Washington-on-the-Brazos.

1843   Texas's invasion of Mexico failed as the Mier Expedition surrendered in Mexico on February 11. The notorious black bean lottery started the random executions of Texas prisoners on March 25.

1845   The word "maverick" came into common use as a reference for unbranded cattle owned by Samuel Maverick. On December 29 Texas joined the Union as the 28th state.

1846   The Mexican War started after United States and Mexican troops skirmished inside the Nueces Strip near Brownsville on April 25.

1848   On February 2 the Treaty of Guadalupe Hidalgo established the Rio Grande as the boundary between Texas and Mexico, ending the Mexican War.

1849   The Neighbors-Ford Trail between Austin and El Paso was blazed.

1850   In compliance with the federal Compromise of 1850, the present boundaries of Texas were established.

1852   Beginning of the King Ranch in Nueces County.

1858   Butterfield Overland Mail coaches first rolled through Texas.

1861   A secession convention met in Austin on January 28. By February 23 Texas ratified a referendum to abandon the Union and join the Confederate States of America.

1865   Upon the ending of the Civil War, Gen. Gordon Granger declared U.S. authority over Texas. On June 19 he proclaimed freedom for Texas slaves, and that date became known as "Juneteenth."

1866   The Goodnight-Loving Trail opened from Fort Belknap, Texas, to Fort Sumner, New Mexico.

1867   The carpetbag era started in Texas with the removal of Governor James W. Throckmorton. The Sutton-Taylor feud erupted in Mason County. The Chisholm Trail connecting San Antonio with Abilene, Kansas, opened.

1869   The state legislature (Texas Reconstruction Convention) in Austin debated the merits of merging West Texas with southern New Mexico and calling it the "Territory of Montezuma." The project failed by a tight vote.

1869   A state of "West Texas" was proposed with San Antonio as its capital. The territory included today's South Texas.

1870   Reconstruction called for organization of the state police. Texas was readmitted to the Union.

1874   The Frontier Battalion (Texas Rangers) was created to protect Texas settlements.

1883   The cowboys went on strike in the Texas panhandle.

1895   The notorious gunslinger John Wesley Hardin was killed in El Paso by Constable John Selman in August.

1898   The Rough Riders trained in San Antonio for service in Cuba during the Spanish-American War.

1900   A hurricane and tidal wave inundated Galveston on September 8-9; it was called the worst disaster in American history.

1901   Oil "gushed" from the Spindletop field near Beaumont.

1905   Texas theaters started showing motion pictures.

1908   Lyndon Baines Johnson was born on August 27 near Stonewall, Texas.

1918   Texas ratified the 18th Amendment, calling for prohibition.

1921   The January 8 discovery of oil on land owned by the University of Texas made it one of the richest schools in the nation.

1925   "Ma" Ferguson became the first female governor of Texas on January 20. On July 30, the largest earthquake ever recorded in Texas took place. So far as we know, the two events were not related.

1935   A new state made from the panhandles of Texas and Oklahoma, called Texlahoma, was proposed on May 25. Congress created Big Bend National Park on June 20.

1936   The Texas Centennial Exposition celebrated 100 years of Texas independence.

1937   The first Dallas Cotton Bowl game was played between Texas Christian University and Marquette.

1941   M. D. Anderson Hospital was authorized at Houston.

1947   A ship explosion in the harbor at Texas City killed 500 and injured 3,000.

1948   Lyndon B. Johnson won the primary election for the U.S. Senate by an eighty-seven vote landslide.

1953   Congress restored the Texas tidelands to the state. Texas and the U.S. government had been arguing over ownership of the tidelands for years. At stake was who owned the area's oil.

1954   The Falcon Dam on the Rio Grande was completed.

1957   Texas opened its first toll highway, connecting Dallas and Fort Worth.

1960   The Houston Oilers joined the American Football League, and the National Football League welcomed the Dallas Cowboys. The Houston Colt .45s (later the Astros) were awarded a major league baseball franchise. On June 1, the U.S. Supreme Court agreed that Texas owned its tidelands, or offshore areas, which contained oil. On July 14 John F. Kennedy chose Lyndon B. Johnson as his vice presidential running mate.

1962   Construction began on the Manned Spacecraft Center at Houston.

1963   Upon the assassination of JFK in Dallas, LBJ became the nation's 36th president. The Chamizal boundary dispute, the greatest ever between the United States and Mexico, was settled, returning 437 acres of El Paso to Mexico.

1964   The Manned Spacecraft Center near Houston became permanent headquarters for U.S. astronauts.

1965   The Astrodome opened in Houston.

1967   Barbara Jordan of Houston was sworn in as the first black senator from Texas.

1971   Audie Murphy, a native of Greenville and the most decorated hero of World War II, died in a plane crash on May 31.

1972   The Washington Senators baseball club moved from Washington, D.C., to Arlington, Texas, becoming the Texas Rangers.

1973   Lyndon Baines Johnson died a of heart attack on January 22 at age sixty-four. The Manned Spacecraft Center in Houston was renamed the Lyndon B. Johnson Space Center. In November Leon Jaworski, a Democrat from Houston, became Watergate special prosecutor. His findings eventually forced President Richard Nixon to resign.

1979   William Clements was sworn in January 16 as the first Republican governor of Texas since Reconstruction.

1991   Ann Richards was sworn in as first female Texas governor since Ma Ferguson.

INTRODUCTION

Gone to Texas

The enemy has demanded our surrender, otherwise the garrison shall be put to the sword. I have answered the demand with a cannon shot, and our flag still waves proudly from the walls.

William Travis, letter to "the people of Texas and all Americans in the world." February 24, 1836, the Alamo.

The letters G.T.T.—written, carved, or spoken—were familiar in the United States during the early 1800s. They meant "Gone to Texas," which is where many farmers, adventurers, and fugitives from the new nation went to start a better life for themselves (or to escape hassles from the law or the bank). Texas was a land of opportunity from the earliest times.

Twelve thousand years ago, in perhaps even more opportune days at the end of the last ice age, the region now known as Texas provided a refuge for hunters and wanderers tramping down ice-free corridors. Archaeologists and others who study these ancient colonists call them paleo-Indians and describe them basically as a stone-age people who left only a few rudimentary weapons and tools to document their existence. In time, these people were succeeded by those known as the Archaic Indians, who conceived a variety of tools and weapons including the bow and arrow. Some of the Archaic Indians ceased their nomadic hunter-gatherer lifestyle and turned to farming.

Anthropologists estimate that some 30,000 Indians, in nine distinct groups or affiliations, lived in the area of Texas when the first Europeans arrived. The Caddos of eastern Texas (and into Arkansas) were probably the largest group. Along the Gulf Coast from north to south lived Attacapas, Karankawas, and Coahuiltecans (who also extended into northeast Mexico and well inland). Lipans roamed the Edwards Plateau, south of the vast domain ruled by Comanches and west of a group reputed to be ritualistic cannibals, the Tonkawas. Wichitas bearing fearsome facial and body tattoos occupied the middle Red River region between the Caddos and Comanches. And Jumanos, first cousins of the Pueblos, frequently settled in cliff dwellings along the upper Rio Grande in west Texas. Less nomadic and warlike than tribes to their east, the Jumanos artfully irrigated and cultivated the earth to raise crops.

Texas history is replete with references to other Indian groups, mainly Shawnees, Cherokees, Seminoles, Delawares, and Kickapoos. These latecomers, driven from or fleeing the expanding United States, entered Texas as refugees. The Shawnees came from Ohio, West Virginia, and Tennessee; the Cherokees from the southern Appalachians; the Seminoles from Florida; the Delawares from Indiana and Missouri after first being evicted from their homelands south of New England. The Kickapoos came to Texas from Wisconsin.

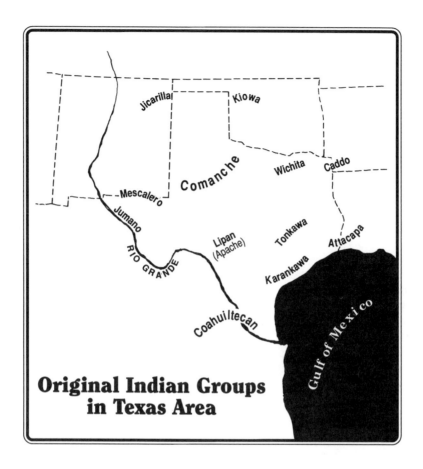

Original Indian Groups in Texas Area

The Cherokees and Seminoles were two of the "five civilized tribes" (Chickasaws, Chocktaws, and Creeks were the others) from the southeastern U.S. forced by the government to lands west of the Mississippi River during the 1830s along the Trail of Tears. Some Seminoles who later served as scouts for the U.S. Army won Congressional Medals of Honor for their service along the Texas-Mexico border from the 1860s to the 1880s.

Of those Indians indigenous to Texas, the Comanches were perhaps the most fearsome. Although their culture embodied tradition, religion, and humanity, their lack of neighborly ways earned them a label as barbarians.

Centuries ago the Comanches followed herds of buffalo down the boundless, windswept plateaus of central North America until they landed on the Texas steppes, better known to Europeans and Americans as the Llano Estacado, or Great Plains. There the hunters encountered a foreign animal that profoundly affected their lives: the mustang. After being released in 1680 by Spanish rancheros fleeing the Pueblo Revolt in northern New Mexico, and with few natural enemies and plenty of grazing lands on the Texas steppes, the horses

3

quickly multiplied into herds so vast and tightly packed that some storytellers claimed surefooted men could cross the plains by walking on the horses' backs. While that may be a slight stretch of the truth, calling the Comanches "Lords of the South Plains," as authors Ernest Wallace and E. Adamson Hoebel did, was no exaggeration.

The Comanches lost no time learning to ride and control the mustangs. From horseback they hammered their southern neighbors, the Lipan Apaches, harassing them near the Nueces, Guadalupe, and Llano rivers. To their northwest and southwest, they sent the Jicarilla and Mescalero Apaches reeling even farther west, toward Arizona and away from such harassment. The Kiowas, who lived north of the Comanches, and the newcomer Kickapoos formed uneasy alliances with these Lords of the South Plains.

With horses the Comanches halted French encroachment in Texas and organized murderous raids against the Spanish deep into Mexico. The mounted spoilers returned home with booty and captives, usually women and young children, and left in their wake death, desolation, wailing survivors, smoldering buildings, and slaughtered livestock.

One notorious escapade occurred in 1836 when a hundred Comanches and Kiowas, with a smattering of Caddos, demanded a cow from Parker's Fort near the Navasota River, a tributary of the Brazos. The whites refused to concede the cow, so the Indians killed seven settlers, scalped and castrated Parker, raped the women, and took two women and three children captive. One of those youngsters, nine-year-old Cynthia Ann Parker, lived with the Comanches for many years, and her story is a classic of Texas history.

Spanish and French Explorers

Few Mexican settlers entered Texas during the early times. Trackless expanses of desert, danger, and loneliness kept most of them from venturing north. And those who crossed the quicksands of the Rio Bravo del Norte (Rio Grande) in rustic ox carts probably wondered if even God could find them so far in the middle of nowhere. The roots of Mexican hesitation to colonize Texas can be traced to the sorts of emigrants Spain dispatched to Mexico; most were soldiers, politicians, and businessmen—adventurers who came as exploiters, not settlers. They sought gold. A typical Spaniard's heartfelt wish was to return to Spain as a rich hacendado.

The huge gold caches Spain stripped from the Aztecs in Mexico and from the Incas in Peru did nothing to dispel the notion that more opulence lay to the north. That's what drove men like Francisco Vásquez de Coronado to penetrate the unknown territory. He and others had heard of the fabulously rich "Seven Cities of Cíbola" from Alvar Núñez Cabeza de Vaca, treasurer of a fleet wrecked during a storm off the Texas coast in 1528.

In an odyssey that lasted several years, Cabeza de Vaca and three other survivors of the wrecked fleet, convinced that no rescue was forthcoming, decided to travel west across what is now Texas. During their years-long odyssey they met and lived with various Indians who frequently regarded the strangers as gods because of their apparently supernatural powers. The travelers encouraged this superstitious belief as a matter of survival. Once, near what is now San Angelo, Cabeza de Vaca performed heart surgery on an Indian. With a stone knife he removed an arrow and stitched the wound closed with deer sinew. The man recovered, and this impressed everyone.

When the wanderers finally crossed the desert into northern Sonora in late March 1536, the weary foursome met a Spanish slaving expedition and came within a trigger pull of being executed. Fortunately, an official intervened in time to save his countrymen, and Cabeza de Vaca then persuaded the Spaniards not to kill or enslave the friendly Indians who had guided his party across the desert.

Upon their return to Mexico City, where the viceroy received the wayfarers as heroes, Cabeza de Vaca reported seeing the Seven Cities of Cíbola from afar during his trek across Texas. How history might have changed if he had been shot or (more commonly) strangled by the slavers. To secure the wealth of these "golden cities," the Spanish organized expeditions called *entradas* and sent missionaries along to carry the Word of God to the untutored natives.

The clamor for gold in the fabled cities aroused Coronado, a Spanish nobleman and soldier, whose *entrada* left Sonora on April 22, 1540, and forded the Rio Grande near what is now Albuquerque. By midyear Coronado had entered the Texas panhandle and scribbled comments in his journal about the wonders of Palo Duro Canyon, then he proceeded to the grassy plains of Kansas. No golden cities embraced him. In 3,000 miles he had found only poor Indians. And he had gazed upon the buffalo.

From the Crown's point of view, Coronado's expedition was a failure. He received no recognition for opening an empire. The greedy Spaniards turned to wealth buried *in* the earth, mining with pick and shovel and gunpowder charges. Mining towns such as Zacatecas, Durango, and Parral sprang up as bastions of Spanish power inside seas of swarming, marauding Indians. Few colonists filled the voids of open, empty, hungry spaces. Spain had neglected to send farmers to the New World.

To the east, the French penetrated the mouth of the Mississippi. Followers of Hernando de Soto reached the vicinity of today's Texarkana in 1542. Other French explorers landed at Lavaca Bay in February, establishing Fort St. Louis near the present site of Vanderbilt, Texas. Some parties traveled inland as well. Even though the fort withered from the onslaught of disease and Indians, the French established a tenuous claim to northeast Texas.

To secure the perimeter of its unknown empire, Spain encouraged colonists to move north. During an *entrada* in 1598, Spanish conquistador Juan de Oñate led 500 men, women, and children into what is now New Mexico. On April 30, near the present-day city limits of El Paso, they celebrated the first North American thanksgiving. This celebration took place more than two decades before the Pilgrim fathers started the New England tradition. When the feasting and baptizing ended, Oñate fastened his cross upon a tree and took possession, *La Toma*, the scribes called it, for God and King Philip of Spain, of all lands watered by the Rio Grande.

Four days later Oñate forded the Rio Grande at a place he called El Paso del Rio del Norte (the Pass Across the River of the North). Oñate's El Paso would become a major metropolis in Texas three centuries later, the largest American city on the Mexican border. And the 1,600-mile route he blazed between Mexico City and Santa Fe became known as El Camino Real (the King's Highway or Royal Road). Because of this, West Texas developed independently from the rest of the vast province.

El Paso del Norte, today's Ciudad Juárez, Chihuahua, was established in 1659. During the New Mexico Pueblo Revolt of 1680, the towns of Ysleta and Socorro were founded near El Paso del Norte as villages for friendly Indians (Tiguas and Piros) who had fled south with the Spanish refugees. Ysleta and much of Socorro are today inside the city of El Paso, Texas.

The Struggle to Colonize

While Spanish Texas was fighting for independence, today's West Texas belonged to New Mexico or Chihuahua. Who controlled it depended upon who was collecting the taxes.

For a while, Spain owned the Louisiana Territory, a gargantuan landscape encompassing the Mississippi River west to the Rocky Mountains and north to the vaguely identified Canadian border. France had ceded that area to Spain in 1762, but the Spanish were unequipped to either consolidate or govern it. They returned it to the French in 1800, and President Thomas Jefferson sized up the situation. He did not want the French threatening American expansion. Fortunately, he caught Napoleon short of finances and purchased the sprawling region in 1803 for $15 million.

This put the Americans up against Spanish Texas to the east and south. To partly fill the Texas vacuum and show the flag, Spain built a few isolated, hastily constructed missions and presidios (forts). The missions were Catholic churches for Indians, usually operated by Franciscan fathers. If Indians were not present, a "mission" did not exist. The presidios offered protection to the missions.

The most important mission was San Antonio de Valero, with its protective presidio, San Antonio de Bexar. What's left of the mission complex today is the Alamo. The accompanying town, Bexar, we now call San Antonio. After secularization, the mission made a natural fort. Soldiers from Alamo del Parras in Coahuila transferred to San Antonio. Some historians suspect the Alamo's name stemmed from the military's point of origin. Others believe it was named for the cottonwoods growing along the San Antonio River, which in Spanish are called *alamo*.

Four additional missions were built at San Antonio. In 1731 the government imported fifteen Canary Island families to strengthen the colony because supplying and protecting the missions was arduous, expensive, and time-consuming. Eventually the crushing expenses encouraged Spain to gradually withdraw from its East Texas holdings. In 1772, the Texas provincial capital became San Antonio.

With Spain barely hanging on to Texas, filibusters struck. A filibuster is a descriptive term rarely used anymore, but newspapers in the 1800s used it frequently to identify invaders, meaning private armies of freebooters illegally organized. Pirates were also called filibusters. Philip Nolan, an Irishman living in the United States, allegedly plotted with Indians to overthrow the province of Texas during the 1790s. In August 1800 he built a Texas fort in the Nacogdoches vicinity and aroused Spanish suspicions. When Nolan went to hunt wild horses near Waco on March 4, 1801, the Spanish caught him, killed him, and dispatched his ears to the Spanish governor. The plot, if one existed, collapsed.

Aaron Burr, a former vice president of the United States who killed Alexander Hamilton in an 1804 duel, allegedly plotted with Gen. James Wilkinson, a military commander of New Orleans. The two planned to politically control a portion of the American Southwest united with Texas and other parts of northern Mexico. But their scheme leaked far and wide and never amounted to more than dreams, shadows, and rumors. The United States arrested Burr and charged him with treason in 1807, but he was not convicted.

Next came Father Miguel Hidalgo y Costilla, the intellectual and emotional author of Mexican independence. When he failed to free Mexico from Spain in 1810-11, one of his lieutenants, José Bernardo Maximiliano Gutiérrez de Lara, decided to slice off a chunk of the weakly defended northern portion of the country: Texas.

With the tacit support of several European governments, and the guiding hand of George Shaler, an agent of the American State Department, Gutiérrez teamed up with August Magee, a disgruntled American army officer stationed in Louisiana. The Gutiérrez-Magee filibustering army of 700 men in 1812 marched under the "Green Flag" and swiftly took Nacogdoches as well as Goliad and San Antonio. Then Magee died.

Gutiérrez assumed command of the Republic of the North. He raised the Green Flag, drafted a constitution, and declared his republic's independence. But Gutiérrez became an egocentric dictator and lost American support. Shaler replaced him with José Alvarez de Toledo y Dublois, a Cuban. On August 18, 1813, near the Medina River not far from San Antonio, a Spanish army decisively crushed the Republic of the North.

This brief republic brings into question the six flags that once flew over Texas. These banners represented Spain, Mexico, France, the Republic of Texas, the Confederacy, and the United States. Perhaps a seventh should be added. The Gutiérrez-Magee Green Flag had as much legitimacy as some of the others.

Meanwhile, Texas boundaries under Spain followed the Gulf of Mexico and Sabine River on the east, the Red River on the north, the Nueces (not the Rio Grande) on the south, and San Antonio on the west. The western line was vague. Six hundred desolate miles, with no settlement except La Junta (a few scattered Spaniards plus some Jumano Indians at the confluence of the Rio Grande and the Conchos) separating San Antonio from Ysleta and Socorro, the oldest towns in present-day Texas.

Mexican hamlets extended to the Rio Grande from Mexico City, but they did not go beyond. Dolores and Laredo for a while were the only towns on the north bank of the Rio Grande, and these flukes of geography owed their existence to holding high ground. Missions and presidios in Texas were staffed primarily by soldiers and religious figures, not settlers.

With Mexico's central government dissolving in chaos, and Texas threatened by French and American filibusters, Mexico faced a serious dilemma: How could it hold Texas when dissension raged from within and foreign occupation threatened from without? The obvious answer was to populate the province, but Mexican colonists were reluctant settlers.

Austin's Settlers

Enter Moses Austin. This hustling Connecticut Yankee had traveled widely and understood banks and mining. (He had failed at both.) As a land developer holding dual American and Spanish citizenship, he visited San Antonio to talk with officials two days before Christmas 1820. But Governor Antonio María Martínez ordered Austin from the province. As Austin prepared to leave, he encountered an old friend (Texas history brims with these fortuitous meetings), Baron Felipe Enrique Neri de Bastrop, whom Texas historian Joe Frantz described as having "as many nationalities as a hound dog." Bastrop intervened with Martínez, and on January 21, 1821, Austin was granted permission to settle 300 families on 200,000 acres in a yet-to-be specified site. Austin had to testify for the good character and behavior of each resident.

The advantages to Spain in this arrangement were obvious. Farmers with families made for reliable, hardworking citizens. They provided Spain a stable, taxpaying commodity, and their loyalty would endear them to the government. Their presence would deter the French and discourage illegal Americans. These colonists would blunt the Comanche scourge ravaging northern Mexico from wide-ranging camps on the Texas plains.

Moses Austin headed home to Missouri, and died of pneumonia three weeks later. His son, Stephen F. Austin, a self-effacing attorney, took up his father's challenge. Stephen received the same terms as his father had in San

Antonio, but when he visited Mexico City he did even better. The taxes would be delayed for six years, and each colonist's family would receive 4,606 acres of high grass, sufficient rain, and abundant game. Furthermore, Austin was appointed civil commandant to oversee the American settlers. He charged each settler twelve and a half cents per acre for surveys, administrative matters, and colony defense, but most families never paid.

Austin fulfilled his first contract in 1822. His settlers farmed the Colorado and Brazos bottomlands and became the "Old Three Hundred," the bedrock of Texas aristocracy.

Other *empresarios* (real estate developers such as Austin) brought in colonists. By the 1830s, the Americans living in Texas numbered 30,000 to 40,000, ten times the number of Mexicans living there.

Mexico had meanwhile expelled the Spanish in 1821. In 1824 the new government incorporated Texas into Coahuila, naming the province Coahuila y Texas (Coahuila and Texas). Those citizens doing business in the courts had to ride several hundred miles to Saltillo, Coahuila, and Texans resented the imposition. Furthermore, while Mexico had a constitution, it did not have a bill of rights. There were no guarantees of freedom of speech, freedom of assembly, or trial by jury.

At a time of tightening tensions, the honest broker Austin found himself in an increasingly difficult situation. He reminded Texans of Mexico's generosity and counseled patience. Although Mexican law required settlers to become Roman Catholics, Mexico seldom enforced the law. The same held true for learning Spanish. After Austin calmed down the Americans, he turned to the Mexican authorities. He pointed out that the Texans had been bighearted as well as dutiful. Now it was time for Mexico to do something for them. The colonists were loyal settlers. They supported the central government and even helped expel American trespassers who crossed the Red River surreptitiously (the first illegal immigrants in Texas).

But not all Texans were as steadfast as Austin's colonists. Over at Nacogdoches, Haden Edwards, an *empresario* lacking Austin's honed sense of integrity, not only smuggled in American illegals, he created for himself the Republic of Fredonia in 1825. Embarrassed settlers from the Austin colony took up arms alongside the Mexican Army. Together they expelled Edwards from Texas and established a Mexican garrison at Nacogdoches.

Yet, as misunderstandings and poor communications multiplied, even Austin could not slow the momentum for revolution. In 1832 the Texans petitioned Mexico City to replace Spanish with English as the language of commerce in Texas. They demanded higher immigration quotas and insisted that Mexican statehood be established in Texas in response to an understanding of the 1824 constitution. A year later Austin returned to Mexico City to personally negotiate these terms with President Antonio López de Santa Anna.

Mexico had already made some concessions. A tariff exemption went into effect, and it permitted the English language in some instances. Foreign immigration had restarted. On the minus side, however, Santa Anna believed in a strong central government with himself as the benevolent but all-powerful dictator. Gradually he reined in state authority, substituting governors handpicked by himself. He denied Austin's demands, and when Austin wrote a letter to San Antonio unwisely suggesting that revolution might be the only alternative, Santa Anna gave Austin some time in a Mexico City jail to reconsider his bad attitude.

The next three years saw considerable skirmishing in Texas with the rebels constantly emerging victorious. In 1835 they thumped Gen. Martín Perfecto de Cós, Santa Anna's brother-in-law who had occupied San Antonio with a 500-man army. Cós surrendered to the rebels and, as a condition of parole, promised never again to fight in Texas.

Furious at such insurrection, Santa Anna stormed into Texas from Mexico with 5,000 men. (In retrospect, an amphibious landing would have made more sense—his troops would have been more rested upon arrival and the Texas rebels would have been closer at hand.) Along the way Santa Anna added to his army by pressing young ranchers into service and even recruiting soldiers from the jails. He promised to bring physicians, but the only medical man in the entire army was the dictator's personal doctor. He promised boats to cross northern rivers, but there were none. Dozens of soldiers drowned while crossing waters swollen by interminable rains. A half-naked fighting force, some of it fresh from the tropics, crunched under a ferocious snowstorm. Soldier accounts from Santa Anna's army read like mail from Valley Forge. Barefoot troopers left bloody tracks on the rocky, frozen ground. But it was a tough, durable, courageous army, and though it faltered and stumbled, it kept going.

Remember the Alamo

On February 23, 1836, Santa Anna entered San Antonio. The rebel force, carousing when it should have been preparing for battle, hurriedly took refuge in the Alamo. The thirteen-day siege began.

Fascinating characters manned the Alamo walls: Col. William Barret Travis, a firebrand, a lawyer, and a seducer of ladies; James Bowie, designer of that wicked blade known as the Bowie knife and reputed to be a slave runner and manslayer; and Davy Crockett, a former Tennessee congressman and spinner of tall tales, but not a natural leader. Travis and Bowie argued over command, resolving nothing until Bowie collapsed from an illness suspected to have been diphtheria. He remained in bed throughout the siege.

Perhaps these three Alamo heroes were all that latter-day historians and folklorists could adequately praise without losing readers and worshippers in a welter of confusing names. Still, the Alamo contained numerous paladins.

One was James B. Bonham, a twenty-nine-year-old South Carolinian. As a courier, he slipped through the Mexican lines twice in a quest for assistance, and failed twice to recruit volunteers. He could have saved himself, with plenty of excuses and no one to fault him, but he chose to return and die with his comrades.

Another defender was Albert Martin, a twenty-eight-year-old Rhode Island native recently of Gonzales, Texas. Captain Martin had already distinguished himself in the revolution, but he was willing again when Travis selected him as the Alamo emissary to meet under a flag of truce with Colonel Almonte, Santa Anna's representative. Travis had only 160 men, and Almonte advised them to surrender or be put to the sword. Travis responded with his famous cannon shot and the "Liberty or Death" missive penned for Sam Houston and the rest of Texas. The letter pleaded for reinforcements, and as the Alamo doors flew open, Martin rode out to deliver it.

Martin reached Gonzales, seventy miles distant, turned over his message to Houston, and set his mind to recruiting Alamo volunteers. Twenty-five men joined him on February 27, and seven more the following day. On the 29th, these thirty-two men shot their way through Mexican lines and entered the Alamo. They were the only reinforcements for the doomed command. Martin and the volunteers knew full well what they were getting into, and they could have avoided the Alamo had they so chosen. Instead they went down in smoke and glory along with the others.

Often it has been cynically stated that if the Alamo had a back door, there would have been no heroes and no battle. The facts are that the Alamo was rife with "back doors," and a sprinkling of men, including couriers who never returned, opened those exits. Yet, 185 defenders deliberately chose to remain, to stand and die. While history has several parallels, the Alamo remains an inspiring example of ideals and brotherhood, of what's really worth living and dying for.

Of those who died defending the Alamo and each other, the youngest was fifteen, the oldest fifty-five. (Crockett, at fifty, was the second oldest.) Thirty-seven came from Tennessee; sixteen from England; fourteen from Pennsylvania; thirteen each from Ireland, Texas, Virginia, and Kentucky. Almost every state contributed somebody, as did Wales, Denmark, France, Germany, Scotland, and Mexico. Eleven were Hispanics, two were Jews, and two were black slaves. There were seven physicians and six attorneys. A poet was in attendance, although anything he wrote died with him. Finally, there were fifteen noncombatants—women and children—all of whom took refuge in the chapel.

Why did this fight happen, you might ask? Some historians believe it gave Sam Houston's Texas army precious time. But time for what? His army would never be ready. So why did the Alamo defenders, who must have known this, not melt into the darkness and fight as guerrillas? For that matter, why didn't

Santa Anna bypass this ragtag assortment of rebels? He surely realized that an Alamo victory, no matter how easily bought, would still have its price—and would be meaningless in terms of ending the rebellion. The only explanation is that both sides were caught up in emotions, and emotions are never a prisoner of logic.

At 4 A.M. on Sunday, March 6, 1836, the bugle sounded and the Mexican troops charged. A sheet of Texas flame buckled the front line. The masses wavered and again pressed forward. Within an hour it was all over.

What made the difference? Primarily numbers and steel. Courage had little to do with it, for both sides showed plenty. The Texans were outnumbered ten to one, but they had accurate rifles. The Mexicans carried awkward, foul-shooting muskets. Both weapons took an inordinate amount of time to reload. But the muskets had bayonets, the rifles did not. The Texans got off perhaps a half-dozen shots each. Then they were backed against the wall by steel, and steel prevailed.

One black slave survived, one Hispanic survived, thirteen of the fifteen noncombatants survived. All were released.

Folklore says Davy Crockett fought to the last and went down swinging his squirrel rifle. Maybe so. Mexican accounts say he and three or four others surrendered. All were executed.

With a pall of black smoke hanging over the Alamo and the bodies burning inside it, Santa Anna turned his attention to the pursuit of Sam Houston and the defeat of the Texas army, which would end the rebellion. First he stopped at Goliad, where Col. James Fannin surrendered 400 Texas men. The prisoners were herded into a field and shot. A few escaped during the melee.

A Tenuous Independence

To the east, Texas was holding an independence convention and Sam Houston was celebrating his birthday, all this while the Alamo cried for help. (Houston had sent Travis and Bowie to destroy the Alamo, not make a stand in it.) Fifty-nine delegates met in Washington-on-the-Brazos (as distinct from Washington on the Potomac), and one of those attending was George C. Childress, a thirty-two-year-old lawyer and editor of Tennessee's largest newspaper, the National Banner and Nashville Advertiser. He had supported Texas radicals with editorials and fund-raising, and his reward was the chairmanship of a committee to draft a declaration of Texas independence.

Childress apparently wrote the document himself and may have had it in his saddlebags when he left Tennessee. The certificate was only briefly debated by the delegates, and within a few hours after discussing it on March 1, 1836, the committee accepted the document. Still the assembly could not sign until March 3 because it took a day to get an engrossed copy. Even then, the document was backdated to March 2 in honor of Sam Houston's forty-third birthday.

All fifty-nine delegates signed, even though several opposed independence. They handled the event so nonchalantly that they laid the document aside and it remained lost for over a half-century until 1896, when it turned up in a Washington (on the Potomac) State Department file.

Incidentally, the two native Texas signers were José Antonio Navarro and the non-English-speaking José Francisco Ruiz. The only native Mexican signer was Lorenzo de Zavala, an *empresario* and soon-to-be first vice president of the Texas republic.

The Alamo sent North Carolina native Jesse B. Badgett to the convention; while there, the Alamo fell. Badgett signed and left for Arkansas. He never returned.

As for the moody Childress, he never afterwards succeeded at anything. Broke, alone, and under severe mental stress in June 1841, he stabbed himself to death in a Galveston boardinghouse. His body still lies somewhere in the city in an unmarked grave.

Meanwhile, the first provisional Texas government had disintegrated. Governor Henry Smith had been impeached. Sam Houston had been retained and then dismissed as leader of an army that barely existed. He showed up in Washington-on-the-Brazos and was again appointed supreme commander in chief. The convention suggested that he visit Gonzales and recruit fighting men.

Former Tennessee Congressman Sam Houston was a tall, striking man, as vain as he was coarse and vulgar. An unhappy marriage led him to resign as governor of Tennessee. Without question he had an alcohol problem—and, some say, an opium habit. He married an Indian woman, abandoned her, came to Texas, and brought his liquor-drinking capacity with him. In Texas he became general of the army, twice president of Texas, and its best-known statesman. Texas without the Alamo would be astonishing; Texas without Sam Houston would be unthinkable.

For a time Sam Houston had an army of 1,400 men. Then the Alamo and Goliad tragedies broke and overnight his force shrunk to 800. Most of the 600 who vanished fled pell-mell for the United States border at the Sabine River in a flight frequently described as the "Runaway Scrape." At its worst it was disgraceful. At its best it represented the understandable consequences of a poorly organized and prosecuted Texas war effort.

Nevertheless, no one questioned the loyalty and courage of those who remained. The army was coming together, and it would fight if Houston gave it a chance. For a while it seemed that he would not.

For a month Santa Anna pursued Houston throughout eastern Texas. Houston burned Gonzales and retreated. The Texas government fled from Washington to Harrisburg—and finally to Galveston Island. Houston chided the politicians for cowardice. President David G. Burnet ordered Houston to stand and fight, but the military leader ignored the order only to face thousands of panicked civilian refugees, in great suffering, heading for the border and blaming his lack of action for their plight. Houston took no one, not even his ranking officers, into his confidence, and military morale plummeted.

At Houston's rear, however, Santa Anna made a tactical blunder. Convinced he could easily defeat any Texas force, the Mexican general divided his firepower into three spearheads, one of which he personally led in pursuit of Houston. While the others searched for the Texas government, they also planned to encircle or cut off Houston.

On April 21, six weeks after the Alamo fell, Santa Anna thought he had the Texas army trapped in a bend of the flooded San Jacinto River near what is now the city of Houston. Actually, the Texans had Santa Anna trapped. Although outnumbered, Houston chose the battle scene, a relatively flat plain. He also burned the bridges behind the Mexican force, which meant there would be no retreat for either army. Whichever side remained standing when the smoke cleared won. The strategy was as simple as that.

Convinced that Houston would attack at sunrise, the Mexican general put his army to work digging breastworks at night. When the dawn broke, Houston slept. As the sun rose higher, Santa Anna concluded the Texans were not coming. Maybe they would charge tomorrow morning. In his confidence and arrogance, he released his troops for a siesta without even posting sentinels, then he retired to his tent with his opium box and Emily, a beautiful twenty-year-old mulatto slave girl.

A few hours later, at about five in the afternoon, a ragged Texas drummer and three fifers struck up "Will You Come to My Bower I Have Shaded for You." Just then, Sam Houston's army slammed into the sleeping Mexican camp with cannons and rifles blazing. They fired until their guns were too hot to reload, and then they stabbed and clubbed. According to Texas accounts, when the battle ended a half-hour later, nine Texans lay on the bloody field beside 630 Mexicans. Houston's army took over 700 Mexican prisoners, including the president and general himself, Santa Anna.

The legendary Yellow Rose of Texas may have played a part in Santa Anna's capture. That she existed, few dispute. Everything else is conjecture. Born a mulatto slave girl (a "high yeller" in Texas slang), Emily Morgan was captured by Santa Anna at Morgan's Point. She sent another slave to warn Houston of the Mexican plans and then kept Santa Anna dallying in his tent long after he should have been worrying about the Texans. She earned her freedom by these acts, but died in obscurity. The "Yellow Rose of Texas" is her anthem, although its modern words do not match historic deeds or events.

Regardless of whether Sam Houston was lucky, brilliant, or received good advice, had he not been victorious at San Jacinto, the rebellion would have folded. There would have been no Mexican War, and no Texas, Nevada, Arizona, California, New Mexico, Colorado, or Utah contributing over a million square miles of territory to the United States. The Battle of San Jacinto shaped North American and world history.

Texas demanded the Rio Grande, not the Nueces, as its southwestern boundary, a border Texas had historically never possessed. Santa Anna agreed and signed two Treaties of Velasco, one of them secret; however, the Mexican congress refused to ratify the treaty, so the Nueces Strip remained in dispute.

Texas sought entrance into the United States, but Congress insisted its admission would upset the balance of free and slaveholding states. The annexation move failed, and Texas became a republic out of necessity rather than preference. While Sam Houston pouted at the rebuff, Mirabeau Lamar, who succeeded Houston as president, was pleased and dreamed of a Texas empire expanding westward to the Pacific.

Lamar repudiated the Houston treaty with the Cherokees, a people who generally behaved themselves in Texas. So they teamed up with Vicente Córdova. In 1838, 300 Indians and a hundred Mexicans occupied an island in the Angelina River and declared their independence. The Texas army dispersed them, but a year later the Texans and Cherokees fought the Battle of the Neches, near Tyler. The Cherokees lost and were driven across the Red River into Indian Territory (Oklahoma), the first of many such Indian banishments from Texas.

Texas Rangers

Texas Rangers recruited to serve as scouts and militia became the best-known Indian fighters to date. Rangers Bigfoot Wallace, John Moore, Samuel Walker, Ben McCulloch, and John Coffee Hays became frontier legends. There were many others.

The rangers were pragmatic, innovative leaders bent on constantly improving their tactics as well as their weapons. Until that time, the single-shot pistol, or the derringer, had been the preferred weapon of duelists and gamblers. Real men carried rifles, muskets, or knives. When Samuel Colt brought out his .34 caliber five-shot Patterson revolver (named for Patterson, New Jersey, the place of manufacture), only the Texas Rangers seemed impressed by its enormous firepower and potential effectiveness for mounted combat. In 1844, Samuel Walker and other rangers defeated eighty Comanches at Nueces Canyon. The Indians feinted, the rangers discharged their single-shot rifles, and the Comanches charged. As the Indians closed in, the rangers opened fire with their Colts, tearing ragged holes in the panicky Comanche lines.

A couple of years later, Capt. Samuel H. Walker set out to improve the weapon. During the Mexican War, he and Samuel Colt attached a trigger guard, added weight so the weapon could be used as a club, and increased the firepower to a .44 caliber six-shot. The Walker Colt gained recognition and popularity during the Mexican War.

The Texas Rangers had saved the Colt Firearms Company and made its namesake revolver famous. Were it not for Texas, where the six-shooter earned its glory, the gunfighter myth might never have emerged.

Statehood, and a Boundary Dispute

Massive immigration had meanwhile come to Texas, much of it from the United States but from Europe as well. The Germans founded New Braunfels in 1844 and Fredericksburg in 1846, migrating in as part of the Adelsverein—the Association of Noblemen at Biebrich on the Rhine. The organization purchased huge Texas land tracts and settled hardy German immigrants. Most of these newcomers followed agricultural pursuits until after the turn of the century.

By 1845 the pressure for Texas annexation could not be denied, and on December 29th, Texas joined the Union. President James K. Polk regarded his election as an annexation mandate. Mexico considered the statehood process tantamount to a declaration of war. Mexico might have accepted Texas statehood if the "original" Spanish province of Texas had been the only territory involved. But Texas and the United States claimed more. Mexico refused to cede the Nueces Strip and gagged at the prospect of Texas extending to the Rio Grande. When the United States sided with Texas and demanded the Rio Grande as the state's boundary, a conflict became inevitable.

On April 24, 1846, a Mexican cavalry patrol crossed the Rio Grande near Brownsville and attacked Gen. Zachary Taylor's advance forces. Blood was shed.

President James K. Polk declared war, and Taylor's army lunged down through central Mexico while Gen. Hugh Scott invaded Vera Cruz. Farther west, Gen. Stephen Kearny left Missouri and conquered Santa Fe. While Kearny went on to capture California, a contingent of 800 Missouri Farm Boys, strung out for miles, out of uniform, and led by Col. Alexander Doniphan, occupied El Paso two days after Christmas 1846. Northern Mexico collapsed. Fourteen months later, on February 24, 1848, Mexico and the United States signed the Treaty of Guadalupe Hidalgo, effectively ending the war.

The United States gained much from that war, including shores washed by the Pacific Ocean. Texas gained the Nueces Strip and the Rio Grande as its southern boundary, but its northern and western borders remained vague.

In March 1848, while trying to get the jump on politicians all over the country, the new Texas legislature organized on paper Santa Fe County with Santa Fe (New Mexico) as the county seat. The county included today's Texas panhandle, the Big Bend, the panhandle of Oklahoma, half of New Mexico, half of Colorado, and portions of Wyoming and Kansas. Texans thought big in those days.

Most American military and political authorities, however, considered Texas jurisdictional claims as terminating at the Pecos River, or thereabouts. The trans-Pecos region belonged to the United States, and Washington alone would make decisions about its ultimate disposition. Until then, El Paso remained a component of New Mexico. A stubborn Texas nevertheless sent emissaries to El Paso.

On March 1, 1850, El Paso voted to abandon its New Mexico heritage and join Texas. Even Dona Ana, fifty miles north of El Paso and then the largest village in southern New Mexico, voted to accept Texas. Congress denied Dona Ana's participation and entry.

The Compromise of 1850 strove for a balance of power between free and slave states, and since El Paso had expressed its willingness to become a part of Texas, Congress paid Texas $10 million to relinquish all additional territorial claims north of El Paso and to accept today's present boundaries. A modern Texas thus emerged, a melting pot of the Old South and the Spanish and Mexican Southwest.

Enterprise and Civil War

By now gold had been discovered in California. Forty-Niners forsook New England and turned the harbors of Galveston and Indianola into flourishing seaports. Numerous gold seekers adopted the southern route across Texas to California because the weather was better than a more northern route, the mountains were less towering, and the landscape was more suited for wagon travel. Texas became a continental way station.

During the mid-1850s, the Butterfield Overland Stage rolled south from Tipton, Missouri, into Texas, stopping at El Paso on its way to San Francisco. The trip took twenty-four days, and the stages averaged four miles per hour. Passengers helped push the stages uphill, and they walked alongside when the coaches forded streams. Along the way they ate slumgullion, a mixed stew. Physicians were rarely available, and there were precious few places to bathe. The close quarters and long days produced the sickest, smelliest travelers one could imagine.

At about the same time, mail coaches rumbled from San Antonio through El Paso to San Diego, California. Because mules did the work, the line was dubbed the "Jackass Mail."

With such fine transportation routes, Texas attracted even more colonists. Since most came from the South, they generally settled in familiar-looking East Texas, where they established plantations and supported their lifestyle with slavery. West Texas, on the other hand (which included the panhandle) attracted Midwesterners and Europeans, few of whom owned slaves. When the national slavery issue could no longer be contained, Texas seceded from the Union. In Texas most residents voted for secession because of states' rights. Black emancipation, except in East and portions of Central Texas, was of secondary importance.

Texas left the Union over the strenuous objections of Sam Houston. Sam was governor, but the legislators swept him aside and installed Lt. Governor Edward Clark in his place. Sixty thousand Texans joined the Confederate Army, while only 2,000 joined the Union Army.

During the Civil War, on a comparative basis, Texas was not a major theater of operations. Brownsville fell into Union possession for a brief period, and Galveston for an even shorter length of time. Politician and Indian agent John R. Baylor rode into El Paso with 300 men of the Texas Second Mounted Rifles. He captured southern New Mexico to forty miles north of El Paso. Gen. Henry H. Sibley and 2,000 Confederate soldiers carried the conquest to Santa Fe; however, at the Battle of Glorieta Pass, the Northern cavalry burned Sibley's supply train. He and his army disappeared back into Texas. El Paso was subsequently occupied by the Union's California Column led by the hard-faced Col. John R. Carleton.

One of the Civil War's great ironies was Texas cotton, perhaps the finest grade anywhere. Because of Union blockades, the South's cotton had difficulty reaching a market. The North had machinery but little cotton, while the South had cotton but little machinery. Enterprising men hauled Texas cotton across the Rio Grande and shipped it from the seaport of Bagdad, Mexico, on freighters with foreign flags. It sold well in Boston or New York and supported the Northern war effort by keeping the factories humming and the soldiers clothed; meanwhile, the Union money that came to Texas from the sale of cotton purchased arms and supplies for the Confederacy.

On the Deep South front, Hood's Texas Brigade, Terry's Texas Rangers, and Ross's Brigade absorbed heavy losses but acquitted themselves well all across the Confederacy. Oddly, the Civil War had already ended when the last battle was fought on May 12-13, 1865, at Palmito Ranch in the Rio Grande Valley. The Texans won.

After the war, Gen. Ulysses S. Grant feared Texas might fight on with the support of French imperial forces currently overrunning Mexico, so he ordered Gen. Philip Sheridan to occupy the state west to San Antonio with the 13th Corps. Sheridan found dispirited and disbanded Confederate soldiers clotting the roads and looting the towns and villages. Liberated blacks were everywhere, homeless, out of work, aimless, sick, hungry, but free and having the right to vote.

Military and political reconstruction became an extension of the war, for Reconstruction was primarily an instrument to punish the white Southerner for failing to integrate the black man into the white mainstream. The North won the shooting war, but lost the Reconstruction (Carpet Bag) aftermath because it lacked the necessary commitment to forcibly reorganize an entire social structure. Had the North been more dedicated and determined, the United States might have avoided the racial disturbances of the 1960s.

To make emancipation work, on March 3, 1865, Congress created the Bureau of Refugees, Freedmen, and Abandoned Lands. Most people called it the "Freedmen's Bureau," and it was administered by the War Department. Its purpose was to establish a system of fair labor laws and wage earnings for black workers. It was supposed to create black schools, provide care for the aged and sick, and adjudicate disputes between blacks and whites.

Reconstruction and the Freedmen's Bureau failed, first because none of the parties wanted it to succeed enough to give it the attention and the patience it required. The army was too small to effectively enforce it, and had no business being an arm of politics. But Reconstruction *was* politics. Second, the Texas countryside had not been militarily overrun and brutalized like most of the South. Its white population circumvented Reconstruction regulations and unleashed terror. And finally, the freed blacks were illiterate and fearful. They congregated around military posts for protection. While most wanted work and tried to find jobs, a large percentage vainly awaited the rumored "forty acres and a mule," a grant never officially promised, a wish never coming true.

Reconstruction ended with Richard Coke's election as a democratic governor in 1874. Even so, Edmund J. Davis, the last Reconstruction governor in Texas and a Texas cavalry officer who fought with the Union, locked himself and his followers in the basement of the capitol building. He appealed to President Ulysses S. Grant for military support, but when an army did not show up, Davis sheepishly withdrew.

Corruption and lawlessness had proliferated during Reconstruction. Every county seemed to have its feud: Sutton-Taylor, the Hoodoo War, the Salt War, Regulators vs. Moderators.

Juan Cortina, a Mexican-Texan and a patriot or renegade, depending upon who offered the opinion, spread his "wars" across southern Texas and northern Mexico near Brownsville and Matamoros. Cortina frequently held high political office in Mexico and threatened to annex the lower Rio Grande Valley back to the motherland.

Times of Transition

The Colt .45 replaced the Bible for settling disputes. Gunfighters such as John Wesley Hardin, Ben Thompson, Jim Miller, John Selman, Luke Short, Jim Courtright, King Fisher, William Longley, and Clay Allison rose to prominence. Only the Texas Rangers restrained them. After 1874 the rangers gradually shifted from fighting Indians to pursuing outlaws. They grimly eliminated gunmen, train robbers, cattle rustlers, revolutionaries, bandits, bank and stage robbers, rioters, strikers, murderers, and feudists. If the rangers did not always show mercy, it should be understood that they seldom received it either. Furthermore, the nearest jail was frequently miles, days, or weeks distant.

After the Civil War, the army once again sought Indian containment. Apaches remained on the perimeter of West Texas, and Kiowas and Comanches thundered around in northern and mid-Texas. They survived because of incredible distances and rugged country, the distractions of the Civil War and its aftermath, and because the buffalo had not yet been decimated.

Buffalo still blanketed the south plains, but contrary to many opinions, they were not slaughtered just to undermine the Indians, although that was a desired by-product. Economics and cheap transportation destroyed the buffalo. The buffalo were killed because eastern tanners and factories demanded hides by the millions, and thousands of eager hunters supplied the product. In 1873, the Atchison, Topeka & Santa Fe Railroad shipped 754,529 hides to eastern markets. When the slaughter ended a few years later, the Indians had been brought to heel as much by fashion designers and machines that needed drive belts as by long-range needle guns.

The army, after the Civil War, enlisted blacks into the 24th and 25th Infantries, and the 9th and 10th Cavalries. The cavalrymen became known as Buffalo Soldiers by Indians who compared their black, kinky hair to the bison's mane. It was a term of respect given by one warrior to another.

Between 1865 and 1881, the 9th and 10th Cavalries constantly pursued the Indians. Along the Mexican border, especially in the middle and lower Rio Grande Valley, the army retained Seminole-Negro scouts, men often descended from former slaves. They spoke Spanish, dressed like Indians or Mexicans, and worshipped like Southern Baptists. Throughout the 1870s, these scouts guided American military expeditions south across the river in pursuit of Indian raiders.

Farther north, at Adobe Walls in the Texas panhandle, nearly 300 Comanches and Kiowas led by Lone Wolf and Quanah Parker could not overrun twenty-eight men and one woman inside an old ruins, a supply post for buffalo hunters. Five days later, the Indians withdrew.

In retaliation, Gen. Ranald S. Mackenzie attacked the main Comanche stronghold in Palo Duro Canyon in 1874-75. He killed very few Indians, but he captured and burned their supplies and shot their horses. To be mobile, to strike from great distances, and retreat onto the trackless plains, the Indians had to have horses. Since the army took to killing all captured horses, the effect on the Indians was as devastating as the buffalo slaughter. Before long the Comanche wars ended.

Cynthia Ann Parker epitomized the rise and fall and tragedy of the Comanche nation. When she was nine years old, around 1835, the Comanches killed her parents and kidnapped her. As the years went by, she assimilated with her captors and married a chief named Peta Nocona. They had two sons, Pecos and Quanah, and a daughter, Prairie Flower. Cynthia—now called Naduah—no longer wished to be rescued or to return at all to white society. Nevertheless, after twenty-five years of living with the Comanches, Texas Rangers captured her and her daughter in 1860. Only Naduah's blue eyes and fair complexion gave away her origin; otherwise, she looked and sounded Indian. She remembered almost no English and made several attempts at escaping back to the prairie, back to the life she embraced. She never saw Peta Nocona again. He died of an infection. Prairie Flower died also. The Texas legislature granted her a pension and a league of land, but none of that brought her happiness. In 1864 she starved herself to death.

Her death, however, did not end the story. Pecos also died, leaving only Quanah as the surviving family member. He adopted his mother's surname,

Parker, and became a Comanche leader. Realizing that war with the whites would ultimately destroy the Comanches, he surrendered in 1874 and assumed senior statesman status. As the last Comanche chief, he led his people across the Red River into Oklahoma and spent his life counseling them and working in their behalf. Under his guidance, the Comanches never jumped the reservation. Quanah traveled across the United States, met hundreds of important people, married seven times, and fathered numerous children. He died in 1911, and is buried alongside his mother in Oklahoma.

Cowboy Culture

With the plains virtually swept free of marauding Indians and hungry buffalo, the cowboy culture flourished across the open land. The roots of that enduring lifestyle go back several centuries. Francisco Vásquez de Coronado likely brought the first cattle to Texas while searching for the Seven Cities of Cíbola. His expedition drove several hundred head of Spanish cattle across the Texas panhandle in 1541. Fifty-seven years later, in 1598, colonizer Juan de Oñate forded 6,000 head of livestock across the Rio Grande at El Paso. After the New Mexico Pueblo Revolt of 1680, cattle escaped their domestic obligations and moved onto the prairie and took cover in river thickets. For nearly 200 years they roamed free and wild.

Until the mid-1860s, the Spanish cattle mixed and multiplied, especially in the lower Rio Grande Valley. The result of so many generations removed from their domestic ancestors was a rangy, ornery, multicolored animal with thin flat thighs, flat ribs, and long, spindly legs—the longhorn. Their tough, stringy meat left little to butcher and cut. Their wide horns looked strong enough to impale a boxcar.

Longhorns could travel long distances, though—those captured walked to market. Early drovers herded the cows from Texas to Louisiana in 1842, and in 1846 Edward Pipes drove a large herd from East Texas to Cincinnati, Ohio. Some cattle went west to California during the gold rush. Others were rounded up from thickets and driven to the Gulf Coast, where they were slaughtered not for meat but for hides, which went to shoe and clothing factories in Boston.

When Civil War veterans returned to the shambles of their former homes, they found unbranded cattle everywhere. Nobody owned them, so anyone could round them up and sell them for $3 to $4 a head. Up north, the Yankees desperately needed beef as well as hides. Chicago markets paid $40 to $60 a head.

The shortest route to market lay in intersecting railroads being built through Kansas and Nebraska. Texans could drive the cattle north toward those railheads by way of the open range. Most drives started from within a lopsided triangle anchored by San Antonio, Corpus Christi, and Laredo. Others originated farther west.

Charles Goodnight and Oliver Loving blazed the 700-mile Goodnight Trail in 1866 from near the Pecos River to Fort Sumner, New Mexico, then north to Colorado. The Chisholm Trail, popular between 1867 and 1871, ran from San Antonio to Abilene, Kansas, then on north into Nebraska and even east to Sedalia, Missouri, terminus for the Missouri Pacific Railroad. The Western Trail went from San Antonio to Dodge City in southwestern Kansas. Most, but not all, cattle drives went north. Jim Stimson, of the New Mexico Land and Cattle Company, drove 20,000 head of longhorns from central Texas to New Mexico in 1882. The Stimson Trail ultimately reached Arizona.

In 1866 some 260,000 longhorns walked to northern markets. By 1880, millions of cattle crossed Oklahoma's Indian Territory, fording rivers and rumbling toward the dinner tables of a nation. Chicago's Union Stockyards opened in 1865, and Texas cattle contributed significantly to the meat-processing industry that grew and thrived there. Chicago served as the major railhead distribution point for the Midwest and East.

The term "cattle baron" came into general use during this period. Stockmen like Shanghai Pierce, George Littlefield, Charles Goodnight, and the Slaughter boys did not become household words overnight, but folks in the cattle business knew these people.

As a rule, cowboys tended to be lean, lithe, and smaller than the average man. Cowboy actor John Wayne looked heroic and every bit a Westerner when sitting on a horse in front of a camera, but his weight would have killed most horses in the Old West. Furthermore, not many cowboys owned their horse, although they usually owned their own saddle. A cowboy generally selected a mount from the ranch "string." Some horses were used for roping, others for night work, branding, cutting, or, occasionally, racing, since cowboys loved to gamble.

A rider's equipment, most of it adopted from Hispanic vaqueros, started with a broad-brimmed hat. The bandana served mainly as a wipe for sweat on a cowboy's face and neck, but it also warmed his ears in cold weather and filtered the air he breathed during dusty trail drives. Leather chaps protected his legs from thorny brush, among other things, and sharp-toed boots with a leather sole made it easy to find the stirrup.

As for six-shooters, cowboys used them to kill snakes, signal for help, or shoot a horse if its rider got "hung up in the stirrup." Movies and books to the contrary, cowboys depended upon each other, and they rarely fought when not faced with the inducements of whiskey, women, or gambling. The holster, worn belt high rather than slung low on the hips, kept the gun secure and out of the way until needed. Since cowboys bounced, climbed, and jumped, the weapon had to be wedged tight in the holster. A fast-draw pretender ran the risk of blowing off his leg or toes if the gun fired prematurely before clearing leather. And ammunition cost quite a bit—usually ten cents a round—so cowboys rarely practiced and were notoriously poor shots.

As abruptly as the longhorn drives began, this golden age of cattle trails ended. Ticks, iron rails, and barbed wire rank among the top villains that brought on change. Longhorns carried the Texas tick, a mite-sized insect that caused an illness known as "Texas Fever." Wherever these Texas steers walked, disaster for someone else's cows usually followed. Yet, like Typhoid Mary, they were immune to the disease they carried.

The intercontinental rails, meanwhile, pushed their way right into Texas, ending the need to drive the cattle to distant railheads. Major lines included the Texas & Pacific; the Southern Pacific; the Missouri, Kansas & Pacific; and the Fort Worth & Denver. While the railroads hauled out beef, they hauled in emigrants from the East who homesteaded the open range, established farms, put down sod houses, and bought machinery. The farmers encircled their land with barbed wire to keep their own cows in and to keep longhorns out.

Fences often blocked roads, schools, and even villages. Farmers fenced out the ranchers, and the ranchers fenced in the farmers. Fences might have made good neighbors but, for a while at least, that adage did not apply in Texas. Bloody conflicts arose, and those who cut fences frequently faced retribution on the spot by gunfire or lynching. Much of the trouble occurred roughly along the 100th meridian, the demarcation line between the farmlands of East Texas and the ranch country of West Texas.

Governor John Ireland called an extra session of the Texas legislature in 1884, and it sponsored a bill making it a felony to cut fences and a misdemeanor to install illegal ones. Those who placed fences across public lands or roads had to install gates every three miles. The Texas Rangers finally brought things under control.

Fencing shut down the open range, and eventually cattlemen started seeing the value of enclosed property. A fence, more than anything else, established land ownership. It protected farms, enclosed livestock, sheltered water holes, and made the boundaries clear. In 1885, the panhandle's XIT Ranch contracted for 6,000 miles of barbed wire, the largest fencing project in the world and a record that still stands. By 1890, the era of the Kansas trail drives had ended.

Barbed wire became one of the cattlemen's best friends. Once they contained their livestock inside fences and erected windmill pumps to keep the animals watered, the ranchers could sit tight and sell their stock only when the price was right. Railroads refined their refrigerated cars, and Texas meat-packing houses and feed lots prospered.

During this time cattlemen began experimenting with genetic improvements to their stock, and that practice continues today. Ranchers brought in Herefords, Durhams, and Angus. The King Ranch developed the Santa Gertrudis by crossing the Brahman with the Shorthorn, and the Beefmaster came about when Tom Lasater, a rancher near Falfurrias, crossed the Hereford, Shorthorn, and Brahman.

The Modern Era

The Spanish-American War began in 1898. Col. Theodore Roosevelt led the Rough Riders, most of whom came from Arizona and New Mexico, with a sprinkling of volunteers from Harvard, Yale, and Princeton. They trained for a month at Fort Sam Houston, but in truth they probably spent as much time listening to Professor Carl Beck's band concerts as they did training. Their two favorite pieces were "Ta-ra-ra-boom-de-ay" and "There'll Be a Hot Time in the Old Town Tonight." According to Dale R. Walker, a Rough Riders historian, the "hot time tune became the semi-official Rough Riders anthem."

Agriculture and ranching remained the mainstays of Texas industry around the turn of the century. By the early 1900s, citrus growing had taken hold in the lower Rio Grande Valley. Cotton grew across Texas from east to west, while sheep ranching spread through the Hill Country and meat-packing plants sprouted from Fort Worth to the panhandle. Texas industry was primarily based on agriculture and cattle.

With a population of 53,000 in 1900, San Antonio registered as the biggest town in Texas. Houston had 45,000; Dallas, 43,000; Galveston, 38,000; and Fort Worth, 27,000. San Antonio owed much of its strength to the military establishment, particularly Fort Sam Houston, then the largest post in the United States.

In 1901, however, the Texas economy started shifting dramatically. The Spindletop Oil Field near Beaumont brought the state its first black gold. This ushered in economic growth far greater than the cattle drives, railroads, or (eventually) even the Dallas Cowboys. The state boomed as one oil strike after another blew in—Petrolia in 1906, Electra in 1911, Burkburnett in 1913, Mexia in 1921, Permian Basin in 1921, and the East Texas Oil Field in 1930. And oil jump-started another Texas industry: petrochemicals and refining. Names like Texaco, Exxon, Gulf, and Mobile became famous and then common.

Howard R. Hughes, a contractor at Spindletop, purchased an improved drill bit for $150 and parlayed that drill's manufacture into $2 million. When Hughes died in 1924, his ambitious son earned even more massive sums and became the richest and perhaps the most eccentric man on earth.

Prior to the oil industry, Houston had been known primarily for mosquitoes, yellow fever, and the San Jacinto battlefield. Suddenly oil refineries and petrochemical plants mushroomed, and the city expanded its ship channel to facilitate the movements of crude oil.

Higher education in Texas grew with its expanding economy. The Texas Agricultural and Mechanical College (Texas A&M) opened in 1876 with forty white male students. A similar institution for blacks started at Prairie View nine years later.

In Austin, classes began at the University of Texas in 1883 after the state set aside two million acres for the school's financial support. But every time the land increased in value, the university's acreage transferred to a less

24

prime area until, eventually, it owned two million acres of nearly worthless desert in West Texas. The $40,000 it generated annually in grazing fees paled in comparison to what lay ahead. In 1919 a group of cowboy drillers struck oil on university lands. Although Texas A&M got one-third of the royalties, the other two-thirds by 1938 had built University of Texas endowments second only to Harvard.

Texas soon developed one of the best systems of road, rail, and air arteries in the nation. It became an easy state to get into and out of. Energy was cheap, taxes low. The state lured tourism as well as business.

Wealth poured into practically every city in Texas except for remote border areas like El Paso and Laredo. Because of oil, Houston surged past San Antonio and Dallas, though the latter city became a financial and fashion center as well as headquarters for numerous insurance companies.

Texas remained a Bible belt. Texas Senator Morris Sheppard pushed prohibition through Congress, and Texas ratified the Eighteenth Amendment in 1918.

James E. "Pa" Ferguson became governor in 1914. His progressive administration improved schools and state agencies, and even the prison system showed a profit. But, upon being re-elected in 1917, the Texas congress impeached him over a quarrel with the University of Texas. Because he could not dismiss objectionable university individuals, "Farmer Jim" vetoed practically the entire school appropriation. His wife, Miriam "Ma" Ferguson, was then twice elected as governor (1924 and 1932).

Another colorful gubernatorial figure was W. Lee "Pappy" O'Daniel, a radio personality who marketed Hillbilly Flour, took on fourteen candidates for the governorship, and beat them without a runoff in 1938. His platform was the Golden Rule, the Ten Commandments, motherhood, God, apple pie, cotton farming, stock raising, and country. He could sing, fiddle, write music, and deliver a sermon or a fireside chat. He wasn't the first, but he was an original "good ol' boy." Despite his poor administrative record, he loved and understood people. In that respect, he understood politics better than most candidates.

Even with oil and colorful figures, however, Texas suffered during the Great Depression. Every relief agency imaginable put people to work. They hired engineers and artists to build and illustrate public buildings, historians to transcribe oral history, librarians to index newspapers, and folks to repair and build roads, bridges, buildings, and conservation projects. Tens of thousands earned meager livings, but they had jobs.

A drought combined with a dust bowl compounded the economic misery, but depression and dust vanished with World War II. Texas built prison camps and ended up with fifteen military bases. Nearly a million Texans served in uniform. Shipbuilding and defense industries came into their own.

In 1902 Texas voted in the poll tax and kept it until 1966, when the United States Supreme Court abolished the practice. These were days of nationwide racial tensions, and Texas experienced its share of bombings, lynchings, and school disruptions. Texas Western College, now the University of Texas at El Paso, already had the highest Hispanic enrollment in the nation. In 1955 it became the first school of higher learning in the state to open its doors to blacks. Ten enrolled without incident.

A resounding tragedy of Texas proportions unfolded before the nation in November 1963. President John F. Kennedy, First Lady Jackie, and Vice President Lyndon B. Johnson visited Dallas to mend the fractured Texas Democratic Party before the 1964 presidential campaign. As President Kennedy's motorcade wound through the streets of Dallas on Friday, November 22, an assassin shot and killed the president. Lyndon Baines Johnson became the 36th president of the United States and passed a string of social programs called the "Great Society."

When oil prices soared during the 1970s, Texas soared with them. Emigrants from the East and Midwest headed for Houston and jobs. Moderate-sized cities like Odessa, Temple, and Midland thrived. Oilmen and bankers epitomized opportunity in Texas. Unfortunately, while banks around the country diversified their investments, Texas banks invested in oil. When the boom turned to bust during the early 1980s, not only did the oil industry go belly-up, so did numerous Texas banks. By 1990 Texas savings and loan organizations had the highest failure rate in the nation.

Texas struggled through the traumatic Kennedy tragedy, and then survived the 1980s oil depression. Its businesses became more diversified in the 1990s. Furthermore, tourism may well become the new oil, and that industry doesn't pollute.

Today Texas remains a state with a big handshake, a wide-open welcome, and an easy, hospitable grace. The wicked, colorful past hasn't been neglected or glossed over. It awaits modern travelers with horses under their hoods instead of under their seats, visitors willing to scratch G.T.T., Gone to Texas, on the back door of their lives.

Unearthing that past and enriching your present is the purpose of this book. So get behind the wheel and let's drive.

ONE

Far West Texas

. . . you cannot sit at home and dream of how you feel about this land. If you really want to know, you have to be here, silent and open to voices that speak of time and space with curves continuous, of hands and leaves, of stones and paws, of water like jade and the stars, and of how all are joined at infinity.

Jim Bones, Jr., *Texas West of the Pecos*
(Texas A&M Press, 1981)

27

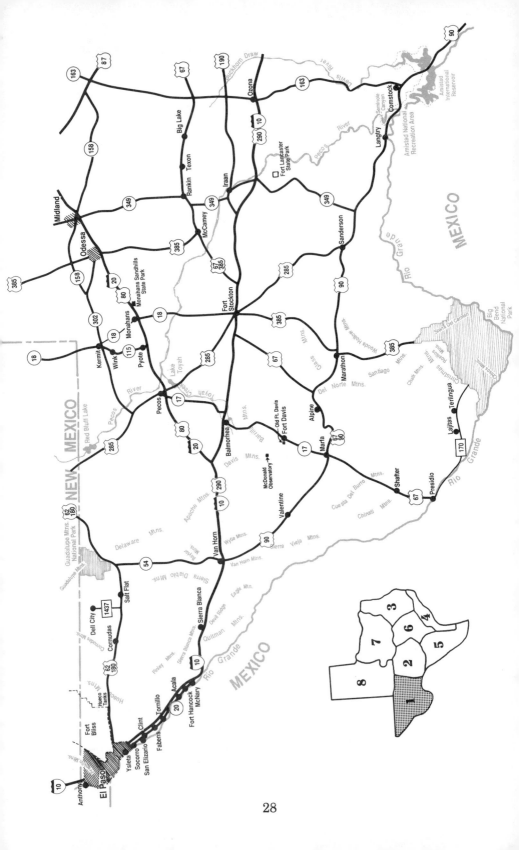

28

F rom deep in the central Mexican interior, between the twin spines of the Sierra Madre Occidental and the Sierra Madre Oriental, an arid arc stretches across the Rio Grande into West Texas and southern New Mexico. This plume is the Chihuahuan Desert, one of the largest arid tracts in North America. It blankets the far west portion of Texas—a region also known as Trans-Pecos Texas. In Texas the desert is bound on the north by the New Mexico line, on the east by the Pecos River, and on the south and west by the Rio Grande. It covers some 30,000 square miles; each mile is different, yet each is the same.

Although the desert appears to have been here forever, in geological terms it is a youngster. Millions of years ago a warm ocean rich and varied in marine life covered West Texas. The decomposed bodies of tiny sea creatures formed thick calcium deposits on the ocean floor, and after many years of mixing with sand and mud they hardened into limestone. Then volcanic action lifted the ocean floor into the sunlight, and plants took root in the mineral-rich soil. Immense savannas spread across the land, and trees grew to enormous heights. Dinosaurs once grazed in the swamps, before mammoths and smaller animals moved in to take their place.

As recently as 4,000 years ago leafy woodlands thrived in this region of Texas. But the Mexican mountain ranges choked off and threw back the clouds. Warm, moist air cools rapidly and condenses into rain as it moves up the slopes, leaving the lower elevations wanting for water. In West Texas this caused the rains to hesitate while the winds dried the air and the sun baked the land until the modern desert formed. Even though the region remains a desert, afternoon rainstorms are common from July through October. When the clouds burst and the water flows, you might hear it storming through the washes and canyons. Its power is enormous and potentially violent, as evidenced by house-sized boulders scattered about in area arroyos.

Covering a total area of 175,000 square miles in the United States and Mexico, the Chihuahuan Desert extends farther south than any other North American desert. It is united primarily by its common drainage into the Rio Grande and includes such diverse terrain as broad plains, mesas, gullies, hills and ridges, and an impassive scattering of stark mountains, some of which reach more than a mile in height. And since it is the highest desert on the continent, it is also the coolest. Visitors should remember that the night air can turn chilly, even in summer. The usual desert surface is gravelly, with thin, pale soil and a scattered assortment of arid-tolerant plants. At low elevations, cactus, creosote, and yucca are common. As the altitude increases, thorny bushes yield to scrubby juniper and madrona, then piñon and ponderosa pine appear. Douglas fir and aspen grow in the highest areas.

Three West Texas mountain ranges illustrate the dramatic transition from harsh to temperate climates. These are the Chisos Mountains in the Big Bend, the Davis Mountains near Fort Davis, and the Guadalupe Mountains that fade into southern New Mexico.

The desert, mountains, and river draw visitors by the tens of thousands to climb the rugged hills, raft the churning river, or experience the rapture of the desert sunset. Monahans Sandhills State Park, toward the eastern limits of the Chihuahuan Desert in Texas, features some magnificent sand dunes, but the desert's great sand dunes lay thirty-five miles south of El Paso, in Samalayuca, Mexico. Big Bend National Park—a classic, visible example of the Chihuahuan Desert at work and play—typifies its harshness, complexity, and beauty. It is a tough place to know, but once you get past that, it's an easy place to love.

The desert requires different methods of adapting. It evokes its own majestic mystery. While some may see it as an empty wasteland—desolate, primitive, and inhospitable to life—others see opportunity in the desert. In the Marfa and Fort Davis area, for instance, ranchers take advantage of the vast prairies of native grasses that provide excellent grazing for their livestock during the rainy seasons, or "monsoons" as the locals call them. Yet, all around this region are parched riverbeds with dust that could not be drier if it lay on the frozen face of the moon.

Archaeological evidence places the arrival of the Suma, Manso, and Jumano Indians in the desert at about 1200 B.C. They survived partially by irrigated farming but mostly by hunting animals and gathering nuts and berries. These natives did not pose a serious detriment to the white man's conquest of this area. They also no longer exist as a people.

The notoriously uncooperative Comanches made "August Moon" raids on settlements in Texas and Mexico, storming through and around the region stretching from Abilene and Odessa to Fort Stockton and Marfa. But even they had limitations on their isolation and preferred the grasslands and abundant water holes of the Great Plains to the desert.

West Texas was the last retreat in the state for Apaches. By the 1880s the survivors of this once-mighty nation had been reduced to hunting rodents. Almost constantly on the run from whites, they occasionally marauded; but mostly they hid from their enemies and simply tried to stay alive in the harsh environment.

In a canyon near the Sierra Diablo, during the cold morning of January 29, 1881, a group of nineteen Texas Rangers led by Capt. George W. Baylor surprised a sleeping group of exhausted Apaches. As the sun rose, the rangers commenced firing. They killed four men, two women, and two children before taking another woman and two children as prisoners. The captive woman received three bullet wounds in her hand, and the baby she held took a wound in the foot. No rangers were hurt. Several Indians escaped. This was the last Indian fight in Texas.

Because of its location, Far West Texas developed historically along with New Mexico. The central corridor of Spanish empire and conquest flowed north out of Old Mexico along the Rio Conchos in Chihuahua. Where that river joined the Rio Grande, at present-day Presidio, Spanish expeditions followed the great river west and north, sometimes exploring, sometimes seeking gold, but almost always enslaving Indians to work in the brutal mines of Santa Barbara, Chihuahua.

In 1581 three priests and nine soldiers trekked through the vicinity of El Paso. The intrepid adventurers carried the word of God to New Mexico in the first documented European penetration of what is now Far West Texas. Seventeen years later, in 1598, Juan de Oñate, a conquistador and colonist who wanted to be governor of New Mexico, ignored the Rio Conchos route and set out with 500 colonists to march north across the fierce Chihuahuan Desert to El Paso. Oñate extended El Camino Real (the King's Highway or Royal Road) from Mexico City through what is now El Paso and into northern New Mexico. This 1,600-mile "interstate" highway stretched to Santa Fe by about 1610 and remained the longest and most heavily traveled road in North America for two centuries.

Beyond the Rio Grande, Spain made little penetration into Far West Texas. The largest villages stood at Ysleta and Socorro (established 1680) and San Elizario (1780s).

West Texas essentially belonged to nobody prior to 1848. Before then, New Mexico claimed an unspecified share of the land, as did Chihuahua and Spanish Texas. But the region had few, if any, voters and taxpayers. Rancorous Apaches and Comanches controlled the desolate countryside, and their political issues and views never attained overriding importance.

After the Missouri Farm Boys led by Col. Alexander Doniphan conquered the area in December 1846, the United States annexed the region as part of New Mexico Territory. Barely more than a year later, after the discovery of gold at Sutter's Mill in California sent pioneers scurrying west to attain their fortunes, the state of Texas laid claim to the area and sent crack Texas Ranger Jack "Coffee" Hays to blaze a trail from San Antonio to El Paso. Hays and his ranger party suffered from thirst and starvation before they wandered into Chihuahua, across the Rio Grande from Presidio, and were lucky the Mexicans did not shoot them. Nearly three months later Hays returned to San Antonio and sheepishly reported that while he did not know of a suitable wagon road to El Paso, he had found a reliable road to Presidio.

Undeterred and without delay, the state dispatched surveyors Robert S. Neighbors from Waco and John S. "Rip" Ford from Austin in March 1849. They rode through Fredericksburg, forded the Pecos River at Horsehead Crossing, threaded their way through Guadalupe Pass, and reached El Paso on May 2. Their route became known as the "upper road," but the Neighbors-Ford trail was not ideally suited to wagon travel.

In late May, Maj. Gen. William J. Worth ordered two United States Army lieutenants, William Henry Chase Whiting and William H. Smith, to find and survey a "lower" El Paso-San Antonio route. Whiting and Smith meandered through the present-day sites of Uvalde and Bracketville before turning north and crossing the Pecos west of Ozona. The officers returned to San Antonio 104 days later to find that Major General Worth had succumbed to a cholera epidemic that swept the town. But that tragedy did not lessen the value of their discovery. The trail they blazed, commonly called the El Paso-San Antonio Road, quickly became more popular than the upper road as an emigrant route because it had better opportunities for water and proved more reliable for year-round wagon travel.

Many emigrants believed these upper and lower roads were well marked, but in most places they were not. The travelers typically wandered several miles to one side or the other of the route to take advantage of water, grass, wood, and hunting opportunities.

Meanwhile, the army had already begun establishing military posts in Far West Texas by 1849, though the region at that time remained under the jurisdiction of the Department of New Mexico. Fort Bliss, known as the Post Opposite El Paso (Mexico) prior to 1854, was the first in the area, and it anchored a line of eleven forts stretching along the Rio Grande south of Santa Fe. The Texas forts of Quitman, Lancaster, and Davis—all charged primarily with protecting wagon trains and travelers heading to California—came along in 1853.

To garrison Fort Bliss, Maj. Jefferson Van Horne set out from San Antonio in June 1849 with 275 men and 2,500 head of livestock. A party of California emigrants tagged along, handily relying on the army for protection. The entire column marched 650 miles to El Paso in 100 days, arriving on September 8, 1949.

John R. Bartlett, an American boundary commissioner riding toward El Paso in November 1850, wrote these remarks in his journal near the spot where he forded the Pecos River: "Barren plains continue. Dried grass and weeds prevail. Many carcasses and skeletons of oxen, and several skeletons of mules, marked our route today, as well as the remains of broken wagons. As the prairie did not furnish us fuel to make our fires, we gathered up fragments of the wagons."

The Butterfield Overland Mail, which began service from St. Louis to San Francisco in September 1858, swept along this same route. It covered the entire 3,000-mile route in twenty-three days and twenty-three hours; it took fifty-five and a quarter hours to travel from the Pecos River to El Paso.

John Russell Bartlett (1805-1886), boundary commissioner for much of the U.S.-Mexico international line. —Rhode Island Historical Society

Waterman L. Ormsby, a special correspondent for the *New York Herald*, rode that first stage all the way to San Francisco and published eight articles about the trip. He wrote that the forty-five-year-old stage driver, Henry Skillman, resembled "portraits of the Wandering Jew, with the exception that he carries several revolvers and bowie knives, dresses in buckskin, and has a sandy head of hair and beard. He loves hard work and adventures, hates 'Injuns,' and knows the country about here pretty well."

At one point when the stage stopped for breakfast, the passengers learned that someone at the last station had failed to pack the coffee and food for the meal. They contented themselves with "jerked beef, raw onions, crackers slightly wormy, and a bit of bacon."

While fares varied, by 1860 it cost $150 to travel one-way over the entire route; shorter trips cost 10¢ a mile, and passengers could carry up to forty pounds of luggage at no extra charge. But transporting mail remained the primary business of the Butterfield Overland Mail Company. It charged 10¢ per half-ounce for "through" letters, and in an average month the stage carried 4,000-6,000 letters. Freight shipments cost $1 per 100 pounds for 100 miles.

The company went out of business when the Civil War started. The federal government ordered United States military post commanders to lower the Stars and Stripes, turn their forts and equipment over to state officials, and march their soldiers east to the Gulf Coast, where ships would transport them to New England.

As Union soldiers trudged toward San Antonio, some of the Texas Mounted Rifles, later reinforced by 2,000 Confederates, entered El Paso in an attempt to conquer New Mexico, Arizona, and California. Within a few months that effort failed, and the starving, thirsty soldiers retreated back across West Texas. Henry Skillman, the former Overland stage driver, became a captain and a spy for the Confederacy and was slain near Presidio, Texas, in 1864 while carrying dispatches.

Within fifteen years after the Civil War, the isolation of Far West Texas was broken by the railroads. From California, the Southern Pacific spun steel rails in 1880 across the blistering sands of Arizona and New Mexico toward El Paso. The Atchison, Topeka & Santa Fe steamed south from Colorado. And the Texas & Pacific laid track west across Texas at the rate of one mile per day.

Ferocious competition broke out among the different railroads, in part because the federal government awarded huge grants of public lands to railroad companies for every mile of track laid. In Texas, where the United States had no public lands, the state put up its own bounty. The state legislature handed the Texas & Pacific twenty sections (each one square mile, or 640 acres) of land per mile of track.

When the Galveston, Harrisburg & San Antonio fell behind, one of the Southern Pacific's "Big Four" investors, C. P. Huntington, purchased a major portion of the GH & SA, making it a Texas subsidiary of the Southern Pacific. That company then merged with the Texas & Pacific, and when their tracks met at Sierra Blanca, eighty miles east of El Paso on December 16, 1881, the first "southern" transcontinental rail hookup had been made.

From those years until well after the turn of the century, railroads raked in enormous profits. They not only monopolized transportation, they controlled rates. They sold their "free land" to farmers and ranchers and earned additional sums by hauling farm and ranch produce. Most cities in Far West Texas started as rail (or oil) towns. While it is easy today to criticize the railroads for their excessive greed, their presence led to substantial development and population growth. Everybody benefited.

Then along came Santa Rita. When that oil well blew in on May 28, 1923, it set off a stampede for black gold similar to the California rush of '49. Tent cities sprang up overnight, populated largely by men with no religion and no faith in anything but Lady Luck. Oil created a rowdy, convulsive, dueling period in West Texas growth. (See Permian Basin and Texon, Big Lake.)

On the heels of the great gushers came the Great Depression, slapping Texas from boom to bust. Although the oil fields remained open, the companies pumped crude from the underground reserves at a reduced rate. Many folks simply sat out this difficult period by remaining on their farms and ranches. The old homestead provided subsistence living, and that was as well as the rest of the country was doing.

A lot of West Texans went to war during the 1940s. El Paso underwent a huge buildup at Fort Bliss. The horse cavalry dismounted in 1943 and became mechanized. The war pulled Far West Texas, as well as the rest of the nation, out of the Great Depression. During and after the war, many American families moved to other parts of the country. In the West especially, including Texas, new residents found homes as people all over the country became less isolated and more mobile.

During the 1950s, West Texas got another economic buzz with the completion of interstate highways I-10 and I-20. Since that time, many of the tiny towns and way stations along the route have shifted their economic bases from oil and agriculture to tourism. In the early 1990s about 20 percent of the nation's cross-country traffic flowed over I-10.

For many years residents of Far West Texas tried to recreate the places they or their families had known in the East. Everybody wanted a green lawn. Trees replaced cactus. They treated the desert as foreign—something to be shunned. And they welcomed smokestack industries because of the high-paying jobs that came with them. Water taken from below the surface was water nobody missed because no one could see the underground levels dropping.

Today that attitude is changing. Water is treated like a precious resource in many places because, in fact, it is. More people are enjoying the desert these days on its own terms, and its beauty is not hard to find. The towns and cities in West Texas are finally coming to terms with the land. Perhaps part of this new approach owes something to our growing appreciation for western history.

A vaquero leads his burros, loaded with chino grass, along the Rio Grande on the way to a trading post. —Museum of the Big Bend, Sul Ross State University, Alpine, Texas

The Rio Grande

The Mississippi, Ohio, Shenandoah, and Colorado rivers invoke images, but not of states; however, when you think of the Rio Grande, you think of Texas. The two are inseparable.

The Rio Grande rises as a clear, snow-fed mountain stream 12,000 feet above sea level in the Rocky Mountains of Colorado. From there it slices New Mexico in half as it rolls south toward the El Paso-Juárez metropolis at the junction of Chihuahua and Texas. The 1848 Treaty of Guadalupe Hidalgo, which ended the Mexican War, established the Rio Grande as the international boundary between Texas and Mexico. The border commences about three miles north and west of downtown El Paso.

The Rio Grande is the fifth-longest river in North America and ranks twentieth in length among rivers of the world. It is 1,885 miles long. It drains a basin of 172,000 square miles. The river flows 170 miles in Colorado, 461 miles in New Mexico, and 1,254 miles in Texas, 107 twisting miles of which negotiate the southern boundary of the Big Bend National Park. Over five million people live along the banks of the Rio Grande.

No one person or group ever explored the Rio Grande as a single unit. Probably the first European to cross the river was Alvar Núñez Cabeza de Vaca in 1535. Five years later Francisco Vázquez de Coronado also crossed it. Juan de Oñate led 500 colonists across the river in 1598. Gov. Juan Bautista de Anza explored it in 1779, as did Zebulon Montgomery Pike in 1806 and John Charles Frémont in 1849. In 1853, boundary commissioners Robert Campbell for the United States and José Salazar for Mexico surveyed and marked the Rio Grande as the international boundary.

The river has had a dozen or more names from the days when Spain, Mexico, France, and the United States thought of the Rio Grande as several different streams. In a sense, the Rio Grande is two streams. It dwindles nearly to puddle status at Presidio and sustains its journey to the Gulf of Mexico only with help from the Rio Conchos coming out of Mexico.

In the United States the river is called the Rio Grande, which translates literally as Big River. Since *rio* is Spanish for river, it would be redundant to say "Rio Grande River." Author and historian Paul Horgan interprets Rio Grande as "Great" River, which suits the river's stature among the world's waterways. In Mexico it is called Rio Bravo, not so much because it is brave as to acknowledge its bold, wild, restless, and turbulent qualities.

The Rio Grande's principal tributaries are the Pecos, Devils, Chama, and Puerco rivers in the United States, and the Conchos, Salado, and San Juan in Mexico. Major cities alongside the river are Santa Fe, Albuquerque, Socorro, Truth or Consequences, Mesilla, and Las Cruces in New Mexico, and El Paso, Presidio, Del Rio, Eagle Pass, Laredo, Rio Grande City, McAllen, and Brownsville in Texas. In Mexico the primary riverside (and thus, border) towns are Ciudad Juárez, Ojinaga, Ciudad Acuna, Piedras Negras, Nuevo Laredo, Camargo, Reynosa, and Matamoros. Mexican states bordering the Rio Grande are Chihuahua, Coahuila, Nuevo Leon, and Tamaulipas. Cuidad Juárez is the largest city on the Rio Grande, and its Texas neighbor, El Paso, is the second largest.

The Rio Grande has never been navigable except near its mouth and, on rare occasions, from the Gulf of Mexico to Laredo. From its origin in Colorado's San Juan Mountains to Albuquerque, the river is primarily a torrent enclosed by spectacular gorges and mountain slopes. South of Albuquerque, however, the land flattens into a desert and the river flows at a slower pace.

Two dams near Truth or Consequences, New Mexico—Elephant Butte, completed in 1916, and Caballo, in 1938—impound the water for use by farmers to irrigate their crops in the Mesilla and El Paso-Juárez valleys. The dams promised a steady supply of irrigation water on demand. By treaty, Mexican farmers near Juárez usually receive 60,000 acre-feet of water per year; however, during years of low snowmelt in the Colorado Rockies, the amount of water available for crop irrigation drops proportionately.

At Presidio the water races toward the canyon walls of Big Bend National Park. South of Redford (formerly Polvo), the Texas Bofecillos and Chihuahua mountains converge to form Colorado Canyon. From there the churning Rio Grande cuts through the limestone formations of Santa Elena, Mariscal, and Boquillas canyons.

Beyond Del Rio, Eagle Pass, and Laredo the Rio Grande skirts huge cattle ranches and farms. Broad, open valleys are the rule in that region, and the river turns brown and sluggish. The scenery caters to area citrus groves, producing a fertile, tropical atmosphere. The river terminates in a true delta at the Gulf of Mexico.

Bancos once posed a serious problem for riverside residents as well as the international boundary. Bancos are wide, often brushy, curves shaped like horseshoes or oxbows that frequently overflowed and altered the main channel of the river. Defining the exact border between the United States and Mexico became a complex issue that the two governments finally resolved with the banco treaty of 1905. It called for straightening the river, slicing through the bancos and awarding the land inside the curves to whichever country they then projected into. The land swap proved about even in terms of acreage gained and lost, and the straighter channel keeps the border consistent.

In 1933 the United States and Mexico approved the Rio Grande Rectification Treaty, which nearly halved the river's lengthy course through the El Paso area by straightening the Texas channel. That work cleared a lot of streamside brush and made the land more suitable for farming. The arable bottomland ushered in King Cotton.

Significant assistance arrived for southeast Texas in 1932, when the United States and Mexico agreed on the Lower Rio Grande Valley Flood Control Project. It called for straightening and raising levees and dredging the channel and floodways. The Mexican-United States Treaty of February 3, 1944, committed both countries to constructing two more dams on the Rio Grande: Falcon and Amistad.

Today the Rio Grande rarely lives up to its name. The dams have choked and tamed its fury and made the river more of a working stream. At times it still dazzles observers with its power and majesty, but increasingly it just looks like a polluted waterway carrying fertilizer and sewage from cities and farms. But it is still a magnificent river in terms of its history and the tragedies that have played out along its banks. Were it not for the Rio Grande, there would be no Texas, or at least not in its present shape and form.

Anthony

Anthony calls itself "the best town in two states" because it sits on the Texas-New Mexico line. It is a farming village as well as a bedroom community of El Paso. In the Franklin Mountains overlooking this village is a peak dubbed "Anthony's Nose" by early Spanish wayfarers. Although the town was organized in 1881 as a Santa Fe railhead called "La Tuna," it later changed its name to honor St. Anthony, the patron saint of the poor.

Franklin Mountains

The Franklin Mountains east of I-10 between Anthony and El Paso reach a height of 7,192 feet. Composed of sedimentary and igneous rocks, these hills are between forty and fifty million years old and measure just three miles wide and seventeen miles long.

Benjamin Franklin Coons (or Coontz), an 1840s developer, named the mountains and the village for himself. Early-day cartographers called the mountains Los Organos, evidently considering them a southern extension of the Organ Mountains near Las Cruces, New Mexico. At one time they were also known as the White Mountains, after an 1840s customs inspector.

Transmountain Road (Texas Highway 375) crosses the Franklins at their lowest point, through Smuggler's Pass. In days past, cattle rustlers sometimes stole Mexican livestock and drove them through this gap from the east side of the mountain. The river thickets provided cover for the thieves and their booty until they could load the cattle onto trains passing through the area. In April 1890 two El Paso policemen and Texas Ranger Charles Fusselman were ambushed after chasing a group of rustlers toward the pass. The *El Paso Herald* reported:

> The three pursuers were going up the canyon, Fusselman in the lead, when they saw a band of about 30 horses apparently grazing on a little bench above. Seeing no men and thinking the thieves had abandoned the stolen horses and fled, they started up to the animals, when suddenly seven rifles belched forth from brush and rocks but a few feet ahead, and Fusselman reeled from his saddle and fell.

Today that canyon, the largest in the Franklins, is known as Fusselman Canyon.

Another significant gorge in the Franklins is McKelligon Canyon, across from William Beaumont Army Medical Center. Workers developed this undedicated park during the Great Depression as a project to create jobs. In McKelligon Canyon are trails and picnic areas and a few scattered mine shafts. Viva El Paso, a brilliant outdoor pageant, takes place in the canyon nearly every day during the summer months. The canyon also hooks up with Mt. Franklin Wilderness Park, the only wilderness park within a city limits anywhere in the United States.

Visitors to El Paso should find time to enjoy a tour on Scenic Drive. The paved two-lane road winds around the southern tip of the Franklins and offers spectacular views, day or night, of downtown El Paso and Ciudad Juárez, as well as the Rio Grande, the Hueco Mountains (thirty miles to the east), and several mountain ranges in Mexico.

Mt. Cristo Rey

West of the Franklins and barely across the Rio Grande in New Mexico is Sierra de Cristo Rey, the Mountain of Christ the King. On its peak stands a forty-foot Cordovan cream limestone figure of the crucifixion. Formerly known as "Mule Driver's Mountain," this and the Franklin Mountains are El Paso's most dominant physical landmarks.

In 1933, to commemorate the nineteenth centennial of the Redemption, Father Lourdes F. Costa, a local priest, suggested placing a cross on the

Mt. Cristo Rey overlooks west El Paso. —Fred Ortiz

40

mountain. The Catholic Church apparently liked the idea and five years later retained Spanish sculptor Urbici Soler, who clung to a scaffold in stormy and pleasant weather at nearly a mile above sea level to carve out his masterpiece with an air chisel.

Visitors can follow a two-mile trail to the cross; however, the trek is arduous and potentially dangerous. A physically fit person can climb the mountain in an hour, but the area is remote and unguarded. Group travel is the safest way to visit the site.

The University of Texas at El Paso

Dominating high ground on the east side of I-10, a mile west of downtown El Paso, is the University of Texas at El Paso (UTEP). It began in 1914 as the State School of Mines and Metallurgy and became Texas Western College in 1949. In 1967 the school achieved university status. Student enrollment tops 16,000 and includes the largest Hispanic population of any university in the nation.

After reading a 1914 article in *National Geographic* about Bhutan, the first dean's wife, Kathleen Worrell, realized a similarity between the terrain around El Paso and the eastern Himalayan kingdom: in both cases craggy, largely barren mountain ranges towered over the nearby villages. Of course, the Himalayas rise 22,000 feet higher than the mountains near El Paso, but loftiness in this case was irrelevant.

At his wife's suggestion, Dean Steven Worrell adopted Bhutanese architecture for the college, and that design theme remains intact today. UT El Paso is the only location outside Bhutan where such striking and beautiful architecture can be found. The massive, sloping walls are shaded by overhanging roofs and girded with deep red bands. The high design of windows and doors was originally intended to discourage marauders, but the campus has never had a problem with such types.

Although the university no longer teaches mining engineering, its athletic teams are known far and wide as "the Miners." The campus is home to the nationally famous Sun Bowl (now the John Hancock Bowl), and the UTEP basketball team usually places within the nation's top twenty each year. In 1966 it won the NCAA championship. Also noteworthy is the university's Centennial Museum, which houses a fine archaeological collection.

El Paso

The first Europeans known to penetrate the El Paso region, the Chamuscado-Rodríguez expedition, came through in 1581. The Spanish described lakes and lagoons in the area, which meant the Rio Grande would have been overflowing at the time.

In 1598 the wealthy conquistador Juan de Oñate brought 500 colonists up from Santa Barbara, Chihuahua, a hamlet near Parral. They struck the Rio

Grande near present-day San Elizario and celebrated the first North American thanksgiving more than two decades before the Pilgrims. Then on May 4 they forded the river near what is now downtown El Paso. Oñate named that crossing El Paso del Rio del Norte, "the Pass Across the River of the North."

Oñate's trail north ended at Santa Fe; southward it stretched all the way to Mexico City. Officially it became El Camino Real—the King's Highway or Royal Road. At 1,600 miles, it was the longest highway in North America. For two centuries the commerce of an empire flowed across it, and each trip brought the explorers, merchants, slavers, and other travelers through the site that later became El Paso, Texas.

The Suma and Manso Indians lived in this section of the Rio Grande Valley. And because of them the Spanish built a mission in 1659 called Nuestra Señora de Guadalupe (Our Lady of Guadalupe) just south of the river. The padres named the village that grew around the mission El Paso del Norte. Today that city is Juárez.

After 1822 increasing numbers of American traders traveled between New Mexico and Missouri over the Santa Fe Trail. Some of the traders went farther south to the Mexican mint in Chihuahua City, Chihuahua, lashing their oxen through El Paso del Norte along the way.

Two of those adventurers, James Magoffin and Hugh Stephenson, married wealthy Spanish women and built their homes north of but adjacent to the Rio Grande. Their estates, and another owned by Ponce de León (not the same adventurer seeking the Fountain of Youth in Florida), strung along in a series of ranches known as Magoffinsville, Stephensonville, and Ponce's Rancho. Ponce de León moved out of El Paso del Norte in 1827 and by 1832 had built his rancho across the river in the heart of what is now downtown El Paso.

Two days after Christmas 1846, during the Mexican War, Col. Alexander Doniphan peacefully marched 800 Missouri Farm Boys into El Paso del Norte and occupied it. The north bank of the Rio Grande passed forever from the feeble grasp of Mexico. The 1848 Treaty of Guadalupe Hidalgo, which ended the Mexican War, brought the Mexican territories of New Mexico and California under United States authority and established the Rio Grande as the border of Texas.

After learning that the U.S. Army planned to locate a fort north of the Rio Grande, developer Benjamin Franklin Coons (or Coontz) leased Ponce's Rancho and rented part of it to the military. He renamed the village Franklin. Since the name suited the town, Coons figured it also fit the mountains that the community would eventually curl around, so they became the Franklins. The discovery of gold in California brought thousands of "forty-niners" streaming westward through Franklin.

In 1850 El Pasoans voted to join Texas rather than remain part of New Mexico. As Congress anguished over organizing the newly acquired Southwest into territories, the slavery issue threatened to divide both the existing nation and the new lands in question. The Compromise of 1850 staved off civil war

42

Nuestra Señora de Guadalupe Mission, Juárez, Chihuahua. —Library of Congress

for another decade. It admitted California as a state and allowed for territorial governments in New Mexico (which included Arizona) and Utah. The legislation also formed the present boundaries of Texas.

Nearly a decade later the Butterfield Overland Mail stage rumbled through Far West Texas on its route between St. Louis and San Francisco, and the company built a major stage station and corrals at Franklin. Indiana-born Anson Mills stepped off one of those stages in 1859 and surveyed a downtown plat. Some of the resulting streets dead-ended while others ran diagonally to form triangular properties, but the layout represented the best deals Mills could work out with landowners. When he changed Franklin's name to El Paso, both sides of the Rio Grande ended up with separate towns of the same name.

In El Paso, Texas, El Paso Street led to El Paso del Norte (Juárez), Mexico, and still does. San Antonio Street headed toward San Antonio, Texas, 600 miles east. The Butterfield Overland Mail Company built its offices on Overland Street, and San Francisco Street pointed the stages toward San Francisco, more than a thousand miles distant. Chihuahua Street showed the way to Chihuahua. Santa Fe Street emerged from Chihuahua and meandered toward Santa Fe.

The same year the American Civil War broke out, 1861, Benito Juárez was elected president of Mexico. The people liked him, but France challenged his authority and installed Archduke Maximilian of Austria as a puppet emperor of Mexico in 1864, sending Juárez to take refuge in El Paso del Norte. With support from the United States, Juárez managed to rally his armies and expel the French from his country. In 1867, five years before his own death, he executed Maximilian and resumed his position as president of Mexico. To honor this great Mexican patriot, El Paso del Norte changed its name in 1888 to Ciudad Juárez (the City of Juárez), leaving only one El Paso on the map—the one in Texas.

When the railroads arrived in 1881, El Paso shifted from a remote frontier community to a thriving and violent city. In all, five different lines converged on the city, and across the border the Mexican Central linked Juárez with Mexico City. Because of these major railroad connections, El Paso and Juárez began their rise as the two largest cities on the Mexican-American border.

El Paso quickly became one large brothel, and city officials "fined" the prostitutes $5 a month as a form of licensing. Early attempts to reform the corruption confined the brothels to only about 80 percent of the city, creating such colorful titles for El Paso as the Tenderloin, the Zone of Toleration, and the Reservation. Finally in 1915 the Texas Supreme Court abolished organized prostitution, ruling that shady ladies could not be forced to live in a particular section of town.

Gunfighters also arrived with the railroads, and the city lurched through five marshals in as many months. Most were dismissed for dereliction of duty. But one of the first who did not abandon his responsibility was City Marshal Dallas Stoudenmire.

On April 14, 1881, Stoudenmire killed four miscreants in five seconds during a shootout at the intersection of San Antonio and El Paso streets. Three days later, at the same intersection, as Marshal Stoudenmire walked his rounds in the company of Doc Cummings, former deputy Bill Johnson tried to ambush the pair using a double-barrel shotgun. He missed, but Stoudenmire and Cummings did not; they killed Johnson with eight bullets. Johnson was buried in a cemetery where the downtown public library stands today. Before building the library the bodies had to be moved, and several people who knew Johnson wanted a last peek, even though he had been dead many years. They pried off the lid to his casket and, according to the newspapers, there lay Bill Johnson looking better than most of the folks staring down at him. Then, before their astonished eyes, his body crumbled to dust.

On September 18, 1882, Marshal Stoudenmire met his end in that same fateful intersection during a wild gun battle with the Manning brothers, who owned a saloon where the Camino Real Paso del Norte Hotel now stands. The two factions had been feuding and had even signed a peace treaty, published

The El Paso County Courthouse as it appeared in 1891. —U.S. International Boundary and Water Commission

"Killin" Jim Miller and his cousin, John Wesley Hardin. Miller killed Bud Frazer in a saloon in Toyah, Texas, and was legally defended by Hardin in El Paso. —Mary Curry and Nina Neven

in the *El Paso Herald*, whereby both parties promised not to threaten each other when passing in the streets. Evidently the treaty broke down.

Famed gunslinger John Wesley Hardin arrived in the early 1890s. His Methodist preacher father named him after John Wesley, the founder of Methodism. His brother Joe was an attorney before being lynched. And John also earned a law degree—while spending nearly fifteen years in the state prison at Huntsville. Shortly before his release his wife died, so Hardin drifted to El Paso, where he hung out his law shingle on the southeast corner of east San Antonio and El Paso streets. It was a prominent but dangerous intersection, if Stoudenmire's experience was any guide.

Martin Mroz was one of Hardin's first clients. New Mexico lawmen accused Mroz of hog rustling and chased him until he took refuge in Juárez. Mroz, who did not look like a cowboy, was married to an attractive blonde named Helen Beulah. He sent her to retain an attorney in El Paso, and Beulah chose John Wesley Hardin. Within a week or so, Hardin had apparently chosen Beulah, too. She decided against returning to her husband.

Affronted by their openness, Mroz began threatening Hardin, who retained El Paso Chief of Police Jeff Milton and three additional lawmen to lure Mroz across the railroad bridge one night on the pretense of meeting his wife. The lawmen shot Mroz dead. He was buried in El Paso's Concordia Cemetery. The newspapers mentioned only two mourners at the funeral: Helen Beulah Mroz and her attorney and affectionate friend, John Wesley Hardin.

John Wesley Hardin drank heavily, and Beulah left him after he beat her. On August 19, 1895, Hardin walked into the Acme Saloon, on the northwest corner of South Mesa and San Antonio, and commenced rolling dice on the bar. "Brown, you have four sixes to beat," he said softly to the grocer rolling dice with him. At that instant constable and gunman John Selman stepped through the door and fired four quick shots from a .45. One bullet missed. The others struck Hardin in the head, chest, and arm. He fell dead. His body lay on the floor for two hours as most of the town filed past to view the body, then they hauled it off to the undertaker where it was washed and photographed. The newspapers said Hardin looked in good shape. He was buried in Concordia Cemetery, one space over from Martin Mroz.

John Selman's murder trial ended in a hung jury. A few months later, while awaiting retrial, Selman argued in an alley with U.S. Deputy Marshal George Scarborough, one of Mroz's killers. Scarborough shot Selman four times, and the old gunfighter died later on the operating table. The state tried Scarborough for murder, but the jury acquitted him. The marshal resigned his commission and went to New Mexico, where he too died on the operating table after being shot by outlaws at Deming, New Mexico, exactly four years to the day after Selman died in El Paso.

The railroads brought more than gunfighters to El Paso. Lines from both Mexico and the United States brought military supplies, soldiers of fortune, war correspondents, and thousands of troopers to town during the Mexican Revolution of 1910-1930.

Revolutionaries led by Pascual Orozco, Francisco Madero, and Pancho Villa gathered across the Rio Grande from where ASARCO (American Smelting and Refining Company) stands today. The first battle of Juárez took place in May 1911; three days later, the city fell. In all, it changed hands six times during the revolution.

After that first battle, Mexican dictator Porfirio Díaz went into exile and Francisco Madero became president of the country. Francisco "Pancho" Villa and one of his wives, Luz Corral, briefly lived at 609 N. Oregon Street in El Paso. The historic site is now a parking lot. Two years later, Madero was assassinated by one of his generals, Victoriano Huerta, who then became president. Villa was forced back into Chihuahua, where, as an outlaw, he raged against Mexico as well as the United States.

The fighting across the river forever changed El Paso. Thousands of Mexican refugees entered the city; most were incarcerated behind barbed wire by the U.S. military—essentially as prisoners of war—since the army didn't know what else to do with them. When the fighting ended, some of the refugees returned home but most remained in this country, building, changing, and improving the city's heritage and culture. The great Mexican exodus into the United States began during the revolution.

From 1880 through the 1930s El Paso's reputation as a health center grew. Sanitariums dotted the foothills of the Franklin Mountains and the town became a "tent city" filled with tuberculars.

From the 1940s to the 1960s El Paso became a gateway for Mexican labor to the farmlands of rural America. Railroads hauled workers from the Mexican interior to the border; once there, they walked across the international bridges and American railroads shunted them to distant locations. While both countries processed Mexican laborers by the tens of thousands, that many more ignored the fees and formalities of time-consuming paperwork and crossed illegally. American farmers, who also didn't care much for paperwork, accepted the Mexicans willingly. Although American laws prohibited illegals from seeking work in the United States, they did not punish Americans for hiring them.

In 1963 the United States and Mexico resolved their century-old Chamizal dispute, whereby the meandering Rio Grande had removed portions of land from Mexico and deposited it in El Paso. The Chamizal Treaty returned 437.18 acres of south El Paso to Mexico, and in return the city received a border highway and a Chamizal National Memorial from the United States government as payment for displacing hundreds of El Pasoans.

The 1980s witnessed a tremendous surge of "maquila" plants in Juárez, and a smaller number of auxiliary plants, warehouses, and offices in El Paso. The maquilas were, and are, primarily assembly plants processing American (and frequently Japanese and European) manufactured products.

At the closing of the twentieth century El Paso can hardly be called a cluster of adobe buildings. Modern residential housing units spread for miles, especially to the east, and shopping centers and road systems are expanding. Even El Paso's downtown, as in the days of old, is thriving economically, primarily because so many Mexican people cross the bridges to shop.

Fort Bliss

Fort Bliss began in 1849 as the "post opposite El Paso," referring to its location across the Rio Grande from the largest city then in the vicinity—El Paso del Norte, Chihuahua (Ciudad Juárez since 1888). The post's mission was to meet American emigrants traveling west at the Pecos River and escort them to El Paso. In 1853 the U.S. Army moved the post three miles east to Magoffinsville, where it became Fort Bliss.

During the Civil War, Fort Bliss surrendered to the State of Texas. A Confederate army marched through intent on conquering the West all the way to the Pacific. But it stumbled during the Battle of Glorieta Pass, north of Santa Fe, and the Southern soldiers retreated back into the Texas interior. For the duration of the war elements of the Union's California Column occupied El Paso.

When the Rio Grande flooded Fort Bliss in 1867, the army moved the post for a third time, to Concordia (Stephensonville). In all, the post moved six times: Its fourth move, in 1878, brought it to downtown El Paso; its fifth move, in 1881, took it two miles to the west, to Hart's Mill; and in 1894 Fort Bliss found its permanent home on the mesa where it remains today.

During the Mexican Revolution, Gen. John J. "Black Jack" Pershing succeeded Gen. Hugh Scott as post commander and Fort Bliss became the largest cavalry post in the nation. The arrival of 50,000-plus troops represented the largest military buildup since the Civil War. Soldiers stood almost

Fort Bliss, Texas, circa 1860. —El Paso Public Library

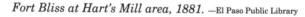

Fort Bliss at Hart's Mill area, 1881. —El Paso Public Library

Machine gun motorcycle, Fort Bliss, Texas, circa 1916. —El Paso Public Library

shoulder to shoulder along that section of the Mexican border. They camped on the courthouse lawn and erected machine gun emplacements around international bridges.

One day the Michigan band passed through the Georgia tent area while playing "Marching Through Georgia." The Georgia boys came boiling out of their quarters and the largest mass fistfight in United States military history took place near downtown El Paso. Nobody was seriously injured, but the doctors worked for hours patching broken noses and busted knuckles. The word then came down that military bands would no longer play tunes calculated to offend the sensibilities of other soldiers.

Pershing led a campaign against Pancho Villa in 1916 known as the Punitive Expedition. Villa evaded Pershing for eleven months, then the general and his troops were called to fight in the world war raging in Europe. Villa remained an outlaw until 1920; three years later he was assassinated on his rancho in Mexico. Pershing became general of the armies in 1919 and served as chief of staff from 1921 to 1924.

From the 1920s through the early 1940s, the best horse shows in the country took place at Fort Bliss. But the cavalry dismounted in 1943 to keep pace with the mechanized world, and the post became an artillery station. Today Fort Bliss is home of the 3rd Cavalry Regiment as well as headquarters for the primary United States Air Defense Center, a training ground for allied troops stationed everywhere in the world. Fort Bliss units won fame in Israel and Saudia Arabia during the Gulf War of 1991 by sending Patriot missiles to knock Iraqui Scud missiles from the nighttime sky.

Several excellent historical museums are located at Fort Bliss.

Ysleta

(To enter Ysleta, take Exit 32 off I-10 and go south three miles.)

Ysleta is the reason El Paso claims over 300 years of history. The town began in 1680 when Pueblo Indians drove 2,000 Spaniards from their homes in northern New Mexico. This was the greatest retreat of European peoples from Indians in the history of North America. The refugees fled south from Santa Fe and Albuquerque, leaving behind their burning villages and haciendas plus their dead relatives.

The Spaniards brought Tigua Indians with them from Isleta Pueblo, still in existence near Albuquerque. Upon reaching El Paso del Norte, the Spanish created a village called Ysleta del Sur (Isleta to the South) twelve miles downstream on the Rio Grande. Isleta and Ysleta are spelled differently but pronounced the same. Both mean "island."

The Ysleta Mission rebuilt in 1910 after the disastrous fire in 1907.
—The Institute of Texan Cultures

51

The town of Ysleta and its mission are the oldest in Texas, although the mission was previously destroyed by water and fire, and then rebuilt. St. Anthony is the mission's patron saint.

Ysleta was twice a county seat but lost the position permanently to El Paso in 1883. The Ysleta Elementary School sits on top of what once was the courthouse. In March 1955 the city of El Paso annexed Ysleta.

Ysleta Mission, 1936. —The Institute of Texan Cultures

(C)1936.

Tigua Indians in ceremonial dress at Ysleta, Texas, 1936. —The Institute of Texan Cultures

Tigua Indians

The Tiguas are the oldest ethnic group in Texas, and during the last 200 years its members have served as scouts for the U.S. Cavalry as well as for the Texas Rangers. Originally they were part of a Rio Grande pueblo (village) culture. After being forced south from Isleta, New Mexico, by the Spanish in 1680, they relocated at Ysleta. The Tiguas built the oldest mission in Texas, Corpus Christi de los Tiguas de Ysleta del Sur. In it the Tiguas still celebrate June 13, their principal feast day, in honor of St. Anthony.

Largely through the untiring efforts of El Paso attorney Tom Diamond, the Tiguas achieved state tribal status in May 1967 and national recognition as a native American tribal group in 1968. They bake bread the old-fashioned way: in outdoor adobe ovens fueled by burning mesquite roots. While most of the Tiguas are proficient in Spanish and English, few recall more than a handful of words in their native language. Since the Tiguas are a city tribe, and the children attend local public schools, severe pressures are placed on their cultural identity.

The Tigua tribe has only several hundred members as of the early 1990s. Their reservation in east El Paso (Ysleta) is just sixty-six acres. They run their own gift shops, administrative offices, workshops, dances, and public restaurant. On New Year's Eve, an Indian assembly elects a governor, lieutenant governor, tribal sheriff, and two at-large council members. These and other officials, such as captains and *mayordomos*, form a tribal council that sets policy and judges community disputes and issues.

In 1991 the Tiguas launched a claim with the U.S. Department of Interior for the return of their ancestral lands. A federal court case is pending. The Indians contend that in 1751 King Charles V of Spain provided them with a four-league grant of land, plus the symbolic Spanish Cane of authority. In 1872 the Texas legislature incorporated Ysleta, but it unincorporated two years later; by then non-Indian settlers had taken the aboriginal lands. In 1983 Tom Diamond asked for return of all former Tigua lands east of El Paso's Franklin Mountains plus all state lands in Hudspeth, Culberson, Jeff Davis, Brewster, and Presidio counties. As a practical matter, the Tiguas are not seeking private land, but they do expect to receive state property plus monetary benefits.

The Purisma Concepcion Church (Socorro Mission), Socorro, Texas.
—The Institute of Texan Cultures

Socorro

(Take Exit 33 off I-10 and drive south one mile to Socorro Road, then go east two miles.)

During the Pueblo Revolt of 1680, Piro Indians fled south from Socorro, New Mexico, with the Spanish refugees. Socorro del Sur was established that same year, five miles east of Ysleta. The Piro Indians lost their tribal identify due to intermarriage and social integration.

The Socorro Mission, with its massive adobe walls and interior shaped in the form of a cross (like the one in Ysleta), is a historical landmark. It and the Ysleta structure are the same age and both are the oldest missions in Texas. Like the Ysleta Mission, the one at Socorro suffered damage from the flooding the Rio Grande, but it has since been restored to much of its original condition. In 1851 United States Boundary Commission employees and local Socorro citizens tried four men for murder. All were found guilty and hanged from cottonwoods in the mission plaza. Socorro is one of the fast-growing tourist towns in the El Paso area.

San Elizario

(Take Exit 33 from I-10 and drive south two miles to Socorro Road, then turn east and follow Socorro Road seven miles, passing through Socorro on the way to San Elizario.)

This community, twenty-one miles east of downtown El Paso, began as the Hacienda de los Tiburcios during the 1700s. By the 1780s a fort (presidio), had been established at San Elizario. The presidio probably housed less than fifty Spanish soldiers at any one time, and most of those likely came from prisons under an agreement by which they promised to serve ten years in the frontier army. The men were abused by their country and superior officers, given little in terms of military equipment, and were buried wherever they happened to fall. Texas owes a great debt to presidio soldiers, and few people have ever heard of them.

The first thanksgiving in North America took place near here on April 30, 1598. Juan de Oñate's colonists, trekking from southern Chihuahua to northern New Mexico, paused to give thanks for their safe journey to the Rio Grande. Their celebration included performing a play, holding a huge feast, and baptizing dozens of local Indians. The ceremony ended with Oñate removing his cross and claiming the area for God and King Philip of Spain.

In 1850 San Elizario became the first county seat of El Paso County. Twenty-seven years later, the El Paso Salt War ended in San Elizario when a mob executed District Judge Charles Howard and two of his friends.

After the railroads bypassed San Elizario in 1881, its growth stalled. But the town's plaza remained intact, and its ancient jail, from which Billy the Kid liberated one of his friends in 1877, still exists. Restoration efforts are ongoing and gift shops are open.

The chapel at San Elizario Mission, 1936. —The Institute of Texan Cultures

Clint, Fabens, Tornillo, Acala, Fort Hancock, McNary

(These six towns are located along Texas 20, which runs parallel to and just to the south of I-10.)

These small farming communities sprang forth in the early 1900s after Elephant Butte Dam in New Mexico (120 miles north of El Paso) came on stream. The reservoir provided irrigation for cotton farming. Acala is named for Acala cotton. Fabens, Clint, and Fort Hancock are the largest villages. World-renowned jockey Willie Shoemaker called Fabens home. Clint received notoriety during the 1940s and 1950s when late-night radio commercials, powerfully broadcast from across the border in Mexico, advised listeners to send their money to "C-L-I-N-T, that's Clint, Texas." Soldiers at Fort Hancock patrolled the Mexican border during the Mexican Revolution (1910-1930), so the military post had but a brief mission. McNary was named for James C. McNary, an El Paso banker nominated as comptroller of the currency in 1923 by President Warren G. Harding. McNary might have gotten the congressional nod, but Harding died before he was approved for the assignment.

Sierra Blanca

Sierra Blanca took root where the Southern Pacific and the Texas & Pacific intersected in 1881. It is the seat of Hudspeth County and was named for the nearby 6,950-foot mountain. The town's attractions are a stucco-covered

The Southern Pacific Depot in Sierra Blanca, under restoration to become a museum.

adobe courthouse and yucca plants that grow fifteen to twenty feet high. The stalks bloom with white clusters in March and April.

On July 13, 1944, B-24 bombers from Biggs Air Force Base in El Paso mistook the town for a practice range, much to the astonishment of the town's residents. Fortunately, nobody was seriously injured by the ten bombs loaded with sand and small charges that struck the community. Five of the bombs hit the railroad tracks and one dropped in the driveway of a downtown service station.

Van Horn

This town is an automotive way station, and travelers who do not stop to eat, sleep, or at least pause for gas and to stretch their legs will miss it. Major Jefferson Van Horne camped at a nearby water hole in 1849, and the Van Horne Wells and the city that sprang from them bear his name, although the town fathers left the final "e" off when they incorporated the town. Before 1881 Van Horn was a way station. The Texas & Pacific Railroad made it a town, and today it is the seat of Culberson County and a major highway junction.

The remains of a Butterfield Overland stage station once stood at Van Horne Wells. Years after that company ceased to exist, in 1879, an Apache war party attacked a group of emigrants in Bass Canyon, twelve miles west of here. The dead were buried at Van Horne Wells.

Mountains surround Van Horn, with the Baylors to the north, the Carrizos and Beaches to the west, the Eagles to the southwest, and the Van Horn and Wylie mountains to the south and southwest. A local landmark called the High Lonesome Peak is also on the south.

The Beach Mountains, named for rancher J. H. Beach, have numerous small caverns as well as trees, wild grapevines, and rock formations. People from Van Horn picnicked here during the early days.

Close inspection of the Eagle Mountains will reveal the prominent peak that resembles an eagle, for which the mountains are named. Below the peak is Eagle Springs. A legend tells of an Indian who betrayed his friends and revealed the location of a treasure to another tribe. This angered the Great Spirit, who turned the treacherous Indian into a stone eagle and ordered him to forever guard this site.

The Culberson County Historical Museum in downtown Van Horn has an ornate hardwood antique bar, complete with mirrors and brass rail. The Sierra Diablo Wildlife Refuge for bighorn sheep is near Van Horn on Texas Highway 54.

US 62/180
El Paso—Guadalupe Mountains National Park
115 miles

Hueco Tanks

Thirty-five miles east of El Paso is a square mile of huge, jumbled syenite rock known as Hueco Tanks. As the rock dissolved unevenly across the centuries, it formed depressions in the ground capable of holding water. By some estimates the tanks could hold 100,000 gallons. In the middle of the desert, this awesome water hole has attracted both animals and humans. Among the rocks are caves, canyons, and overhanging cliffs. Prehistoric Indians camped nearby, and two of their cultures (Jornada and Mogollon) adorned the rock walls with art (as did early Europeans). Much of the art remains uninterpreted, but it pertains basically to Pueblo and Mescalero influences.

Comanche Cave is the largest in the complex, and historians say the art found there tells of an Indian massacre. One interpretation claims Mexican cavalry trapped and killed 150 Apaches; another says Tigua Indians were involved.

Early wagon trains rested here, as did the Butterfield Overland Mail. A portion of the stage's line shack still exists. Since the 1950s, both El Paso County and the Tigua Indians have attempted to turn the Hueco area into a visitors' site. Those efforts failed, and today the tanks are part of the Texas State Parks and Wildlife system.

Cornudas

This site once served as a resting place for passengers on the Butterfield Overland stage. Apparently that purpose is Cornudas's destiny because it still serves a similar purpose for modern travelers and truckers. The name comes from the nearby Cornudas Mountains, and it appeared frequently on reports from rangers, government workers, the military, travelers, and stage drivers.

Dell City

Thirteen miles north of US 62/180, on Farm Road 1437, is Dell City. The region is known as the "Valley of Hidden Waters" because of the vast underground resource discovered in 1948. Although the population numbers less than a thousand people, the cotton and vegetable farms they work are massive. About 25,000 sheep winter in this area.

Salt Flat

Ninety miles east of El Paso on US 62/180 are extensive surface salt deposits in a desert bolson (a depression with no natural drainage) at the foot of the Guadalupe Mountains. White men first used these flats in the mid-1600s, and the Indians likely used them, too. Salt served an important function in meat preservation, in addition to its value as a seasoning. Perhaps even more crucial to the men who dug precious metals from the ground, salt was necessary for smelting silver. Silver mines in northern Mexico consumed tremendous quantities, and to meet this need at least two well-traveled salt trails jutted up from Mexico and fanned out through the El Paso region.

In 1851 boundary commissioner John R. Bartlett found a wagon train stalled near here in dire need of fresh water. Soldiers from Fort Bliss rescued the travelers by hauling water from El Paso and placing barrels every ten miles.

In the 1860s, corrupt El Paso politicians formed a "salt ring" and began charging fees for salt removal, the injustice of which led to the infamous El Paso Salt War of the 1860s and 1870s. The fighting finally ended in San Elizario with the surrender of a squad of Texas Rangers. Political assassinations and a congressional investigation followed, leading to numerous indictments and the resurrection of Fort Bliss.

Guadalupe Mountains National Park

During the Permian period, nearly a quarter-billion years ago when warm inland seas covered this region, the skeletal remains of tiny marine organisms gradually built a limy reef thousands of feet thick. Movement of the earth's crust tilted the southwestern edge of the reef upward a mile and a half, giving rise to the great cliffs of the Guadalupe Mountains. For centuries travelers have marveled at the landmark features of these mountains. The 2,000-foot prowlike face of El Capitan is the most photographed mountain in Texas, although Guadalupe Peak, at 8,749 feet, is the highest point in the state.

In the late 1840s, when Apaches dominated this region, the upper trail linking El Paso with Austin meandered alongside the area that became Guadalupe Mountains National Park. The nearby Pine Springs served as a stage station, and the first meeting of the Butterfield Overland cross-country coaches—one from St. Louis, the other from San Francisco—occurred near this site in 1858.

In 1869 Capt. Felix McKittrick settled in the canyon that now bears his name. The gorge later became the cornerstone of the 76,293-acre national park, which was dedicated in 1972. In it are numerous deep canyons as well as timber-rich regions and springs. Over eighty miles of marked trails zigzag across the park's mountain ridges. Deer, elk, and mountain lions roam its more primitive areas. The visitor's center has maps, books, and other information needed for touring the park.

I-10
Junction of I-20—Ozona
182 miles

Balmorhea

In 1906 a trio of Chicago land promoters purchased a $14,000 tract of rolling Far West Texas plains and sold it to Easterners. The three developers (Balcom, Morrow, and Rhea) dubbed the plat after themselves: Bal-mor-hea. With thousands of cheap acres available for homesteading, the company enticed eastern buyers with a free train ride to view the property. Alfalfa was the principal crop. To better serve the community's needs, the developers built a forty-foot dam and reservoir in 1917 a mile and a half southeast of Balmorhea to store water from local springs as well as Madera Canyon in the Davis Mountains.

The region's greatest asset was San Solomon Springs (originally Mescalero Springs), which gushed forth at a rate of 26 million gallons per day. In 1927 the Bureau of Reclamation dredged the springs and constructed the main canal to give farming a boost.

During the Great Depression, 300 young men with the CCC (Civilian Conservation Corps) built Balmorhea State Park from the bounty of San Solomon Springs. Covering 68,000 square feet, the spring-fed swimming pool is on of the world's largest. The park is home to two rare and endangered desert fishes: the Comanche Springs pupfish and the Pecos mosquito fish.

Fort Stockton

Shipwrecked Spanish sailor Alvar Núñez Cabeza de Vaca wandered through this area in 1534. Jesuit priests named the place St. Gall in 1854, but development did not begin in this Pecos County seat until Camp Stockton opened in 1858. A year later the camp became Fort Stockton. Its soldiers protected emigrant roads and intercepted Indians along the nearby trail used by Comanche raiders. In 1881 the town growing around the military post officially became Fort Stockton. More than a hundred years after the U.S. Army abandoned the post (in 1886), local efforts are under way to reconstruct it.

Paisano Pete, the pride of Fort Stockton, Texas.

Sheriff Andrew Jackson Royal terrorized Fort Stockton from 1892 to 1894. Six men fell before his fast guns. To rid the town of his ruthlessness, the leading citizens met secretly and drew separately for a black bean. Whoever got the bean was supposed to kill Sheriff Royal with a shotgun. Royal met his death in November 1894 and the slaying was never solved.

Farming and ranching thrived after the Kansas City & Orient Railroad reached Fort Stockton in 1912. The world's largest gas and oil wells went in at Fort Stockton, as did the world's second-deepest man-drilled hole. In the mid-1950s several water wells west of Fort Stockton tapped the aquifer feeding Comanche Springs and pumped it dry, but they still managed to keep the Olympic-size swimming pool at Comanche Springs full.

The world's largest roadrunner is Paisano Pete—a fine sculpture of concrete and wood in the middle of Fort Stockton. Standing eleven feet high and twenty feet long, Pete is one of the most photographed subjects in West Texas.

The Annie Riggs Hotel Museum at Fort Stockton. This old hotel was built in 1899 and served as a stagecoach stop. The local historical society restored the building and now maintains the museum.

The old Riggs Hotel is now the excellent Riggs Museum. Travelers may also want to visit the courthouse square, the restored Grey Mule Saloon, and the old Fort Cemetery.

Iraan (US 190)

(Iraan is on US 190, fourteen miles northeast of the I-10 and US 190 junction.)

In 1927 Ira Yates and his wife, Ann, purchased a ranch and put down "Discovery Well A No. 1." A year later their gusher came in, spraying oil across tent cities for miles around.

Most oil workers slept in a red barn on the Yates property, so the community for awhile was called "Red Barn"; however, as a sprawling town site developed, the residents sponsored a contest for a new name. They chose to combine the names of the founders, Ira and Ann, and Iraan (pronounced Ira-Ann) arose.

Artist-illustrator Vincent T. Hamlin designed and sketched the cartoon "Alley Oop" while living in Iraan. Oop's favorite dinosaur, Dinny, is now the leading attraction at Iraan's Fantasyland. In model form, he weighs 80,000 pounds, stands sixteen feet tall, and stretches sixty-five feet long.

Fort Lancaster

Fort Lancaster stood on the east bank of Live Oak Creek a half-mile upstream from its junction with the Pecos River, along the San Antonio-El Paso Road near a crossing called Indian Ford. The infantry post was one of four established on that route in 1855 to ensure safe passage for emigrants, mail carriers, and freighters.

Fort Lancaster, Texas. —The Institute of Texan Cultures

63

It began as a meager camp of tents and canvas-roofed picket houses, but after the first year about twenty-five structures, many made of stone, gave the post a more substantial feel. Seventy-four enlisted men and four officers comprised the usual staff.

The stage road near the fort was so steep that mules had to be unhitched, blindfolded, and led one-by-one off the mesa. Coaches had to be lowered with block and tackle.

On March 19, 1861, in response to Texas seceding from the Union a month earlier, the U.S. Army abandoned the post and returned east to brace for the Civil War. Except for brief interludes, the military did not reoccupy Fort Lancaster after 1871. In the 1920s, the army removed all bodies from the cemetery except two—one was "Little Margaret," possibly the child of a soldier, and the other was an unknown Texas Ranger.

On May 17, 1968, Fort Lancaster was designated one of five historic forts in Texas. It is preserved and interpreted for visitors by the Texas Parks and Wildlife Department.

Ozona

As the only town in Crockett County, Ozona is the county seat. It is also the largest unincorporated city in Texas managed entirely by a county government. The community gets its name from the clearness and freshness of the atmosphere. Stock growers own several of the prominent homes in this region, which ranks high in wool production.

There is a Crockett County Historical Museum, plus a monument to Davy Crockett in the center of town. Nearby US 290 overlooks scenic Pecos Valley.

US 90
Van Horn—Marathon
130 miles

Valentine

On February 14, 1882, the Southern Pacific created a new community while laying track in West Texas. In honor of the day, the workers called the town Valentine. The local post office does a brisk business early each February. Valentine cards received by the first of the month are postmarked on or before the 14th with a special Valentine Day's cancellation.

Because Ozona is the county seat of Crockett County, this Davy Crockett Monument stands in the town square.

Marfa

Marfa and Alpine are gateways to the Davis Mountains and Big Bend country.

Marfa gets its name from a character created by the Russian novelist Dostoyevsky. The Southern Pacific's chief engineer's wife was reading *The Brothers Karamazov* as the railroad laid tracks through here. She liked the servant Marfa in the Karamazov household, and when the railroad reached a watering spot in 1882 and needed a name for it, Marfa won the honor.

Hollywood chose this location to film the movie *Giant* in the mid-1950s. It starred James Dean, Rock Hudson, and Elizabeth Taylor, but Dean both lost his life and achieved immortal fame in his fateful car crash before the movie was released in 1956.

Marfa has always been cattle country, and it remains so today. However, soaring (hang gliding) has lately attracted considerable attention. Three national soaring championships and one world championship were staged during the 1980s. Golf is a growing sport here, too. The Marfa municipal golf course is over a mile above sea level—the highest course in Texas.

The eerie Marfa Lights are a mysterious phenomenon dating back to ancient Indians and wagon trains. Between two and six lights appear almost every night at dusk a short distance above the horizon. The lightbulb-sized luminaries move vertically and horizontally, sometimes at great speed, and glow white, blue, and occasionally red. Each year thousands of people observe them by looking south from marked roadside parking areas nine miles east of Marfa on US 90.

Highland Street in Marfa, Texas, 1940s. The Presidio County courthouse is on the far right. —Museum of the Big Bend, Sul Ross State University, Alpine, Texas

The 82nd Field Artillery on maneuvers near Marfa, Texas, circa 1928.
—El Paso Public Library

Marfa is home to the Chinati (Art) Foundation, named for the nearby Chinati (Black Bird) Mountains. It opened in 1979 and occupies 350 acres of the old Fort D. A. Russell. The foundation is working to establish one of the world's largest permanent art exhibits.

Fort D. A. Russell

As forts go, D. A. Russell arrived late. When the Mexican Revolution started in 1910, the U.S. War Department established Camp Marfa and ordered several troops of the 1st Cavalry there to protect the town and the border against insurgents. In addition, the soldiers offered asylum to Mexican refugees fleeing Ojinaga and transported them by train to El Paso. The post later became Fort D. A. Russell in honor of David Ashley Russell, a veteran of the Mexican War.

In December 1932 the military deactivated the fort. Louie, the oldest horse in the regiment, was given a military review. Less than three years later the fort was reactivated and enlarged to include an artillery brigade. During the Second World War Fort D. A. Russell served as a German prisoner-of-war camp, but it was closed for good in December 1945. In 1949 the post transferred to private ownership. Many of the old buildings remain intact.

67

Alpine

Alpine, established as Murphyville in 1883, is in Brewster County, the largest and most mountainous county in Texas. In this cattle country "large" spreads are those over 200,000 acres. Out of sight but not out of mind are orchards in the canyons west of town. They produce pecans, apples, and peaches.

A star of the community was the Holland Hotel built by Trost and Trost, El Paso's famous architects. The three-story building opened in 1912 during a mercury mining boom, and for nearly half a century it was the business, social, and cultural center of Alpine. The building closed in 1969, but reopened as a restored Holland Hotel in 1985.

After being postponed by the First World War, Sul Ross Normal College opened in 1920 on 100 acres of Hancock Hill. Lawrence Sullivan "Sul" Ross was a colorful Texas soldier, governor of the state, and later president of Texas A&M University. On the first morning of registration at Sul Ross Normal School, cowboys wearing boots, spurs, and bandanas enrolled with a kind of idle curiosity. Within a week every professor on staff knew the name of every student. Two years later, in 1923, the school became Sul Ross State Teachers College. In 1943 only thirty-three students graduated because of World War II. The following year just eighteen students were enrolled. But that changed when the WAACS (Women's Army Auxiliary Corps) arrived in groups of 200 for two months of training each. After the war, returning veterans flocked to school on the GI Bill and the student population grew steadily. In 1949 the school's name was shortened to Sul Ross State College, and twenty years later it achieved university status.

Main Street in Alpine, 1924. The large white building is the Holland Hotel.
—Museum of the Big Bend, Sul Ross State University, Alpine, Texas

Cowboys and a chuck wagon during a drive from Hudspeth Ranch in Val Verde County to Alpine, Nov. 29-Dec. 20, 1926. The ranch owner and second man on the right is Congressman Claude Hudspeth. —The Institute of Texan Cultures

Texas Rangers camped in the Alpine area of the Big Bend, 1880s. —Division of Manuscripts, Library, University of Oklahoma

Now covering 600 acres, Sul Ross is the only four-year institution of higher learning within 200 miles of Alpine. It offers programs in range animal science, range and wildlife management, biology, geology, and Chihuahuan Desert and Big Bend studies. It is the birthplace of the National Intercollegiate Rodeo Association (NIRA).

Noteworthy sites around here include the Woodward Agate Ranch sixteen miles south of Alpine on Texas 118, which will interest rockhounds; the unique western murals on the inside walls at the Southern Pacific depot and in the 1930s-style post office; and the Museum of the Big Bend on the Sul Ross State University campus, one of the finest museums in West Texas.

Marathon

A sea captain in 1882 said this area reminded him of Marathon, Greece, so he named the place after it when the Texas & New Orleans Railroad arrived. Like Alpine and Marfa, Marathon is a gateway to the Big Bend.

The old Gage Hotel, designed in 1927 by El Paso's great architect, Henry Trost, has been restored to its original splendor. While not all of the nineteen bedrooms have private baths, they each have colorful names, like Panther Junction, Dagger Mesa, and Stillwell's Crossing. Alfred Gage, once the largest landowner in Texas, ordered the hotel built, and it's said that he bought and sold over a million head of livestock in the lobby.

Fort Davis established an auxiliary post in 1881 called Fort Pena Colorado to interrupt the flow of Comanches across the Marathon Basin. Today it is a county park five miles south of Marathon. Pena Colorado was abandoned in 1893.

Texas 17
Marfa—McDonald Observatory
32 miles

Fort Davis National Historic Site

Fort Davis was named for Jefferson Davis, secretary of war and later president of the Confederacy. The post of Fort Davis, established in 1854, guarded the trail between San Antonio and El Paso and protected travelers from marauding Comanches and Apaches. The army abandoned the fort during the Civil War but sent black federal troops known as "buffalo soldiers" to reoccupy it in 1867. One of these was George Jordan of Company K of the 9th Cavalry.

In 1879 the twenty-eight-year-old Jordan was part of a 200-man force that engaged Mescalero Apaches during a battle in the Guadalupe Mountains. The army promoted him to sergeant, and in May 1880 he led a detachment of men that successfully defended Fort Tularosa against attacks by Victorio's Apaches. A short time later he and his company out-maneuvered and out-fought Indians at Carrizo Canyon. For his bravery and leadership, the government awarded Sergeant Jordan the Congressional Medal of Honor in 1890. He was one of seventeen black soldiers so honored for service during the Indian Wars.

Perhaps the most famous and brilliant officer ever to serve at Fort Davis was Gen. Benjamin Grierson. After the Civil War he organized the 10th Cavalry, a black unit, and brought it to Fort Davis to begin a relentless pursuit of the Apache renegade Victorio. The 10th so thoroughly destroyed Victorio's fighting career in Texas that the Apache leader fled to Mexico, where Mexican federal forces killed him.

The 10th Cavalry went to Arizona in 1885. The following is from an account by Helen Fuller Davis, who wrote on behalf of her husband, Lt. William Davis:

> The twelve troops of cavalry and long train of wagons for carrying camp equipage made a train—when stretched out—about two miles long; one of the three battalions taking the lead and then falling to the rear the next morning. This rotation gave them an equal chance of being first and avoiding the dust. Though we passed over unbroken ground, the dust was terrible for those in the rear. The soldiers fastened their handkerchiefs to their hats to protect their eyes.

By the end of the Indian Wars, in 1891, Fort Davis deactivated. People from San Antonio used the buildings for summer homes until the 1920s, when movie mogul Jack Hoxie turned portions of the location into a movie set. A few films were shot here prior to 1929, then things sort of died down until Judge David Simmons of Houston got local citizens involved in a massive restoration effort after 1946. In 1961 Congress authorized the National Park Service to take charge of the former fort and restore its buildings.

Visitors now wind through the fort's museum and reconstructed barracks. Around twilight you can hear bugles and hoofbeats, muffled commands, and band music echoing across the parade ground in a haunting rendition of days past.

Fort Davis

The town of Fort Davis grew up around the military post and attracted its share of hard characters. One was Jesse Evans, who befriended Billy the Kid in Lincoln County, New Mexico. Another was John Selman, who later killed John Wesley Hardin in El Paso. But in Fort Davis, during the wild 1880s, more gunmen than these terrorized the town.

71

Relief came only after Sgt. L. B. Caruthers and a group of Texas Rangers suppressed the lawlessness. On July 1, 1880, six rangers fought the outlaws. The following is from Sgt. Ed Sieker's official report:

We shot at them and a running fight lasted for one and one-half miles. We discovered they were concealed behind a ledge of rocks, as a solid volley was fired at our little band. A shot cut [Ranger] Carson's hat brim and another passed under his leg, wounding his horse. At forty yards, Carson shot one of the [outlaw] party in the side, but the man was determined and kept shooting. When I saw him stick his head up to shoot, I shot him between the eyes. [Ranger] Bingham was about 35 yards to my rear, when he was shot through the heart. We charged their stronghold and they surrendered. Had I known Bingham was dead I would have killed them all.

In 1875 Fort Davis became the seat of Presidio County, which eventually yielded five additional counties carved from its area. Within fifteen years the

Fort Davis, circa 1915. Cavalry units from Marfa and Fort D. A. Russell are in Fort Davis on maneuvers. Note the Catholic church in the background.
—Museum of the Big Bend, Sul Ross State University, Alpine, Texas

Front Street, Fort Davis, Texas, circa 1880s. —Museum of the Big Bend, Sul Ross State University, Alpine, Texas

town boasted seven mercantile stores, four hotels, a bakery, a lumber yard, a drug store, and nine saloons and gambling establishments. No wonder it was popular with ranchers and cowboys.

The first courthouse cost $2,700 to build and soon became known as the "Bat Cave Courthouse" because of its cellar where prisoners were kept. The later 1880 courthouse had a stone dungeon under the sheriff's office, which prisoners entered through a trapdoor in the floor before shuffling down a ladder. The only ventilation was two small holes in the sheriff's floor. Although the prison was generally known as the "Bat Cave Jail," it never had bats.

The railroads bypassed Fort Davis, giving rise instead to such towns as Marfa. In 1884 the county seat moved to Marfa. But when Jeff Davis County was created in 1887, its seat was established at Fort Davis. Thus, Fort Davis became the only town in Texas to serve as the seat of government for two different counties.

After the soldiers left in 1891, the high altitude and spectacular scenery of the Davis Mountains made the place a haven for those afflicted with respiratory disorders, specifically asthma and tuberculosis. Summer visitors also started arriving to escape the heat in other parts of Texas, and apples became a commercial crop.

Davis Mountains State Park, just northwest of town, features peaks that tower more than a mile above sea level, wildflowers and huge trees, and chattering streams plowing through broad, green-belted canyons.

The Civilian Conservation Corps (CCC) built Indian Lodge in 1933, making adobe bricks on site and cutting timber in the canyons. In 1967 the lodge was updated with baths, a swimming pool, a restaurant, and twenty-four additional guest rooms.

Bloys annual camp meeting started on October 10, 1890, after the Reverend William Bloys came to Fort Davis to minister the Presbyterian church. His pulpit was an Arbuckle Coffee crate and he drew only thirty-six people to the first meeting. But he started one of the Southwest's great continuing traditions. The weeklong meetings now draw well over a thousand souls and are held in Skillman's Grove, seventeen miles west of Fort Davis on Texas 166. The ministers range from Baptists and Methodists to Presbyterians and Disciples of Christ.

Visitors who like to travel off the beaten path are invited to the Chihuahuan Desert Research Institute, three and one-half miles southeast of Fort Davis on Texas 118. A nature trail leads through a botanical garden in the institute's arboretum, which exhibits over 500 species of Chihuahuan plants.

Kitchen staff at a Baptist camp meeting, 1921. At one time the food was served at no cost. Today, collections are taken for expenses. —Museum of the Big Bend, Sul Ross State University, Alpine, Texas

The community's mile-high altitude and scenic views make Fort Davis an ideal vacation site. The Neill Museum, the Overland Trail Museum, and the historic Limpia Hotel are open to the public. The courthouse is a visual delight, and don't miss the 1,400-pound monument to Jefferson Davis. The Prude Ranch is both working and guest, and it is a safe and sane place for young people on vacation as well as a great spot for seminars or stargazing. But only the dinner hall has a television. A seventy-four-mile scenic drive loops past Indian Lodge, through the Davis Mountains State Park, and along the beautiful Madera Canyon.

McDonald Observatory (Texas 118)

When banker William Johnson McDonald of Paris, Texas, died in 1926, he left over $1 million to the University of Texas for the construction of an observatory. His relatives contested the will on the grounds that McDonald lacked his full mental faculties, and the trial ended in a hung jury. An out-of-court settlement gave the university $840,000.

The university built the observatory in 1932 on the 6,791-foot peak of Mt. Locke, named for Mrs. Violet Locke McIvor, a local ranching woman who donated 200 acres on the gently sloping flat-topped mountain. Clear air, a high ratio of cloudless nights, and the distance from concentrations of artificial lights made the location practically perfect for viewing the stars. All the university needed was a suitable expert to run the observatory.

Eleven years earlier, Otto Struve had immigrated to the United States from Russia and earned his doctorate from the University of Chicago. Struve arranged a thirty-year partnership between the University of Texas and the University of Chicago, and the 82-inch Otto Struve Memorial Telescope resulted from the union. At the time of its installation, on May 5, 1939, it ranked as the second-largest telescope in existence, and it remains the workhorse of the observatory. The observatory's location in the Davis Mountains of West Texas made it the farthest south of all major observatories in the United States. From there, scientists discovered Miranda, a moon of Uranus; Nereid, a moon of Neptune; and evaluated the atmosphere on Triton, another of Neptune's moons. They also determined that frost comprised the polar caps on Mars.

Today the observatory includes a "millimeter wave dish" to study gas and particles between stars in the Milky Way, a 30-inch telescope to study lunar occultations, a "laser ranging telescope" to measure our moon accurately within inches, and a 107-inch telescope that ranks among only a dozen or so in the world. With it scientists can analyze planet atmospheres, chemically analyze stars, and study the mysterious quasars. Plans are under way for even larger telescopes before the end of the century.

By use of this observatory, astronomers hope to better understand the evolution and possibly the future of the universe. They do this by studying galaxies, planets, stars, quasars, asteroids, and comets.

The McDonald Observatory's visitor's center contains a small museum displaying a meteorite that weighs 1,530 pounds. The center also offers video programs and sometimes conducts "star parties." The large dome is frequently open to the public, and well worth the visit.

Texas 67
Marfa—Presidio
61 miles

Shafter

Shafter is a ghost town forty miles south of Marfa named for William Rufus Shafter, a profane, egocentric, physically prepossessing man charged with clearing the area of revolutionaries and Indians. He provided the strongest and most determined protection the town of Shafter ever had.

Three hundred men once worked the silver mines at Shafter. In the 1860s burros toted ore to a nearby smelter in Mexico. Mining ceased in 1952. Visitors may be interested in touring the beautifully restored Sacred Heart Catholic Church.

Presidio (La Junta)

Since the first people ambled through this area in ancient times, the junction of the Rio Conchos and the Rio Grande marked it as a special place. The Spanish named the settlement on the north bank of the Rio Grande La Junta. After 1848 it became known as Presidio for the forty-room adobe fort built around a patio by Ben Leaton, a former scalp hunter who encouraged Indians to raid Mexico. He died in 1851, and the next two owners, Edward Hal and John Burgess, were mysteriously murdered. Today at Fort Leaton State Historic Site, twenty-four of the original forty rooms have been restored, complete with cottonwood beams, and the others are undergoing restoration.

In 1913, journalist John Reed described Presidio, Texas, as "a straggling and indescribably desolate village." Were it not for the flow it receives from the Rio Conchos, the Rio Grande would likely go dry before it reaches the gulf.

Frequent floods along the Rio Conchos after the turn of the century caused the international boundary (the Rio Grande) to occasionally shift. To correct this condition, the United States and Mexico forged a treaty in 1970 that

General William R. Shafter. His black soldiers protected the border from marauding Indians and revolutionaries. —National Archives

Fort Leaton, Texas, near Presidio, 1936. —The Institute of Texan Cultures

allowed for straightening the Rio Grande. In swapping land known as the "Ojinaga Tract," Texas transferred nearly 2,000 acres to Mexico and received about 300 in exchange.

Ranch Road 170
Presidio—Big Bend
60 miles

Lajitas

Ranch Road 170 (also known as El Camino del Rio or the River Road) twists through the Chinati Mountains as it follows the Rio Grande through canyons of primitive grandeur. At Lajitas, which means "flagstones," lies a rustic village established in 1915 by soldiers assigned to protect this strip of border from Mexican outlaws who forded the river here.

Lajitas has been restored or recreated to its original splendor. The village remains tiny in spite of the large number of visitors who stroll through the Lajitas Museum and Desert Gardens. Arrangements can be made in Lajitas for Rio Grande float trips through remote canyons.

Terlingua

Terlingua refers either to three languages (native American, Spanish, English), or to three separate tribes of local Indians. Take your pick. During the early 1800s, a few Mexican sheepherders and Comanches roamed the area.

The discovery of cinnabar, a red stone containing mercury, in 1889 brought forth the Terlingua Mines, which flourished between 1900 and 1942. In 1903, Howard E. Perry, a Chicago industrialist, accepted land in payment for a debt.

Looking south across the Rio Grande into Mexico from Lajitas, Texas, July 4, 1957. Mexican ranchers are crossing into Texas as honored guests of an annual barbecue and celebration at the Rex Ivey Ranch. —Harry Ransom Humanities Research Center, UT Austin

The little man with a battered hat opened the Perry Quicksilver Mine and essentially built the town. The 2,000 or so mostly Hispanic miners and their families called him Chapito (the Little Man) or El Patron (the Boss). The mines folded in 1942 when mercury was no longer profitable, but not before yielding about 5,000 tons of quicksilver (mercury).

Perry died at age eighty-six, and some people believe his spirit haunts the Chisos (Ghost) Mountains.

In 1967, Wick Fowler, Frank Tolbert, and others hosted the "First Annual Championship Chili Cook Off" in Terlingua. The event has become a yearly festival attracting chili chefs from all over the world.

Big Bend National Park

If you seek immense solitude, diversity, and remote locations with spectacular natural beauty, Big Bend National Park is the place for you. Although it attracts 200,000 visitors per year, its sequestered locale makes it one of the least visited of all national parks.

The Big Bend is the last great wilderness area in Texas. Volcanic eruptions up to sixty-five million years ago, during the last days of the dinosaurs, gave rise to the Chisos Mountains, and they steered the Rio Grande around high ground to form its big bend. Across the park's southern boundary the river runs sometimes passive and sometimes slashing. The Boquillas, Mariscal, and Santa Elena canyons reveal geologic history that documents one-fifth of the earth's existence. Arroyos in many of the broad and arid valleys expose deeper strata of brightly colored clay and rock.

Comanches and Mescalero Apaches were the dominant Indian forces in the Big Bend. During the 1840s, the Florida Seminoles were ordered to Indian Territory (Oklahoma), where they went through constant conflicts with other Indians. Seeking to escape the rigid demands placed on them by the United States, the Seminole warrior Coacoochee (Wild Cat) led a small group of refugees toward Mexico. Along the way they united with black Seminoles as well as a band of Kickapoos. They took up residence at Nacimiento de los Negroes in Coahuila, Mexico, south of the Big Bend. For years afterward, until Coacoochee died of smallpox in 1857, these black Seminoles raided Comanches and Apaches as well as a few white settlements in the Big Bend. Strangely, these Indians so detested by the U.S. Army were later hired as scouts to track down and fight their former comrades.

A branch of the Comanche War Trail cut through the Big Bend. With the help of Presidio trader Ben Leaton, the Indians swapped their booty for guns, liquor, and tobacco. Later, between 1910 and 1930, Mexican bandits operated along the Big Bend international border and burned the village of Glenn Springs in May 1916.

When Boundary Commissioner William Emory passed through the area in 1853, he sent Lt. Nathaniel Michler to survey the Big Bend. Michler's crew walked and boated 125 miles along the river, bouncing their skiffs repeatedly off the canyon walls. The going was tough and they were lucky to lose only one man, who drowned.

A Texas Ranger floated a survey party down Santa Elena Canyon in 1881, and eight years later a U.S. Geological Survey crew floated all the way from Presidio to Langtry, the first known explorers to do so. With modern equipment, and if the water is high enough, such trips today are relatively common.

Meanwhile, the Big Bend had become a ranching paradise, first to the Mexican vaqueros and then, by the 1880s, to Texas cowboys. By World War

Santa Elena Canyon cut by the Rio Grande. The Chisos foothills are in the background. Circa 1930s. —Museum of the Big Bend, Sul Ross State University, Alpine, Texas

I sheep and goat operations had moved in, and irrigated farming made a modest headway. Miners, too, found lucrative diggings in the Big Bend country. In addition to silver, they found gold, mercury, zinc, copper, coal, and lead. In turn, the availability of minerals gave rise to the transportation industry.

Big Bend State Park was established in 1933 under the short-lived name of Texas Canyons State Park. Meanwhile, President Franklin D. Roosevelt needed projects for his Civilian Conservation Corps, the CCC. Discussion of an international park in cooperation with Mexico led nowhere, so, on June 20, 1935, Congress established the Big Bend National Park. By 1943 the state

A lone rider follows the only trail across Mariscal Canyon in Big Bend. Mexico is on the left and Texas is on the right. —Museum of the Big Bend, Sul Ross State University, Alpine, Texas

lands had been transferred to the federal government, and in 1944 the national park opened with 708,221 acres. Additional lands are currently being considered.

The park typifies the scenery, plant, and animal life of Mexico, specifically the Chihuahuan Desert, more than that of the United States. The view to the south is dominated by the rugged Sierra del Carmen, Fronteriza, and other mountain ranges in Mexico.

Big Bend cannot be seen in just a few hours. There are several hundred miles of trails, a hundred miles of paved road, and 175 miles of dirt road. Check in at the visitor's center, and discuss your plans with a park ranger.

US 90

Sanderson—Comstock

88 miles

Sanderson

Sanderson was named in honor of a construction engineer for the Galveston, Harrisburg & San Antonio Railroad. Originally named Strawbridge in 1882, the town became Sanderson that same year. Of historical interest is the Terrell County Memorial Museum. Thirty miles east is a buffalo ranch offering daily tours. Perhaps the most visited local site is the Cedar Grove Cemetery, featuring the graves of two train robbers killed at Baxter's Curve east of Sanderson.

Street scene, Sanderson, Texas, circa 1913. —Museum of the Big Bend, Sul Ross State University, Alpine, Texas

Langtry

There are three versions of how Langtry got its name. One says that in 1881 an official of the Galveston, Harrisburg & San Antonio changed the town's name from Eagle Nest to Langtry. A second, related version says a civil engineer for the railroad named Langtry supervised Chinese laborers. The third and most famous version says Judge Roy Bean named the town in honor of the actress he so admired, Lillie Langtry.

This last version is probably correct, but keep in mind that Judge Bean was never known for telling the truth. A self promoter with a strong sense of humor, Bean was as unscrupulous as he was audacious and shrewd. There is no evidence that Judge Roy Bean ever hanged or shot anybody, but he remains an interesting figure from an interesting time.

Roy Bean hailed from Kentucky. After a series of adventures, he wound up tending bar in Langtry. On August 2, 1882, Capt. T. L. Oglesby of the Texas Rangers ordained Bean as a justice of the peace. He promoted himself as the "Law West of the Pecos," an assertion that made his position seem important, dynamic, and more effective than he actually was. Most of Bean's decisions were practical. A few were bizarre.

In addition to performing marriages, he was known for granting divorces, claiming he had a right to rectify his errors. He generally chose juries from bar customers, and on one occasion is reported to have fined a defendant $40 and

Judge Roy Bean holds court for horse thieves, in Langtry, Texas, circa 1900. One thief sits on the porch with Bean while court officers guard two more thieves, mounted at left, along with the stolen horse. —The Institute of Texan Cultures

This old relic is located in the little town of Langtry, Texas, which was the abode of Judge Roy Bean---a "Saloon," and also a "Hall of Justice," he being the only Peace Officer west of the Pecos river, at the time this photo was made, about 1900, and shows Judge Bean holding court, trying a horse-thief. Left of the picture is the stolen horse. On horses, guarded by officers are two other horse thieves, supposed partners of the one on trial.

a round of drinks. He freed a man who had slain a Chinese railroad laborer, defending his action by claiming he found nothing in his (single) law book stating it was illegal to kill a Chinaman.

Bean had a way of justifying almost anything he wanted. In 1896 the governor of Texas sent Texas Rangers to El Paso to prevent a boxing match between world heavyweight contenders Bob Fitzsimmons and Peter Maher. The governors of New Mexico and Arizona had also outlawed fighting (as had almost every state in the Union), and even officials in Chihuahua threatened to arrest anyone fighting there. Just when it looked like the fight was cancelled, Roy Bean loaded everyone, including the Texas Rangers, onto a train and guided the sporting event onto an island in the Rio Grande, where the uncertain international boundary kept authorities from intervening. With a couple dozen rangers and Roy Bean as the only witnesses, Fitzsimmons apparently won the world heavyweight championship by a knockout in less than two minutes of the first round.

On March 16, 1903, Bean died in his saloon of lung and heart complications. His lifelong ambition, other than embracing Lillie Langtry, was to cheat people. His fascination for the famed English actress was so great that Bean named his saloon after her stage name, the Jersey Lily. However, the itinerant sign painter, who accepted the job for food and drink, added and extra "l" in Lily; the old sign still says "The Jersey Lilly."

Bean and Langtry never met. He wrote her letters, which she never acknowledged. In 1904, she visited Langtry, but it was too late to meet her greatest fan—the spirit of the colorful old justice had already left for that great courtroom in the sky.

Langtry is now a tourist center complete with a Judge Roy Bean visitor's center.

Seminole Canyon

Twenty miles east of Langtry is Seminole Canyon State Park. Rock art in the park dates back 4,000 years. But long before that, perhaps a hundred million years ago, an ancient sea covered this region. The skeletons of marine life formed huge limestone slabs across the sea floor. Later, that sea floor rose into the air, and over time it eroded. Rivers cut deep canyons and scooped out pockets in the limestone. The present arid climate that dominates this region settled in more than 8,000 years ago.

There are hundreds of caves penetrating the bluffs along the lower Pecos and Devils rivers. In these cliffside shelters, prehistoric inhabitants laid down trash and other human debris. These people, whoever they were, expressed themselves through rock art, leaving bizarre and mystifying clues to their identity. Experts come from all over the world to study the art.

Comstock

Comstock began in 1882 with a railroad sidecar serving as its post office. The town was named for a Southern Pacific section foreman. The trains originally crossed the nearby Pecos River through a series of underground tunnels. Then, in 1890, the Southern Pacific began construction of a high bridge across the Pecos River gorge to shorten the route by eleven miles. Touted as the "eighth wonder of the world," workers spent eighty-seven days building the bridge, which opened for traffic in 1892. A marvel of engineering, the bridge stood 321 feet high, stretched 2,180 feet long—the world's longest—and cost $1.2 million. To pay for costs, the railroad charged an extra fifty cents just to cross the bridge.

A highway bridge spans the Pecos today. It is 273 feet above the river and doesn't cost a cent to drive across.

I-20
I-10 Junction—Odessa
126 miles

Pecos

The town of Pecos started as a station on the Texas & Pacific Railroad in 1881. Two years later Reeves County was created and Pecos moved from the Pecos River bottoms to its present location, where it became the county seat.

Pecos hosted the world's first rodeo on July 4, 1883. Trav Windham, foreman of the Lazy Y, roped and tied a steer on Oak Street in 22 seconds.

In 1896 former Texas Ranger R. S. Johnson constructed a red sandstone two-story saloon with attached furnished rooms. Soon afterward, gunman Barney Riggs killed cowboys Bill Earnhart and John Denson in the saloon. Floor tags mark the spot where each fell. Eight years later, in 1904, Johnson added the three-story Orient Hotel, which is today the cornerstone of the magnificent West-of-the-Pecos Museum and Park.

Gunslinger and cowboy Clay Allison, one of the West's deadliest manslayers, moved to Pecos in 1880 and became a rancher. A year later, while returning from town with supplies, he fell off his buckboard and died when the wagon's wheels crushed his skull. Allison is buried in the park portion of the West-of-the-Pecos Museum.

If you like gourmet cantaloupes, you'll love those grown in Pecos. A cantaloupe festival is held each August during the harvest.

Clay Allison was one of the most dangerous gunmen who ever lived, a terror to the people of Texas and New Mexico. He died in 1887 near Pecos when he fell off a wagon and a wheel crushed his skull.
—El Paso Public Library

The Legend of Pecos Bill

Pecos Bill is a familiar legend in Texas. Nobody really knows the "true" story of the mythical cowboy—most tales were fabricated in bunkhouses and alongside campfires. We know only that as the tales passed from one ranch to another, new verses and versions crept in.

Storytellers generally agree that Bill was the youngest of eighteen children when a flood on the Pecos separated him from his family. Coyotes raised him, and by the time Bill grew to manhood he had learned to ride everything from tornadoes to mountain lions. During a drought, Pecos Bill took a stick and dug the Rio Grande. It's said that Bill finally died from "laughing at all the dudes who called themselves cowboys."

Pecos River

Pecos is an Indian word meaning "crooked," an apt description of this river. It rises in the Sangre de Cristo uplift in north-central New Mexico and winds south 260 miles before entering Texas. There the river turns brackish and does little more than relieve constipation of those foolish enough to drink from it. A ford called "Horsehead Crossing" took its name from the hundreds of bleached horse skulls that once lined both banks. Apparently the alkaline water killed them.

Historically, travelers heading west across Texas had to cross the Pecos. They still do, but now they have bridges. Several of the great trail drives forded the Pecos, especially at Horsehead Crossing. Today the Pecos has so many diversions and impoundments that it barely resembles the raging torrent of former times.

When cowboys and emigrants spoke of "crossing the Pecos" or referred to lands "west of the Pecos," they meant entering a territory lacking law and civilization. In these parts, "Pecosin" once referred to killing a man and throwing his body in the Pecos River.

A Southern Pacific Railroad train crossing a bridge over the Pecos River. —The Institute of Texan Cultures

Pyote

Pyote may be a misspelling of Peyote, a potent hallucinogen derived from a variety of cactus. Another version of the name's origin claims Chinese railroad laborers could not pronounce "coyote," and said "pyote" instead. Who knows? The town started during the 1880s and is best known for Pyote Air Force Base (Rattlesnake Bomber Base), where miles of bombers and fighters sat and rusted following World War II.

Located north of Pyote on Texas 115 are the tiny oil towns of Wink and Kermit. Wink is the first syllable of Winkler County. In 1910, Kermit was named for the son of former President Theodore Roosevelt.

Monahans

The Texas & Pacific Railroad launched this community in 1881 as a water stop between Big Spring and the Pecos River. Today it is oil and gas that keep the place going. Many of the wells are drilled at a slant to draw the valuable resources from beneath every part of town.

The Million Barrel Museum started in 1928 as an oil storage facility. Today it is known as one of the better oil museums in the country.

Monahans Sandhills State Park

Established as a state park in 1956, Monahans Sandhills consists of 3,840 acres of sand dunes, some of which mound to seventy feet or more in height. One of the nation's largest oak forests thrives here, but unlike the popular conception of oaks, these Harvard Oaks seldom reach over three feet in height. Their roots, however, shoot down into the earth some ninety feet, causing some people to suspect these oaks are growing in the wrong direction. The park has an excellent interpretive visitor's center.

Permian Basin

The Permian Basin covers 100,000 square miles and includes much of West Texas as well as southern New Mexico. It gets its name from the Permian age of 200 million years ago. Although people likely visited this area more than a thousand years ago, they probably did not take up residence here until much later. Spanish explorers sketched it on maps centuries before "forty-niners" hustled across it and the empire builders laid rails across it, but through those years only Comanches and Apaches dominated it. Dryland farmers grieved over its meager yield. Until the 1920s most of the Permian towns were connected only by the railroad.

When the drillers first arrived, their goal was water; oil meant bad news. But improved refining techniques and a growing need for petroleum products ushered in a new age, and oil began to assume its modern role in technology and the economy. The first commercial oil strike occurred in 1920 on the basin's eastern edge. The excitement picked up the following year when the founders of the Texon Oil and Land Company drilled their first well. They had sought investors in New York, many of whom were Catholic, and a local priest recommended prayers to Santa Rita, the patron saint of the impossible. They christened their well Santa Rita #1, and twenty-one months later she started producing oil and gas.

The oil-producing area of the Permian Basin is 250 miles wide and 300 miles long. In the early days, gas flowed in such enormous quantities that surface facilities could not pump, cap, or store it. The waste was unimaginable. Flares lit up the night sky for miles. One flare burned steadily for twenty years.

Throughout its history, the Permian Basin has experienced lean and prosperous years. Much of its oil, however, still lies in the darkness awaiting a dream and a drill. (See Far West introduction, Texon, and Big Lake.)

Odessa

Russian workers on the Texas & Pacific Railroad saw a resemblance between the steppe country they had known in Ukraine and the region around what is now Odessa, Texas. They suggested naming the railroad siding Odessa after the southern Ukrainian port city on the Black Sea. The town that grew from the siding stood geologically and geographically in the heart of the Permian Basin.

Railroad officials wanted to import and settle hardworking German Methodists in this area. Civic leaders cooperated by banning liquor, but the Methodists did not arrive. Once that became apparent, the sheriff allegedly opened the first saloon.

Although the region contains tremendous reserves of gas and oil, a glut in the market economically devastated Odessa during the 1970s. Fortunately, it had largely recovered by the late 1980s.

While Odessa has an oil-worker "roughneck" reputation in comparison to its neighbor, Midland, a town of finance, Odessa has made strides in the arts. The Art Institute for the Permian Basin features regional artists and traveling exhibits. Odessa College has an authentic replica of the Shakespearean Globe Theatre. The Presidential Museum caters to the U.S. presidency and its political campaigns.

Some 20,000 years ago, a nickel-iron meteorite collided with the earth and dished out a crater 500 feet in diameter. As centuries passed, windblown dirt covered the crater but did not conceal it from either scientists or tourism promoters. Today a nature trail winds through the Odessa Meteor Crater.

McCamey—Big Lake

McCamey

An oil drifter named George McCamey hit a gusher in 1920 and asked the Orient Railroad to construct a siding. Upon completion of the spur, the railroad left a boxcar with a rough, handpainted sign on it spelling out McCamey. The Burleson-Johns Township Company laid out town lots, and the community boomed for a short period. Some oil is still sought, but livestock shipping presently has the economic upper hand. McCamey is home to the Mendoza Trail Museum and the Santa Fe Park with its pecan and elm trees. Travelers driving across King Mountain Mesa will enjoy the scenic vista.

The world's deepest oil well in 1930, located in Texon, Texas, was owned by the Texon Oil and Land Company. —Eugene C. Barker Texas History Center, UT Austin

Rankin

Rankin is the seat of Upton County and was named for F. E. Rankin, who discovered underground water here in 1911. The town serves ranchers and oil workers. The restored Yates Hotel, built in 1927, now houses the Rankin Museum.

Texon, Big Lake

About a hundred years ago, Big Lake attorney Rupert P. Wicker leased 431,360 acres (674 sections) of University of Texas land in Reagan County. He subleased much of the property to oil prospectors, which allowed him to pay the rent, and he invested what he had left over into a well of his own. Wicker sold oil permits to Frank T. Pickrell and El Pasoan Haymon Krupp, who organized the Texon Oil and Land Company and set aside 200,000 acres for themselves. Then they spudded in the Santa Rita on January 8, 1921, just minutes before their drilling permit expired. For over two years their well produced little more than dirt. Then, on May 28, 1923, the venture paid off. Oil blew everywhere, and West Texas, as well as the University of Texas, was changed forever by Santa Rita #1.

Within a year, seventeen producing wells flourished in and around Texon as the field spread ten miles east toward Big Lake. In 1925 the McCamey Pool followed the Santa Rita's success. Crane, Howard, and other nearby counties joyously welcomed discoveries in 1926.

Texon was named for the Texon Land and Oil Company, and the town served as headquarters for the Big Lake Oil Field. When Santa Rita roared in, Texon had no structures except two small wooden shacks and an oil derrick. A hamburger and cold drink stand was not only the sole restaurant but for a while the only business. Texon, however, was not an ordinary oil boom town. Workers brought their families to live here. Soon the town had a modern hospital, a library, schools, churches, and even a golf course and tennis court.

Big Lake started in 1911 as a stop for the Orient Railroad. Its name was taken not from underground lakes of oil, as one might suspect, but for broad, shallow depressions that formed lakes during intemperate rains. (See Far West introduction and Permian Basin.)

TWO

Hill Country

I thought: Now I know why I am not a revolutionary—have never had a desire to kick over old, established things. It's because the hill country does not teach you the need for change. The land is always so satisfying that you want it to remain the same forever as a kind of handy immortality.

Elroy Bode, *This Favored Place*
(Shearer Publications, 1983)

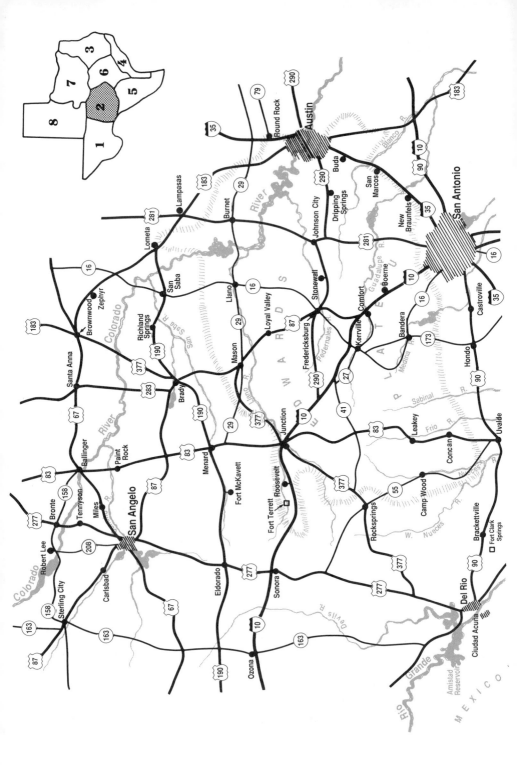

The Hill Country is near the middle of Texas. It belongs to neither South nor West.

In a sense, Lyndon Baines Johnson "owned" the Hill Country, or sometimes liked to think he did. Kerrville became the home of the "Blue Yodler," Jimmie Rodgers. Author A. C. Greene spends much of his time in the Hill Country, and Fred Gipson, author of *Old Yeller*, lived along the Llano River. Yet, for every famous name here, a dozen more literary and artistic talents deserve mention as well.

While all the regions of Texas are unique and scenic, the Hill Country is blessed with a special charm. Perhaps that is why the many artists who have chosen to live there love it.

Artists and poets think of the Hill Country as an attitude, a region of "unravished quietness." To some, it is an idea as much as a place—both emerging from the modest hills, narrow rivers (the Guadalupe, Pedernales, and Colorado), and cool nights with stars blanketing the silent earth.

Its downside is soil so thin that even fingernails can't scratch it. Cattle get along well enough, but the stony, shallow outcroppings have discouraged all but the most stubborn farmers. Hill Country owes its relatively low population (compared to most parts of Texas) and its lack of industry and big business to the poor soil. But the ranchers and writers seem satisfied with the Hill Country's clear, gurgling waters, struggling farms, picturesque villages, old-country languages, and its gentle, easy lifestyle.

One feature in the Hill Country that visitors always notice is dry-laid rock fences, some of which reach heights of five or six feet and enclose several acres. Most were built by German and Norwegian settlers between 1850 and 1900; however, the walls have less to do with ethnic background than with the availability of raw materials. The pioneers had plenty of rocks, and they had a source of cheap labor in their growing families. But they did not have wood for fenceposts or barbed wire to string between them, and the hard ground discouraged any digging of postholes. When other means of fencing became available and economical, the settlers stopped building rock fences.

Eons ago south-central Texas lay covered with warm, shallow seas. As the skeletal remains of countless marine creatures formed enormous deposits resemblant of a layer cake, the mass twisted and groaned until it finally heaved upward and broke. The eastern portion sloped downward and became a coastal plain. As the seas drained out, the Hill Country emerged. Geologists call it the Edwards Plateau, a geologic fault zone. The palisades on the eastern and southern fringes of Hill Country are known as the Balcones Escarpment. The plateau itself is flatter, averaging 2,000 feet above sea level and generally comprising the western and northern portions of Hill Country.

Hill Country is sandwiched between high plains, relentless desert, and rolling coastal lowlands. The hills that give this place its shape and character never grew into mountains, and few of its streams ever achieved the width and depth we usually associate with "real" rivers.

Austin anchors the eastern edge of Hill Country. But as the seat of Texas government and center of the state's higher education system, Austin's cosmopolitan nature sets it aside from the rest of this region.

Some folks claim that San Antonio is in Hill Country. The point is arguable, but in this book it is relegated to the Brush Country of South Texas. Uvalde marks the southeastern extreme of Hill Country, while San Angelo neatly locks in the northwestern corner.

Flowers here are eternal. In March and April, Indian paintbrush, yellow coreopsis, Indian blankets, and daisies—the mystical robes of spring—replenish the spirits of residents and visitors alike. And the bluebonnet is a Texas legend in itself.

The tale of the bluebonnet grew from a mouth-parching drought that once shriveled the Hill Country. While discussing the matter with the Great Spirit, a Comanche chief learned the drought would be lifted only when someone's dearest possession had been placed on the highest knoll as an offering. That night, as the tribe slept, the chief's daughter laid her favorite doll—adorned with the bright feathers of a blue jay for its bonnet—on the summit. This touched the Great Spirit. The rains came and the drought was broken, and in good faith the Spirit left behind the sign of his covenant. When the tribe awoke the next morning, the hills were adorned with bluebonnets.

The Hill Country also grows cedars, mesquite, post oak and live oak, wiry range grasses, and an occasional cactus. Plums, blackberries, dewberries, and persimmons grow wild along the watercourses. While cattlemen and farmers dominate the eastern portion of Hill Country, goats and sheep thrive on the rocky highlands of the western section.

Indians have always played a major role in the Hill Country. Historians Ernest Wallace and E. Adamson Hoebel called the Comanches who rode through the Hill Country and made it their headquarters the "Lords of the South Plains." They knew there was little to conquer or own here, so they did little more than take note of the scenery and drink from the springs bubbling up between rocks or standing in quiet pools. The Comanches saw ghosts haunting rocky faces along the ridges and escarpments, and they kept riding.

By the mid-1800s, Hill Country lay astride the path of American empire. Texans carved a trail angling toward El Paso from Austin through the Hill

Country. But water along that route was sparse, and wagons rolling across the rough landscape broke down often as their wooden-spoked wheels constantly creaked and groaned against the unyielding stony ground.

Highways showed little improvement over the next hundred years; they twisted and turned according to the demands of the terrain until I-10 shouldered its way through the region. The interstate remains the only major thoroughfare.

Since its settlement, Hill Country has belonged largely to the Germans. They fled their homeland to escape peasant revolts, feudal slavery, draft laws, fragmentation of farms, the potato blight, and overpopulation. Some sought comfort in the British Isles while others disappeared into Russia and Latin America. But most migrated to the United States. Those who came to Texas left behind their ancestral lands in the middle and high German provinces of Nassau, Wetterau, Upper Hesse-Darmstadt, Electoral Hesse, and Alsace. Of course, many ethnic groups, particularly Hispanics, today outnumber the residents of Germanic descent, but the invigorating charm of the latter group enlivens the area in a special way.

Early American developers actively sought German settlers, which they widely believed were the best farmers in the world. Much of that perception stemmed from the superior quality of German houses and the neat, orderly layout of their farms and fences. The Germans generally showed little interest in politics; their gift to America was their work ethic and their strong communal and family tradition and heritage.

Throughout the 1830s and 1840s considerable literature praising Texas for its fertile land and invigorating climate infiltrated Germany. Friedrich Ernst of Oldenburg accepted an Austin colony grant in the Mill Valley and, with a steady stream of German immigrants pouring in, his farm soon grew into a village called Industry.

Even so, most migrants might never have left Germany had it not been for several German organizations that encouraged immigration to Texas. Wealthy, titled Germans who bought Texas lands and sold them to their countrymen operated a society called *Verein zum Schutze deutscher Einwanderer.* Unmarried males paid $120 for 160 acres and agreed to live in a Texas home and cultivate the earth for three years. Married men paid $240 and received 320 acres.

The society negotiated the Fisher-Miller grant, a huge Hill Country tract bound on its south by the Llano River. Incredibly, the society sent two German investigators to examine the land, but upon disembarking at Indianola they never traveled within 300 miles of their destination. They naively assumed all of Texas looked just like the southeastern part of the state, so they returned home and praised Fisher-Miller as excellent for farmers. Of course, the region then was terribly isolated and inhabited by warlike Comanches and Apaches. It had little moisture and consisted of stony soil repugnant to the plow. Still, the immigrants arrived. New Braunfels was founded in 1845 by German settlers.

Empresario Henri Castro brought 2,000 settlers from Germany (along with a few French immigrants) to Castroville in 1844, providing Medina County with a German nucleus.

Nassau-born Baron Ottfried Hans Freiherr von Meusebach, who soon changed his name to John O. Meusebach, arrived in Texas in 1847 to assist German immigrants. He was a mining engineer, an economist, and a scholar knowledgeable in forestry and finance who spoke five languages, including fluent English. Since Comanches threatened the Fisher-Miller enterprise, Meusebach left Fredericksburg with a military company of twenty men, plus volunteers and surveyors. Indian agent Robert S. Neighbors assisted at San Saba when Meusebach negotiated a peace treaty with Comanche leaders Buffalo Hump, Santana, and Old Owl in March 1847.

A legend still intact says negotiations continued into the first of April, at which time the women of Fredericksburg noticed roaring campfires high in the hills and became fearful. To calm the children, mothers explained that the

An 1888 drawing of John Ottfried Meusebach.
—The Institute of Texan Cultures

Fredericksburg, Texas, R. M. Burrier & Company building, 1890s.
—The Institute of Texan Cultures

fires were the work of the Easter Bunny boiling dyes for its Easter eggs. On Easter Sunday, while the church bells tolled, Fredericksburg learned that the flames were actually peace fires in celebration of the agreement. The treaty was ratified in Fredericksburg shortly thereafter. Until the Civil War, at least, the Germans remained unmolested, and the Indians freely came and went inside the white settlements. Today the residents of Fredericksburg still light traditional springtime "peace" fires in the hills.

During the Civil War, Germans and Mormons frequently declared their neutrality, though an overwhelming majority of each group fought for the Confederacy. Most Germans did not own slaves but believed the federal government should pay the owners for freed slaves. In August 1862, sixty-five Germans fled Kendall County for Mexico with Confederates close behind. During an ambush nineteen died; six others were later executed.

When the war broke out Robert E. Lee commanded the Hill Country's Fort Mason. On the night before he left to assume command of Southern armies, Lee showed his appreciation to the people of Mason by inviting them to a ball in his quarters. But Lee, apparently preoccupied with the difficult choice he had made and the thought of the bloodshed that lay ahead, did not dance.

As soldiers left the Hill Country to fight, the Indians grew restless. At last the Comanches and Apaches hoped to free themselves of the white men. They captured Herman Lehmann and fourteen-year-old Alice Todd. Lehmann did not return for nine years, and Miss Todd never returned.

After the Civil War the Hill Country went through a spate of longhorn cattle drives. The Western (Dodge City) Trail passed slightly west of San Antonio. It entered the Hill Country roughly by way of today's I-10 and then generally followed what are now Texas highways 87 and 283 north toward Oklahoma.

Next came the railroads. The Atchison, Topeka & Santa Fe skirted the north rim of Hill Country. A century later Amtrak looped around its southern border. The Fredericksburg & Northern Railroad dug a 920-foot tunnel in Kendall County. It operated thirty years and remains one of only two main-line rail tunnels in the state.

One of the strangest tales ever to float out of the Hill Country concerned the federal government's efforts to use local bats as dive bombers during World War II. In 1942, Lytle S. Adams, a Pennsylvania physician, suggested the concept to Franklin D. Roosevelt. The president liked it, and Project X-Ray was born. Researchers trapped small free-tailed bats in large numbers throughout Hill Country caves. The U.S. Navy leased four caves and sent U.S. Marines from Corpus Christi to guard them.

Experiments with captured bats involved attaching a string to their chests with a surgical clip. On the other end of the string dangled a one-ounce device capable of burning an incendiary flame for eight minutes. The bats were to be air-dropped from canisters at 1,000 feet; then they would spread out over twenty miles and eventually land, creating thousands of fires. But, for reasons unknown, the project was abruptly terminated in 1943.

In modern times, the Hill Country is not just a crossroads but a place where people come together to tell stories, work, and visit. Practically every village is a tourist center.But there is little incentive for increasing the permanent populations. The residents share their huge caverns, their spring waters, and their magnificent sunrises and sunsets with visitors, but when the tourists return home, the locals get on with living, content to be alone.

So the Hill Country remains what author Elroy Bode called "This Favored Place." The land has always brought out the best.

Devils River

Spanish explorer Gaspar Castaño de Sosa in 1590 supposedly called this stream "Laxas" because of its slack or feeble quality. But the name it carries today originated more than two and a half centuries later with Capt. John Coffee Hays of the Texas Rangers. After riding across desolate country for days, he encountered a deep, crooked crevice in the ground. He looked to its bottom and saw water. "What's the name of this place," he asked a local resident. "San Pedro's Hell," came the reply. "Well," said Hays recounting afterwards, "it looked like the Devil's River to me."

After rising in Crockett County and flowing 100 miles south to the Rio Grande, the river empties into the Amistad (Friendship) Reservoir.

Sonora

Sonora, between San Angelo and Del Rio, marks the western slope of the Edwards Plateau and the desert border of the Texas Hill Country. It developed during the late 1840s as a trading post for emigrants and a stopover for stage coaches traveling on the San Antonio-El Paso Road.

The Apaches lived here until the U.S. Army established Fort Terrett in 1852 thirty miles to the east. Otherwise, the earliest residents of this community likely hailed from the Mexican state of Sonora, hence the name. E. M. Kirkland brought in sheep in 1879, and eleven years later Sonora became the seat of Sutton County. Some folks had unknowingly settled on land owned by a New York firm, so they had to either move or repurchase their own property.

Railroads hesitated at first to enter the Hill Country because the terrain required higher than usual construction expenses and there was a lack of marketable goods. Then a man named Tillman gouged out a 250-foot wide path between Sonora and Brady, a hundred miles to the northeast. Holding pens, wells, and windmills along the way permitted thousands of cattle to walk from Sonora to the railhead at Brady.

Today's Sonora remains a headquarters for cattle and sheep operations. Attractive homes line the wide, shady main street. A couple of attractions worth seeing include the Miers Home Museum, built in 1888, and the Caverns of Sonora, a subterranean mile and a half of unbelievable beauty with regularly scheduled guided tours.

Roosevelt

This small community grew from the infantry post established on the east bank of the North Llano River in 1852. The troops of Fort Terrett built their post of stone and named it after Lt. John Terrett, who died in the Battle of Monterrey during the Mexican War in 1846. The army abandoned the post after just two years, and its rock buildings became foundations for nearby ranch houses.

Junction

Junction is a transition community. To its west lies dry desert; but here the hills are green and covered with trees. Local residents call this the "Land of the Living Waters," and the town's name comes from the junction of the North and South Llano rivers. With the organization of Kimble County in 1876, Junction superseded Kimbleville, a couple miles east of the river forks, as the county seat. Junction's courthouse went up in 1878, replacing a brush arbor and blacksmith shop where officials formerly met.

The small village lay thirty miles from the little-used Spanish road opened in 1808 connecting San Antonio with Santa Fe. At that time Apaches and Jumanos dominated this territory, then Comanches moved in during the mid-nineteenth century.

The area's remoteness, its rivers, and heavy brush made Kimble County into what Texas Ranger H. B. Waddill called "a thief's stronghold. A man that isn't a thorough expert at stealing," he said, "is looked upon as an enemy." Nearby Fort Terrett (1852-54) and Fort McKavett (1852-59, 1868-83) offered settlers their only defense against Indian marauders.

Judge A. McFarland noted the honest citizens were arming themselves at such a rate that stores could not keep rifles and ammunition in stock. He urged a force of rangers to restore law and order. Maj. John B. Jones rode to the headwaters of the South Llano, and on April 18, 1877, ordered four detachments to converge on Junction from different directions. The arrival of law inspired the town's citizens to offer their assistance.

John B. Jones. —Eugene C. Barker Texas History Center, UT Austin

The Frontier Battalion went to work immediately. Within two weeks they made forty arrests on charges ranging from cattle and horse rustling to murder and prison escape. Some criminals awaited trial while chained to trees. At Pegleg Station, ten miles southwest of town, Sgt. James Gillett and three other rangers rushed an outlaw hideout where they killed alleged murderer Dick Dublin and captured four desperados. Indictments implicated a corrupt sheriff and county judge, both of whom resigned from office.

As Junction became relatively quiet and law-abiding, Young P. Oliver purchased a section of land containing hundreds of pecan trees and became a pioneer of the industry in 1896. One giant tree known as "Old Oliver" produced nearly 400 pounds of soft-shelled pecans per year until 1935, when its bountiful yield fell victim to a flood. Fortunately, however, thanks to timely grafting, Old Oliver's descendants live on and pecan harvesting is now a major industry in Kimble County.

Junction is also a center for wool and mohair production, as well as a popular fishing, camping, canoeing, and hunting area. A scenic bluff known as "Lovers Leap" overlooks the town from the east. Another landmark east of town is Teacup Mountain, which naturally resembles a teacup. While in Junction, visit the Kimball County Historical Museum for a more in-depth look at the area's past.

Llano River

Llano is Spanish for "plains." In that language the double *l* is pronounced as *y*, but most of the locals pronounce the river LAN-no. The river's north and south forks join near Junction, and from there it flows a hundred miles northeast until draining into the Colorado River.

Kerrville

Kerrville sits on a section of Cretaceous limestone known as Trinity Rocks, which accumulated at the bottom of a warm, quiet sea 180 million years ago. Eventually that sea floor rose into the sunshine, and today's residents claim that the area has the most ideal climate in the nation. Cedars and live oaks dot the hillsides while cypress trees grow tall in the green valleys. White-tailed deer are so numerous that highway signs warn motorists to be careful.

Texas independence veteran Joshua Brown opened a way station here called Brownsborough in 1848. After becoming the seat of Kerr County in 1856, however, the name was changed first to Kerrsville and then Kerrville.

Cypress shingle production provided the economic strength of Kerrville for many years until Capt. Charles Schreiner opened a general store in 1869. His business swiftly became the largest mercantile in the Southwest. Other Germans also flowed into Kerrville from San Antonio during its early years, and many of them raised cattle as well as sheep and goats.

When the San Antonio & Aransas Pass Railroad built northwest toward the high plains from San Antonio, competition broke out between Fredericksburg and Kerrville as to which town would get the much-valued resource. Charles Schreiner put his considerable reputation and prestige on the line for Kerrville, but the issue remained in doubt until the railroad reached Comfort. To Schreiner's relief, the tracks followed the Guadalupe River toward Kerrville, but the tonnage and traffic fell short of the railroad's expectations and the enterprise never moved so much as a mile beyond Kerrville.

The community's reputation as a health center gained such acceptance that in 1937 the Kerrville State Sanatorium opened on 620 acres. A tuberculosis center exclusively for Negroes operated there until World War II.

In more recent times, several Texas businessmen grew concerned over fine Western art being locked up in private collections. They convinced the Cowboy Artists of America to establish a museum in Kerrville, and the facility opened its doors to the public in 1983. It spotlights contemporary works and showcases important historical artists such as Frederic Remington and Charles M. Russell. Located on ten acres, the museum resembles a fortress and has nearly 15,000 square feet of space.

Kerrville also has a Hill Country Museum, a classic car and wax museum, and numerous camps for children. The internationally famous Kerrville Folk Music Festival takes place in May and June of each year. And there are dude ranches as well as religious bivouacs in the area. Kerrville State Park encompasses 500 green acres along the Guadalupe River.

Guadalupe River

The Spanish explorer Domingo Terán named this stream San Agustín, but Alonso de León prevailed in 1689 when he renamed it the Guadalupe, after Nuestra Señora de Guadalupe (Our Lady of Guadalupe). Like many streams in the Hill Country, this one has north and south forks. They unite ten miles west of Kerrville.

The Guadalupe River is a working watercourse with numerous dams. Its principal tributaries are the San Marcos, which joins it east of San Antonio, and the Comal, entering it south of Victoria. In all, it drains about 6,000 square miles and flows southeast about 250 miles until it reaches San Antonio Bay at the gulf, just north of the Aransas National Wildlife Refuge.

Comfort, Boerne

In 1854 a group of German settlers traveling west from New Braunfels were so taken by the relaxed scenery of the Guadalupe River that they called their resting site Camp Comfort. Soon permanent buildings replaced temporary shelters, and now some have been restored to form the perimeters of the historic walking district along High Street.

Near this spot is one historical monument called "True to the Union." During the Civil War, sixty-five Germans fled Comfort and various Hill Country communities and headed toward Mexico. Confederates ambushed them along the Nueces River, killing nineteen and wounding nine, whom they later executed. (See the Hill Country introduction for additional information.)

Boerne grew out of Tusculum, which was laid out in 1849 by five members of the Communist Colony of Bettina. When they abandoned Tusculum in 1851, the new town was named in honor of Ludwig Boerne, a German poet, historian, and political refugee living in West Texas. The Cascade Caverns are nearby, as is Guadalupe River State Park. Boerne is primarily a recreation area.

Texas 90
Del Rio—San Antonio
152 miles

Del Rio

Del Rio straddles a dividing line between the Hill Country and the Brush Country while managing still to keep a leg in Far West Texas. It is called the "Queen City of the Rio Grande" and the "Wool and Mohair Capital of the United States." Ciudad Acuña is its Mexican neighbor across the Rio Grande in Coahuila.

The village began as San Felipe del Rio after seventeenth-century Spanish explorers paused here on the Day of San Felipe, the first Mexican martyr. By the time San Felipe became a part of Texas, however, the state already had a village by that name. The town agreed to change its name to Del Rio, but a section of the community is still called San Felipe.

Del Rio has always been a major crossroads: The San Antonio-El Paso Wagon Road went through it, as did a hookup between Chihuahua and the Texas port of Indianola. Stagecoaches, wagons, and ox carts crossed this Chihuahua road, which remained an important route until the railroads arrived in the early 1880s.

San Felipe Springs supplied an enormous amount of water to the community, and irrigation came into its own after tapping the resources of the Rio Grande, the Pecos, and the Devils River as well. In 1969, Presidents Richard Nixon and Díaz Ordaz dedicated the international Amistad (Friendship) Dam on the Rio Grande twelve miles north of Del Rio.

Near Del Rio is Parida Cave, a rock shelter overlooking Amistad Reservoir. Archaeologists have recorded human use of the cave dating back 8,000 years. It is administered by the National Park Service and is accessible only by boat.

Since the 1970s, Del Rio has concentrated on luring American and European industrial and assembly businesses (maquila plants). Meanwhile, the town remains a gateway into and out of Mexico, as well as a recreation resort.

The Whitehead Memorial Museum is open to the public, as is the Val Verde Winery and San Felipe Springs and Moore Park. A downtown walking-tour brochure is available through the local chamber of commerce.

Fort Clark

The troops who first used this post in 1852 called it Fort Riley. But it became Fort Clark after only one month to honor Maj. John B. Clark, who died serving his country during the Mexican War. The fort denied the Comanches watering privileges at Las Moras Springs (now Fort Clark Springs).

Seminole Indian scouts. A combination black and Indian, they guarded the border and led military excursions into northern Mexico. They were some of America's finest fighting men.
—National Archives

As stone buildings gradually replaced the fort's original wooden shacks, Secretary of War William W. Balknap and Gen. William Tecumseh Sherman met here with Col. Ranald Mackenzie and 1st Lt. John Lapham Bullis to destroy the Kickapoo and Lipan Apache camps across the Mexican border in Coahuila. They launched their successful foray from Fort Clark on May 16, 1873, penetrating seventy miles into Mexico during the process.

In post-Civil War years Fort Clark served as a home base for Seminole-Negro Indian Scouts. These proud, independent people descended from slaves who had fled a miserable existence on southeastern plantations to Florida when it still belonged to Spain. Most intermarried with native Seminoles who accepted them as equals. After Florida became part of the United States in 1819, the Seminole-Negroes escaped federal authority (and slave status) by fleeing to the Mexican border, often living and working on both sides of the international line. They spoke Spanish as well as English. Throughout the 1870s and 1880s, approximately 150 Seminole-Negroes signed on as scouts with the United States Army. Several of them won Congressional Medals of Honor while accompanying expeditions into Mexico. A Seminole-Negro Cemetery lies between Fort Clark and Brackettville.

Fort Clark later became home to such significant military leaders as John Bankhead Magruder, George Patton, and Jonathan Wainwright. Wainwright became the commanding officer at Fort Clark during World War II, before his transfer to the Philippines and subsequent capture by the Japanese.

Fort Clark no longer exists as a post. It is primarily a resort-retirement community.

Brackettville

Brackettville, on the fringes of the Hill Country and the Chihuahuan Desert, arose in 1852 as a stage stop, supply post, and recreation area for Fort Clark.

The Spanish visited this vicinity in the late 1600s as they searched for La Salle, the French explorer who threatened their claim to this land simply by his presence and nationality. According to legend, the Spanish found one French survivor of La Salle's party living as an Indian king.

Although Brackettville is currently a trade center for ranches and farms, it is best known as a movie site. *Arrowhead*, staring Charlton Heston and Jack Palance, was filmed here in 1950. In 1955 *Last Command* and *Five Bold Women* went before the cameras. Two years later construction started on John Wayne's "Alamo Village" at J. T. "Happy" Shahan's ranch. Filming of *The Alamo* began in 1959, one month before the construction was finished for this largest and most complete set ever built in the United States (at a then-record cost of $12 million). After the two armies of actors squared off and the Alamo fell, the set became home to regular country-western shows staged during the summer months. The biggest bash occurs on Labor Day.

107

Cowboys still ride in the dusty streets of San Antonio in this re-created (movie) town near Brackettville, Texas. —Happy Shahan's Alamo Village

Uvalde

The upper Nueces River brought Spanish explorers into modern-day Uvalde County. Fernando del Bosque and Fr. Juan Larios led an expedition through this area and on May 14, 1675, performed the second Mass ever held in Texas (the first took place on April 30, 1598, near El Paso). A thousand Indians attended.

The Spanish established two missions that failed because of Comanche and Apache uprisings. In 1790 Capt. Juan de Ugalde smashed the Comanches in Ugalde Canyon. Over the years, popular parlance corrupted the young officer's name to Uvalde. But settlement did not take hold for another half century. In 1853 a village called Encina arose from a ranch on the Leona River. Three years later it became the county seat and changed its name to Uvalde.

The Texas & New Orleans Railroad steamed through in 1881. By 1910 the San Antonio, Uvalde & Gulf Railroad had arrived. The Uvalde & Northern

Senator Lyndon Baines Johnson, President Harry Truman, former vice president John Nance Garner, and Speaker of the House Sam Rayburn. —Sam Rayburn Library

reached town in 1914, and by that time the village had become headquarters for mining companies as well as sheep and cattle ranches.

Throughout its early history, Uvalde was home to fascinating characters. Three were King Fisher, Pat Garrett, and John Nance "Cactus Jack" Garner. Fisher, an alleged cattle rustler and murderer, repeatedly found himself arrested and brought to trial, but the court never convicted him. He became acting sheriff of Uvalde County in 1883 and was killed in San Antonio a year later. Pat Garrett, the tall slayer of New Mexico's Billy the Kid, spent a few years in Uvalde during the late 1880s and early 1890s. John Nance Garner was Franklin Delano Roosevelt's vice president from 1933 to 1941. He lived and died in Uvalde, and the Garner Memorial Museum honors his accomplishments. Another worthy stop for visitors is the Uvalde Grand Opera House, which has been restored in all its 1890 spendor.

Hondo

In Spanish, Hondo means "deep creek," and the Southern Pacific created it in the 1880s as a railroad siding. Though the bed of Hondo Creek is now rock hard, when dinosaurs roamed this area they stepped in soft mud and left enormous footprints to intrigue later life-forms (humans). Today Hondo is home to the World Championship Corn Shucking Contest. The Medina County Historical Museum occupies the former train depot.

Castroville

At first glance, the name of this community would seem to have a Latin or Hispanic background. Actually, its founder was Henri Castro of Paris, France. In 1844 he settled Castroville with immigrants from the Alsace-Lorraine region between France and Germany. These colonists were Alsatians, a German dialect group with plenty of French influence. Most of the settlers farmed and each received a town lot and a forty-acre farm. This largest concentration of Alsatians outside Europe is now into its fifth generation as Texans.

Castro, a French Jew of Spanish-Portuguese ancestry, helped the Republic of Texas negotiate a $7 million loan from France. By 1842, he had become an *empresario* with plans to colonize 600 families in the lower Rio Grande country southwest of San Antonio. He was to receive one section of land (640 acres) for every 10 families settled.

After recruiting all over Europe, Castro finally amassed 2,000 pilgrims and organized twenty-seven ships to carry them across the Atlantic. Delayed by storms and suffering understandable hardships, the passengers arriving at Texas ports became disgusted with the man who brought them there. As charges of fraud began stacking up against Castro, the colonists stranded on the coast began moving inland. Their descendants today live in pockets along the central and coastal communities of Texas. A few Germans, French, Americans, and Mexicans made it to the 17,500 acres of fertile land on the Medina River that became Castroville.

Comanches and Lipan Apaches frequently stalked Castroville and almost destroyed the Alsatian colonies of Quihi and D'Hanis. As though the Indians and droughts were not distressing enough, in 1849 locusts and cholera brought further grief. The survivors carried off a victim a day for six weeks to Cross Hill (Mount Gentilz Cemetery).

Castroville in 1850 was the twelfth-largest town in Texas. Thirty years later the Southern Pacific bypassed it. The villagers persevered in their box-style rock-and-timber houses, in the process preserving for America a bit of northeastern France. Alongside streets named for Old World capitals, one finds these unpretentious peak-roofed peasant houses and tall-steepled churches. Castroville is called the "Little Alsace of Texas."

110

Henri Castro.
—Eugene C. Barker
Texas History Center,
UT Austin

Those with nostalgia for the frontier will enjoy the Landmark Inn State Historic Structure. With its former lead-lined bathtubs, it once served stage travelers. Now it has been restored in a style befitting the 1940s. The St. Louis Catholic Church, Mt. Gentilz Cemetery, and the Castroville Regional Park are also worthy tourist sites.

Medina River

When Spanish explorer Alonso de León passed by in 1689, he named this river for Pedro Medina, a Spanish engineer. In 1721 the Marquis de Aguayo defined the Medina as the western boundary of Texas. It remained so until the 1830s.

The Medina flows southeast for 115 miles before becoming a tributary of the San Antonio River a few miles south of San Antonio.

On August 18, 1813, the Gutiérrez-Magee Expedition met defeat by Spanish royalist forces at the Battle of Medina River. Of the nearly 3,000 men that clashed, one-tenth that many survivors fled toward Louisiana.

Uvalde—Rocksprings
69 miles

Camp Wood

This site started as the San Lorenzo de la Santa Cruz Mission near the Nueces River Canyon. It was founded then quickly abandoned by Franciscan missionaries in 1762. The United States Army established Camp Wood here in 1857 but pulled out the troops four years later. The Texas Rangers occupied the camp on an occasional basis for years thereafter.

Rocksprings

At 2,450 feet above sea level, Rocksprings is the highest point in the Hill Country. The marvelous springs attracted settlers by 1891, but the site is perhaps best remembered for the tornado in 1927 that destroyed the village and killed sixty-seven people. The Angora Goat Breeders' Association maintains the Rocksprings Museum.

US 83
Uvalde—Leakey
41 miles

Concan, Leakey

Concan, on the scenic Frio River Canyon, was named after "coon can," a popular Mexican gambling game. Comanches and Apaches once roamed here, but now the area is known for its scenic rugged canyons, Angora goats, and ranching.

John Leakey built a cabin in the Frio River Canyon in 1857. Soon, the town that bears his name grew around it. Garner State Park is nearby, as is Horsecollar Bluff with its scenic view of the Frio River.

Frio River

The Spanish in 1689 called this river the Rio Sarco. Later its name was changed to Rio Frio, the "Cold River." Rising northwest of Uvalde, the Frio River drains 7,000 square miles and flows southeast for 200 miles until emptying into Choke Canyon Lake, halfway between San Antonio and Corpus Christi.

US 90—Bandera
28 miles

Bandera

This community began as a camp for harvesting cypress shingles in 1853. A Mormon colony followed a year later, and soon a large group of Poles moved in. The St. Stanislaus Catholic Church, built in 1876 and beautifully restored to its original condition, is the meeting place for one of the oldest Polish parishes in the United States.

During the Great Depression, folks who had cash and felt a pressing need to escape San Antonio's summer heat headed for Bandera, where they spent their money and pretended to be cowboys. Since there were more city folks with cash than there were cattle, the working outfits gradually converted to dude outfits. By World War II, dude ranches provided a substantial source of local revenue.

Today Bandera still has plenty of ranches, both working and guest. The Frontier Times Museum displays fine antiques from the Old West. According to legend, John Wilkes Booth once taught school in Bandera.

US 190
Eldorado—San Saba
130 miles

Eldorado

Eldorado began in 1859 as a ranching headquarters and later became the seat of Schleicher County. The extensive fossil fields southwest of town feature ancient sea creatures.

San Saba River

Three tiny streams unite to form the San Saba River in eastern Schleicher County. It flows east a hundred miles past Fort McKavett and the community of Menard to join the Colorado River eight miles east of San Saba. The river is best known for the Mission Santa Cruz de San Saba and the San Saba Presidio. San Saba is Spanish for "Holy Sabbath."

Fort McKavett

This post began in 1852 as Camp San Saba before it was renamed for Capt. Henry McKavett, who died during the Mexican War. The troops deserted the post during the Civil War and reoccupied it in 1868, when Col. Ranald Mackenzie used it to neutralize Comanches on the high plains. Once the most attractive army post in Texas, Fort McKavett had twelve officers' quarters, barracks for eight companies of infantry, and all the necessary support facilities. Although the army permanently abandoned the post in 1883, it has been restored and is today an official Texas historic site.

Menard

San Antonio in the early 1750s represented the deepest penetration of Spanish power into Texas. But far to the northwest, along the San Saba River, Lipan Apaches had requested a mission, evidently believing it would protect them from Comanches. In April 1757, Col. Diego Ortíz de Parilla, with a company of soldiers and five priests, headed for the San Saba. There, in the heart of Apachería, at present-day Menard, the Spanish hoped to convert the Lipans and open the area for settlement, thereby extending their power. They built the Mission Santa Cruz de San Saba of logs and surrounded it with a palisade. Then they constructed the Presidio San Saba, a fort on the northwest edge of today's Menard.

In early March 1758 the Apaches unexplainably disappeared from the mission. Colonel Parilla advised Padre Terreros and the others to take refuge in the presidio. Terreros said he would think about it, but by the 16th his time to think had come and gone. Most accounts say about 2,000 horseback-riding Comanches surrounded the walls. Armed primarily with lances and bows, but wearing painted faces and dressed in barbaric splendor, the Indians demanded admittance to the mission.

Reluctantly yet foolishly the priests opened the gates—and started handing out presents. Within an hour the bloodletting commenced. Padre Molina and two others took refuge in the church, praying passionately. While other mission structures burned around them, they remained safe in the church because its green logs refused to ignite. Since the building contained little of value, the Comanches paid it scant attention. Molina and his two companions were the only survivors.

Colonel Parilla dispatched thirty soldiers to end the massacre, but the Comanches slaughtered them. As for the presidio, it suffered only threats since the Indians rarely made frontal attacks against entrenched positions.

An outraged arm of the government in San Antonio demanded the Comanches be punished for murdering priests and destroying a mission. In August 1759 Colonel Parilla led 600 men, the largest Spanish army ever to roam about in Texas during those days, out onto the Great Plains in search of the culprits. The army destroyed a Tonkawa village and then tangled with what Parilla described as a combined force of 6,000 Indians. While his Indian allies fled, Parilla's military remnants slashed their way out, abandoning their cannons and supplies and retreating back to San Antonio. It was the worst military defeat ever suffered by Spain in Texas prior to the Texas Revolution.

The Spanish mounted no additional serious campaigns against the Comanches in Texas. San Saba at Menard had been a high-water mark for the Spanish, who never rebuilt the mission and within a few years abandoned the presidio. Today the remains of the presidio serve as a county park.

Calf Creek, Brady

Jim Bowie and his brother Rezin, while seeking what has since been called the Lost Jim Bowie Silver Mine, are said to have stood off some 200 Indians for nine days near Calf Creek in 1831.

Brady, organized during the 1860s, is closer than any other Texas town to being the exact geographical center of the state. The Dodge City Cattle Trail passed through here, and the trail northeast out of Sonora, the longest fenced cattle trail (actually a corridor) in the world, terminated here. (See Sonora.)

Richland Springs, San Saba

In 1850 sheepherder John Duncan built a private fort at what is now Richland Springs. For some years afterwards, travelers and emigrants sought protection from the Comanches there.

West of the confluence of the San Saba and Colorado rivers, the settlement of San Saba arose in 1854. During the late 1870s, two mobs vied for control of the area. One was a gang of powerful, loyal, and well-organized rustlers who coerced court witnesses into testifying favorably on their impeccable behavior or whereabouts during any given time. The other mob was comprised of wealthy ranchers who paid informants and retained an entourage of cowboys, lawyers, preachers, and lawmen. By 1879 the rustlers suffered losses from gunmen and lynchings. The Texas Rangers repeatedly tried to intervene, but they were helpless because no one on either side talked. There were no apparent eyewitnesses to murder.

The violence between these two groups alternately tapered off and flared up. Over the years, nefarious residents died from gunfire or from verdicts handed down by the mobs. Finally, in the late 1890s, with both mobs out of control, people began opening up to the Rangers. Numerous indictments led to ineffective trials, the first of which ended with a hung jury because one juror held out for acquittal; in the second, two jurors blocked a conviction. But the indictments continued. One ranger vowed that if he couldn't get convictions, he would try to scare the guilty parties to death. Soon the system started to work and several of the early-day mobsters went to prison. The trials and violence finally ended about 1903.

Today San Saba is a quiet ranching community famous as the "Pecan Capital of the World." And, even though descendants of the San Saba mobs still reside there, the old resentments have died out. Few talk of past grievances. They'd rather discuss friendships.

Five blocks east of the courthouse is the San Saba County Historical Museum.

US 87

San Angelo—Sterling City
43 miles

Concho River

The Concho River rises in three main branches. The North Concho runs seventy-five miles; the Middle, about ninety; and the South, forty. They converge from the northwest, the west, and the south at San Angelo, where they form the Concho River, which flows another forty miles until it empties into the Colorado River.

Concho means "shell" in Spanish, and the name likely refers to mussel shells in the stream bed. The Spanish in 1650 called it Rio de las Nueces (River of the Walnuts) and later Rio Florida. Today the Concho River provides water for recreation and irrigation. Numerous dams make the stream a working river.

Fort Concho

Fort Concho was established in 1867 at the site of an ancient Comanche watering hole where the forks of the Concho River join. Many travelers passed nearby on the Comanche War Trail, the San Antonio-El Paso Road, the Goodnight-Loving Cattle Trail, and the old Butterfield Trail. Forts Concho, Griffin, and Richardson formed a line 220 miles long, with no telegraph. Each acted as a supply center for the destruction of Comanche power not only in Texas, but also in New and Old Mexico.

The post opened as "Permanent Camp," then changed to Camp Hatch in honor of Maj. John Hatch, an inspector who recommended a move from Fort Chadbourne to this post. But he did not want the post named after him, so the army changed its name to Camp Kelly, after an officer who died of malaria. In February 1869 it became Fort Concho.

Major Hatch liked adobe buildings and put the soldiers to work for weeks carefully forming and drying mud bricks. They had barely laid foundations for the new buildings when heavy rains ruined everything. The bricks returned to soft mud and from then on the troops referred to the major as "Adobe Hatch." German artisans from Fredericksburg were then hired to construct a stone fort.

General Ranald Mackenzie, without question the toughest, most successful, and brilliant Indian fighter that America ever produced.
—National Archives

During its lifetime Fort Concho had at least three outstanding commanders: Col. Ranald Mackenzie, Col. Benjamin H. Grierson, and Col. William Rufus Shafter. These three rotated duty posts. In September 1872, Mackenzie led troops from Richardson and Concho to a fight near Palo Duro Canyon in which they burned 262 Comanche lodges and captured 127 women and children plus 3,000 horses. Although the Indians returned that night to stampede the horses and get them back, the captive women and children remained securely interred at Fort Concho until the following spring, when they were delivered to the reservation at Fort Sill, Oklahoma.

Back at Concho, Mackenzie organized the 4th Cavalry Regiment and led it to Fort Clark where, with his Seminole-Negro scouts in the lead, he raided Mexico on May 17, 1873, burning Kickapoo and Lipan Indian villages. No sooner had this affair calmed down than Indians began killing buffalo hunters on the south and central ranges. Quanah Parker led the Comanches and Lone Wolf guided the Kiowas while Stone Calf and White Shield kept the Cheyennes active. The military closed in on them from a ring of Texas forts.

Mackenzie had overall command, and he left Fort Concho with eight companies of cavalry and three of infantry. In late September 1874, he successfully tracked Quanah Parker and hundreds of Comanches to their home inside Palo Duro Canyon in the Texas panhandle. The outcome signaled the end of Indian troubles in Texas. Furthermore, Mackenzie captured nearly 1,500 horses. This time he shot them.

Colonels Grierson and Shafter worked out of Concho in 1874, both remaining active until the Victorio wars ended during the early 1880s. Fort Concho ceased operations in 1889. The band marched away playing "The Girl I Left Behind Me."

In 1905 the Concho Realty Company purchased the fort's structures for $15,000 and sold them to private individuals. In 1930 Ginevra Wood Carson of San Angelo aroused the community's conscience and started a preservation movement for Fort Concho. Before long the post had become a living museum supervised by the Fort Concho Museum board, a group of San Angelo residents. The post was designated a national historic landmark in 1961. A forty-acre park contains sixteen original buildings. The restored old fort is one of the more successful military tourist attractions in Texas.

San Angelo

Fort Concho contributed to the creation of a raucous village across the Concho River. The community originally called itself San Angela before masculinizing the name to San Angelo.

San Angelo appealed to buffalo hunters, cowboys, sheep ranchers, and soldiers. Its streets housed saloons and brothels before churches and stores, then more saloons and brothels. One brothel on Concho Street, "Miss Hatties," became an institution. It had the finest indoor plumbing in San Angelo. The saloon occupied the main floor while the upstairs, popularly known as "the cowboy hotel," featured rooms named after the working girls. The door to Miss Blue's room even had a peephole, since she was one of the more vigorous employees. Today the main floor is a gift and antique shop, and the upstairs has been converted into a museum. Visitors may walk freely from room to room, but they cannot remove their clothes.

When the Santa Fe Railroad went through San Angelo in 1888, the post knew its time had come. Within a year, Fort Concho was abandoned and the soldiers were reassigned elsewhere.

During World War II the government commissioned San Angelo Army Air Field, better known as Concho Field. It trained soldiers in navigational techniques as well as operating the Norden Bombsight. The field closed in 1946 and has been superseded by Goodfellow Air Force Base. In the mid-1980s Goodfellow became a headquarters for U.S. Air Force military intelligence.

San Angelo is a major recreation area as well as a shipping center for livestock. After the city coined its nickname, "Oasis of West Texas," San Angelo citizens approved a $2.1 million bond to make the name stick. The Concho River beautification project started in 1980. Four miles of trails and parks now line the river, some with fountains, picnic tables, footbridges, and waterfalls plus a parking area for a municipal golf course.

Elmer Kelton, the internationally renowned Western fiction writer, has lived in San Angelo all his life.

Walking along Concho Street is the best way to appreciate the restored buildings and take advantage of the shops and museums. Nearby is the Concho River Walk, Fort Concho itself, the General Telephone Exhibit Museum, and the Museum of Fine Arts. The Producers Livestock Auction Company handles the second-largest livestock auction in the state.

Carlsbad

This community was created in 1908 when ranchers dug wells and found mineral water. The name stemmed from the spa at Karlsbad, Germany. The Texas Tuberculosis Sanatorium opened at Carlsbad in 1912 with a 1,000-bed capacity. A famous resident was Katherine Ann Porter, author of *Ship of Fools* and *The Leaning Tower*. In 1969, the sanatorium was converted into a home for mentally retarded adults.

Sterling City

For such an ordinary, unexciting name, Sterling City is a community of mystery and legend. In 1654, the Spanish sought pearls in the Llano River. A legend claims outlaws Jesse and Frank James hid here during the 1870s. Another mystery is Tower Hill. Settlers in 1864 found the ruins of a rock fort on its summit. Inside were muzzle-loading muskets, a skeleton, and jewelry.

San Angelo—Robert Lee

Robert Lee

In 1889 two Confederate veterans named this settlement Robert Lee in honor of the Southern general. Graves of Civil War veterans are in the local cemetery. Oil was discovered in 1942. Spence Reservoir is nearby.

San Angelo—Fort Chadbourne

Tennyson, Bronte

The town of Tennyson took its name in 1880 from Alfred Lord Tennyson, the English poet. Nearby Mt. Margaret is a permanent memorial to a young girl killed by Indians. A cross marks her grave.

Bronte started in 1887 on a branch of the Chisholm Trail. The settlement was named for the famed English writer Charlotte Bronte.

Fort Chadbourne

Ten miles north of Bronte, Fort Chadbourne was established in 1852 on the east bank of Oak Creek. The post protected the Butterfield Overland Mail. Bad water forced the post's abandonment in 1859.

In 1861, Texas secessionists waited at the fort for the last eastbound Butterfield coach. Famed publisher and abolitionist Horace Greeley was supposed to be on board from California. However, Greeley changed his mind and sailed home by ship.

Federal troops returned to Fort Chadbourne in 1867, but the water had not improved, so they transferred to Fort Concho.

San Angelo—Ballinger

Miles, Ballinger

When Jonathan Miles of San Angelo donated $5,000 to get a railroad from Ballinger to San Angelo, the railroad named one of the settlements Miles, Texas. Today, the old opera house has been restored, as have numerous historic buildings.

Ballinger, on the Colorado River, began first as Hutchings, then switched to Gresham. In 1886 it became Ballinger. It honored William Pitt Ballinger, an attorney for the Santa Fe Railroad. The old and beautiful Carnegie Library is restored and is still in use. There is a striking statue on the courthouse lawn of Charles H. Noyes, a local cowboy killed in a range accident. The sculptor was the world-renowned Pompeo Coppini.

In recent years the lake at Ballinger has silted, causing residents to consider either closing the town or switching to Lake Spence, fifty miles distant on the Colorado River, for their water supply. Lake Spence has a salty flavor.

Ballinger—Paint Rock

Paint Rock

Indian pictographs, a stone-age art gallery, are found along a one-mile stretch of the limestone cliffs lining the Concho River Canyon. Preserved are pictorial records of the Shawnee, Delaware, Cherokee, Kickapoo, Comanche, and Lipan Apache. One set describes a Comanche victory at the Mission Santa Cruz de San Saba. Over 1,500 Indian paintings are here, the largest collection in Texas and one of the most significant in the United States.

"Lady in Blue" miracles occurred in the vicinity of Paint Rock. Mother Maria de Agreda never left her convent in Spain, but she visited the American Southwest on many occasions, as attested to by Texas Indians who watched her descend from the sky. Mother Maria described the American Southwest to her superiors, and she repeatedly asked the Franciscan Order to establish missions among the Indians.

Ballinger—Brownwood

Santa Anna

This community is not named after the Mexican dictator, but for nearby Santa Anna Mountain, which was likely named for the dictator. Soldiers, settlers, rangers, surveyors, and Indians used the peak as a landmark and observation post. The town, which dated back to the 1860s, was originally called Gap, for a gap in the mountain. The Wire Road (Earl Van Dorn Trail) extended from San Antonio to Camp Colorado, eight miles north of Santa Anna. The Santa Fe Railroad arrived in 1886.

Brownwood

Brownwood grew up in the heart of Comanche country and was county seat of Brown County in 1857. During the 1870s and 1880s, the town and county went through the fence-cutting wars as the area became a rendezvous for thieves, rustlers, and murderers. Texas Rangers frequently restored order.

Brownwood became the largest cotton-buying center west of Fort Worth. Oil strikes occurred during the 1920s.

Oil, cattle, sheep, and tourism are still the leading businesses. Worthwhile visits can be made to the Brown County Museum of History, the Camp Bowie Memorial Park, and the Douglas MacArthur Academy of Freedom.

Brownwood—Austin

Zephyr

This small community was founded around 1863. Zephyr is best known for a 1909 tornado that killed 32 people.

Lometa

The Santa Fe Railroad built a siding called Montvale in 1885. However, since a Montvale already existed in Texas, a Hispanic sheepherder suggested "Lometa," Spanish for "Little Mountain," a nearby landmark. The townspeople resolved never to permit saloons in the village, which explains partly why it still lives up to its name "little."

Lampasas

"Burleson" was created in the early 1850s on the Sulphur Fork of the Lampasas River. By 1856, the year stagecoaches came to town, the community name had changed to Lampasas.

Since a local spring had medicinal qualities, the village was originally known as a health center. Folks were so healthy, the story goes, that they had to shoot one another to start a cemetery. Some residents still equate the graveyard's creation with the Horrell brothers: Matt, Tom, Merritt, Ben, and Sam. They tangled with the state police in Jerry Scott's saloon. When the gunfight ended, four policemen were dead and a badly wounded Matt was in jail. When he recovered, his brothers broke him out of jail and the entire clan fled to Lincoln County, New Mexico, where for the next few years they engaged in the "Horrell War" shortly before Billy the Kid and the Lincoln County War.

By 1874 the Horrells were back in Lampasas and squabbling with a ranching neighbor, John Pinkney Calhoun Higgins, better known as "Pink" Higgins. Pink accused the Horrells of stealing his livestock, and the Horrell-Higgins feud was on.

After Pink killed Merritt Horrell in Scott's Saloon, two raging battles took place in Lampasas before the Texas Rangers restored order. Maj. John B. Jones talked both parties into signing a July-August 1877 peace treaty, and in the history of Texas feuding, this is the only treaty that ever held. The Horrell-Higgins feud was over.

The Gulf, Colorado & Santa Fe Railroad reached Lampasas in 1882. The Houston & Texas Central (Texas & New Orleans) followed in the early 1900s.

Lampasas is now a major ranching crossroads. The area is popular with fishermen, who try their luck in the Lampasas and Colorado rivers. The town has a historic downtown area featuring limestone structures of the 1880s. The Keystone Square Museum is housed in an early frontier building.

Lampasas River

This river winds for a hundred miles from western Hamilton County to the Little River in Bell County. Lampasas is Spanish for "lilies," which is not a descriptive term. Many historians suspect the Spanish confused the Lampasas River with the Salado (salty) River.

Fort Mason—Burnet

Fort Mason

On July 6, 1851, Fort Mason was established on "Post Hill" overlooking the San Saba and Llano rivers. It was one of several "middle line" forts strung from the Red River to the Rio Grande. Settlements arced across the center of Texas, and Mason protected villages in territory controlled by Comanches, Lipan Apaches, and Kiowas. Overall the fort lasted nearly nineteen years, although it had several periods of inactivity.

Mason was a cavalry post as well as an administrative and command center. Twenty of its officers rose to the rank of general during the Civil War. Some of their names were Col. Albert Sidney Johnson, Maj. Earl Van Dorn, Edmund Kirby Smith, Col. Robert E. Lee, John Bell Hood, and Maj. John P. Hatch. Four officers became Union generals, one of whom was George H. Thomas, the "Rock of Chickamauga."

Lt. John Bell Hood took his men on a 500-mile march in July 1857. They killed up to twenty Comanches. Only two soldiers were killed and a half-dozen wounded.

Capt. Charles Travis, the only son of Alamo hero William Barret Travis, was accused of gambling, lying, and slander. The army dismissed him in 1856 and he died of tuberculosis in 1860 at the age of thirty-one.

U.S. Dragoons stationed here would have been right at home in a John Wayne movie. They wore gaudy uniforms, kept their hair long, and sported beards. Col. Charles Augustus May, one of many commanding officers, was six feet, four inches tall. His beard covered his chest, and hair from his head dangled to his hips. He was a brave, eccentric, flamboyant, and remarkable officer, and stories about him circulate to this day.

From 1856 to 1861, the 2nd Cavalry garrisoned Fort Mason. Each company had horses of an identical color, and since there were ten companies, the parades were striking indeed. The entire period bore testimony of one Indian fight after another. Mason was the most active military post in the nation.

During the Civil War, Fort Mason guarded Union prisoners of war. After Reconstruction, the post fought a few Indians, but spent most of its energy chasing outlaws and rustlers. By 1869, the fort was abandoned. Today Fort Mason has been largely reconstructed. The walls are a tourist site a few blocks south of the Mason County Courthouse.

Mason

Mason, named for the fort, was built along Centennial and Comanche creeks. The town had its share of ne'er-do-wells, outlaws, murderers, thieves and rustlers, but it took the Mason County War, oftentimes known as the Hoodoo War, to bring it statewide attention.

In February 1875, Sheriff John Clark arrested nine men for cattle theft. When four broke jail, the vigilantes shot one and lynched three. Of the three dangling from ropes, one staved off strangulation until friends cut him down. A final prisoner escaped in the melee.

Author and historian C. L. Sonnichsen claimed the masked vigilantes borrowed the Hoodoo name from the Ku Klux Klan, infamous for its "ambushes and midnight hangings," tactics in the Texas case designed to "get rid of the thieves and outlaws who had been holding a carnival of lawlessness." Of course, other factions believe the Hoodoos were Confederates smarting from Reconstruction and determined to take vengeance upon former Unionists, especially Germans.

Two months later, deputy sheriff John Worley and prisoner Tim Williamson were attacked by a dozen blackfaced vigilantes. Williamson was shot to death. His slaying so infuriated friend and former Texas Ranger Scott Cooley that Cooley organized his own vigilantes and extracted vengeance. At least twelve men were shot to death in separate incidents. Cooley even scalped one victim.

On September 28, Maj. John B. Jones rode into town with twenty men of Company A of the Texas Rangers. Things got quiet. Then Company A transferred to other trouble spots, and the Hoodoo War flared again. Finally, after 1876, with so much blood on the land, there weren't enough enemies left to fight one another. To this day, no suspects in Mason County were ever convicted of murder.

Mason today is a ranching and tourist center, a headquarters for rock hunters. The Mason County Historical Museum is housed in an 1870s schoolhouse. The restored Seaquist Home has tours by appointment.

Sixteen miles south of Mason on US 87 is Loyal Valley, birthplace of one of the most fascinating men in Texas history. Germans settled here, people who refused to desert the Union. Hence the name, Loyal Valley.

Herman Lehmann was born here on June 5, 1859. He never went to school and spoke only German, but at the age of eleven he and his younger brother Willie were captured by Apaches. Willie returned home nine days later, but Herman was adopted by his Apache captor, Carnoviste, and became a warrior. Lehmann took part in raids against Texas Rangers, Mexicans, Americans, and Comanches. After Carnoviste was slain, Lehmann joined the Comanches and fought in several battles against the U.S. Cavalry.

When the Comanches surrendered at Fort Sill, Oklahoma, in 1874, Lehmann was eventually recognized as white and forcibly returned to his white family near Loyal Valley, who had thought he was dead. He had to relearn German as well as English, but he never learned to sleep in a bed. Lehmann frequently dressed like an Indian, emitted "war hoops" during religious revivals, and had to be restrained by his brother Willie from slaughtering neighborhood livestock.

Captain James B. Gillett and Herman Lehmann in 1924 at the Gunter Hotel in San Antonio during an Old Trail Riders reunion. Lehmann was captured by Apaches and spent nine years with them and Comanches as a warrior. As a Texas Ranger, Gillett once shot Lehmann's horse out from under him. —Harry Ransom Humanities Research Center, UT Austin

Nevertheless, Lehmann was likeable, easy-going, and something of a Texas celebrity. He married twice, the second time fathering two sons and three daughters. The government gave him land in Oklahoma because he was a Comanche. Herman Lehmann died on February 2, 1932, and is buried in Loyal Valley.

Llano

No place in the state can lay claim to more picturesque scenery than Llano, a community that bills itself as the "Deer Capital of Texas." The first settlers arrived about 1855. Iron ore was discovered in 1880. Then came mineral finds of copper, lead, zinc, asbestos, and even a trace of gold. None of this proved commercially successful, although rock hounds still find this region a delightful and productive place to visit. Llanite in particular is unique to the Llano area. It is a dark pink granite with inclusions of sky-blue quartz crystals.

Near Llano are the remains of the Communist Colony of Bettina, established in 1847. The settlers were German intellectuals from the universities of Heidelberg and Geissen. With their motto of "friendship, freedom and equality," they sailed from Hamburg, landed at Galveston, and migrated to New Braunfels. After the peace treaty with the Comanches had been signed, the colonists moved to Bettina, named in honor of Bettina von Arnin, a German thinker. Within a year, the members drifted away because few wanted to work.

Fort Croghan

This post was three miles south of today's Burnet, Texas. In 1849 Henry McCulloch and a squad of Texas Rangers built McCulloch's Station, a fort. Within a few months the site became a federal post. It had several different names over the years—Camp Croghan, Camp Hamilton, and then Fort Croghan. Col. George Croghan was an inspector general. The post was abandoned during the mid-1850s, and the buildings were used as civilian residences. The ruins are a historic site.

Burnet

This village lies in one of the world's most ancient geologic areas, but its actual birth began with Fort Croghan. The town was originally called Hamilton Valley, but it was renamed for David Burnet, president of Texas during the eight most turbulent months of the republic's existence. Stone for the state capitol in Austin came from Granite Mountain near Burnet. Today there is excellent fishing on the Highland Lakes. Black Rock Park and Longhorn Cavern State Park are near Burnet.

Fredericksburg

The Pedernales River Valley awoke one morning in May 1846 to the heavy creak of wagons disturbing the quiet countryside. Developer John O. Meusebach was bringing 120 emigrants in from New Braunfels. The Pedernales was in Indian country, of course, but Meusebach, whom the Comanches called El Sol Colorado (the Red Sun), would make a deal with twenty Comanche chiefs for land north of the Llano River.

Baron Ottfried Hans Von Meusebach dropped his title and became John O. Meusebach on the day he sailed for Texas. Upon arriving in New Braunfels, he learned that the Adelsverein Society, founded in Germany to promote immigration, had not yet fulfilled its destiny of turning three million acres of the Fisher-Miller Grant into a thriving frontier. New Braunfels was a way station, and by 1845 another was needed. Within months, Meusebach led his

Fredericksburg, Texas, about 1890. —The Institute of Texan Cultures

Charles Henry Nimitz, a founder of Fredericksburg, Texas, with his grandson, Chester William Nimitz. Young Chester had recently graduated from the U.S. Naval Academy in 1905. —Admiral Nimitz Museum State Historical Park, Fredericksburg

people to 10,000 acres on the Pedernales. The outpost was named Fredericksburg after Prince Frederick of Prussia, a patron of the Adelsverein.

By 1847, Mormons founded a nearby village called Zodiac. That same year, Meusebach solidified his peace treaty with the Comanches.

Fort Martin Scott opened to protect Fredericksburg in December 1848. The 1st Infantry guarded travelers along the Fredericksburg-San Antonio Road. While the fort was a source of hard cash for the civilians, due to Meusebach's treaty with the Indians few soldiers were really necessary. It was manned infrequently after 1852 and abandoned completely after the Civil War.

The Bismarck Saloon and saloon hangers-on, Fredericksburg, Texas. —The Institute of Texan Cultures

For years Fredericksburg represented the last rest stop before El Paso, 500 miles west. But forty-niners were a mixed blessing. While they were a source of cash, their diseases, especially cholera and typhoid, kept the cemetery full.

Ninety-six percent of Fredericksburg voted *against* secession. Union sentiment ran high in the town. While the Germans owned no black slaves, and generally found the practice repugnant, the settlers believed solutions could be found to the slavery practice short of war.

After the war, the San Antonio & Aransas Pass Railroad sought a route to the High Plains. Fredericksburg and Kerrville were in contention, and in November 1913 the iron horse arrived in Fredericksburg.

In the years since, Fredericksburg has found its destiny primarily as a tourist town. A European atmosphere pervades. German is frequently spoken and ancient customs abound. Older buildings have been restored. The Easter Fires are still celebrated, as are Schuetzenfests (marksmanship tournaments), Oktoberfests, and Kristkindl Markets.

Since Fleet Admiral Chester Nimitz, a United States hero in World War II, was born in Fredericksburg, a state historic site honors his memory and his exploits. Nearby is Enchanted Rock State Park, a massive dome of solid granite. It is 500 feet high and covers 640 acres. Modern visitors hold it in as much awe and reverence as the prehistoric Indians and early settlers did.

Various parks and Sunday houses abound. There is a Pioneer Memorial Library, a Pioneer Museum Complex, and a Texas Children's Museum. The Oberhellmann Vineyards & Winery has complimentary tours and tastings.

(Additional information about German settlers can be found in the Hill Country introduction.)

Stonewall and Johnson City

These two towns represent "LBJ Country." The former congressman, senator, vice president, and 36th president of the United States was born and is buried here. During his presidency, the LBJ Ranch was the Texas White House. Johnson brought world-renowned leaders here to discuss national and international problems.

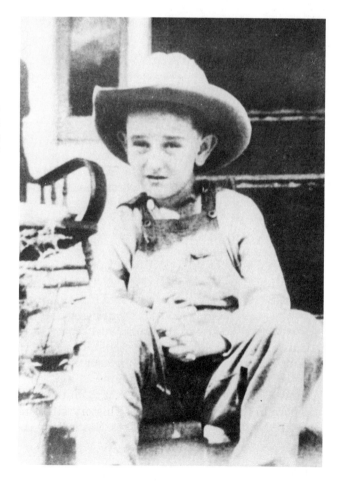

Lyndon B. Johnson at age five. —Lyndon Baines Johnson Library

Stonewall was established in 1870 and named for Gen. Thomas "Stonewall" Jackson. Had Lyndon Johnson not come along, Stonewall would likely be better known today for its delicious peaches.

The Johnson City area was settled in 1856 by James and Martha Provost. By the mid-1860s, Tom Johnson, Lyndon's great uncle, had obtained the property. A year later, Sam Ealy Johnson, Sr., Lyndon's grandfather, moved in. After the Civil War, the two brothers did well in the cattle driving business, earning sufficient money to purchase additional land for pens and pastures along the Pedernales. The brothers made four cattle drives up the Chisholm Trail to Abilene, Kansas.

Sam Ealy Johnson, Jr., took a different path than his father. By 1913 he lived in a small frame home and had five children, one of whom was Lyndon. Sam was also a state representative, and the Johnson home was frequently filled with elected officials. Mrs. Johnson added to the clamor. She was a college-educated lady who conducted elocution, debate, and declamation

Rebekah Baines Johnson and Samuel Ealy Johnson, Jr., parents of Lyndon B. Johnson, 1936. —Lyndon Baines Johnson Library

The restored birthplace of Lyndon B. Johnson, which is a tour site in the Lyndon Baines Johnson National Historic Park near Stonewall.

lessons on the porch and in the parlor. Lyndon obviously had some strong influences prior to his entering what is now Southwest Texas State University at San Marcos.

Stonewall and Johnson City are home to the 500-acre Lyndon Baines Johnson National Historical Park, which contains two sections, one in each community. Tours (walking and bus) are available to the replica of Johnson's four-room birthplace, the ranch, the towns, and the grave site.

Pedernales River

President Lyndon Johnson made the Pedernales famous. When he visited the Western White House (his Johnson City ranch), the media often got photo opportunities and interviews during his strolls along the river. He loved the Pedernales, spent a lot of time there, and it influenced his ideas and presidency.

The Pedernales, which means flint rock or arrowhead, can be stepped across in many places. Other than in the Hill Country, it would not likely even qualify as a river. Still, it meanders 106 miles and empties into the Colorado River in western Travis County.

A popular visiting and camping site is Pedernales Falls State Park, a 4,800-acre area set aside for visitors plus turkeys, deer, raccoons, armadillos and jackrabbits. The river slices through the park for six miles and then borders a very spectacular gorge for another three. Tubers and swimmers have designated areas. Primitive trails several miles long appeal to hardy hikers.

Dripping Springs

By the 1850s, this area was thickly settled. There was timber, water, and fertile soil. However, unlike most other parts of this region, the Germans did not predominate. Southern states furnished a majority of the settlers.

Colorado River

The word *colorado* is Spanish for "red" (red mud, in this instance), but the Colorado's waters are clear and always have been. Chances are that the Colorado and the Brazos had their names interchanged during periods of Spanish exploration. Indians called the Colorado the Kanahatino or the Pashohono, depending upon which tribes were in evidence. Spaniards also called the Colorado the San Clemente. Texans tend to pronounce it "Colo-RAY-do," apparently to remind visitors that the state of Colorado has nothing to do with this river.

The Colorado rises near La Mesa in the High Plains of West Texas not too far from New Mexico. It flows generally southeast for 650 miles until it spills into Matagorda Bay. Principal tributaries are the Pedernales, Llano, San Saba, and Concho rivers. The drainage basin is 38,000 square miles, the largest of any river totally within Texas. In spite of size, the drainage is light. In fact, for the first hundred miles of its journey, the Colorado struggles to keep enough water between its banks to be called a river.

Several of Stephen F. Austin's Old Three Hundred colonists settled on the Colorado's banks, but most preferred its tributaries. The state capital of Austin (the largest city on the river) was established in 1839. In 1844, President Antonio López de Santa Anna, under intense pressure from French and English diplomats who did not want Texas annexed by the United States, agreed to recognize the Colorado River as the Republic of Texas boundary.

The slow current led to a logjam (called "the raft") fifteen miles upstream from the river's mouth, halting navigation inland for settlers. Although shallow draught vessels did at times make it to Austin, the Civil War and subsequent railroads ended the Colorado's possibilities as a transportation line.

Once the Concho and other tributaries join the Colorado, the river shows its power. A 1935 flood took 400 lives. Roughly twenty major rampages in recorded history have given the Colorado Valley its shape and character.

A need for flood control and rice irrigation led to the creation of the Colorado River Authority (divided into Lower, Central, and Upper districts) in the 1930s. In 1937, the Lower Colorado River Authority built Buchanan Dam as its first project. This dam became a cornerstone of efforts to control the river and bring electricity to rural areas in Central Texas. Thus began a period of six dam constructions that would manage the Colorado and create the Highland Lakes of Buchanan (highest and broadest), LBJ, Marble Falls, Travis (the largest), Austin, and Town. The Highland Lakes have spurred growth in the city of Austin. Citizens celebrate the river every year with festivals and fireworks. Today the highly managed Colorado ebbs and flows and, occasionally, demonstrates its great power. In the spring of 1957, sixty-five-mile-long Lake Travis rose thirteen feet in twenty-four hours when torrential rains poured down.

A variety of river-cruise tour boats are available.

Austin

Austin balances on the eastern edge of the Hill Country where the Gulf Coastal Plain breaks away from the Balcones Escarpment, a crusty region that could in fact be interpreted as Central Texas. It sprawls across a bend in the Colorado. While Stephen F. Austin had a colony here in 1835, Jacob Harrell was the first to settle. Harrell resided in a tent near present Congress Avenue. He and other residents named the village Waterloo in 1838. Two nearby communities were Montopolis and Parthenia. They drew their water from Elizabeth Springs, later Barton Springs.

In 1836, Washington-on-the-Brazos was capital of the Texas Republic, but President Sam Houston ordered it moved to Columbia, and three months later to the city of Houston. President Mirabeau Lamar, however, disliked Sam Houston and the city that bore Houston's name. Furthermore, Lamar wanted the capital away from the humidity and malaria of the gulf region and closer to the Texas interior, near fertile soil, an invigorating climate, and good drinking water.

The remote republic of Texas could be more easily governed from a capital situated in the hinterlands rather than along the Gulf Coast. Even after moving to Austin, it still wasn't all that distant from Houston and the Atlantic, but it was as far as a city could safely get from the coast in those days, so it would have to do.

President Lamar appointed a commission in 1839 to select a capital, giving his committee authority to evaluate the Colorado River region as an intersection of major north-south, east-west trade routes. The commission chose Waterloo, and their report was nothing if not grandiloquent: "The imagination of even the romantic will not be disappointed on viewing the valley of the Colorado, and the fertile and gracefully undulating woodlands and luxurious prairies at a distance from it."

Construction started on 700 acres purchased by the republic. The Colorado River would be the southern boundary, and Waller Creek (today's East Avenue) the eastern. Shoal Creek (Western Avenue) formed the west boundary. Except for Congress Avenue, north-south streets were named for Texas Rivers. For awhile Congress was the widest street in the world, three times wider than its present width.

East-west streets were named for Texas trees (but were later given numbers), except for Water Avenue, College Avenue, and North Avenue. North Avenue marked the northern limits of the city.

As time passed, the street system went awry. The city's core remained sensible and ordered, the blocks at right angles. But when the city expanded outside its original limits, as enclosed roughly by today's I-35, 1st Street, Martin Luther King Boulevard, and West Avenue, the streets wandered off, drifted, radiated in first one direction, then another. Once outside the core, Austin was (and is) easy to get lost in.

A temporary capitol arose on Colorado Street between Hickory (8th) and Ash (9th), a one-story wooden building with a stockade for protection against Indians. Government offices were in place by October 1839. The president lived in a two-story pine house.

By 1840 the French had an embassy in Waterloo. The town's population was 856, and there was talk of a name change. Waterloo became Austin, in honor of Stephen F. Austin.

Sam Houston became president again in 1841. He considered Austin an unsafe location, his suspicions being verified in 1842 when the Mexican Army reoccupied San Antonio, seventy-five miles south. Houston summoned congress to Houston, but the capital could not be physically there unless state records (archives) were transferred too. So Houston ordered the Texas Rangers to remove them from Austin. On the night of December 30, 1842, as the papers were surreptitiously being loaded in wagons, Angelina Eberly, an Austin boardinghouse lady, discovered the theft and fired a warning cannon. The chase was on. The archives were overtaken and recovered near Round Rock. The farcical struggle has since become known in Texas history as the Archives War.

Anson Jones, the architect of annexation to the United States, assumed the Texas presidency in 1844. He called for a convention in Austin to draft an ordinance of annexation to the United States, plus a constitution for the state of Texas. When all that had been settled, Jones, as the last president of the Republic of Texas, swore in James Pinkney Henderson as the first governor of the state of Texas. By popular vote in 1850, the citizens of Texas retained Austin as the state capital.

A new state capitol cornerstone was laid on July 3, 1852, by the Masonic Fraternity of the Grand Lodge of Texas. Two thousand people stood in respectful attendance.

Upon completion of the capitol, dedicated in 1853, a visitor described it thus: "The Capitol Building was on a commanding eminence, and faced south,

The capitol under construction in Austin. —Archives Division, Texas State Library

at the head of a street known as Congress Avenue. It was built of soft white stone, and although without any pretensions of architectural beauty, yet, from the material of which it was composed, and its striking situation, it presented quite a commanding appearance."

A sign over the gate warned, "Horses prohibited on capitol grounds."

For nearly thirty years the government of Texas conducted business in the capitol. But that ended on a cold, rainy afternoon in November 1881. The building caught fire, and firemen saved only the limestone and the lot.

For a while the Texas government met in the Travis County Courthouse, as well as the jail. Governor Oran Roberts built a temporary capitol on the southwest corner of Congress Avenue and Mesquite (11th) Street, but portions collapsed even before it was finished. Still, it sufficed until a more durable building was ready.

The Texas constitution stipulated that a new capitol building could be constructed only through the sale of public land, so property was surveyed and appraised at fifty cents an acre. A firm called Taylor, Babcock and Company purchased three million acres of panhandle land. The XIT Ranch arose from that transaction. (See Channing.)

Newspapers insisted that the Texas structure should be second in size only to the national Capitol in Washington, D.C. It should be larger and finer than the German Reichstag or the English parliament building.

Texas supplied convict labor for the capitol's construction, the number of individuals not exceeding 1,000 for the quarrying of limestone. The contractor agreed to board, clothe, and feed them. Guards were not in uniform, but they were armed, mounted, and assisted by bloodhounds.

The International Association of Granite Cutters boycotted the job, which meant there were no skilled craftsmen showing the convicts what to do. The contractor then circumvented the boycott by hiring sixty-two granite cutters from Scotland and paying them $4 per day. The builder was in violation of the federal Alien Contract Labor Law, and the courts fined him $8,000 plus costs. But the work continued.

In April 1888 over 2,000 people attended the capitol dedication. The largest state capitol in the nation, it was built of red granite from Marble Falls and towered seven feet higher than the national Capitol. Senator Temple Houston, the youngest son of old Sam Houston, intoned the dedication speech. It wasn't brief.

Backtracking to the Civil War, Austin had voted against secession in 1860. Still, the city raised a company of light infantry for the Confederate Army and dispatched a few volunteers to join Terry's Texas Rangers. A percussion cap factory was constructed.

Following the war, Gen. George Armstrong Custer and his wife, Libbie, arrived in Austin to supervise Reconstruction. Their quarters were in the deserted Asylum for the Blind. Although the flamboyant Custer's duties were to militarily govern the state, he was just as well known for disciplining his

Flamboyant George Custer as he appeared in Texas after the Civil War.
—National Archives

troops. Those guilty of crimes had their heads shaved and their backs stripped to receive floggings of twenty-five lashes.

As a general rule, Custer was popular among Texans. Upon his death at the Little Bighorn in 1876, the Texas legislature passed a resolution of condolences. As for the Asylum for the Blind, the Custer building has been restored and is a part of the University of Texas at Austin.

The Houston & Texas Central Railroad arrived in 1871. Close behind was the International & Great Northern in 1876, which brought the first cold beer to Austin. The Missouri, Kansas & Texas Railroad arrived in 1909.

Ben Thompson was one of those people the trains frequently hauled in and out. Although born in Knottingley, England, in 1842, he moved to Austin when he was nine. He wounded his first man with bird shot, survived the legal inquiry, and drifted to New Orleans, where he killed a man. Meanwhile, after being a gambler all his life, he learned the printer's trade while staying abreast of the art of manslaying.

Thompson joined the Confederacy during the Civil War. When the conflict ended, he smuggled whiskey, gambled, and within a year sold his talents to Emperor Maximilian in Mexico. That didn't last long, and back in Austin a military court sentenced Thompson to prison for threatening a justice of the peace. He was released in two years and for a while drove cattle up the Chisholm Trail.

Thompson returned to Austin in 1879 and campaigned for city marshal. By then he had slain eight men. He challenged anyone to prove he had ever been dishonest or had failed to "protect the timid, weak, or defenseless from the aggressions and wrongs of the overbearing and strong." He lost the election.

Thompson was elected city marshal two years later in 1881. While he had always been a dandy, sporting a cane, gloves, and stovepipe hat, he did bring respectable law enforcement to Austin. Still, he had his erratic, even bullying moments. He stopped trains for moving slowly through town and threatened the engineers with six-shooters. He shot up a banquet of the Texas Cattle Raisers Association.

Under civic pressure, Thompson stepped aside as marshal. He then moved to San Antonio and killed Jack Harris during a gambling incident. In March 1884, he and gunman King Fisher were ambushed and slain in a San Antonio variety theatre.

Austin easily survived Ben Thompson and went on to construct a dam and power plant on the Colorado River in 1900. In 1937, a series of dams created the Highland Lakes, which have since provided outstanding recreational and scenic opportunities.

All the while, interesting things were happening in education. What is now the University of Texas at Austin started out in 1839 as just words on paper. The school was endowed with 231,400 acres of public land. On September 6, 1881, Austin was selected as the main university site. The Austin campus consisted of a 40-acre tract on College Hill. Today the university's buildings, equipment, and stock are worth billions of dollars. In one of those ironies to end all ironies, the legislature kept swapping the university lands until the school owned nothing but worthless desert in West Texas. When oil was discovered beneath that barren desert topsoil, the university became very rich.

In addition to the University of Texas, the city of Austin has St. Edward's University, Huston-Tillotson College, Concordia Lutheran College, Austin Community College, and and two theological seminaries.

High technology arrived in Austin with companies like Tracor, a home-grown corporation, and IBM, Motorola, Texas Instruments, Fisher Controls, Data General, and Radian.

Scores of talented musicians call Austin home. Among them are Willie Nelson and the late Stevie Ray Vaughan. Austin has its Aqua Music Festival in July and August, and its South by Southwest Music Festival is usually in March.

For history buffs, Austin has walking and driving tours. No one should miss the Greek Revival mansions of Abner Cook, Austin's master builder, projects that included the governor's mansion. There is the Lyndon B. Johnson Library, the Harry Ransom Humanities Research Center, the Texas State Library and Archives, the Daughters of the Republic of Texas (and the Confederacy) Museum, the state capitol complex, Oakwood Cemetery (where frontier figures and gunfighters are buried), the Barker Texas History Center, the George Washington Carver Museum, and the Lorenzo de Zavala State Archives and Library. The list of architectural landmarks, parks, art centers, and sporting outlets defies cataloging.

I-35
Austin—San Antonio
80 miles

Buda

Although settlers arrived in the 1840s, a town called Dupre did not arise until 1889, when the International Great Northern Railroad needed a siding. That same year the town's name switched to Buda, probably a mistranslation of *viuda*, a Spanish word for "widow." A widow operated the settlement's only hotel. Local legends insist that a ghostly Lady in White guards a nearby buried treasure.

San Marcos River

Only fifty miles long, the San Marcos is one of the shortest rivers in Texas. Due to a fault caused by collision forces of the Balcones Escarpment and the Gulf Plains, a huge spring gushed forth with nearly a million daily gallons of cool, fresh water. It formed the San Marcos River and flowed southeast, joining the Guadalupe River west of Gonzales.

Spanish explorer Alonso de León named the stream in 1689. In addition to being occasionally misidentified as the Colorado, it has also been called Los Inocentes (the Innocents), San Agustín, and the Marquis de Aguayo.

Glass-bottomed boats from San Marcos currently cruise over Aquarena Springs, the foundation of the river. A re-created frontier village and mission ruins are nearby.

San Marcos

The town is built around Aquarena Springs, the beginnings of the San Marcos River. In the mid-1750s, this site was the temporary location of the San Xavier Mission and the presidio of San Francisco Xavier. San Marcos de Neve, a Spanish villa, was established in 1808 by Manuel Antonio Cordéro y Bustamante as a link in defense settlements between San Antonio and Nacogdoches. However, the villa was never a success. A flood damaged it in June 1808, and repeated Comanche attacks made life difficult. It was abandoned in 1812. In 1851, William Lindsey, Edward Burleson, and Eli T. Merriman purchased the Juan Martín Veramendi land grant and laid out the village of San Marcos.

San Marcos (Saint Mark) evolved quickly into a county seat and commercial center, a gateway to the Hill Country. The Southwest Texas State Teachers College became Southwest Texas State University, with magnificent buildings that are throwbacks to the Old South. During World War II, the San Marcos Air Force Base opened. It closed at war's end, but reopened in 1950 as a helicopter training center.

Historic sites are Aquarena Springs, the Bevin Street Historic District with its nineteenth century homes shaded by live oaks, a re-created Indian village, the San Marcos River Walkway, and Wonder World, an earthquake-formed cave.

Comal River

The Comal River stems from a number of large limestone fissure springs in New Braunfels and flows four miles into the Guadalupe River. It is said to be the shortest river carrying a large body of water in the United States. The shieldlike leaves of the giant caladium plant add a tropical aspect to the stream.

The river has often been misidentified as the Guadalupe. *Comal* is Spanish for "flat dish," perhaps a reference to the New Braunfels Valley.

New Braunfels

When the Fisher-Miller grant (see Hill Country introduction) proved to be too deep in Indian country to be readily settled, Prince Carl purchased a league of land on the Comal River. A contingent of German settlers were given ten-acre plots for farming, plus building lots. The settlement was named for Braunfels on the Lahn, the prince's hometown in Germany.

Indian troubles never threatened Braunfels, and the village became a supply center as well as a jumping-off point for settlements such as Fredericksburg. A log building was both church and school, and New Braunfels was one of the first communities in Texas to assess taxes for public schooling. Over the years the town has been a successful timber, farming, and ranching center.

The Baetge House is a fine example of fachwerk construction, but there are many historic homes and churches, as well as the Faust Hotel and Prince Solms Inn. Visitors will want to see the Natural Bridge Caverns and Wildlife Ranch, the Museum of Texas Handmade Furniture, and a former log fortress now known as the Sophienburg Museum. Guided float trips on the Guadalupe River are also available.

THREE

Pineywoods

Texans call deep east Texas the Piney Woods. This is a different world from the rest of Texas. Here the rain falls more than 50 inches a year and has created a forested region that runs 75 to 125 miles westward from the Louisiana border, ending in the Post Oak belt, and south from the Red River to about 25 miles from the Gulf of Mexico, enclosing an area of 16 million acres. This is an extension of the Southern forest into Texas, and it is also an extension—cultural as well as topographical—of the Deep South across the Texas line.

T. R. Fehrenbach, *Texas: A Salute from Above*
(Portland House, 1990)

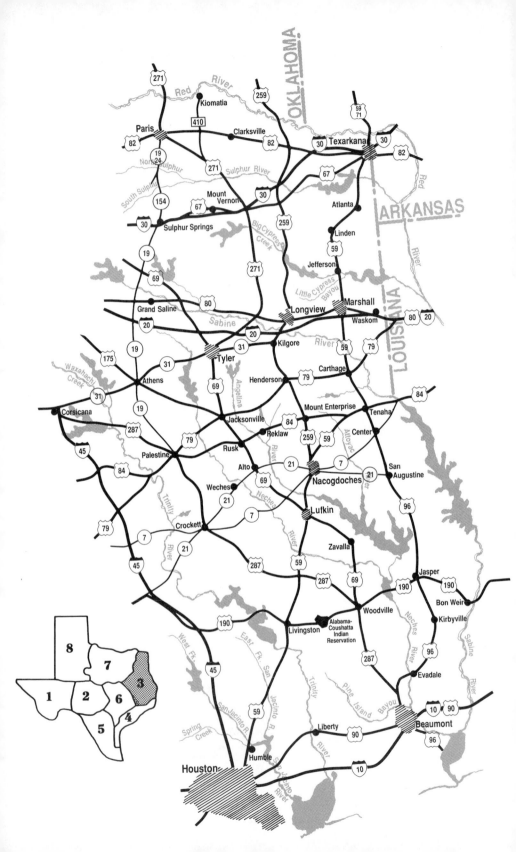

F or our purposes, the Pineywoods country is East Texas. It lies between the Red River on the north and I-10 on the south. Its western boundary follows I-45 north out of Houston to Corsicana (southeast of Dallas), then jogs east to Athens on Texas 31, and from there it follows Texas Highways 19, 154, and 19/24 north to Paris, with US 271 finishing the boundary on to Oklahoma. On the east, the northern Pineywoods portion of Texas meets the straight-line north-south running border of southwestern Arkansas and northern Louisiana while the southern portion conforms to the irregular boundary formed by the Toledo Bend Reservoir and the Sabine River.

Geologically, the Pineywoods is sinking—not fast, but losing elevation nevertheless. For the last 50 or 60 million years, the rivers we know today as the Sabine, Trinity, Brazos, and Colorado have dumped sediments that added land to the southeastern Texas shoreline, extending it farther into the gulf. This process buried the limestones and shales deposited millions of years earlier in the shallow sea that became the Gulf of Mexico. Eventually, according to Darwin Spearing in his *Roadside Geology of Texas*, "these rocks were buried deeply where they could be cooked at the right temperatures to generate gas and oil." Those rocks are covered by Pineywoods soil.

The Pineywoods country—some 50,000 square miles—begins among 200 species of wild trees and shrubs, mostly varieties of oaks and pines. Into this terrain of humid greenery came the first paleo-Indians. They arrived 37,000 years ago. By the time the Spanish and French arrived in the sixteenth century, three Amerind groups—the Caddos, the Karankawas, and the Attacapas—dominated the region. The latter two practiced ritualistic cannibalism, but the Caddos created a more refined culture. They farmed, fished, and developed an enriched artistic base. The Caddo word *tayshas* meant "friend," according to the Spanish, and from that realization sprang the name "Texas."

Explorer Hernando de Soto penetrated East Texas in 1542, the same year he died and was buried along the Mississippi River. Frenchman René Robert Cavelier, Sieur de La Salle, entered East Texas in 1685, two years before his mutinous crew murdered him. To protect the land Spain claimed for itself from further encroachment by the French, the Spanish ultimately built six missions in the region.

Meanwhile, the French and Spanish empires were crumbling. In 1762 France ceded the vast Louisiana Territory to Spain. But the Spanish could neither consolidate nor govern it, so they returned it to France in 1800, and three years later President Thomas Jefferson purchased the unexplored territory for $15 million. Texas, of course, remained part of Spanish territory, which led Spain and the United States to argue over exactly where the border between Louisiana and Texas fell. Should it be the Sabine River, or some other line? On November 6, 1806, U.S. Gen. James Wilkinson and Spain's Lt. Col. Simón de Herrera narrowed the disputed border to a vacant strip of "neutral ground" along the present boundary.

Spain forbid anyone from residing within twenty leagues of that neutral ground; however, a few Mexican ne'er-do-wells and numerous Americans, many of them outlaws, entered the area and made life and commerce hazardous for legitimate enterprises. Perhaps as many Americans resided in the Pineywoods (specifically Shelby, Panola, and Harrison counties) as lawful residents who settled in the Spanish province of Texas.

In 1810 and 1812 the two governments dispatched joint military expeditions, with only limited success, into the neutral ground to expel illegal aliens. With the 1819 Adams-Oñis Treaty (oftentimes called the Florida Treaty), the Americans took possession of the disputed territory and the neutral ground disappeared.

By that time there were two major overland routes to Texas: one crossed the Red River at the northeastern corner of the state; the other crossed the Sabine River and followed the Old San Antonio Road (roughly Texas Highway 21) through San Augustine, Nacogdoches, Alto, Crockett, and Bastrop into San Antonio. The key to travel through East Texas in those days was the fords. While roads over land might wander in all directions, they converged at river crossings. At the fords, travelers could usually find ferries, inns, and trading posts.

Meanwhile, the Alabama Indians had migrated to the Neches River in East Texas from their homelands in the southeastern United States after the French and Indian War ended in 1763; they did not want to be dominated by the English. The Coushattas followed in 1807 and established two villages on the nearby Trinity River.

About a quarter of the Cherokee people, also native to the southeastern United States and divided in their loyalty to the new country, intruded into East Texas in 1820, settling in present Cherokee, Rusk, Smith, and Van Zandt counties. When the Texas legislature in 1839 voided a treaty guaranteeing them title to their land, Gen. Kelsey H. Douglass drove them to join the rest of the Cherokee nation, by then relocated in Oklahoma. The Caddos, Anadarkos, Wacos, and Tonkawas had been placed on reservations along the Brazos River, but by 1859 they, too, were escorted to Indian Territory (Oklahoma).

Nacogdoches, established by Europeans in 1716, is today the oldest community in the *original* province and state of Texas. The Old San Antonio

Road, often called El Camino Real, stretched like a worn thread northeast from the Rio Grande for 500 miles across Texas to Nacogdoches and beyond.

As the Spanish empire and then Mexican rule retreated, and the Americans made their presence felt, most American emigrants avoided the Pineywoods or hustled through it quickly. Americans generally wanted farms, and they sought the blackland prairie. But the green, murky vastness of the Pineywoods remained the domain of Indians, for a while; the new settlers stuck to well-traveled forest pathways until the threats were gone and the countryside opened.

The Americans tamed and settled the land, prevailing where the Spanish and Mexicans could not. There are three reasons for this: 1) East Texas was closer to the United States than to Mexican population centers; 2) the Spanish were not as interested in establishing commerce as they were in keeping the French out; 3) the Spanish never understood, and therefore could never love, the Pineywoods country. In its moss, bayous, and dense forest, the Spanish found no comforting reminders of Spain or Mexico. While legitimate American settlers avoided East Texas for the time being, they at least understood it. To the Spanish, East Texas was a foreign, inhospitable land.

The American settlers were largely "farmers" and "planters," minute distinctions but nevertheless valid. Farmers saw their land as a family enterprise. They usually performed their own work, lived alongside their plows, and ate what they raised. (Historian T. R. Fehrenbach once defined a farm as containing less than twenty slaves.) Planters, however, from which we derive the word "plantation," operated with grandiose values. They brought in slaves, often numbering a hundred or more, cleared the forests to make room for commercial agriculture, and settled themselves along the rivers. They traveled in buggies and lived a genteel lifestyle. Cotton and sugar plantations shipped their produce to market along the major waterways.

Everything had its price, however. Plantations and farms were not ordinarily as romantic as present-day Americans, remote from the frontier, believe. *Gone With the Wind* was a great love story, but red-welt mosquito bites on Scarlett's legs, face, and arms might have dampened Rhett's ardor. Mosquito storms forced families to shut their houses tight during the hottest and most humid summer nights. Sometimes they lit smoky fires to thwart the pests.

Life on the frontier tested pioneers in subtle as well as obvious ways. Doctors were scarce, and such dreadful illnesses as malaria were common, as was the "summer complaint" (dysentery). Smallpox, diphtheria, and whooping cough often ravaged the population.

A slave belt girdled the eastern third or more of the state. At the peak of slavery, perhaps 100,000 slaves lived in Texas; the farther west one traveled, the fewer slaves one saw. When the climate turned arid and the soil rocky, and the rivers became too shallow for transportation, the plantation economy faltered. There was little substance in terms of cash crops and little need for slaves. Post-Civil War Reconstruction devastated the blacks as much as it did the whites. Many continued working for their former masters at room and board wages. Others drifted, clotting the roads and byways.

The railroads helped create a new social fabric. In 1870 Texas had only 500 miles of track. By 1890 the trackage exceeded 8,000 miles. Railroads quickly surpassed river traffic, and they led to the creation of sawmill towns, rail yards, and businesses where employees earned weekly or monthly wages. Lumber was the state's first important manufacturing industry. Texarkana and Tyler arose, as did numerous other villages.

Early in the twentieth century, Texas began running short of hardwood lumber. The large, century-old pine trees had been cut and quietly relegated to a nostalgic part of the past. Other resources surfaced to supplement the state's economy.

In 1901, Spindletop proved that East Texas had oil in abundance. Three decades later the field claimed the greatest reservoir of "discovered" oil on the planet. It blew in on September 5, 1930, near Henderson. Another strike followed in December with the Bateman #1 at Kilgore. Oddly, although hundreds of wildcatters rushed to the area, the major companies hesitated as their geologists dismissed the discoveries as two wells tapping small individual pools instead of a large field. As a result, it was independents rather than large corporations that developed this huge oil empire. The East Texas Oil Field covers more than 140,000 acres in its roughly forty-two-mile length and four-to twelve-mile width; it extends under the counties of Gregg, Rusk, Upshur, Cherokee, and Smith.

With so much oil production, marketing became a problem. The price per barrel plummeted from over a dollar to just ten cents. On occasion it even dipped to four cents a barrel. To generate a profit, everybody pumped more oil—at substantial waste.

On August 17, 1931, Gov. Ross Sterling ordered all East Texas wells temporarily closed until sane production schedules could be established and accepted. To enforce the edict, he declared martial law and sent in the National Guard and the Texas Rangers. One of those rangers was Sgt. M. T. Gonzaullas, better known as "Lone Wolf."

After the rowdiness died down and oil production resumed, Gonzaullas became a well-known figure around Kilgore. He always wore boots and a Stetson and carried two revolvers plus a submachine gun. A local oil man, impressed by the peace Sergeant Gonzaullas brought to the fields, purchased a new Chrysler for the ranger. The specially equipped car came complete with armor plating, bulletproof glass, and a mount for the submachine gun.

The field reopened to higher oil prices and reduced production on September 5, nearly three weeks after the governor had closed it down. This led to about three years of bootleg sales known as "hot oil" production. It amounted to oil pumped and shipped illegally to dozens of tiny but legal oil refineries manufacturing cheap gasoline. The practice ended when even large refineries started making cheap gasoline, and *all* refineries had to account for the source of their crude.

The troops were withdrawn, and oil production passed into the hands of the Railroad Commission. By 1938 the major oil companies controlled 80 percent of the field. Over the following forty-two years more than five billion barrels of oil had been removed from the ground, and the reserves today contain an estimated billion more—enough to last until 2030. Currently about 10,000 wells do the work once done by 32,000.

The Indians, explorers, settlers, and much of the oil—all of which contributed to the rich history of East Texas—are now gone. Today most people around here rely on oil, lumber, agriculture, cattle, and tourism to maintain their livelihoods. While the Big Thicket is but a shade (forgive the pun) of its former shadowy self, East Texas still has four national forests. But the Texas past and tradition are everywhere. Around each bend in the road you'll see the plantations, the old cemeteries, and the quaint farms and villages that made the Pineywoods country what it is today.

EAST TEXAS
(Northern Portion)

The boundaries are the Red River on the north, Arkansas and Louisiana on the east, and US 84 on the south. The western edge is held down by Texas 19 from Palestine north to I-30, Texas 154 north to Texas 19/24 into Paris, and US 271 north to the Red River.

US 82
Texarkana—Paris
90 miles

Texarkana

Caddo Indians originally lived at Texarkana, the village being a crossroads for the Great Southwest Trail, a line of travel for Indians trading between the Mississippi River and the South and West. There are seventy Indian ceremonial mounds near Texarkana.

Texarkana was a strategic location in the Pineywoods. Since the town was split between Texas and Arkansas, it became Texarkana on December 8, 1873. The state line extended down Main Street. The Bi-State Justice Center (housing the courts and jails) straddles today's line.

Railheads from the Cairo & Fulton Railroad, which had crossed Arkansas, touched noses with the Texas & Pacific advancing from the Red River to Texarkana in January 1874. By the 1940s there were eight railroad outlets, all taking advantage of the timber, the fertile fields, and the mineral wealth.

Cullen Baker, an ex-Confederate soldier turned desperado, made things lively around Texarkana during the Reconstruction era. He murdered dozens of people, most of them Negroes, but was himself slain in 1869 when a group of vigilantes caught him. One of his slayers was his father-in-law.

On the responsible side, H. Ross Perot came out of Texarkana, as did the ragtime musician Scott Joplin. A mural at Third and Main streets depicts Joplin's Pulitzer Prize-winning accomplishments.

The Texarkana Historical Society and Museum is especially strong with its Caddo Indian artifact display.

Clarksville

President Andrew Jackson commissioned James Clark, salt trader and Indian fighter, to supply food to the Choctaw and Chickasaw Indians during their removal to Oklahoma. In 1833, he laid out Clarksville in Red River County, one of the original Texas counties. The Texas & Pacific arrived in 1872, but the town showed little progress until the East Texas Oil Field brought prosperity.

Col. Charles DeMorse, the Father of Texas Journalism, founded the *Northern Standard* in Clarksville. On the town square, a marker honors the Methodist circuit rider William Stevenson. He carried Protestantism deep into Spanish Texas.

Kiomatia

This hamlet is eighteen miles north of US 82 on Farm Road 410. Established near a buffalo crossing in a bend of the Red River, it was initially considered part of Arkansas Territory. Kiomatia and the nearby village of Jonesborough served as centers for the landmark known on both banks of the Red River as Pecan Point.

By 1811, American fugitives from justice lived in this vicinity, most of them disembarking from flatboats. These travelers used Pecan Point as a way station rather than a village, and the towns of Clarksville and Paris were largely settled by these migrants.

The Pecan Point Plantation arose during the 1830s. Before the river destroyed it following the Civil War, the plantation encompassed a thousand acres and included cotton presses, cabins for a hundred slaves, and an overseer's house. Owner John Watson was known as "the Prince of Pecan Point" because of his lavish entertaining.

150

Paris

The land between the Red and Sulphur rivers provided a setting for Paris, first known as Pinhook. Today Paris is a fresh and modern Texas town, perhaps because two major fires destroyed the old buildings.

On the eastern side is Crockett Circle. Davy Crockett, traveling toward his death at the Alamo, spent a night here beneath a live oak tree.

John Chisum, the famous New Mexico cattle baron and Lincoln County War figure, is buried in Paris.

Miss Frances Willard organized the Texas Woman's Christian Temperance Union in 1882. When none of the churches permitted temperance meetings, Miss Willard rented the opera house.

The Hay Meadow Massacre trial was held in the Paris federal court. Since the court had jurisdiction over Indian Territory as well as portions of Kansas, it charged twenty men with murdering U.S. officers in No Man's Land (the Oklahoma panhandle). Eight were convicted and sentenced to be hanged.

Today, Paris is a shipping and processing center. It occupies a hub of the blacklands prairie, and its long-fibered cotton is known as Paris Cotton. The Victorian home of Confederate Gen. Sam Bell Maxey is a state historic structure.

I-30
Texarkana—Sulphur Springs
105 miles

Mount Vernon

In 1849, settler Stephen Keith donated twenty-four acres for a town called Lone Star. However, when Lone Star became the county seat, the commissioner's court abolished saloons, gambling, and racing. Lone Star soon became Mount Vernon in honor of George Washington's Virginia home. Mount Vernon today is best known for its dairy farms and Holstein cattle herds.

Sulphur Springs

This town, originally known as Bright Star, was a popular camping site for teamsters hauling goods from Jefferson. By 1871, the town sought additional methods to attract tourists, so the name was switched to Sulphur Springs. Mineral springs had great advertising appeal as health resorts.

After the turn of the century, the first Monday in every month was set aside as Trades Day. Farmers crowded the business section to swap animals, hay, and produce. Hopkins is the leading dairy county in the United States.

US 59
Texarkana—Jefferson
59 miles

Atlanta

The Texas & Pacific Railroad established this village in 1872, and the residents named it after their hometown, Atlanta, Georgia. Atlanta pine and hardwood lumber kept the Red River Valley booming until the turn of the century, when the opening of the Rodessa, Louisiana, oil fields added a fresh impetus.

Lake Wright Patman, the Atlanta State Park, and a farm tour of Natural Food Associates are worth experiencing.

Linden

This town lies in the heart of the lumbering region and was named by a Major Wood in 1852 for his Tennessee hometown. The *Cass County Sun* started operations in 1875 using an old Washington press purchased in Shreveport, Louisiana. In 1864, when Federals threatened to invade the county, residents dumped the press into the Red River. That led to a lot of additional work, as the Unionists never arrived. The press was dragged out and the local newspaper continued publishing.

Jefferson

One has a choice of 1836 or 1840 for the creation of Jefferson, although few dispute that it originated on Big Cypress Creek at the edge of Caddo Lake. The town was born with the Republic of Texas in 1836 and named for Thomas Jefferson. Unlike other county seats, it was not laid out around a square but at right angles to the Big Cypress Bayou.

A mass of driftwood and trees obstructed the Red River for seventy-five miles, and this barrier was called the Red River Raft. It backed up the waters of Big Cypress and created Caddo Lake, thereby making the bayou possible. Because of this raft, Jefferson became the principal river port in Texas. Its

152

wharfs sagged with northeast Texas items anticipating markets in New Orleans. Captain William Perry opened Caddo Lake and Big Cypress Bayou to navigation and arranged to bring in the *Llama*, the first steamboat to Jefferson.

A single steamboat shipment in those days could fetch a $20,000 profit, and money like this helped transform Jefferson into a Southern belle town. Architecture styles included Greek Revival and Neoclassic, plus Victorian and Italianate.

The first beer brewed in Texas originated in Jefferson, although its brand name, if it had one, has been forgotten. In 1867, Jefferson was the first town in Texas to use gas for artificial light. There were fancy brothels, banks, churches, theaters, and the *Jefferson Jimplecute*, a newspaper. Regional discoveries of iron ore lured a smelter and a plow works to Jefferson. Ice was manufactured on a commercial scale in 1868, but the ammonia refrigerant patent was sold to outside interests a year later.

By 1870 Jefferson was second only to Galveston in volume of trade. It was a busy inland port with up to 200 steamboats docking a year, and the sixth-largest Texas city in terms of population. Early homes were furnished with goods shipped from Philadelphia, New Orleans, and St. Louis. Although fire destroyed the business section in 1866, the town recovered within four years. In 1874, however, the raft was removed, blasted away by the U.S. Army Corps of Engineers using newly invented nitroglycerin nicknamed (in Jefferson) "Uncle Sam's Toothpullers." The water level dropped eight feet, and Jefferson ceased to be a significant port city with an exuberant, prosperous lifestyle.

The Texas & Pacific might have saved Jefferson had the town's political leaders been more astute. They wanted grass and not railroad tracks in the streets, so Jefferson refused to contribute land in exchange for rails, as other cities as well as the state of Texas and the national government had done. Jay Gould, the railroad tycoon, allegedly wrote "the end of Jefferson" in the Excelsior House register and vowed that grass would indeed flourish in the streets of Jefferson. He was almost correct. The railroad spun its rails to Marshall, and Jefferson went into a slumber.

Today, Jefferson is old-fashioned and unpretentious, a quiet town incredibly rich in history, a town rescued by thirty-five women of the Jesse Allen Wise Garden Club. Going after tourists as only determined women can do, the garden club organized Jefferson's Dogwood Trail as well as the Jefferson Historical Pilgrimage.

Visitors frequently stay at the Historic Inn, Excelsior House, Hotel Jefferson, or at one of over two-dozen bed-and-breakfast hotels. Jay Gould's eighty-eight-foot private railroad car, the *Atlanta*, saved and refurbished from a Rusk County weed patch by the garden club in 1950, is on display across from the Excelsior House. There are tours of historic homes, a Bayou Queen River Boat tour, surrey and trolley rides, and the Jefferson Historical Society Museum.

Louisiana State Line—Grand Saline

Waskom

Powellton, established in 1850, became Waskom Station in 1872, named for the man who brought in the Southern Pacific. In 1881, it dropped the second part of its name. The Waskom Gas Field was discovered in 1924. Today's top attraction is the Travel Information Center and a remarkable store and museum called T. C. Lindsey & Company.

Marshall

Marshall was established in 1839 and named for Chief Justice John Marshall. Although known as the "Athens of East Texas," it was the largest and most prosperous town in the whole state when Texas seceded in 1861.

In 1862, fearing Confederate armies might not penetrate beyond the east bank of the Mississippi once Vicksburg had fallen, the governors of Texas, Missouri, Louisiana, and Arkansas met in Marshall. They made plans for a defense of the West and forwarded copies to President Jefferson Davis. When Vicksburg fell a year later, Gen. Edmund Kirby Smith called another conference at Marshall on August 15, 1863. This one ended with Marshall becoming the seat of civil authority west of the Mississippi River. As a fortified city, and with Smith as commander in chief, Marshall housed the wartime capitol of Missouri and the headquarters of the Trans-Mississippi Postal Department.

When Lee surrendered in April 1865, Union Gen. John Pope offered General Smith the same terms as Lee. Smith rejected the terms and summoned delegates for another Marshall meeting on May 15. With the trans-Mississippi army disintegrating, the governors tried dictating their own peace terms to the North. They were unacceptable, and Marshall ceased to be the trans-Mississippi authority.

Marshall is presently a center for foundries, industry, and lumber. It is one of the nation's largest manufacturers of glazed pottery.

During Christmas 1987, Marshall started its Wonderland of Lights. By Christmas 1990 there were two million tiny white lights burning, 100,000 of them on the festival crown jewel, the Harrison County Historic Courthouse Museum. Visitors should also tour the Ginocchio National Historic District, the Michelson-Reves Art Museum, and the Starr Family State Historic Site.

Longview

This area was a Mexican land grant and by the 1850s had been settled by planters migrating in from the Old South. Surveyors for the Texas & Pacific Railroad named it Longview for the long distances visually observed from the village. For a while its industries were a foundry and a wagon factory, but the discovery of oil during the 1930s provided a broader base.

Stroh Brewing Company on Cotton Street is the largest brewery in Texas. The city's broad agricultural and industrial foundation was helped along by the "Big Inch" petroleum products pipeline. Longview lies in the heart of the East Texas Oil Field (see Pineywoods introduction). The East Texas Chamber of Commerce is headquartered here. The Caddo Indian Museum, the Gregg County Historical Museum, and the Longview Museum and Arts Center are all worth seeing.

Grand Saline

The name means "big salt." Cherokees and Caddos mined these deposits in prehistoric times. Local settler John Jordan filed his claim in 1843 and blazed a trail into Grand Saline from Nacogdoches. With two iron kettles, he started a salt works. The settlement was originally called "Jordan's Saline."

Salt still makes the city thrive. The underground dome is one and a half miles wide and three miles deep. It could supply the world's salt needs for 20,000 years.

A salt-block building known as the Salt Palace was built in 1975. The Grand Saline Museum is housed in the public library.

Texas 31
Kilgore—Athens
61 miles

Kilgore

The Missouri-Pacific Railroad named this tiny village for Constantine Buckley Kilgore in 1872. The gentleman was an attorney, Presbyterian and Mason, a hero in the Civil War, and a federal judge in Indian Territory.

After the well dubbed Bateman #1 struck oil in December 1930, 5,000 laborers, gamblers, and prostitutes reached the town almost overnight. The city was incorporated, and Texas Rangers as well as the National Guard

Captain Manuel T. "Lone Wolf" Gonzaullas, one of the most famous Texas Rangers of his time, after he had become chief of the Department of Public Safety Crime Detection Laboratory in 1937. —The Institute of Texan Cultures

provided order. Manuel T. "Lone Wolf" Gonzaullas, a veteran Texas Ranger, prowled the streets forcing idlers to turn up their palms. Those with calloused palms went free. Those with smooth hands were gamblers or thugs, and Gonzaullas hauled them to a Baptist church he used for a jail. At one time he had 300 men shackled in the aisles to a heavy log chain called a "trotline."

In 1930, oil men drilled through the terrazzo floor of the demolished Kilgore National Bank. The downtown block (1.2 acres) once contained the greatest concentration of oil wells in the world, and considering that the wells cost $35,000 each, that block had a lot of money invested in it.

The original derricks were wooden, but humidity rotted their pine beams. By the mid-1930s, steel had come into use, but even these became obsolete and yielded to the "work over" rigs, which reworked completed wells. Kilgore's forest of steel gradually dropped from 1,100 to 1.

Kilgore College is home to the world-famous Kilgore Rangerettes. The fifty-three-member precision drill and dance team formed in 1940 and has since performed at football games throughout the nation. The college maintains a showcase display of rangerette history.

The East Texas Oil Museum at Kilgore is the best of its kind.

Tyler

President John Tyler is responsible for this town's name, and the community was founded on a site where the Cherokees had displaced the Caddos. But the Cherokees themselves were uprooted in 1839.

The Battle of the Neches began in July 1839 a few miles west of Tyler. When it ceased near Grand Saline, at least a hundred Cherokees had been slain or wounded. Several Indian villages had been destroyed and the crops burned. While a few Indians reached Oklahoma, those attempting to skirt the Texans

John Tyler. —Library of Congress

and enter Mexico were overtaken and killed. And so ended the Cherokee-Texas wars.

During the Civil War, Tyler was a Confederate stronghold. Nearby Camp Ford was the largest prisoner of war compound west of the Mississippi. Over 6,000 Union troops were incarcerated there.

Tyler originally was a shipping center for fruit. It was later an oil capital and headquarters for East Texas Oil Field corporations.

The rose industry has made Tyler famous. For years, one-half of all United States rose bushes were grown within ten miles of Tyler. A famous product is the Tyler Rose, as well as the "Lady Bird Johnson" Rose. At twenty-two acres, the Municipal Rose Garden is the nation's largest rose showcase. Tyler's annual Texas Rose Festival is the state's largest floral event.

Tyler also has a museum of art, the Carnegie History Center, the Caldwell Zoo, and the Goodman-LeGrand Home.

Athens

Nobody is sure if the town gets its name from Athens, Greece, or Athens, Georgia, but Athens it became, after being called Alfred. In 1850 it replaced the county seats of Buffalo and Centerville.

The former Comanche captive Cynthia Ann Parker and her daughter, Prairie Flower, died in Athens.

Athens is known for its fine pottery and brick making. An Old Fiddlers' Reunion each spring draws thousands of country music lovers.

US 79
Louisiana State Line—Palestine
107 miles

Carthage

Carthage was named for Carthage, Missouri, and today is known for its gas, oil, and chicken processing. Four miles east of town, a life-sized statue marks the grave of country-western singer Jim Reeves, an East Texas native who died in a 1964 plane crash. The Panola County Historical Jail Museum is the town's primary tourist attraction.

Henderson

James Pinckney Henderson, Texas patriot and European diplomat for the Republic of Texas, was honored in 1843 by lending his good name to this town. Although it grew rapidly, a fire destroyed most of it in 1860.

In 1926 Columbus "Dad" Joiner, in his mid-sixties and suffering from rheumatic fever, walked into Rusk County and spoke of his dream of tapping the largest oil field in the world. During the next four years he searched the county for just the right spot, finally settling on the Daisy Bradford farm near Henderson. Following two dry holes, the Daisy Bradford #3 yielded a promising core sample. Within a week 5,000 people converged on the Bradford farm, hopefully waiting for a gusher and some even burning their truck tires to keep warm. Several days later the drill penetrated the trapped reserves and the gusher roared forth. In addition to the oil, a wondrous supply of coal reserves has added to Henderson's economy.

A bronze statue of Gen. Thomas Jefferson Rusk guards the town square. A Missouri Pacific Railroad depot houses a Depot Museum and Children's Discovery Center. The Howard-Dickinson House has been refurbished.

On March 18, 1937, the greatest school disaster in United States history struck a few miles northwest of Henderson, in the small town of New London. The West Rusk Consolidated High School blew up that afternoon, killing 297 students, teachers, and visitors. Since natural gas is odorless, nobody realized that a leak in the school's system allowed the volatile vapor to accumulate inside the building. The sudden, devastating explosion led to legislation requiring that all natural gas used in homes and businesses throughout the United States have the smell of rotten eggs added so its presence can be detected in the air. The odor is virtually impossible to ignore.

Eighteen miles northeast of Henderson, on Texas 43, is the Harmony Hill Ghost Town. Known as Nip and Tuck before a storm destroyed it in 1906, a cemetery is our main reminder of the town that once existed.

Jacksonville

This town began in the middle of an 1880s iron rush. Up near Mount Selman, ten miles north of Jacksonville, is Kellough Monument, which commemorates East Texans killed by Indians on October 5, 1836.

Palestine

Fort Houston, founded in 1835, became a town called Palestine in 1846. The town took its name from Palestine, Illinois. Survivors of the Fort Parker massacre fled to Fort Houston in 1836. The Palestine Salt Dome is one of the largest in the United States.

NASA balloons from the nearby Scientific Balloon Base study the upper atmosphere and outer space. The Davy Dogwood Park offers 400 acres of

159

forest, streams, and meadows. The Museum of East Texas Culture is worth examining, and visitors should ride the Texas State Railroad. An old steam engine operated by the Texas Department of Parks and Wildlife pulls passengers through 25.5 miles of woodlands to Rusk.

US 84

Louisiana State Line—Rusk

71 miles

Tenaha

This tiny village in Shelby County, a portion of the former "neutral ground" explained in the Pineywoods introduction, had for decades been habitually stocked with flint-eyed individuals who took the law into their own hands. The Regulators and Moderators fought a savage feud, dealing summary justice to violators of their unwritten codes.

In 1840 Charles Jackson killed Joseph Goodbread during an argument over forged land certificates. A jury acquitted Jackson, who then organized a band of Regulators to suppress crime. They burned so many homes that a rival group of Moderators arose to curb the Regulators. Jackson was ambushed and slain. Charles Moorman took Jackson's place.

Moorman's Regulators waylaid and slaughtered the killers of Jackson. For a while Moorman dominated the whole county. He defied the courts and even considered overthrowing the Republic of Texas. After ordering several families from the region, he found himself face to face with a reinvigorated group of Moderators. Both factions now numbered perhaps 150 riders each, and they waged relentless war upon each other.

A fed-up President Sam Houston issued a proclamation on August 15, 1844, calling upon both factions to disarm. Six hundred militiamen enforced the edict. Ten ringleaders from both sides were brought to San Augustine and forced to sign a treaty of peace. It held, and the Regulator-Moderator feud ended that same year.

Mount Enterprise

This little community was named for its slight elevation over the surrounding land and the business enterprise shown by the Vinson brothers who settled here in 1832. Lumber was its major industry.

Reklaw

The Cherokee Indians roamed this land practically until the Texas & New Orleans Railroad arrived. Iron Mountain dominated the area and attracted miners, prospectors, and settlers in the early 1860s. Only a ghost town remains.

Rusk

In 1846 only one family lived here, but that was enough to name the site Rusk, after Thomas Jefferson Rusk. Although born in South Carolina, Rusk studied law and moved to Texas, becoming in 1835 the inspector general of the Texas revolutionary army. Rusk signed the Declaration of Texas Independence and fought in the Battle of San Jacinto. After statehood he was elected to the U.S. Senate, defended the justice of the Mexican War, and was almost a candidate for the presidency of the United States. After his wife died he committed suicide in Nacogdoches in 1857. He was buried there in Oak Grove Cemetery.

The Rusk settlement grew rapidly and was known as the birthplace of two Texas governors: James Stephen Hogg and Thomas M. Campbell. The Texas State Railroad Park is not only the nation's narrowest state park, but Rusk is its termination point. A narrow-gauge steam locomotive connects Rusk with Palestine.

The Footbridge Garden Park contains a 546-foot footbridge, reputedly the nation's longest. It was built in 1861 and was used for crossing the valley. The old Rusk penitentiary is still intact.

Texas 7
Center—Nacogdoches
32 miles

Center

This town had a central location in Shelby County, so the founders named it Center. The nearby "neutral ground" furnished many of the county's settlers, and Shelbyville in particular (ten miles east on Texas 87) saw a lot of action and death during the Regulator-Moderator feud (see Tenaha).

Center's courthouse was modeled after an old Irish castle. The county museum is delightful.

Nacogdoches

Nacogdoches is the hub of a pine belt extending across East Texas. A swathe of iron-rich soil six miles wide extends across the county from east to west. As the iron oxidizes, it takes on a rusty red color.

The Nacogdoche Indians originally occupied Nacogdoches. They were a Caddoan tribe, one of nine major members of the Hasinai confederacy. The La Salle Expedition visited the area in 1685. In June 1716, Domingo Ramón, a Spanish military captain, founded the mission of Nuestra Señora de Guadalupe de los Nacogdoches. Other nearby missions were also established.

Nacogdoches was a final hookup of the Old San Antonio Road (El Camino Real), which reached catercornered across Texas from south of the Rio Grande. Two years later, the Spanish suspected a French invasion and fled. The Marquis de Aguayo rebuilt the mission in 1721, but the Marquis de Rubí, after an inspection of Texas, said Spain should distinguish between real and imaginary dominions, and recommended the abandonment of East Texas in 1773.

Displaced persons settled in San Antonio and on the Rio Grande. Louisiana-born Antonio Gil Ibarvo (Ybarvo) submitted petitions for a return to East Texas. They were approved, and in April 1779 he and his followers re-entered Nacogdoches.

Antonio Gil Ybarvo and settlers from Bucareli arrive at the abandoned mission of Nacogdoches, Texas, 1779. —The Institute of Texan Cultures

162

The administration of Ibarvo is controversial, as historians believe his chief interest lay in smuggling contraband between Louisiana and the Texas Indians. Ibarvo built the Old Stone Fort and designed it to serve as a defensive post, military headquarters, and trading post. In 1806, over a thousand soldiers were stationed here while Spain and the United States signed agreements. Four years later, Governor Manuel de Salceda spent three months in Nacogdoches, making this province the seat of government.

Still, Spain could not control the area, and Nacogdoches played a major role in every conspiracy that shook Texas. Filibusters streamed through because Nacogdoches was a major eastern gateway into Texas, a way station for desperate men. Philip Nolan's group was here. Dr. James Long and 300 followers were expelled after they had declared a republic of Texas. The Fredonian Rebellion appeared in 1826. *Empresarios* passed back and forth through Nacogdoches. In 1832, the Battle of Nacogdoches broke out over national recognition of Antonio López de Santa Anna. Santa Anna was a "liberal" who supported American immigration into Texas.

Meanwhile, Samuel Davenport, a trader, purchased the Old Stone Fort. He welcomed the Gutiérrez-Magee Expedition, helped them capture portions of Texas, but fortunately wasn't around when the Spanish army destroyed the filibusters at Medina. Davenport fled into Louisiana.

Old Stone Fort, Nacogdoches, Texas, 1885. The men are unidentified, and the building was likely used for a jail as well as a storehouse. —Nacogdoches Historical Society

The fort passed from one master to another and was the scene of revolts, counter-revolts, riots, and meetings. Sam Houston, James Bowie, Davy Crockett, and Thomas Rusk took their perfunctory oaths of allegiance to Texas inside the walls. Vincente Cordova finally had ownership, but he assisted Cherokees in rising up against the Texans. As a result, half of the stone fort was awarded to Mrs. Zachariah Fenley, whose relatives controlled it until 1900, when the Perkins brothers purchased it, demolishing it in 1902 because Nacogdoches needed a drugstore. The Old Stone Fort was rebuilt in 1907, only to be destroyed once more. In 1936, as a centennial project, the fort was rebuilt on the Stephen F. Austin University campus.

Nacogdoches was the second-largest city in Texas by the beginning of the nineteenth century. Advertising claims still refer to it the "oldest" city in Texas.

La Calle del Norte (North Street) is the oldest public thoroughfare in the United States, a trail used by prehistoric Indian tribes. Millard's Crossing is a restored group of nineteenth century buildings. The Oak Grove Cemetery dates from 1837 and contains the graves of four signers of the Texas Declaration of Independence. The Sterne-Hoya Home (Hoya Memorial Museum) was built in 1828. Sam Houston was baptized in it.

Nacogdoches is a city proud of its heritage. There is a strong lumber commitment, a powerful agribusiness, and exceptional progress in shipping and academics. The Stephen F. Austin State University is a regional educational prize. While the streets are relatively narrow and congested, this is a city that lives by its fantastic history, its tourism, and its subdued lifestyle.

Texas 21
Louisiana State Line—Crockett
115 miles

San Augustine

In 1716, Father Antonio Margil de Jesús established the mission of Nuestra Señora de los Dolores de los Ais. Like the Caddos, the Ais Indians were a branch of the Hasinai confederacy. They were distrusted by both Indians and Europeans and were later placed on the Wichita Reservation in Oklahoma.

Due to French incursions the mission was abandoned in 1719, only to be rebuilt in San Augustine by the Marquis de Aguayo in 1721. Somewhere around 1794, Philip Nolan and Antonio Leal settled the area, in the process trapping wild mustangs for shipment to Louisiana. By the early 1800s, the village had undergone considerable settlement and was known as the Ayish Bayou District. It became San Augustine in 1834.

When the Texas Revolution broke out, San Augustine was an educational center. The University of San Augustine was chartered in 1837. An 1890 fire destroyed the village, but the town quickly rebuilt. San Augustine is often known as "The Cradle of Texas" because so many Texas heroes slept here. Historical markers identify the mission site. The Old Town Well is restored. The Ezekiel W. Cullen Home is open for visitors.

Alto

This was the highest point between the Angelina and Neches rivers, so the settlers gave it a Spanish name, Alto, meaning "high." The town was formerly a stop on the Old San Antonio Road.

Nine miles west of Alto are the Caddo Indian Mounds. The site consists of a large village area, a burial mound, and two temple mounds. The Caddos settled here in A.D. 800 and drew local native groups into economic and social dependence for 500 years. By the year 1100 they reached their zenith, attaining the most highly developed prehistoric culture known within today's Texas. But for disputed reasons, by 1300 the Caddos abandoned the location. In 1939 scientists started excavating the mounds. The results are still coming in. The site is a state historic park.

Weches

Herein lies the site of the Mission San Francisco de los Tejas. The mission was built in 1690, but abandoned in 1693. It was re-established in 1716, and the name lengthened to Nuestro Padre San Francisco de los Tejas. The church represented the earliest and most eastern mission in Texas.

Crockett

A settler donated a town site in 1837 and named it for his friend Davy Crockett. A fortified log fort served as a courthouse, but it and everything else burned in 1865. When the Houston & Great Northern Railroad built through in 1872, a lumbering interest started developing.

The town is filled with pecan trees, and the economy is based on agriculture plus some industry. Davy Crockett is, of course, a household name. There is a Davy Crockett Memorial Park, a Davy Crockett Spring, and a Davy Crockett National Forest.

Lufkin

Lufkin, hemmed in by pine forests, was established in 1882 as a depot for the Houston, East & West Texas Railroad. It was named for railroad civil engineer E. P. Lufkin. The town site consisted of 360 acres, but on November 10, 1885, two railroads divided up the land and arranged the sale of lots. Excursion trains chugged in from Houston, Shreveport, and Tyler. A barbecue was held, and on November 24 the lots were sold at auction. By the early 1900s

A sculpture across from the Museum of East Texas in Lufkin, depicting an artist's concept of a Franciscan father, Angelina, and an Indian. Angelina was a Hainai girl who so impressed early Spanish missionaries that they took her to Mission San Juan Bautista on the Rio Grande and educated her. The Angelina River is named in her honor.

the town had become an industrial center with wood and paper mills. Even today, Lufkin remains a home to vast lumber and wood-product enterprises.

The Forestry Museum is open every day, as is the Medford Collection of Western Art. The Museum of East Texas is a must visit.

Livingston

This community started as Springfield in 1839, but changed its name to Livingston, for a town in Alabama, in 1846. A fire destroyed the business center in 1902, but oil discoveries and plenty of lumber production gave the community a strong and vigorous economic life. The Polk County Historical Museum is a fine one.

Humble

Humble, a few miles north of Houston, was turned into an agricultural and lumber-shipping region by the Texas & New Orleans Railroad. Pleasant S. Humble, a local settler, operated a ferry across the San Jacinto River in 1865. Only a crude house or two existed here until 1902, when the town of Humble came into existence.

Oil was discovered in 1902. Three years later, Humble sat in the middle of the largest producing field in Texas. The Humble Oil Field was actually a salt dome unsuccessfully evaluated for oil until January 7, 1905. By April, the field was pumping two million barrels a day. In 1914-15, additional wells plunged deeper into the salt strata. Production reached a million barrels annually prior to the 1940s.

The Humble Oil Company arose in 1911 with a small refinery in Humble, the total capital being $150,000. On March 1, 1917, the firm reorganized as the Humble Oil and Refining Company, with capital of $1 million. The Humble Pipe Line Company, a subsidiary, once was a nationwide transporter of crude oil. The company built a products line from Baytown to Dallas, and from West Texas to the Gulf Coast. During World War II, Humble produced more oil than any firm in the United States. The company operated in every important oil field in Texas. Its refineries spread across the nation. A fleet of oceangoing tankers, tows, and barges established Humble's place in world commerce.

Humble moved to Houston in 1963 when it built a forty-four-story Houston building and consolidated 3,500 of its Houston employees. On January 1, 1973, Humble changed its name to Exxon Company, U.S.A.

The Humble Historical Museum naturally places emphasis on oil, but other historical factors are covered too. The Houston International Airport is just west of Humble.

Zavalla

The map should spell this town with one " l," as it was named for Lorenzo de Zavala. He was born in Yucatan, spent three years in Mexican imprisonment, represented his state at the Spanish Cortes (parliament) in Madrid, was a member of the Mexican Constituent Congress and the Mexican Senate, governor of the state of Mexico, minister of the Mexican treasury, again governor of Mexico, member of the Mexican Chamber of Deputies, minister to France, and a Texas revolutionary. He signed the Texas Declaration of Independence, fought in Sam Houston's army, and was wounded at San Jacinto. In between all this, Zavala was an *empresario*. His colonists settled today's tiny village of Zavalla. There is a Texas monument on his grave in San Jacinto Park.

Zavalla lies inside the Angelina National Forest.

The Angelina River near Jasper.

The historic restored Belle-Jim Hotel in Jasper, Texas, as it looks today.

US 190
Jasper—Livingston
93 miles

Jasper

The town was organized in the early 1830s and for a while was known as Bevil Settlement. In 1835 it became Jasper in honor of Sgt. William Jasper, a South Carolina hero of the American Revolution. Two Jasper residents, George W. Smyth and Stephen H. Everitt, signed the Texas Declaration of Independence, and Everitt also helped draft the republic's constitution. General George Custer was once a familiar figure in Jasper. Lumbering, farming, and ranching were originally the main industries, but with numerous lakes in the vicinity, Jasper has now become a sporting and tourist paradise.

Stephen Williams, the only known soldier of the American Revolution to be buried in Texas, lies in Jasper.

Woodville

Woodville is surrounded by woods, a sawmill and tourist area named for George T. Woods, the second governor of Texas. The Texas & New Orleans Railroad built through in the 1880s. Of must-see importance is the Heritage Village Museum as well as the Shivers Library and Museum.

Alabama-Coushatta Indian Reservation

The name refers to two tribes, the Alabamas and the Coushattas, who originally lived as woodland neighbors in the state of Alabama. They were of the Muskhogean linguistic stock like the Choctaws, Creeks, and Chickasaws. DeSoto mentioned them in 1541.

Culturally these tribes have always been one people with mutually understandable languages (except for a few isolated words). Until about 1840 they used aboriginal Indian names, but because of property ownership and other legal entanglements created by living in a white man's world, they gradually adopted Anglo names. Incidentally, the "Alabama" name derives from a combination of words meaning "vegetable gatherers."

After the French abandoned Mobile Bay and the pressures of British expansion mounted, a four-way split in the Alabama tribe occurred. One faction moved into Texas and settled along the Neches River. The Coushatta followed the Alabama, entering Texas about 1807 and settling on the Trinity River. Altogether both tribes probably included fewer than 2,000 people.

Prior to the Battle of San Jacinto, most Alabamas left Texas, returning later to find whites had appropriated their lands. For the next sixteen years, the Alabama Indians were wanderers.

In 1854, primarily through the assistance of Sam Houston, the Alabamas received 1,280 acres where the reservation is today. However, even Houston was unable to get 640 acres for the Coushattas. Many subsequently left Texas while others stayed and intermarried with the Alabamas.

Until the Houston-Shreveport Railroad reached Polk County in 1881 and provided a few job opportunities, the Alabama-Coushattas were destitute. A Presbyterian mission arrived the same year, and it brought Christianity, teachers, and educational benefits. Another factor was Judge J. C. Feagin, a resident of Livingston. He chastised state authorities for the economic and social blight suffered by the tribes.

In 1928, the federal government purchased and donated an additional 3,071 acres alongside the reservation. It has since provided Indian revenue from timber, gas, and oil production. The deed was collectively allocated to the Alabamas and Coushattas, and Alabama-Coushatta has since been the official title of this reservation. As for religion, most of the Indians attend the Presbyterian, Baptist, or Assembly of God churches.

Still, the Alabama-Coushattas remained isolated by language and poverty until 1960, when they discovered tourism. A visitor program started. Today, the reservation has about 550 Indians living on 4,766 acres. The tribes conduct tours of the Big Thicket by land rover and by train. Indian dances are regularly performed, and there is a museum, campground, and small lake. Crafts are always on display in the Living Indian Village and gift shops.

An engraving of a frontiersman trading with Indians.
—The Institute of Texan Cultures

Jasper—Beaumont

Kirbyville

Kirbyville is named for John Henry Kirby, who is remembered primarily as a lumberman, but who was also an able lawyer, businessman, and banker. In and around Kirbyville, he owned twelve sawmills and logging camps, altogether employing 16,000 people. He even coaxed railroads into the forests, and lumbering has since been a major occupation.

Evadale

John H. Kirby (see Kirbyville) named this village for Miss Eva Dale, a teacher of music at the Southeast Texas Male and Female College at Jasper. It is near the site of Richardson's Bluff on the Neches, a dangerous crossing during the Runaway Scrape in 1836.

The Big Thicket

This area once extended from the Sabine River to as far west as the Brazos and as far south as the coastal prairie of South Texas. Later, the Trinity River and not the Brazos became the western Thicket border. Early migrants from Louisiana found their way blocked by nearly impenetrable growths.

The region, which includes several counties, consisted of long-leaf yellow pines whose needles and branches covered the ground so that no other woody growth could survive. This layer even absorbed the rain, creating seepy and swampy areas. The swamps then supported a growth of hardwood trees and vegetation that came to be called "thickets." These thickets weren't *everywhere*, but travelers would encounter so many that to them the whole landscape was a big thicket. Due to intense lumbering, however, the thickets essentially disappeared after the early 1900s.

While the Big Thicket once encompassed more than three million acres, less than three hundred thousand remain today. On the other hand, most of the carnivorous plants are still around, even if the panthers and several animal and bird species are not.

In 1966 U.S. Senator Ralph Yarborough introduced a congressional bill calling for a Big Thicket Park. Eight years later, in 1974, congress approved an 84,550-acre Big Thicket National Park. Instead of preserving a massive area, however, the park is a "string of pearls." It is essentially a band of forest extending as a narrow corridor down through Jasper and Tyler counties until striking Beaumont, at which point it curls northwest in patches and groups. A final portion reinforces the Alabama-Coushatta Reservation.

Beaumont—Houston

Liberty

The French and Spanish once contested this area. The French influence so upset the Spanish that prior to 1757 the Spanish built a military highway called the Atascosito Road from Refugio and Goliad to Atascosito, a Spanish settlement and military outpost on the Trinity River near today's Liberty. The road passed three miles northeast of the present town.

The French were not intimidated, however. A group of Napoleonic exiles (a motley assortment of Americans, Poles, Spaniards, French, Mexicans, and pirates) left Philadelphia, sailed to Galveston, and received help from the noted pirate Jean Laffite. They then sailed to the Trinity River destination of Moss Bluff just south of today's Liberty. The French called the site Champ d'Asile. On May 11, 1818, they issued a manifesto of "natural rights" and commenced building log fortifications. Of course, the Spanish promptly marched against them. The invaders retreated back to Galveston and took a ship to New Orleans.

Next to arrive were unauthorized American squatters. An *empresario* group known as the Galveston Bay and Texas Land Company was not recognized by Mexico, so the participants were refused admission into Stephen F. Austin's colony. Therefore, they illegally settled at Atascosito in 1830 and renamed it Liberty. Although the village was not acknowledged by Mexican authorities, and land titles were dissolved, the town continued to grow. A thousand residents existed there by 1835, most of them working at lumbering or on riverboats.

After 1880, state and federal efforts dredged a Trinity River waterway into Liberty, a barge channel of 236 miles. By 1940, Liberty had become a substantial inland port. The region is still 60 percent forested, although the county has pumped nearly 400 million barrels of oil since 1905. A historical marker identifies Sam Houston's law office. The Sam Houston Regional Library & Research Center draws Texas scholars from all over the nation.

FOUR

Gulf Coast

The Texas coastline is a big, beautiful, long, curved, sandy rim on the edge of the Gulf of Mexico. The rim itself is a string of elongated sandy beads, called barrier islands, that separate the mainland coast from Gulf waters. The coastline is not static. It moves and changes, growing here, retreating there, shifting one way then another.

Darwin Spearing, *Roadside Geology of Texas*
(Mountain Press Publishing Company, 1991)

The Texas Gulf Coast is served by splendid roadways. You can drive the entire length along three major highways: I-10 between Orange and Houston; US 59 between Houston and Victoria; and US 77 between Victoria and Brownsville. From these highways, however, you will only occasionally glimpse the ocean. To reach the shoreline, take any of the numerous eastbound or southbound routes from the highways mentioned.

The Gulf Coast in Texas arcs 367 miles as the crow flies. (Along the major highways between Brownsville and Orange you'll travel about 460 miles.) The gulf's total shoreline, including islands, bays, and river mouths, measures some 3,360 miles. All along the Texas coast lies a series of narrow sandbars. These are usually called barrier islands, even though some of them are actually peninsulas; they protect the mainland against ravaging storms and tidal waves. The longest, Padre Island, runs from Corpus Christi to the southern tip of the state near Brownsville; it is 113 miles long.

Some geologists believe barrier islands may be formed in one or more of three ways. In the first way, sand piles upon more sand in the offshore area until finally the accumulation rises above sea level. In the second way, waves lap against the land at such an angle that they shift the sediments laterally, in a process known geologically as longshore drift, to form a spit; if the ocean erodes a portion of the spit, separating it from the mainland, a barrier island results. In the third way, a rise in sea level may overtake the existing shoreline and permanently fill the area behind that headland or beach with water, creating lagoons between the mainland and the now-isolated spits or barrier islands.

In geologic terms, changes along the Texas coast have occurred rapidly. Just a mere 135,000 years ago, when the weather was warm and there was little polar ice, the Gulf of Mexico extended twenty to fifty miles farther inland than it does today. The rivers responded by building higher floodplains. Then, about 18,000 years ago, colder temperatures greatly expanded the polar regions, locking up much of the water supply in icy glacial fingers that extended deep into the North American continent. This caused the sea level to drop and the Texas shoreline to extend seaward beyond its present position. During that most recent ice age, the streams flowing into the gulf from Texas cut deeply into the former floodplain. When the ice age ended and the glaciers melted, the gulf rose to its present level and drowned the river mouths. Some of the sandbars became barrier islands, and new bays, bayous, and lagoons formed along the Texas coast.

Nowadays great cities have arisen and there are twenty-eight man-made ports along this coast. After dredging the harbors to remove silt and deepen the channels, fifteen were made suitable for smaller ships and barges while thirteen can accommodate oceangoing vessels.

Although the Gulf Coast has its charms and hidden beauties, not all of it is glitz, and almost none of it compares with the Riviera. White sandy beaches are relatively few, and even these are disappearing due to neglect, erosion, and overdevelopment. So what do tourists get for their time and money? Well, there are 7,000 square miles of water, plus a plentiful supply of bracing gulf air to restore dragging spirits and put spring and joy into the stride of any visitor.

Industries are anchored soundly on the coast but rarely intrude upon the business of water; however, their presence should not be minimized. Dams on the rivers that feed the gulf impede the flow of sediments and retard nature's strengthening or maintenance of the islands. And the gulf itself has become polluted from waste dumps, offshore platforms, and oil spills.

Still, the shoreline is more than a commodity, it is an emotion. It is power, peace, tranquility, romance, and coming to terms with life, death, and eternity—all wrapped up in whitecapped packages. By state law, Gulf Coast beaches are free and open to the public. A fence never stands between people and the ocean, even though 30 percent of all Texas residents live within only a few miles of the sea.

To walk along the Texas Gulf Coast is to ponder riddles unmastered and mysteries unsolved. Who knows how many Spanish galleons once blew ashore on these barrier islands? If there is actually a graveyard of ships, it is likely the Gulf Coast.

From June to November, and especially during August and September, furious storms wash the Gulf Coast. The Spanish learned this as dozens of their treasure-laden vessels were whipped onto the churning surf, frequently along Padre Island. Hurricanes were unknown to the first Europeans who visited the Americas. They only knew tropical storms such as cyclones or typhoons. The word "hurricane" belongs distinctly to the New World. The Mayans called the intensely destructive storms "hunraken," while Caribbean natives used "aracan," "urican," and "huiranvucan" to describe them. Between 1900 and 1980, thirty-one hurricanes and a dozen or two lesser tropical storms struck the Texas coast.

While the high winds of a hurricane often cause great damage, it is tidal waves that really wreak havoc. They range from ten to twenty-five feet in height and are apt to slam ashore even before the winds become menacing. But modern weather forecasting makes it virtually impossible for hurricane-force storms to strike without warning.

During the California Gold Rush of the late 1840s and 1850s, fortune-seeking forty-niners shipped out of New England and landed on the Texas Gulf Coast prepared to strike out overland to the Pacific coast. Thriving ports of entry sprang up along the shores of Texas prior to and following the Civil War as the growing and restless nation sought new lands and resources. Never a people to let opportunities slip by, the Americans who came to Texas saw the ports as a way to ship cattle and cotton, and later oil. Eventually military bases diversified the economy, and heavy industry came along to fight the wars and support the peace.

Today, the gulf generates a third of the state's wealth. The shrimping industry is vigorous. At least 40 percent of the nation's petrochemicals are refined along or near the coast. In terms of quality and volume of materials handled, Texas harbors rank among the nation's highest.

The Texas Gulf Coast, with its fascinating past and unlimited future, is the vortex of immense wealth and tremendous popularity. Yet, those seeking solitude to ponder the tomorrows while wading the waters of yesterday will find ample space along the Texas coast.

I-10
Sabine River—Beaumont
28 miles

Sabine River

The Sabine River forms two-thirds of the border between Louisiana and Texas. In times past this 360-mile waterway (the third longest in Texas) has been an international line between the United States and Spain, the United States and Mexico, and the United States and the Republic of Texas. Sabine is Spanish for "cypress," a reference to thick growths along the final course of the stream. The Sabine River forms Sabine Lake, which is drained through Sabine Pass into the Gulf of Mexico.

Before trains and trucks took over, the river floated logs to the sea. In recent years the waterway has been deepened as far north as Orange, providing additional facilities for shipping as well as industry.

Golden Triangle

Orange, Port Arthur, and Beaumont form what natives call the "Golden Triangle." Twentieth-century oil, industry, tourist, and shipping aspects have turned this triangle into an economic juggernaut.

Orange

The pirate Jean Laffite is said to have used this site for a repair base. Orange, which overlooks the Sabine River, was called Green's Bluff in 1830. In 1840, Green's Bluff became Madison, in honor of President James Madison. By 1852, Madison had become the seat of Orange County (named for an orange grove). The post office, however, couldn't make a distinction between Madison and Madisonville, so the settlement incorporated and became Orange in 1858.

For a while lumbering was practically the only industry in Orange, but oil strikes diversified things in 1913. Shipbuilding became a thriving enterprise. When World War II ended, the United States Navy established a mile-long

The Orange Rifles at the Orange, Texas, railroad station, preparing to depart for the Mexican border, circa 1912. —The Institute of Texan Cultures

A destroyer being launched on the Sabine River near Orange, 1943.
—The Institute of Texan Cultures

A fire in the oil fields at Orange, 1922. —The Institute of Texan Cultures

berthing facility for its reserve fleet. One hundred and fifty rusting, weary warships lived out their retirement years in Orange.

Orange (as well as the entire Golden Triangle) is known for its Cajuns, who comprise 20 percent of the population. Their story begins in 1775, when Britain expelled 7,000 French-speaking Acadians from Nova Scotia on Canada's Atlantic coast. They drifted to the swamps, prairies, and bayous of Louisiana. After the Texas Company (Texaco) opened a refinery in the Golden Triangle in 1902, many Acadians-Cadiens-Cajuns transferred there for work, a trend accentuated by the Great Depression.

Visitors to Orange should see the W. H. Stark House, constructed in 1894, and the Stark Museum of Art, as well as the First Presbyterian Church with its distinctive copper dome. The church was built in 1912.

Neches River

Travelers can be assured that conditions along this river are far different than a few centuries ago when the Spanish considered this the Cannibal Coast. The Attacapa Indians took their name from two Choctaw words meaning "eaters of men." Although their villages occupied both sides of the Neches River near Beaumont, the Indians were fishermen as well as hunters. As a people they no longer exist. They were not a particularly loved race.

Neches rises in Van Zandt County, and after forming more county lines than any other river in the state, it empties 260 miles east into the Gulf of Mexico. The river drains over 10,000 square miles. The Hasinai Indians called it "Snow River," but Spanish explorer Alonso de León named it Neches after a nearby tribe of Indians in 1689. From 1819 until 1836, some authorities, especially in the United States, believed the Neches, and not the Sabine, actually marked the western boundary of the United States. The river has several dams as well as a tributary canal feeding the Gulf Intercoastal Waterway.

Evadale

Evadale overlooks a ferry site on the Neches River north of Beaumont on US 960. Panicked Texas families crossed here while fleeing Santa Anna during the 1836 Runaway Scrape.

Beaumont

Oil and petrochemicals in themselves are descriptions of Beaumont, although the city has an ample number of paper, rice, food processing, and lumber mills.

French and Spanish fur trappers arrived during the early 1800s. Trevis Bluff was the first permanent settlement, and it became Beaumont by 1835.

Beaumont, Texas, in 1901, after Spindletop came in big. —Windmill Museum

Within a few years, Beaumont was pre-eminent in the lumber industry and was a shipping center for sugar cane, cattle, and cotton.

By 1901 Beaumont had 9,000 people, one of whom was Curt Hamill. His grimy derrick searched for oil five miles south of town. When the drill reached 1,160 feet on a chilly January morning, mud and oil squirted 150 feet into the sky. Since no one knew how to staunch the flow, nearly a million barrels were squandered. Spindletop brought in the age of liquid fuel.

The town (and the nation) was jubilant. Beaumont land sold for thousands of dollars an acre. Five hundred derricks cluttered the landscape. Oil, which had once brought $1.13 a barrel, dropped to a few cents a barrel. (Good drinking water sold for over $5 a barrel.) At least ten million barrels of oil spilled on the ground or were burned in flares.

Three years later, the boom ended. Production had dropped to 10,000 barrels daily by 1904.

Today, the oil is almost depleted. The hill where Spindletop sat is flat, having collapsed as the oil pumped out. Even Gladys City (a suburb of

The Spindletop Oil Field after the

Beaumont named for a nine-year-old schoolgirl) is almost a meadowlands, its memory kept alive as a re-created village of shops and offices at Beaumont's Lamar University. A Spindletop Museum is nearby.

Beaumont was also home to Babe Didrikson Zaharias, the world's greatest female athlete during the first half of the twentieth century. A Beaumont memorial and museum honors her exploits.

US 96

Beaumont—Port Arthur

17 miles

Nederland

The community was platted for Dutch colonists in 1898, and they in turn were joined by Cajuns a few years later. Nederlanders built a forty-foot-high windmill in 1969. It is a local landmark.

fire of April 16, 1903. —The Institute of Texan Cultures

Port Arthur

Port Arthur, nine miles inland from the Gulf of Mexico, started as the tiny fishing village of Aurora in the early 1840s. Arthur E. Stillwell, president of the Kansas City Southern Railroad, envisioned greater growth for the village, so by 1900 he had revamped the city and given it his first name. A canal twenty-five feet deep was dredged, and oceangoing vessels started arriving.

Oil was pumped to Port Arthur from Spindletop. Shipping facilitated the construction of petrochemical facilities, especially oil refineries. A Port Arthur motto proudly proclaimed, "We Oil the World." Nearly a million barrels of crude oil were refined daily.

In 1938 Port Arthur and Orange completed a "Rainbow Bridge" across the Neches River and subsequent salt marshes. Its two lanes extended 1.5 miles (including approaches). The bridge's 177-foot clearance satisfied requirements that any U.S. Navy ship could pass beneath it. This was the first cable-stayed bridge built on Texas highways.

As numerous Acadians moved into the area, Port Arthur became known as the "Cajun Capital."

Port Arthur attractions include Sabine Pass Battleground State Historical Park, Sea Rim State Park, and the McFaddin and Texas Point National

Wildlife Refuges. The Port Arthur Historical Museum is fascinating. Furthermore, visitors should not miss the Pompeiian Villa, a mansion built in 1900 for Isaac Ellwood, the "Barbed-Wire King."

Texas 87
Port Arthur—Port Bolivar
74 miles

Sabine Pass

This narrow inlet drains Sabine Lake into the Gulf of Mexico. The inlet is best known for the Battle of Sabine Pass on September 5, 1863. Union Gen. Nathaniel P. Banks sent four gunboats to silence Fort Sabine, an earthen bulwark with six cannons manned by forty-six Irishmen led by Richard W. "Dick" Dowling. Dick owned a saloon called "The Finish" in Houston. He joined the Confederate Army, held the rank of 1st lieutenant, and participated in the recapture of Galveston on January 1, 1863. Three weeks later Gen. John B. Magruder ordered Dowling to spike the guns at Ford Sabine. Like Travis and Bowie at the Alamo, however, Dowling disobeyed orders. But unlike Travis and Bowie, he put up a successful defense. Confederate fire knocked all Union ships out of action. Nineteen Federals were slain.

Three hundred and fifteen prisoners and two boats were captured in what the *Handbook of Texas* described as "the most spectacular military engagement in Texas during the Civil War." Surviving Federals returned to New Orleans.

The exact ruins of Fort Sabine have never been determined, so in 1936 the Texas Centennial Commission erected a monument to Dowling and his comrades at Sabine Pass.

Port Arthur annexed Sabine Pass in 1978.

Port Bolivar

Dr. James Long and a group of filibusters established a mud fort here from 1819 to 1821. Long then left his wife and entered Mexico, only to die there.

Jane Wilkinson Long gave birth to a child while avoiding the Indians. Because her's was the first Anglo baby born in what would become Texas, she is known as the "Mother of Texas." A free, twenty-four-hour ferry connects Port Bolivar with Galveston.

Jane Long, the "Mother of Texas," and her companion firing a cannon at Port Bolivar to scare away the Indians. —Hendricks Long Publishing Company, Dallas

Beaumont—Pasadena
75 miles

Anahuac

(Seven miles south of I-10. Take Texas 124 south, then go west on Texas 65.)

Anahuac, at the head of Trinity Bay (an extension of Galveston Bay), is difficult to pronounce and even more challenging to spell. Nobody is sure what it means. The village started in 1821 as a port of entry for American colonists heading for Mexico. Travelers called it Perry's Point until 1825. In 1830, Juan Davis Bradburn, a Kentuckian and commander of the Mexican garrison, established Fort Anahuac and made it his headquarters. He confiscated land, impressed slaves, and annulled laws. Bradburn was despised by both Mexicans and Texans, and as the Texans fumed, he locked a local firebrand named William Travis in a brick kiln.

These troubles led to the Turtle Bayou Resolutions, named for the village of Turtle Bayou at the tip of Trinity Bay. The resolutions supported the Mexican constitution as well as incoming President Antonio López de Santa Anna, but they deplored a local disregarding of laws by Mexican authorities.

Mexico finally relieved Bradburn of command and the area remained quiet until June 1835, when Travis and twenty-five men demanded and received a surrender of the Mexican garrison. These and other troubles at Anahuac helped spark the Texas War for Independence.

Baytown

Baytown got its start by swallowing the nearby communities of Goose Creek and Pelly in the 1820s. Although the Confederates built a shipyard at Goose Creek in 1864, Baytown showed little promise until the discovery of oil in 1916. Baytown today is a shipping and industrial complex.

San Jacinto River

The San Jacinto River is barely 100 miles in length, even when taking its branches into consideration. The river twists through eastern Texas before emptying into Lake Houston and San Jacinto Bay. The Spanish discovered the stream in 1746. In 1836, Gen. Sam Houston defeated Gen. Antonio López de Santa Anna along its banks (see Pasadena). The battle ended the Texas Revolution and made Texas a republic.

Pasadena

(Pasadena is just east of Houston. From I-10, take the East Sam Houston Parkway nine miles south.)

Pasadena was laid out in 1896 and envisioned as a fruit and vegetable area. The Houston ship channel, however, changed Pasadena into an industrial complex similar to Baytown.

Pasadena and Deer Park, the eastern suburbs of Houston, form the core of the San Jacinto battlefield. On April 21, 1836, Santa Anna, with 900 men (the figure is arguable), believed Sam Houston's forces had been trapped in a bend of the San Jacinto River. The Mexicans expected a charge at dawn. When it didn't happen, the Mexicans waited until noon and then napped. Meanwhile, at Vince's Bayou in Pasadena, Deaf Smith, one of Houston's trusted lieutenants, burned the bridges behind the Mexican forces, denying both armies an escape route. At three o'clock in the afternoon, Houston straightened his lines, placing his cavalry on the right and the artillery in the center. Infantry flanked each side. Then the army marched forward, walking squarely into the

Mexican positions before being noticed. Twenty minutes later it was all over. Mexican dead littered the battlefield. Santa Anna became Houston's prisoner. Texas liberty was assured.

By following Federal Road through the Washburn Tunnel near I-10, visitors pass the point of Santa Anna's capture.

In 1891, the San Jacinto Chapter of the Daughters of the Republic of Texas started a $10,000 fund-raising drive to purchase the San Jacinto battlefield. By 1900, the area belonged to them. Thirty years later, with federal assistance, they built a tower higher than the Washington Monument. In April 1939 the fifty-seven-story San Jacinto Monument, complete with visitors center, galleries, and tours, was dedicated.

Near the battlefield, alongside the Houston ship channel and Buffalo Bayou, is the battleship *Texas*. Congress offered this sole surviving dreadnought-class battleship to Texas after World War II. School children and civic organizations donated funds to tow it in. As a tourist attraction today, this 35,000-ton lady draws nearly as many visitors as the San Jacinto battlefield.

An early monument at the San Jacinto battlefield, 1910. The visitors have just arrived by boat. —Houston Metropolitan Research Center, Houston Public Library

Sam Houston. He did it all for Texas. —Archives Division, Texas State Library

Houston—Galveston

Houston

In 1836, Augustus C. and John K. Allen, New York land speculators living in Texas since 1832, wanted to build a town capable of becoming the seat of Texas government. They selected a Karankawa Indian site at the head of Buffalo Bayou, named it Houston after the victorious general of the Texas revolutionary armies, and set about advertising this town that existed only on paper as "the commercial emporium of Texas."

Almost from the outset, however, this town called Houston, chosen by luck, logic, and perhaps a roll of the dice, developed into a major trading center. Buffalo Bayou flowed from Houston into Galveston Bay. The bayou was deep when compared with most other channels. It was fairly wide, of near-constant depth and with substantial banks. It even ran east and west, appealing to the fertile Brazos Valley country because the Brazos River was too undependable as a navigational lane. While oceangoing vessels could not sail into Houston proper due to the shallowness of Buffalo Bayou, barges and tiny steamboats could transport goods from Houston via the bayou to Galveston and return. Galveston, of course, had easier access to ocean facilities. Houston's strength was land connections plus limited access to water.

Because Houston was such a splendid potential seaport, although fifty miles from the ocean, immigrants started arriving immediately. In 1837 the state capital took up quarters in Houston, increasing the population to 1,200. But the mud and miserable weather caused grumbling among the politicians, all except Sam Houston, who rather liked his namesake town. Still, when a yellow fever epidemic wiped out 10 percent of the population in 1839, the capital shifted to Austin.

Houston was platted in a typical gridiron pattern, the most efficient approach for commercial purposes. Broad boulevards ran parallel and perpendicular to the bayou. Water Street extended alongside the riverfront.

Development of a ship channel started in 1840 with construction of the first dock. Houston became an important shipping point for cotton. Over 2,000 people had settled on this nine square miles of city by 1850.

Houston Marsh Rice reached Houston in 1839 as a barkeeper who shifted his talents and interests to cotton as well as real estate and railroads. The Civil War made him a millionaire as his cotton wagons successfully ran Union blockades to Mexico. Before he left Houston in 1863, later becoming a murder victim, he provided for the creation of Rice Institute. Rice University is one of America's premier schools.

Although the community suffered from periodic floods and another yellow fever epidemic in 1867, the ship channel construction continued. Buffalo Bayou was widened and deepened in 1869. When a hurricane and tidal wave destroyed Galveston in 1900, Houston was the major port in Texas.

Roads leading to the Texas interior were another matter. When the rains came, as they always did, the highways turned to mud. When the clouds cleared, the mud dried and the roads turned to powder. Dust and mud invaded everything, and there were discussions of plank roads, log roads, rock roads, and even shell roads. However, nothing solved the mud/dust dilemma until paving came along many years later.

Railroads contributed a crucial transportation factor, for a growing seaport needed land connections. By the mid-1850s, Houston advertised itself as a place "Where Eleven Railroads Meet the Sea."

Buffalo Bayou with a railroad bridge in the background. —The Institute of Texan Cultures

The Capitol Hotel in Houston before it was renamed The Rice, circa 1889.
—Houston Metropolitan Research Center, Houston Public Library

The steamboat Lizzie *loading cotton on Buffalo Bayou in 1900.*
—Houston Metropolitan Research Center, Houston Public Library

The William O. Mary *was the first oceangoing vessel to sail up the new ship channel into Houston. It had a cargo of gas mains for Houston Heights.* —Houston Metropolitan Research Center, Houston Public Library

Fire destroyed portions of Houston in 1859 and 1860, but industry continued to build. The city manufactured carriages, barbed wire, beer, brick, tile, cigars, and bottles. In 1885 over 23,000 people lived in Houston. By 1900 the population had jumped to 45,000.

During the Civil War, Houston had a reputation for blockade running. Although no fighting took place, the city sucked in its breath in 1862 when Federals captured Galveston Island. A year later Houston became headquarters for the Trans-Mississippi Department of the Confederacy, although what that title meant, and how it influenced the war's outcome, length, or ferocity, if at all, is conjecture.

According to David McComb's *Houston: The Bayou City*, Houston was a cauldron of refugees during the war. Hard economic times also arrived as evidenced by a newspaper story written when Gen. John B. Magruder accepted a sword for returning Galveston to the Confederacy:

> *Magruder, wearing a 'gorgeous' uniform, accepted the sword, and with an 'unfortunate lisp' promised the crowd on Main Street that it would never be*

sheathed while the enemy trod on Confederate soil. After the music, speeches and cheers, however, the sword, borrowed for the occasion from a Mexican War veteran, had to be returned to its owner—a sad commentary on the economic condition of Houston and the State.

The 34th Iowa Regiment, along with elements of the 114th Ohio Regiment, arrived on June 20, 1865, to occupy Houston for the North. The town remained orderly, and Reconstruction presented no serious problems.

Smallpox, yellow fever, and cholera continued to take a heavy toll, and newspaper notices advised residents to "thoroughly cleanse the stomach and bowels." The community created a board of health and passed a pure milk ordinance.

The narrow, tortuous Buffalo Bayou, with its snags, sandbars, and overhanging trees, was dug wider and deeper, but still only the smallest of oceangoing steamers could get through. More dredging commenced after the

Senator Thomas Jefferson Rusk. He was as much a father of Texas independence as Sam Houston.
—Texas State Archives

Civil War. The *Weekly Telegraph* argued that Houston could be the leading city in Texas if it had an adequate ship channel. Without it, Houston would be "a small commercial town gradually growing due to her railroads and manufacturing, but destined never, in our lifetime, to grow much beyond what she is now."

In 1870 the federal government declared Houston a port of entry and ordered a survey of its harbor possibilities. Lt. H. M. Adams determined that a ship channel could be dug six feet deep and one hundred feet wide. The federal government kicked in $10,000 (its first grant), and work commenced again along Buffalo Bayou.

In 1914, Houston became an official ocean port. A deepwater harbor and turning basin were completed.

Gunslingers, who seemed so prevalent around Texas, for the most part seemed to have avoided Houston. Maybe that's because Houston was better known for cotton, shipping, oil, and finance. Newspapers described the city as filled with "oaths, blasphemy, and drunkenness." A popular new drink was

Main Street, Houston, looking north from Preston Avenue, 1915.
—Houston Metropolitan Research Center, Houston Public Library

"Kiss Me Quick and Go!" A grand jury described dueling as "ungentlemanly." The city had ordinances against carrying firearms, and in 1842 the newspapers reported that no duels had occurred in four years. Counterfeiting, however, was almost a craze.

Legal hangings occasionally transpired, as did lynchings. Before 1850, criminals could be whipped, fined, or jailed. Whippings and hangings were popular pastimes for observers.

The discovery of oil convinced several petroleum companies to build refineries in the city. Houston became a leading petrochemical and natural gas center. Even tourism went big-time in 1928 when Houston hosted the Democratic National Convention. In a rousing speech, Franklin D. Roosevelt nominated his friend Al Smith of New York for president of the United States.

Meanwhile, major construction started on the south edge of the business district. During the 1970s, the pace quickened. Houston became a city of concrete canyons.

Main Street, Houston, looking south from Preston Avenue, 1915.
—Houston Metropolitan Research Center, Houston Public Library

197

The Market House in Houston, 1889. —Houston Metropolitan Research Center, Houston Public Library

"The Bayou City," as a title, seemed old-fashioned and unprogressive, so Houston's leaders changed it to "the International City."

Twenty-three colleges and universities graced the city, with Rice being the best known. The Baylor School of Medicine opened, as did a dental branch of the University of Texas. The city acquired fine-art centers, ballets, symphonies, and operas.

Houston's Astrodome, the first domed, air-conditioned stadium, home to the Houston Oilers football team, opened in 1965. Today the Astrodome caters to many sports.

During the 1980s, with plummeting oil prices, Houston entered an economic slump, the central area threatening to become a ghost town. Bank closings and savings and loan failures hit Texas, and especially Houston. However, even before the decade ended, Houston was surging forward again. Today the city is anticipating a bright future.

Historic places to visit in Houston include the Antique Car Museum, Bayou Bend Collection, Children's Museum, Contemporary Arts Museum, Gallery of Texas (Sam Houston Historical Park), Houston Museum of Natural Sciences, Menil Museum, Museum of Fine Arts, Museum of Mexican Sciences, and the Railroad Train Museum.

Other historical assets are the Old Market Square (Allen's Landing), Armand Bayou Nature Center, Astrodomain (includes the Astrodome),

Astroworld/Waterworld, Christ Church Cathedral, the Civic Center, Clear Lake Queen, Fame City, Hermann Park Zoo, Houston Arboretum and Nature Center, Houston Garden Center, Houston Underground, Miller Outdoor Theatre, Orange Show, Port of Houston, Rothka Chapel, and the Texas Medical Center. Of course, the Johnson Space Center and San Jacinto Battleground State Historic Park are nearby.

Lyndon B. Johnson Space Center—NASA
(Houston's Mission Control)

The Manned Space Center, command post for spaceflights by United States astronauts, opened in 1961. While located in nearby Clear Lake, a Houston suburb, it employed over 10,000 workers and directed the first landing of astronauts on the moon in 1969. It was renamed the Lyndon B. Johnson Space Center in 1973.

Today the Lyndon B. Johnson Space Center complex not only directs the Space Shuttle project but also interprets the moon and stars as well as making itself available to tourists. A visitor's center exhibits fragments of the moon brought back by astronauts. Additional buildings display spacecraft plus films of spaceflights. Apollo and Mercury command modules are present, as is the Lunar Roving Vehicle trainer.

Texas City

Texas City was known as Shoal Point prior to 1891. Port construction began in 1893 with the dredging of an eight-foot channel, and the first oceangoing vessel arrived in 1904. The town never took off, however, until World War II, when it developed into an industrial arm of Galveston.

This community is best remembered for the harbor explosion on April 16, 1947. Workers were loading a French cargo vessel with ammonium nitrate fertilizer, a brown crystalline powder capable of detonating when hot unless open space is available to disperse heat. Safety precautions were ignored, and the fertilizer exploded.

An orange-black fireball blotted out the sun and shot down two light aircraft. The explosion collapsed every house within a one-mile radius. It not only destroyed the fire department, it set refineries ablaze. A nearby ship blew up. Over 500 people died and emergency rooms were jammed for two days. The city rebuilt however, and has regained strength as a shipping and industrial center.

The Texas City Dike extends five miles into Galveston Bay and is a popular tourist attraction. Other popular spots are the College of the Mainland Art Gallery and the Frank B. Davison Home, a Victorian structure with period furniture and archives dating back to 1897.

Galveston

Cabeza de Vaca called it "Malhado," the island of doom. In 1785, however, Spanish surveyors named it after Count Bernardo de Gálvez, viceroy of Mexico.

Galveston is a sand-barrier island, thirty-two miles long and three miles wide at its broadest point. It is fifty miles southeast of Houston and two miles from the coast.

Historically, the island was once a pirate stronghold, with Jean Laffite being the most successful freebooter. (Laffite never claimed to be a pirate, only a privateer who preyed on foreign vessels.) Galveston was his headquarters during the early 1800s, and although he captured and sold practically every imaginable item, slaves were his speciality. In this respect, he worked closely with the brothers Resin and James Bowie, the latter a hero of the Alamo.

Bernardo de Gálvez, Spanish governor of Louisiana and the man for whom Galveston Island is named. —Nettie Lee Benson Latin American Collection, UT Austin

An 1804 oil portrait of pirate Jean Laffite, painted when he was 22 years old.
—The Institute of Texan Cultures

Laffite captured slave ships sailing from Africa. Dealers from the Southern states, principally Mississippi, purchased slaves by the pound. Since the importation of blacks was illegal, the Bowie boys walked them to New Orleans and surrendered them to federal customs officials, who paid a reward for getting slaves off the market. American officials then auctioned the slaves back to the Bowies, the transaction making the slaves legal and free to be resold. The Bowies became wealthy.

Around 1821 the American warship *Enterprise* visited Galveston. The captain ordered Laffite to leave, and Laffite left. No one knows exactly where he went or what eventually happened to him.

Galveston became a Mexican port of entry in 1825, but Texans used it as headquarters for the republic's navy during the 1836 war for independence. Over 2,000 Mexican prisoners were briefly incarcerated in Galveston, and Santa Anna passed through while in captivity.

As a city, Galveston was founded by Canadian-born Michel B. Menard in 1836. From the beginning Galveston was a shipping and receiving point on the eastern part of the island. The primary export was cotton. Although slow to industrialize, Galveston was often described as the New York City of Texas.

Texas didn't adopt a banking system until after the Civil War. Cotton and commission houses in Galveston handled paperwork that, in spite of its doubtful legality, seems to have been accepted everywhere. This put the town in direct competition with Houston. A trade war intensified when railroads reached both places during the 1850s.

The Galveston waterfront in 1855. —The Institute of Texan Cultures

An engraving of ships in Galveston harbor, 1879. —The Institute of Texan Cultures

In 1862, the United States Navy captured Galveston, but Confederates shortly retook it in a land-sea battle more noted for its blunders than brilliance. The Civil War ended with Galveston surging in population.

The immediate postwar years were difficult. Yellow fever swept Texas in 1867, a disaster immobilizing Galveston, the largest city in the state. The epidemic infected three-fourths of the Galveston population and killed nearly 2,000 people. Bankers hesitated to lend money, as any borrower could be dead before making the first payment.

As a port of entry, Galveston attracted emigrants from all over the world. More languages were spoken here than anywhere outside of New York and London. Extravagance came easy.

Greek Revival architecture became nationally known as the "Galveston Style." After the Civil War, the Galveston Style went Victorian. A Gothic craze virtually dominated architecture, with gingerbread trim added to houses and showing up on furniture, steamboats, and even newspaper advertisements.

The 1890s Galveston home of John Trube, built to resemble a Danish castle. —The Institute of Texan Cultures

After the turn of the century, the Renaissance styles gained acceptance. Spanish Revival and Neo-Classical periods followed. Galveston rarely did anything in modest measures.

Those same years were rowdy and frequently despairing for Galveston, times when it truly earned its nickname of "Sin City of the Gulf Coast." Killing was practically an industry, as were brawling, gambling, and prostitution. John L. Sullivan, heavyweight boxing champion of the world, fought an exhibition in an opera house. Sullivan knocked his man down three times in fifty-five seconds. The opponent wisely decided he'd had enough.

A large force of Texas Rangers worked Galveston during the 1930s and 1940s. Slot-machine busts made for newspaper copy all over the nation.

As Galveston grew, it knew few bounds or limits except those imposed by nature, and nature showed how imposing it could be on September 8, 1900. A hurricane swept across Puerto Rico, Cuba, and Florida, then veered toward Galveston. The storm killed more people than any previous natural disaster

Storm damage to a Galveston church after the hurricane of 1900.
—San Antonio Conservation Society

in United States history. Twelve thousand people died on the island, 6,000 in the city. Nearly 4,000 homes were destroyed. The mainland bridge was swept away. Economic losses amounted to $30 million.

In 1915 another hurricane struck the city. This time Galveston was better protected and only eight people died. Since then hurricanes have visited in 1919, 1932, 1941, 1943, 1949, 1957, 1961, and 1983. Only a few people died in these. Hurricane Alicia in 1983, for instance, killed no one, but it caused an estimated $300 million in property damages.

Part of Galveston's success story today is the Strand, one of the greatest historical preservation triumphs in the United States. The Strand comprised six blocks between 19th and 25th streets, the most important commercial real estate in Texas between 1875 and 1900. Five of the largest and wealthiest banking houses in Texas once buttressed the Strand. Today these marvelous old buildings have been impeccably restored. The historic area swarms with cafes, boutiques, galleries, and antique shops. Other than the port, the Strand is probably the greatest income-producing part of Galveston.

Henry Rosenberg, banker, merchant, and diplomat, died in 1893 and left a portion of his estate to endow a free public library in Galveston. The Rosenberg Library opened in June 1904. During the following year a branch opened for the benefit of Negroes, the first such library in the United States. The Rosenberg Library ranks as one of the finest libraries in the country. It has tremendous book and archival collections.

There is the Port of Galveston, always a tourist item, plus excursion boats, fishing piers, yacht basins, and beaches. There is a Railroad Museum, Automobile Museum, a County Historical Museum, and a Texas Heroes Monument. A list of historic homes and churches would go on practically forever. Tour guides are always available.

US 59

Houston—Refugio

150 miles

Sugar Land

People in Sugar Land describe their community as the sweetest town in Texas. That's appropriate, of course, because its main industry, the Imperial Sugar Company, is "the oldest business in continuous operation at one spot in the state."

Samuel May Williams, merchant, banker, and financier of the Texas Revolution (he was also Stephen F. Austin's secretary), settled a league of land

The Beach Hotel in Galveston. —Frank Leslie, *Illustrated Weekly*, May 31, 1890.

in 1828 on Oyster Creek and called it the Oakland Plantation. He brought in slaves and produced enough sugar for local consumption. After Williams died, Benjamin Franklin Terry and W. J. Kyle named the property Sugar Land and induced a railroad to market the product.

Kyle died in 1862. Terry, a delegate to the secession convention, participated in the Battle of Manassas. Shortly afterwards, he returned to Houston and formed Terry's Texas Rangers, a Confederate force. He was killed in Kentucky while leading a charge on December 17, 1861. Sugar Land then passed to Col. E. H. Cunningham, who built a sugar refinery in 1890.

Businessman I. H. Kempner bought everybody out in 1907. Since he had spent many a night in New York's Imperial Hotel, Kempner named his sugar operation "Imperial."

The Kempners still own the Imperial sugar business although sugar here nowadays is not so much grown as it is refined. The Sugar Land refining capacity is four million pounds daily, the sugar being brought in from Hawaii, Australia, Africa, Florida, Louisiana, and South Texas.

The Imperial Sugar Company is open for tours. The LPGA (Ladies Professional Golf Association) has its hall of fame in Sugar Land.

206

I. H. Kempner, instrumental in forming the Galveston Cotton Exchange as well as the sugar industry in Sugar Land, Texas. —The Institute of Texan Cultures

Richmond

This area was settled in 1822 by the Old Three Hundred and named by the brothers Henry and Randal Jones for their hometown of Richmond, Virginia. They picked a bend in the Brazos because it offered an easy ford. Most of the early settlers were Southern plantation owners. Northerners flooded into the region after the Civil War, and that led to trouble.

Richmond was the seat of Fort Bend County, and two political factions arose during the 1880s. A black-dominated Republican government had gained control during Reconstruction. The Democrats opposed them, a class of people not only 90 percent white, but composed of the county's wealthier residents.

The Jaybird-Woodpecker War, or Feud, erupted. The Jaybirds were the Democrats and the Woodpeckers the Republicans. Strangely, both sides vied

A statue commemorating the Jaybird-Woodpecker Feud on the city hall lawn, Richmond, Texas. —Darrell Jepson

for the Negro vote during the 1888 county elections. A Jaybird leader was slain. Democrats were told to quit seeking black support. As a result, the Jaybirds met in Richmond on September 6 and warned most blacks to leave the county.

By now the Texas Rangers were assisting with the peace. The Woodpeckers remained in political control of the county. Two additional fights took place in town, and this time a couple of Woodpeckers died.

On August 16, 1889, the Battle of Richmond commenced, most of the fighting taking place around the courthouse, the National Hotel, and the McFarlane residence. After twenty minutes of shooting, the Woodpeckers retreated inside the courthouse and the Jaybirds controlled the town.

With armed Woodpeckers and Jaybirds rushing to Richmond, Governor Lawrence S. Ross declared martial law and sent state guardsmen to separate the combatants. Then Ross himself arrived to act as mediator. The Fort Bend County government was completely reorganized. Most Woodpeckers resigned from office or were removed and replaced by Jaybirds. Whites now controlled the county.

A Richmond mass meeting of October 3, 1889, drafted a county constitution giving permanent political control to white people. The Jaybird Democratic Organization of Fort Bend County was organized and 441 white men signed the membership roll. A city-hall obelisk is presently topped with a jaybird.

When Carrie Nation began her crusade against "demon rum," the drive began in Richmond.

Richmond and Rosenberg are now essentially one city, the municipalities having merged because they are only brief distances apart. Together they create an unusual variety of ethnic and cultural groups. A Confederate Museum is available, as is the Fort Bend County Historical Museum, one of the finest small museums in the state.

Texas patriots Erastus (Deaf) Smith, republic President Mirabeau B. Lamar, and the "Mother of Texas," Mrs. Jane Long, are buried in Richmond.

Rosenberg

This site was a shipping point on the Brazos River until 1883, when it was named for Henry Rosenberg, a Galveston merchant, banker, diplomat, politician, Episcopal church leader, and civic benefactor. The Gulf, Colorado & Santa Fe Railroad came to town the same year. Oil was discovered during the 1920s, and Rosenberg became a boomtown. Nowadays it and Richmond are regional trade centers.

Victoria

The "City of the Roses," as it is oftentimes called, has always been a crossroads of history more than just a rest stop on the San Antonio-Indianola Road. Martín de León established it in 1824 for Guadalupe Victoria, one-time president of Mexico. De León colonized it with German, Irish, Italian, and Hispanic residents. It had five alcaldes (mayors) before entering the Republic of Texas. Santa Anna's army passed through after the Mexicans massacred James Fannin's Texas troops at Goliad. Although Victoria was incorporated in 1839, Comanches struck it a year later, killing several citizens. Cholera ravaged much of the population in 1846.

General John B. Magruder destroyed the Victoria & Port Lavaca Railroad in 1861. It was rebuilt as part of the San Antonio Mexican Gulf Railroad in 1866.

Victoria's Memorial Square contains graves of early pioneers. Also of interest are the Texas Zoo, Riverside Park, the Nave Art Museum, and the McNamara Historical Museum.

Commerce Street, Refugio, Texas, 1908. —The Institute of Texan Cultures

Refugio

Refugio is located forty-one miles southwest of Victoria on US 77.

In 1790, Franciscan fathers established the last Spanish mission in Texas. Nuestra Señora del Refugio (Our Lady of Refuge) turned out to be misnamed.

Its four square leagues were distributed in 1834 to Irish and Mexican colonists. In March 1836, during the war for independence, Texas Capt. James Fannin sent Amon King and twenty-eight men to lead the Refugio residents to safety in Goliad. Mexican Gen. José Urrea's cavalry cut him off, and King took refuge in the Refugio mission while calling on Fannin for aid.

Fannin sent William Ward and one hundred men, but neither Ward nor King could agree on who should command, so King withdrew from the mission, became lost, and was captured and killed. Fannin then ordered Ward, who had been under bombardment for several days, to retreat to Victoria. He obeyed, but at Victoria he and his men were captured by Mexican forces and sent to Goliad, where they were shot along with Fannin and other Texans during the infamous Goliad Massacre.

Altogether, Refugio had lost one-fourth of its male population. Four years later, when Refugio became the county seat, there were not enough males available to operate the government. Even so, in 1842, Mexican regulars invaded the town and carried off all but two of the men into Mexico. Refugio's historical museum commemorates these events.

The Aransas National Wildlife Refuge is thirty-eight miles east of Refugio.

East Columbia—Blessing
45 miles

East Columbia and West Columbia

Josiah Hughes Bell, a friend of Stephen F. Austin and a developer in the same mode, started a Brazos River port called Bell's Landing around 1823. It specialized in cotton and sugar plantations. Shortly afterwards the Landing became Marion and then Columbia. In 1826, Bell laid out another village two miles west and called it Columbia. The earlier community became East

The Patton Plantation home and outbuildings at West Columbia, circa 1890. The plantation was later sold to the Hogg family and became known as the Varner-Hogg Plantation. —The Institute of Texan Cultures

Columbia (it declined after the Civil War), and the later one West Columbia. Today, when someone mentions "Columbia," they generally mean the western one.

Columbia was the first capital of the republic (1836). The first congress swore in the first Texas president (Sam Houston) in Columbia. The Texas Congress also wrote a constitution and bylaws providing for a military, judiciary, postal service, and financial organization. However, on November 30, 1836, the capital moved to Houston because Columbia lacked adequate accommodations. Stephen F. Austin, who was secretary of state, died in Columbia on December 27 that year.

The Varner-Hogg Plantation, a two-story colonial antebellum mansion, is nearby. Governor James Hogg lived there in 1901. His children restored the structure in 1920.

Brazosport Area

To reach the Brazosport area, take Texas 36 south from Texas 35.

Brazosport is essentially a nine-city industrial complex. Among these is Jones Creek, with its well-preserved home of Emily Perry, the only sister of Stephen F. Austin. She kept a special room for her brother. Freeport is three miles farther, and it dominates the Brazosport region.

The most historic Brazosport community is Surfside, the original site of Velasco. Austin's colonists landed at Velasco in 1821. They were the first of 25,000. Colonel Don Domingo de Ugartechea commanded the Velasco fort in 1832 when John Austin, no relation to Stephen F., loaded three cannons on a small ship and sailed to attack Anahuac. However, the Velasco fort denied him access to the gulf from the Brazos River. Austin promptly divided his forces, sending riflemen by land to flank the fort while he attacked the post with cannon fire from shipboard. The fort finally fell after eleven hours of fighting. Colonel de Ugartechea fired the last futile government rounds himself when his men, shot to pieces by Texas snipers, refused to approach their own artillery.

When the Texas war for independence ended, the Treaty of Velasco was signed here on May 14, 1836, between Mexican President Santa Anna and Texas Interim President David Burnet.

Actually there were two treaties: one public, the other secret. The public treaty stipulated that hostilities would cease, Santa Anna would not again take up arms against Texas, Mexican forces would withdraw beyond the Rio Grande, property would be restored, prisoners would be exchanged, Santa Anna would be repatriated to Mexico, and the victorious Texas army would not approach closer than five leagues to the retreating Mexican forces.

The secret treaty was somewhat different: Santa Anna would be released immediately and would use his influence for the recognition of Texas independence, he promised not to attack Texas again, he would give orders for the withdrawal of Mexican forces from Texas, he would pressure the Mexican government to favorably receive a Texas mission, and he would work for a treaty of commerce and limits whereby the Texas boundary would be established no farther south than the Rio Grande.

Unfortunately, the Mexican government voided all agreements signed by Santa Anna as a captive, and the Texans did not immediately release Santa Anna to return home. Both sides had thus violated the agreements, and the border issue festered until the Treaty of Guadalupe Hidalgo in 1848 ended the Mexican War.

A hurricane destroyed Velasco in 1875.

Matagorda

Matagorda is located twenty-two miles south of Texas 35 on Texas 60.

When *empresario* Stephen F. Austin started seeking settlers for his Mexican land grants during the 1820s, he made his capital San Felipe de Austin and began spreading farmers out along the Brazos and Colorado River bottoms. The colony needed a port city too, so in 1829 Matagorda had been established complete with log fort and rudimentary dwellings. By the 1830s, Matagorda had become the gateway port into Texas as well as the closest port city to New Orleans. Mexico placed a customshouse there in 1831.

Matagorda funnelled supplies into Texas during the revolution, but it was also briefly occupied in 1836 by Gen. José Urrea. The city was deserted. After the Mexican Army left, the city revived. In 1837, it became the county seat as well as a center for the slave trade, as the first of hundreds of slave ships tied up in the harbor.

The Civil War brought sad times to Matagorda. The Matagorda Coast Guards went off to fight, and practically all were slain. Another group of forty men left Matagorda in a sailboat to engage a supposedly invading Union army. But the boat capsized in freezing water and twenty-two died. They lie in a Matagorda common grave.

When the war ended, Matagorda only briefly recovered. Dog Island, a reef two or three miles from Matagorda, prevented large ships from docking at the port. At least three hurricanes swept the city (in 1854, 1875, and 1886), and periodic yellow fever epidemics did not do it any favors. When the Cane Belt Railroad (later Gulf, Colorado & Santa Fe) arrived in 1898, it could not save the town. Matagorda died because better ports arose along the Texas Gulf Coast.

Matagorda Island

Islands somehow lend themselves to tall tales, legends of pirates, shipwrecks, mutiny, lost men, lost dreams, and lost souls. So it is with Matagorda Island, a few miles south of the village of Matagorda.

Some historians believe Cabeza de Vaca landed on Matagorda Island instead of Galveston. Maybe so. However, there isn't much question that the

La Salle Expedition reached there in 1685. La Salle had sought the Mississippi's mouth, missed it, and discovered Matagorda instead.

The thirty-mile-long barrier island of Matagorda began its "historic" life with the name Purgatory. In 1839, Texas established the town of Calhoun as a customs port. But business was lax, so the village withered. Then a ranching center sprang up called Saluria. It survived a hurricane only to be torched by retreating Confederates in 1864.

As a region of few if any comforts, Matagorda has never been a resort. The marshes, snakes, mosquitoes, and general remoteness have seen to that. In 1934, the Bureau of Reclamation cut a barge channel from the mouth of the Colorado River across Matagorda Island and into the gulf. It helped turn Bay City into a seaport.

During World War II the air force used the island as a bombing and gunnery range. Although the aircraft are now gone, the craters are still visible. Matagorda Island presently belongs largely to the Department of Interior. Cattle-ranching operations once flourished there, but the Aransas National Wildlife Refuge ordered them out by summer 1991.

Blessing

Jonathan Pierce described this railroad crossroads as a "blessing" in 1902, and the name stuck. Pierce and his brother, "Shanghai" Pierce, one of the great individuals in Texas history, built the Matagorda Ranch with land extending for miles up and down the coast. Blessing was a ranching headquarters.

Texas 316
Port Lavaca—Indianola
14 miles

Lavaca River

This river flows seventy-five miles into Lavaca Bay from the southwestern corner of Fayette County. It established the western boundary of Stephen F. Austin's original colony. In Spanish the name Lavaca means "cow," but in this case some authorities suspect it might have referred to the buffalo.

Port Lavaca

The origins of Port Lavaca, which sits on a bluff overlooking Lavaca Bay, are more confused than most. Spain unloaded supplies here for the Texas interior by 1815. Surveyors reached the area by the early 1830s, and the town, then known simply as Lavaca, was a functioning seaport by the time of the Texas Revolution. It's population surged in 1840, however, after Comanches raided and destroyed Linnville, three miles upstream. The survivors fled to Lavaca while Linnville returned to the soil. By the mid-1840s, Lavaca was called Port Lavaca.

A major wharf was constructed in 1846 just in time for portions of Gen. Zachary Taylor's army to march through on their way to the Mexican War. Cotton was then the largest export, with salted cattle hides second on the list.

During the following year, the Harris and Morgan Steamship Line out of New Orleans opened offices in Port Lavaca, and it briefly seemed that the city had no way to go but up. But Port Lavaca increased its dockage fees in 1849, and the company moved to Indianola. Other shippers, traders, and merchants followed. A savage tropical storm hit Port Lavaca in 1851 and destroyed everything. But the town rebuilt.

Captain Dan Shea of the Van Dorn Guards patrolled the Port Lavaca waterway during the Civil War. On October 31, 1862, a Captain Renshaw led two Union warships to Port Lavaca and demanded the port's surrender. On the following day, both sides waited ninety minutes for women and children to clear the town. Then the shelling started, with the Federals finally withdrawing.

After Indianola was abandoned, primarily due to storm damage, the county seat again shifted to Port Lavaca in 1886. Even so, times had changed. Port Lavaca's glory never returned, even though an intercoastal canal cut through the old reefs that had so plagued earlier shipping.

The port now has oil and chemical industries, as well as recreational opportunities. Fishermen and duck hunters visit in great numbers.

The old Port Lavaca Causeway is now a state recreation park with a visitors center and fishing pier. Nearby is the La Salle Monument, the Indianola County Historic Park, and the Halfmoon Reef Lighthouse. And the Calhoun County Museum is worth a visit by the historically curious.

Indianola

Indianola was once the most popular entry point in Texas. La Salle may have landed here.

When Prince Karl zu Solms-Braunfels undertook a project for settling thousands of Germans in Texas, he chose Indian Point on Matagorda Bay. A storehouse was erected three miles south at Powderhorn Point, which German immigrants called Karlshafen. By 1836, over 3,000 Germans had come ashore. Most of those not already inland lived on the beach, where they

215

battled mosquitoes and yellow fever. Boardinghouses were not constructed until 1847, but by then Indian Point had become a community. There were wharfs, businesses, and warehouses.

Cattle drives from central Texas to the Kansas railheads were still futuristic concepts, but a few dreamers were already looking eastward. On September 24, 1848, the schooner *Louise Antoinette* sailed with 120 head for New Orleans. The shipping of cattle to Louisiana from Indian Point thereafter became a common occurrence.

Port Lavaca and Indian Point were but ten miles apart and struggling for supremacy when Port Lavaca made a serious mistake: it raised its docking charges. Large shippers moved to Indian Point, and so did most of the businessmen. This caused a push for a new name for the town in 1849. Indian was retained, Point was dropped. "Ola," meaning "wave" in Spanish, was added. This rising city would be Indianola.

The United States Army chose Indianola for its Quartermaster and Subsistence Department in 1850. The government wharf was 250 feet long.

John R. Bartlett, American boundary commissioner in 1851, called Indianola the most promising port in America and predicted it would eventually rival New York and Boston harbors. Commission supplies poured through Indianola.

Until the Civil War, the United States supplied Texas military posts through the Indianola port. The great camel experiment started here in 1856

Crewmen trying to load a camel on a boat. In 1856, Secretary of War Jefferson Davis tried a "camel experiment" to see if camels could replace horses for the U.S. Army in the Southwest. The camels were unloaded at the port of Indianola, Texas, and trekked through San Antonio and El Paso to California. The experiment was successful, but the impending Civil War aborted additional camel caravans.
—The Institute of Texan Cultures

when Secretary of War Jefferson Davis wondered if camels could outperform horses and mules in the desert. They actually succeeded, but the Civil War intervened and the camel experiment was discarded. The camels were turned loose in the deserts of California and Arizona.

The Civil War brought Indianola traffic to a standstill. A federal blockade stopped ships from entering or leaving. Wagon trains went out of business also. The town was bombarded at least twice by Federal warships, and looted on each occasion. The Texans reluctantly destroyed warehouses, wharfs, bridges, and railroads to keep them out of Union hands.

When the war ended, trade resumed. The town seemed once again headed for greatness. There were stores, shops, professional offices, churches, schools, and hotels like the Casimer House with its splendid furnishings and chandeliers.

But 1875 marked the beginning of the end. On September 15, the rain started. By daylight most of the town was underwater, some of it five feet in depth. For a while, people thought the worst was over. But late that night the wind changed direction and water torrents roared through town. When the sun came up, a town of 2,000 residents was destroyed, with nearly 300 people dead.

The stunned village managed to rebuild. Then, ten years later, on August 20, 1886, a hurricane and fire slashed through Indianola. This time there was nothing left to save. The town was gone. Only a historical marker identifies the site today.

The Matagorda Island State Park and Wildlife Management Area is but a few miles southeast of Indianola, as is nearby Port O'Connor (originally named Alligator Head). A hurricane nearly destroyed Port O'Connor in 1961.

Texas 35
Tivoli—Corpus Christi
64 miles

Tivoli

Col. Newton C. Gullett owned the 20,000-acre Tivoli Ranch, which took its name from a New Orleans street. The land was subdivided and developed in 1892. Tivoli became an agricultural center.

Fulton, Rockport

Rockport is the most historic of these two communities. A ledge of shellrock projecting into Aransas Bay gave it the name Rocky Point, later changed to Aransas Pass and then Rockport. Fulton, a few miles north along the coast, was the 1860s residence of Col. George Ware Fulton.

Prior to the Civil War, W. S. Hall slaughtered 11,000 head of cattle just for the hide and tallow, which he shipped to market. After the war, the local cattlemen constructed the Big Wharf, which was a thousand-foot-long, forty-foot-wide ramp whereby cattle could be easily loaded for shipment to eastern markets. Hall figured the livestock were too valuable for such senseless waste, so he built a packery near Rockport. Other ranchers recognized the enormous economic opportunities and joined him.

According to Keith Guthrie, author of *Texas Forgotten Ports*, at least a dozen large packeries and a half-dozen smaller ones were soon operating in the Rockport-Fulton area. Forty men in one plant could process over 200 head of cattle each day.

By 1875, most ranchers were sending their cattle to market via trains. Packinghouses sought out larger cities. As communities, Rockport and Fulton began to fade. People moved away. For a while the shipping business in wool stayed active, but gradually that even folded. The 1888 arrival of the San Antonio & Aransas Pass Railroad could not halt the decline, although it did introduce tourists to one of the most beautiful seaports in America.

Since those heady days, the palatial three-story Fulton Mansion in Fulton, built at a cost of $100,000, has been restored. Today it is a magnificent state historic site.

Rockport attractions include Copano Bay Causeway State Park, a state champion live oak at Goose Island State Park near Rockport, and the Aransas National Wildlife Refuge, twelve miles across the bay from Rockport.

Aransas Pass

Aransas Pass, a gateway city on the mainland, is named for a natural cut, a pass (gap, strait) between nearby Mustang and St. Joseph's islands. This strait is an entrance from the gulf to Aransas Bay, a body of water lying between Matagorda Island and the coast. The town was laid out as Aransas Harbor (Harbor City) in 1835, but it was there largely because nearby Harbor Island had no credible, deepwater outlet to the sea except by way of the strait of Aransas Pass.

The push for a deepwater harbor had its start with the creation of railroads, specifically the Texas-Mexican Railroad, which was chartered in 1875 and absorbed by the Mexican National Railways. Seaborne commodities brought into the city of Aransas Pass would then be transferred by railroad to Mexico. But first the Aransas Pass strait would have to be deepened.

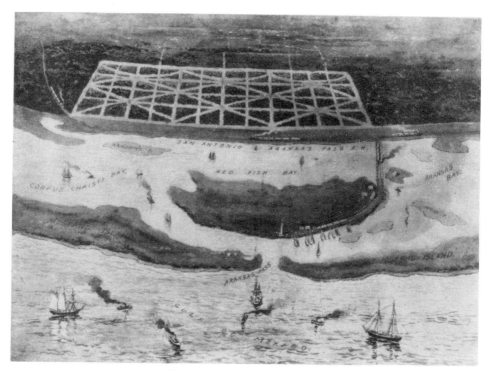

An 1890 engraving of Aransas Pass, Texas, shows Harbor Island and portions of Mustang and St. Joseph's islands. In the background is a proposed plan for the town of Aransas Pass. —The Institute of Texan Cultures

Congress authorized a deepening of Aransas Pass in 1879, but most of the funds allocated went to stop erosion from Mustang Island. In 1890, a private corporation known as the Aransas Harbor City and Improvement Company announced it would deepen the strait, but its real purpose was to sell land. A stampede of settlers took place as thousands entered Aransas Pass and lived in tents while they purchased lots. The scheme finally fell apart and Aransas Pass lost more people than it had taken in.

The Army Corps of Engineers put their talents and skills to work for a deepwater port starting in 1899. They deepened the strait and in the process built a channel across Harbor Island. Material dredged off the gulf floor was piled on Harbor Island, raising the island's surface by eight feet. On September 12, 1912, the ocean liner *Brinkburn* sailed through the strait to Harbor Island, taking 10,000 bales of cotton on board and kicking off a weeklong celebration.

Land speculation again returned to Aransas Pass, but so did hurricanes. One struck in 1916, and another in 1919. Damage was severe each time, and the latter storm led to construction of a seawall.

The Aransas Pass Courthouse. —Frank Leslie, *Illustrated Weekly*, October 18, 1890.

Intense competition now arose between Aransas Pass and Corpus Christi as to who would be *the* deep water port in that vicinity of the gulf. Congress decided in favor of Corpus Christi and in 1922 allocated appropriations for the construction of a first-class harbor and seaport.

Harbor Island became little more than an oil terminal. The city of Aransas Pass declined, only to be rescued by shrimpers. Shrimping and fishing gradually forced an expansion of the harbor. Aransas Pass is now home to the largest shrimp fleet on the Gulf Coast. The Seamen's Memorial Tower pays tribute to fishermen lost at sea.

A causeway (Texas 361) and free ferry connect Aransas Pass with Port Aransas on the north end of Mustang Island. A driving tour of Conn Brown Harbor is a must.

Corpus Christi

Corpus Christi is twenty-two miles southwest of Aransas Pass at the junction of I-37 and US 181. The city lies at the west end of Corpus Christi Bay and is built on two levels: one at sea level, the other on a forty-foot bluff, a precipice seldom recognizable in today's city. Mustang and Padre islands shelter the town from the Gulf of Mexico.

Karankawa Indians once lived here. In 1519 Alonso Alvarez de Piñeda became the first European explorer in the area. Since he arrived on the feast day of Corpus Christi (Body of Christ), he named the bay in Christ's honor. For the next 200 years, the region was sparsely settled by ranchers.

Three centuries later, during the early 1830s, Henry Lawrence Kinney, a Pennsylvania merchant, politician, self-promoter, and adventurer, opened a trading post on the site of today's Corpus Christi. Since it was within the disputed Nueces Strip claimed by both Mexico and Texas, Kinney turned his post into a fort. His private army averaged between forty and sixty stout-hearted types, few of whom were gentlemen.

Although mud flats interrupted oceangoing vessels, lighters (shallow-draft boats) brought a variety of trade items to Corpus Christi, most of which were sold to Texas, Mexico, or one of the various revolutionary or filibustering factions. Gen. Zachary Taylor and his army marched through in 1845, stocked up on Kinney's supplies, and stayed long enough to establish a tent city that became Corpus Christi. Before long Kinney was calling his town the "Naples of the Gulf."

As the community grew, it dreamed of becoming a major seaport. There was talk of a channel across the mud flats that would link up with Aransas Pass. To get money and publicity, Kinney sponsored the first state fair in Texas. It flopped, and the richest man in Texas was now losing his influence as well as his money. He seized San Juan in Nicaragua and was military governor for sixteen days before being forced out. His wife divorced him because of his mistress. An unhappy Kinney died in Matamoros in 1862, victim of a mysterious gunshot.

The Corpus Christi & San Diego Railroad came through in 1873. Stockyards and hideyards arose. Other railroads arrived, and the town became a wool center.

Meanwhile, Aransas Pass and Corpus Christi struggled for deepwater port supremacy—and Corpus Christi won. Thanks in large part to the backing of Richard King, of the King Ranch, Congress in 1922 designated Corpus Christi as the area's port. The harbor deepening was completed in 1926. Toll rates were 25 cents per ton of lead and 50 cents for copper. Horses, mules, and cattle were 40 cents each, and cotton was 5 cents per hundred pounds.

In 1923, the city struck its first natural gas. By the 1930s several oil wells came in, and for the first time Corpus Christi showed signs of becoming a metropolis. Forty thousand airmen trained at the U.S. Naval Air Station in Corpus Christi during World War II.

Since World War II, natural gas and the city's port facilities have turned the economy toward petrochemicals, grain, cotton, ores, seafood, aluminum, glass, and tourism. Instead of being just the "Naples of the Gulf," the town is now also known as the "Sparkling City by the Sea" and the "Texas Riviera."

Corpus Christi attractions include the International Kite Museum, the Museum of Oriental Cultures, and Mustang Island State Park. Cruises on the paddlewheeler *Flagship* are offered around the bay, and tours are available at the U.S. Naval Air Station. At scheduled times, the Texas-Mexican Railway travels the 157 miles between Corpus Christi and Laredo.

Corpus Christi after the 1919 hurricane. —Corpus Christi Public Library

A coastal scene on Padre Island. —The Institute of Texan Cultures

Padre Island

The longest barrier island in the United States is Padre Island. Barrier islands are thin strips of land that protect the mainland from storms. They shield 13 percent of the earth's coastlines.

The Gulf of Mexico lies to the east of Padre Island. Between the mainland and Padre is the Laguna Madre, an enclosed, shallow waterway.

Padre Island is a sandbar extending 113 miles from the mouth of the Rio Grande to Corpus Christi. It includes brief stretches of Park Road 22 at the north end (from Corpus Christi) and Park Road 100 (from Brownsville and Port Isabel) on the south. Casual drivers are advised not to drive the entire length of the island, as much of it is isolated, rugged, and can be traversed only with trepidation even by four-wheel-drive vehicles.

The Laguna Madre (Mother Lagoon) is practically tideless, with only the wind appearing to affect it. Since the evaporation rate is high, the waters are unusually saline. No rivers flow into the lagoon, and only the rain replenishes it. The lagoon is frequently dredged, and fishermen and water enthusiasts enjoy the water.

The Texas shoreline has been developing for sixty million years. Along this arc is a string of barrier islands, and all of these, including Padre Island, were formed in roughly the same way: rivers emptying into the gulf were slowed by the ocean. The river sediment dropped to the bottom, built up, and created islands, all shaped by wind, rain, and tides. The Padre Island dunes, which occasionally reach thirty-five feet in height, are the largest on the Texas coast and migrate up to seven feet per month.

Most of Padre Island's sand consists of quartz, a common rock mineral. Crushed shells form a portion of the mineral sand. Across millions of years, the waves, current, and rain have turned these rocks and shells into tiny granular shapes.

The island averages thirty-seven annual inches of rain, which usually arrives in heavy downpours. While a variety of plants thrive here, including blankets of wildflowers, only the hardy survive the salt spray and ocean winds. Since grazing ended in 1971, bluestem grass has made a comeback.

The Spanish originally charted Padre Island as three islands because two narrow necks were sometimes inundated. In 1766, Diego Ortíz Parilla and twenty-five assistants surveyed the island from north to south. They called the northern part Isla de Corpus Christi and the southern part San Carlos de las Malaguitas.

Karankawas (called Kronks by the Texans) were the original inhabitants. These tall, tattooed people were hunters and gatherers with nomadic lifestyles. They made bows and arrows out of cedar and they built eighteen-foot canoes from logs. Eventually they vanished by rejecting assimilation and becoming victims of Spanish and Texan diseases and swords.

Three out of twenty Spanish galleons—the *Santa María de Yciar, Espíritu Santo,* and *San Esteban*—sailing from Vera Cruz were wrecked on Padre Island in April 1554. Three hundred survivors, including Doña Juana Ponce

A gulfside casino on Padre Island, 1927. —The Institute of Texan Cultures

de León, a lady of great beauty, perished while struggling 350 miles south toward Tampico. Only Fri Marcos de Mena and a grandee named Francisco Vásquez survived.

Marcos de Mena had five arrows in him due to unpleasant Indian behavior. Convinced of his imminent death, the priest dug his own grave and laid down inside it. After a couple days, he decided he was too hungry to die. So he got up and started walking, eventually arriving at Tampico.

Vásquez hid in the hole of a ship and occasionally dodged among sand dunes while awaiting rescue. Although he assisted his saviors with salvage efforts, much of the wreckage and treasure reportedly still lies beneath the silent water or is perhaps covered by sand. The Federal Antiquities Act of 1906 forbids the removal of historical or archaeological items from federal parks.

Spain granted the island to Padre Nicolás Balli in 1800. Although Balli called the place Isla Blanca (White Island), and other explorers called it Islas Blancas (White Islands), mistaking the towering dunes for a chain of small islands, most wayfarers referred to it as Padre Island. By 1811 the padre had established residence and was grazing cattle.

Balli and his nephew built a ranching headquarters on South Padre twenty-five miles from the island's southern tip. Nothing remains of it today.

The last of the Balli family left the island by 1844, and it was next visited by Capt. Ben McCulloch and a company of Texas Rangers. Ranger Lt. George Gordon charted the Laguna Madre.

The island remained deserted until John V. Singer, brother of Isaac Singer, who built the Singer Sewing Machine Company, wrecked the *Alice Sadell* there in 1844. Singer re-established the Balli ranch, buying half the island from Balli's heirs.

Since John Singer could not abide the South, he left the island in 1861. Fearing Confederates might confiscate his money, he allegedly buried $80,000 and his wife's emerald necklace in a screw-top jar beneath a live oak on the ranch. When he returned years later, the area had been swept flat by a hurricane. So far as is known, the money and the necklace are still there.

Ranching partners Richard King and Mifflin Kenedy bought 12,000 acres on Padre Island after the Civil War. An 1880 storm forced them out.

By the 1880s, Patrick Dunn, known as the Duke of Padre Island, had entrenched himself on North Padre Island as a cattle baron. By 1926 he owned most of the land and claimed it with line camps spaced fifteen miles apart. He built a mansion on the northern stump of the island and sold businessman Sam Robertson (a former scout for Gen. John J. Pershing) most of the southern portion. Robertson constructed the Surfside Inn (The Casino), as well as the Twenty-Five Mile Hotel on the island's southern end. Robertson also built a wooden causeway from the mainland to the northern end of the island in 1927.

Robertson went broke during the Great Depression and sold out to brothers Albert and Frank Jones. They lost everything when a storm demolished the causeway in 1932 and blew away most of the island's buildings.

The government used Padre Island for bombing practice during World War II. Between those craters and the cattle (until 1971), most of the island's vegetation disappeared. Lately the grass has been returning.

Today, the primary business of Padre Island is tourism on the north and south extremes of the island. Condominiums, subdivisions, and resorts seem to have taken over, the tourism helped along by the Queen Isabella Causeway, built during the late 1970s. It is the longest bridge in Texas.

Portions of Padre Island, especially where the Singers settled, became Padre Island National Seashore. It extends between the north and south portions of the island, an eighty-mile-long strip of isolated beaches, dunes, tidal flats, and grasslands. It isn't quite like the Karankawa Indians found it, but it's close.

FIVE

Brush Country

Spanish Texas was a successful failure. The missionaries never converted the bulk of the Indian population to Christianity nor made them vassals of the Spanish king; the soldiers never wrestled the land from the native inhabitants; Spanish immigrants did not settle the province in large numbers and turn it into a replica of Spain; and, in the end, the territory slipped away from Spanish control.

Odie B. Faulk, *The Last Years of Spanish Texas*
(Mouton, 1964)

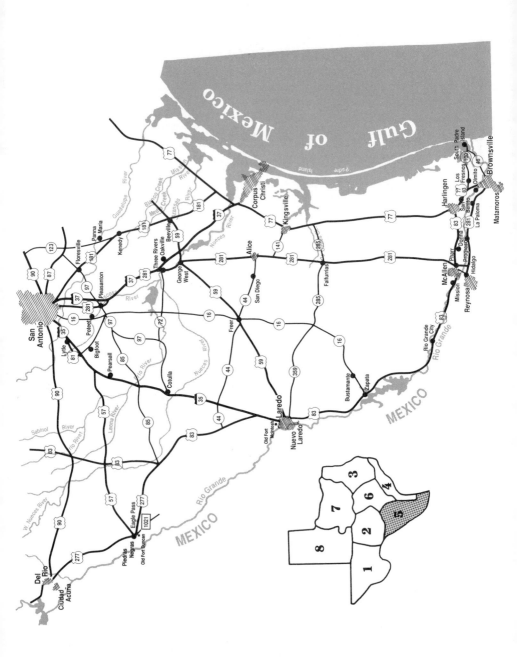

The Brush Country has additional descriptive names: Spanish Texas, South Texas—even Extreme South Texas, meaning the lower Rio Grande Valley. Here, that valley—also called Delta Country—is a part of the Brush Country. As for the term "brush," it is more common among Anglos than Hispanics, who say "chaparral" for the same meaning; usage is a matter of preference and language orientation.

The Nueces River nearly severs the Brush Country in two as it flows across it from west to east. Historically that section of land between the Nueces and the Rio Grande has been called the Nueces Strip; on occasion it has also been referred to it as the Mustang Desert.

The Brush Country contains twenty million acres of subtropical, dryland vegetation. Most of it unfurls south from San Antonio toward the Rio Grande and extends east almost to the coast. The northern boundary of Brush Country runs along US 90 between Del Rio and San Antonio; its northeastern border follows US 181 southeast out of San Antonio until it meets US 77 just north of Corpus Christi; its eastern border is US 77 to Raymondville, then due east along Texas 186 to the Gulf Coast; and its southwestern border is the Rio Grande.

The most recent prehistoric vegetation in the Brush Country consisted primarily of bunchgrass growing amidst post oak, live oak, and mesquite. But early ranchers understood little about sustaining the natural plant life, and most of the bunchgrass died out from being overgrazed. The encompassing brush—mostly mesquite, prickly pear, and dwarf oaks—has grown in dense thickets. A portion of the area has been reseeded with buffalo grass.

Brownsville, Laredo, and especially San Antonio are the Brush Country's chief trading centers. Since the advent of European culture during the early 1700s, South Texas has primarily catered to stock raising with an emphasis on cattle, sheep, horses, and goats.

Citrus, predominantly oranges and grapefruit, covers the southeastern portion of the Brush Country in the lower Rio Grande Valley. The valley is geographically a part of the Brush Country, but irrigation has made it principally agricultural.

During the early 1800s, Lipan Apaches controlled the northern section of the Brush Country while the Coahuiltecans populated the middle and lower

*José de Escandón,
the founder of Laredo.*
—Laredo Public Library

regions. The Coahuiltecans, however, were timid and impoverished. They prevailed neither against the Spanish nor other Indians; in the end they vanished as a people, victims of battle, disease, and assimilation.

When Europeans arrived during the seventeenth and eighteenth centuries, they saw South Texas merely as territory to be crossed in the process of traveling from one point to another. Into this void came José de Escandón, better known as El Conde, the Count. In the 1740s Spain promoted him to lieutenant general and charged him with colonizing the province of Nuevo Santander, today's northeastern Mexico and that area later known as the Nueces Strip.

By 1747 Escandón had proposed settlements on the south bank of the Rio Grande, including Camargo (across from Rio Grande City), Guerrero (near Eagle Pass), and Reynosa (across from McAllen). During this era of conquest, it was no accident that Spanish settlements (except Laredo and Dolores, two flukes of history) kept to the south bank of the Rio Grande. The settlers wanted to remain a part of the Mexican motherland. On the north bank, little stood between the Spanish settlers and eternity except tribes of unfriendly Apaches and Comanches.

Both France and Spain originally claimed Nuevo Santander; however, after the United States purchased Louisiana Territory in 1803, France's influence in the Southwest diminished. Mexico booted out Spain in 1821, leaving just the Americans and the Mexicans struggling for supremacy.

The province of Texas at that time existed north of the Nueces and east of San Antonio. Meanwhile, explorers had lanced across the Rio Grande from Guerrero and laid foundations for El Camino Real, but not the same one that winds near El Paso bound for Santa Fe. The trail through the Texas Brush Country has been called the Broad Road, the Old San Antonio Road, and, more colorfully, the Old Spanish Trail. Although its original starting point was Mexico City, its structure involved crisscrossing routes instead of just one pair of ruts, all of which converged in San Antonio.

Domingo Terán de los Rios, the first Spanish governor of the province of Texas, blazed the trail and crossed the Rio Grande near Eagle Pass in 1691. After pausing in San Antonio, he extended the road to Nacogdoches. The trail also served as a major trade route connecting missions and presidios.

The Nueces Strip evolved into a series of headquarters for huge cattle empires owned by a smattering of rancheros holding land entitlements containing millions of acres. Until 1821, Spain granted most of the land. Then Mexico took over.

The grants succeededed only because of the vaqueros—rugged cowboys with sun-stained skin the color of tobacco juice. They rode for the brands, the hacendados, and the vast feudal landholdings. Vaqueros gave us such traditional cowboy garb as the boots, spurs, hats, chaps, and bandanas. Through them, Spanish words rode into the English language: rodeo, *la reata* (lariat), sombrero, ramada, bronco. American cowboys still call jails by the slang term "hoosegow," for the Spanish *juzgado*.

Gen. Antonio López de Santa Anna, Mexico's president from 1833 to 1836 (and three subsequent times during the 1840s and 1850s), drafted vaqueros and peons into his army as it struggled across the Brush Country to San Antonio, where it conquered the Alamo in 1836. Following that victory, however, Santa Anna met defeat at San Jacinto. The Treaty of Velasco ended the war and granted Texas its independence. But most of the Brush Country remained disputed territory. Texas claimed it as far as the Rio Grande; Mexico disagreed, insisting the new republic's border lay at the Nueces river.

During its nine years as the Lone Star Republic, Texas claimed the Nueces Strip as its own. Both Texas and Mexico invaded it, but neither dominated it— and neither built any communities upon it. When Texas joined the Union on December 29, 1845, a contentious dispute between the two countries over that land between the Nueces and the Rio Grande heated to fever pitch.

The Mexican War at its core was fought to establish jurisdiction over the Nueces Strip. Texas and the United States demanded the Rio Grande as the southern border of the new state and the growing country. If Mexico had conceded just the Nueces Strip, the Americans might have been satisfied with the gain and restrained themselves, temporarily at least, from further conquest. At that time Mexico still owned all or parts of California, Arizona, New Mexico, Nevada, Colorado, and West Texas, but the war changed all that.

Even if Mexico had relinquished the Rio Grande "to its source," the North American map might still be different. There would have been no war, and Mexico, at a bare minimum, would have retained California, Arizona, Nevada, and half of New Mexico and Colorado.

After the war, as discussed in the historical overview ("Gone to Texas") at the front of this book, filibusters exploited Mexican military weakness. They attempted to establish empires for themselves. The Burr conspiracy and the Republic of the Rio Grande were but two examples.

Leander McNelly, Texas Ranger.
—The Institute of Texan Cultures

As the United States took possession of the Brush Country after the Mexican War, and the Rio Grande became accepted by all parties as the legitimate international boundary, additional border issues soon rose to the forefront. In the lower Rio Grande Valley, for instance, the river meandered across the deltalike landscape, continually readjusting its channel. Every time the river changed its course, so did the international boundary. Or did it? Nobody was certain. Understandings and agreements were vague. With surveyors unable to define and mark the *exact* border, pockets of the seesawing river became "no man's land." Outlaws, particularly cattle rustlers and murderers, infested those regions. Mexican bandits, displaced Indians, and revolutionaries made the river thickets and curves unsafe for travelers and area residents.

Leander H. McNelly, a former theology student, formed a group of Texas Rangers and invaded the Brush Country to rout the dangerous inhabitants. McNelly took very few prisoners. His habit of dumping dead outlaws in town plazas proved disconcerting to other badmen, and the desperados holed up in "no man's land" gradually faded away.

When the Treaty of Guadalupe Hidalgo ended the Mexican War in 1848, the United States received generous compensation in the way of lands. But its obligations increased, too. One responsibility called for preventing Indian attacks upon Mexico from the United States.

Congress approved a string of military posts throughout the Brush Country and along or near the Rio Grande: Forts Brown, Ringgold, McIntosh, Duncan. Although the treaty article requiring protection of Mexican citizens from Indians was rescinded a few years later during negotiations of the Gadsden Purchase, the United States Army faced another dilemma: how to prevent Mexico's Indians from raiding Texans in the Brush Country.

After more than two decades of fighting a losing battle, Secretary of War George W. McCrary issued an order on June 1, 1877, to Gen. William Tecumseh Sherman. This order authorized the Army, when in close pursuit, to follow marauders "across the Rio Grande and to overtake and punish them." This led to numerous skirmishes in Mexico between Indians and the United States Army and between Mexican soldiers and the United States Army. The order ceased in the late 1880s, after the Apache leader Geronimo surrendered to the Army in Arizona.

But the problem of a constantly shifting U.S.-Mexico border remained. In 1905 the two countries forged a treaty for the elimination of bancos. These horseshoe bends in the Rio Grande were where most channel changes occurred during floods. The treaty authorized a straight line to be cut across the neck of each bend. Those lands that protruded into the United States or Mexico prior to straightening the channel passed into the possession of that country. The river, and the international boundary, became exact and eliminated outlaw enclaves.

General William Tecumseh Sherman suppressed the Texas Indians just as unmercifully as he had the South. He once said that if he owned Texas and Hell, he would sell Texas and live in Hell.
—National Archives

As law and order returned to the Brush Country, a struggle arose over the legalities of long-standing Mexican land grants. By treaty language these were respected in the United States. But the whole system was chaotic. Some grants had been approved by Spain or Mexico, while others were still in various stages of development. Many grants had been sloppily measured and defined. Several had been abandoned, or sold. Disputes existed among residents over who owned what, and how much. Only a court system could resolve the mess, and while much has been said and written about Hispanics being cheated out of their rightful, legal property, the courts faced substantial dilemmas and made credible decisions. In Texas, most cases did not involve Anglo vs. Hispanic, but Hispanic vs. Hispanic.

Meanwhile, the longhorn came into its own. As soldiers, Indians, rangers, and outlaws fought, thousands of wily longhorns hid in river thickets, all the while interbreeding and producing the world's toughest, meanest cattle. These were wild, ownerless stock, the property of anyone willing to rope and drag them to the branding fire. From there they were driven to market. The rest is history—and legend.

The word "maverick," meaning one who follows his own trail, perhaps even kicking over the traces now and then, arose from these wild cattle. It seems that Samuel Maverick, a lawyer and signatory of the Texas Declaration of Independence, entered the cattle business prior to the Civil War and marked his stock with the MK brand. But he didn't bother branding his original herd, so when a cowboy encountered an unbranded steer, he considered it one of Maverick's, or "a maverick."

A little-known irony grew from the overabundance of cattle in Texas after the Civil War. A cow's hide was worth more than its meat, and its bones were generally ground into fertilizer. Gulf Coast industries processed the hides and tallow, then shipped both to market in New York and New Orleans. The meat usually rotted on Texas rangeland. Only the advent of refrigerated boxcars in 1869 made the meat valuable for shipping after slaughter.

Today, the Brush Country remains one of the least populated areas of Texas. Entire counties have, at best, a few thousand people gathered in isolated towns. Like the El Paso Southwest, the Brush County is predominantly Hispanic in population. But it is still cattle country. It grows some of the finest beef, the best citrus, and the most nutritious vegetables in the world.

I-35

San Antonio—Laredo

154 miles

San Antonio River

The river begins with a cluster of springs just north of San Antonio. Some two hundred miles east of there it joins the Guadalupe River.

Alvar Núñez Cabeza de Vaca crossed the San Antonio River in 1535. Alonso de León called it Arroyo de León in 1689, but in 1691 Domingo Terán de los Rios named it San Antonio de Padua.

The mission of San Antonio de Valero was established on the east bank of the river in 1718, while the presidio of San Antonio de Bexar stood on the opposite bank. San Antonio thereafter became the principal city in Texas partly because of the plentiful water. Goliad was established along the river, as were various *empresario* grants.

During the Texas war for independence, numerous engagements took place alongside the river: the Alamo, Grass Fight, Siege of Bexar, Battle of Concepción, and Goliad.

The San Antonio River in Brackenridge Park, August 1936. —The Institute of Texan Cultures

By 1939 San Antonio began beautifying the riverbanks and eventually built along fifteen miles of the river as it flows through the city. The San Antonio River Walk and the Alamo are two of the most popular tourist sites in Texas.

San Antonio

In 1970 historian and writer Charles Ramsdell described San Antonio as "not well ordered, not wholly beautiful, not wholly anything. It is, and has been always, a meeting place, on the verge between France and Spain, between Spain and England, between the Indian and the white, between the South and West, the old and the new."

In short, San Antonio has always been, and remains, a city of contradictions. It lacks the oil wealth of Houston, the financial strength and professional football team of Dallas, the political sophistication of Austin, the cow town relaxation of Fort Worth, the remoteness of Lubbock and Amarillo, and the aloofness of El Paso. But it attracts more tourists than any town in the state.

Although 150 miles from Mexico, San Antonio calls itself a border town. Although 150 miles also from the ocean (at Corpus Christi), San Antonio's Sea

San Juan Capistrano Mission, San Antonio. —The Institute of Texan Cultures

World could lead one to think it has a world-class beach. The San Antonio River flowing along the River Walk is dinky and trivial by non-Texas standards, yet tourists flock from everywhere just to ride upon its waters. The Alamo is a constant storm center of controversy, a shadow of its former size. But in Texas, the Alamo is hallowed ground.

Domingo Terán de los Rios, the first Spanish governor of Texas, recorded in his diary on June 12, 1691: "We camped on the banks of a stream adorned by a great stand of trees. I named it San Antonio de Padua because we reached it on his day." Thus was born the city of San Antonio. Of course, nobody lived there for a while. The christening came a quarter-century later when, on May 1, 1718, Governor Martín de Alarcón formally founded the adobe mission called San Antonio de Valero. Since there was no such thing as a Spanish mission without Indians, this one catered to the Pamaya, Jarame, and Payaya who lived nearby. The tag "de Valero" honored the marquís of Valero, the viceroy of Mexico. Today this mission is called the Alamo.

The Spanish also built Fort San Antonio de Bexar (pronounced "Bear"), to protect the mission from marauding Apaches and Comanches. Other missions constructed in San Antonio during the 1700s were San Antonio de Concepción, Espada, San José, and San Juan Capistrano.

A hurricane destroyed the Valero mission in 1724, and it was rebuilt in what is now Alamo Plaza. Nearly three hundred Indians lived there. Fifty years later, in 1793, with secularization, the priests and Indians were gone and troops took up quarters in the former church. A stand of cottonwoods (alamo trees) grew in the immediate vicinity, and these trees likely gave the Alamo its name. The city's first hospital (1807-1812) was the Alamo's "Long Barracks." Another barracks, the "Low Barracks," stood along the south wall, originally a mission granary.

Two hundred Spanish residents and six hundred Indians lived at or near the Alamo Plaza and the Mission San José. On March 9, 1731, sixteen families of Canary Islanders moved to the city. Their descendants are everywhere. On the ninth day of each March the Cathedral of San Fernando holds a requiem in their memory.

José Bernardo Gutiérrez de Lara, a sketch by José Cisneros. —The Institute of Texan Cultures

San Antonio, circa 1840. —The Institute of Texan Cultures

Lt. Zebulon Montgomery Pike, twenty-eight years old and perhaps the first American to visit San Antonio, arrived on June 7, 1807. He had been captured by Mexican forces in New Mexico while wandering next to the Rio Grande when he was supposed to be surveying the headwaters of the Red River. Pike spent seven days in San Antonio before returning to the United States. San Antonio had about 2,000 residents then, mostly living in grass-roofed adobe houses.

In March 1813 the city fell to an 800-man filibustering expedition led by Gutiérrez de Lara and Samuel Kemper. Gutiérrez was born in the Mexican state of Tamaulipas, while Kemper, a Virginian, signed on with Gutiérrez to lead the American volunteers. The victors soon argued with one another, however, and the occupation disintegrated.

The 1820s were the years of Stephen F. Austin. He and other *empresarios* received permission from Texas Governor Antonio María Martínez in San Antonio to bring American emigrants into Texas. Within fifteen years the Americans began considering independence, so Mexican President Santa Anna sent his brother-in-law, Gen. Martín de Cós, to occupy San Antonio and show the flag.

Three hundred Texas rebels surrounded San Antonio and rallied under Ben Milam, who delivered a rousing speech arguing that while Texans squatted in the miserable rain, warm brothels less than two miles away beckoned them. Milam finally led his followers inside the town. In December

239

1835 the Texans charged, but Milam, the only casualty, died from a musket ball. Cós retreated into the Alamo, where he later surrendered.

Most of the victors marched south for an assault on Matamoros. After reaching Goliad, however, they reconsidered their options and ceased their advance.

Meanwhile, Santa Anna gathered his army and began marching north from Mexico. To counter that assault, Sam Houston, commander of the Texas forces, sent James Bowie and thirty-one volunteers to San Antonio on January 19, 1836. Their mission was to destroy the Alamo so the Mexicans could not occupy it. Instead of obeying orders, however, Bowie decided to defend the Alamo.

In February the frustrated Houston sent William Barret Travis and thirty Texas regulars to destroy the Alamo. Travis also disobeyed his commander. He would stand and fight. By the middle of the month, sixteen Tennessee Mounted Volunteers rode into San Antonio to support its defenders. Among them was Davy Crockett, a renowned politician, bear hunter, and storyteller.

Benjamin Rush Milam, slain during the 1835 battle of San Antonio.
—Archives Division, Texas State Library

Portrait of Jim Bowie.
—Texas State Archives

General Santa Anna's vanguard entered San Antonio on February 23 and shortly afterwards raised the flag of No Quarter. Roughly 170 Texas rebels, plus 15 noncombatants, took refuge inside the Alamo.

Bowie and Travis quarreled over leadership, but Bowie also fought ill health, probably diphtheria, and ended up in bed never to recover. Travis assumed command by default.

The Alamo complex occupied four acres. In the weeks prior to Santa Anna's arrival, the Americans made little effort to strengthen their defensive positions along the forts crumbling walls. Evidently they expected reinforcements. As the Mexican Army tightened its iron siege, Travis wrote one of the most dramatic messages in military history. He addressed it to the "people of Texas and all Americans in the world."

> *I am besieged by a thousand or more Mexicans under Santa Anna. I have sustained a continual bombardment for 24 hours and have not lost a man. The enemy has demanded our surrender, otherwise the*

William Barret Travis.
—Texas State Archives

garrison will be put to the sword. I have answered the demand with a cannon shot, and our flag still waves proudly from the walls. I shall not surrender nor retreat. I call upon you in the name of liberty, patriotism and everything dear to the American character, to come to our aid. The enemy is receiving reinforcements daily and will no doubt increase to three or four thousand within four or five days. I am determined to sustain myself as long as possible and die like a soldier. Victory or death.

Travis dispatched perhaps a dozen couriers over the next few days, most of whom never returned. On February 27, thirty-one men from Gonzales, Texas, cut their way through Mexican lines and entered the Alamo. They were the only reinforcements.

As Santa Anna slowly tightened his grip, those inside the Alamo realized that they would stand alone and the old mission would become their gravestone. Travis called everyone into the courtyard. He explained the hopeless situation and offered any who wanted out an opportunity to leave. But he needed to be sure of those who chose to remain, so he drew a line in the sand with his sword and asked all who would stand with him to cross over. Bowie was carried over on his litter. Only the Frenchman Louis Rose, a member of Bowie's volunteers, slipped over the wall. He died fifteen years later in Louisiana.

Except for sporadic small arms fire and occasional cannonading, the fighting had a lackadaisical quality during much of the struggle. But on March

242

The Alamo, 1829. —The Library of the Daughters of the Republic of Texas at the Alamo

The final battle of the (re-created) Alamo was fought right here near Bracketville, Texas, with John Wayne as Davy Crockett in 1959. Five thousand men worked one year and eleven months building the replica, the stockade, and the little town of San Antonio. —Happy Shahan's Alamo Village

6, after thirteen days of siege, at four o'clock in the morning, the Mexicans charged. Their band played the haunting "Deguello," a reminder of no quarter. A sheet of rifle fire belched from the walls, and, for a moment, the Mexican line buckled, then wavered, then pressed forward again. Mexican soldiers breached the northwest wall and within an hour, perhaps less, the battle ended. Travis died early in the fighting. Bowie was bayonetted on his sickbed.

By Texas accounts, Davy Crockett was the last to fall, and he went down swinging his trusty rifle. By Mexican accounts, Crockett and four others surrendered. Santa Anna ordered them tortured and executed.

In all, 185 defenders died at the Alamo during the final battle. Santa Anna spared two of the wounded survivors, one Hispanic and one black slave. One unidentified man died later of his wounds. Of the fifteen women and children noncombatants inside the chapel, two died during the fight; the others were released. Unknown are the losses among Santa Anna's troops. Probably they totalled a few hundred rather than the widely reported thousands.

Santa Anna led his forces east in search of Gen. Sam Houston. The two armies collided about six weeks later at San Jacinto (near present-day

Mexican General and President Antonio López de Santa Anna, a self-serving and ultimately tragic figure.
—Texas State Archives

General Adrian Woll. —The Institute of Texan Cultures

Houston), where the Texans defeated the Mexican Army and captured Santa Anna. The Battle of San Jacinto essentially made Texas into a republic.

Meanwhile, Texas forces ineptly invaded Mexico, and the Mexican regulars made frequent incursions into Texas. Down in Mexico City, Santa Anna still smouldered over his Texas humiliation. He sent Gen. Rafael Vásquez and a force of nearly four hundred to attack and occupy San Antonio. But Vásquez found the town practically deserted in that early March of 1842, so his troops looted what they could and after two days retired toward the Rio Grande.

In the months that followed, Lt. Col. Ramón Valera brushed against the outskirts of San Antonio but did not enter the city. Col. Antonio Canales, instrumental in the defunct Republic of the Rio Grande fiasco (see Laredo), swung near the Nueces River, clashed frequently with Texas forces, then headed for the Rio Grande and safety. Finally, Adrian Woll, a Frenchman and former aide-de-camp to Santa Anna, recruited over a thousand men for an invasion and conquest of San Antonio. The attack commenced in September 1842. Woll took the town and defended it twice against counterattacks. Still, the forces marshalling against him were gathering strength. So after ten days, the last and longest period San Antonio was ever be held by Mexico, the occupation army vanished.

The Comanches, however, had been raiding San Antonio unremittingly. Yet, it was they who tired first and sought peace. Three leaders of the Southern Comanches appeared at San Antonio in January 1840 and requested a council. The Texans told the Indians to bring all of their white captives to the "Council House" (courthouse) on March 19.

Hugh McLeod and William G. Cooke headed the Texas delegation. They were supported by three companies of infantry. Only sixty-five Comanches attended, including twelve warriors and twelve chiefs; the rest were mostly women and children.

As a demonstration of good faith, the Indians released Matilda Lockhart. Two years earlier, at age thirteen, she and four of Mitchell Putnam's children had been captured and taken to Comanche strongholds in the Guadalupe Mountains. Settlers had made two unsuccessful expeditions to rescue them. Matilda said her captors raped and beat her repeatedly. Her body bore scars, bruises, and severe burns. Mary Maverick, who supported Matilda upon her release, wrote that "both nostrils were wide open, denuded of flesh."

The Indians insisted Matilda Lockhart was their only white captive, but she claimed the Indians planned to release others one at a time for ransom. McLeod and Cooke demanded the release of the Putnam children and other captives, and, when the Indians stalled, the troops attempted to place the Comanches under arrest until they complied with their demands.

A skirmish known as the Council House Fight ensued, resulting in the deaths of seven whites and thirty-five Indians, including all the chiefs. Twenty-eight Indian women and children plus two old men were taken into custody. The Texans sent one of the Indian women to announce their terms to the other Comanches, and this apparently resulted in freedom for two or three of the white captives. Accounts of this incident vary, though, and some say the Southern Comanches, furious over a perceived lack of good faith shown by the whites, put thirteen of their captives to death. Years of bitter recriminations among whites and Indians alike prolonged the Indian Wars in Texas by another three decades.

Later in the 1840s, during the Mexican War, San Antonio remained relatively tranquil. The same held true during the Civil War. When it commenced in 1861, Gen. David Twiggs, from his federal headquarters in San Antonio, ordered all military posts in Texas surrendered to state authorities. The fighting never reached San Antonio.

The Galveston, Harrisburg & San Antonio Railroad reached San Antonio in 1877 and overnight changed this tiny outpost into a city. Gas lights and telephone service began operating in 1882. Sarah Bernhardt called San Antonio the "art center of Texas" in 1887. Three years later residents could travel across the city on electric streetcars.

General David E. Twiggs.
—U.S. Army Military History Institute

Although San Antonio is known predominantly for the Alamo, the River Walk, and its Spanish-Mexican character, it is known only slightly less as one of the world's great military towns. During the Spanish and Mexican periods, San Antonio functioned as a seat of military power. Then, in 1873, the United States Congress created a headquarters military post at San Antonio to serve as a supply and rendezvous depot for forts along the border as well as the frontier.

Construction began in 1875 on the 92-acre site. By 1876 workers had completed a quadrangle, and ten years later fifteen sets of officers quarters stood on the grounds. In 1890 the post received the name Fort Sam Houston, and it remains the oldest active post in San Antonio.

The fort has seen its share of famous visitors and residents. In December 1885 and January 1886 the quadrangle held Apache leaders Geronimo and Natchez, along with thirty-one men, women, and children, before the army shipped them to Fort Pickens, Florida. During the Spanish-American War, Col. Leonard Wood and Theodore Roosevelt trained Rough Riders at the fort.

247

Colonel Theodore Roosevelt and two of his Rough Riders in front of Concepcion Mission, San Antonio, Texas, 1898. —The Institute of Texan Cultures

They remained about a month before transferring on to Florida. And 1st Lt. Dwight D. Eisenhower was stationed at Fort Sam Houston when he met Mamie Geneva Doud, who lived in Colorado but had come to San Antonio on vacation. They married on July 1, 1916, and lived briefly on the post in a two-room apartment with no kitchen.

The U.S. military also launched its air force from Fort Sam Houston. The army's first airplane arrived in seventeen boxes in 1910. This biplane, purchased from the Wright brothers, flew 150 feet off the ground. By 1915 the United States Army Air Corps (actually the aviation section of the Signal Corps) had grown to include six planes, all housed at Fort Sam Houston. These aircraft went with Black Jack Pershing a year later to chase Pancho Villa in Chihuahua, Mexico, during the Punitive Expedition. The first airborne maneuvers were conducted at Fort Sam Houston in 1942. The triangular form of the infantry division was also perfected there.

San Antonio's Kelly Air Force Base, named for Lt. George E. M. Kelly, the first military pilot ever killed in an aircraft accident (in 1911), served as a repair and supply depot. It employed the largest single number of civilians in the Southwest. Charles Lindbergh received flight training here, and Jimmy Doolittle stopped by when he spanned the continent for the first time in daylight hours.

Lackland Air Force Base once involved so many people that it held the distinction of being the largest air force reservation in the United States. As a basic training facility, most air force personnel pass through its gates at one time or another. This writer spent three months there as a private in basic training from June to August 1948.

Other military installations in the San Antonio area include Brooks Air Force Base, known for its School of Aviation Medicine, and Randolph Air Force Base, better known as Randolph Field, which is headquarters for the Air Training Command (ATC).

Tourists visiting San Antonio today can choose from a variety of historical and entertaining pastimes. The Alamo is the heart of downtown.

Paseo del Rio (the River Walk) is best approached from the Commerce Street Bridge, although the river is accessible from any downtown bridge. The approximately two-mile walk passes shops, restaurants, theaters, tropical trees, and shrubbery. You can rent a variety of boats, or you can simply stroll along the walk, pausing at whatever interests you.

La Villita or "the Neighborhood" is an architectural wonderland. It opens at the corner of Villita and South Presa and extends for several blocks. Inside are lush tropical plants, restored mansions, and life out of another time and place.

The Main Plaza features the San Fernando Cathedral, whereas the Military Plaza focuses on the Spanish Governor's Palace. Near the plazas are the First Presbyterian Church, the Old Ursuline Convent, the Nat Lewis House, and the First National Bank. The bank is representative of the 1880s.

Germantown stretches along King William and Washington streets. If you like early Victorian architecture, you'll enjoy the King William area. Also worth seeing are the Steves Homestead, the Irish Flat, and the famous Menger Hotel.

Brackenridge Park has a touring train with stations at Witte Museum, the San Antonio Zoo, the Oriental Sunken Gardens, and the Texas Pioneer and Trail Drivers Memorial Hall.

Nobody should leave San Antonio without visiting the Buckhorn Hall of Horns. "Old Tex" has a spread of eight feet. A deer antler displays seventy-eight points, a world record. Allow plenty of time to see this collection that started way back in 1884.

The list of things to see and do in San Antonio is endless, including Sea World, the Institute of Texan Cultures, military bases, art museums, universities, Mexican fiestas, and parks. It's difficult to get bored in San Antonio.

Lytle, Bigfoot, Pearsall, Cotulla

Some twenty or so miles southwest of San Antonio along I-35 is Lytle, which began as a ranch and blossomed briefly as a rail center. It lost momentum when the rails left.

Bigfoot, east of the interstate on Farm Road 462, is named for the famed Texas Ranger William A. A. "Bigfoot" Wallace, who spent his last years here. A small museum in town features Bigfoot relics.

Pearsall started in 1880 with the arrival of railroads, but is better known for the wanderings of the Frenchman La Salle searching for Spanish settlements in 1685. Today this area produces over fifty million pounds of peanuts annually.

Cotulla, named for Polish immigrant Joseph Cotulla, is a crossroads in Texas history, specifically those treks of the Spanish and French. Local legend claims that a thousand mustangs were once rounded up near here to fulfill an Argentine contract.

Laredo

In 1755, when this region was part of the Spanish province of Nuevo Santander, the man responsible for colonizing northeastern Mexico, José de Escandón, granted Thomás Sánchez fifteen leagues of land for a ranch. Seven years later a mission opened to Christianize the Indians, and the settlement that grew around it became Villa de San Agustin de Laredo, named for a coastal village in Santander, Spain.

The Mexican president and general of its army, Antonio López de Santa Anna, passed through here in 1836 en route to the showdown at the Alamo, and Manuel Gonzáles entertained Santa Anna in his Laredo home.

Nearly three years later, on November 5, 1838, Mexican attorney Antonio Canales and Col. Antonio Zapata declared opposition to the central government. Laredo joined the revolution the following summer, and Texans Reuben Ross and S. W. Jordan recruited 180 volunteers by promising each man $25 a month, a half league of land, and all the booty each could carry. This little army shot up northern Mexico, winning the battles of Guerrero, Mier, and Alcantro Creek. The revolutionaries could have taken Matamoros and Monterrey but for the hesitation of Canales. Ross and Jordan abandoned Mexico in 1840.

Canales responded by creating the Republic of the Rio Grande early in 1840, with Laredo as its capital. The republic included Coahuila, Nuevo Leon, Tamaulipas, and today's lower Rio Grande Valley of Texas, although a subsequent convention added New Mexico, Chihuahua, Durango, and Zacatecas. Canales devised a flag, wrote a constitution, appointed a president, and named himself commander in chief of the military.

Gen. Mariano Arista rushed north with a Centralist army from Mexico City, however, and effectively spiked the new republic. Arista marched into Laredo on March 19, 1840, driving Canales to Lipantitlan on the Nueces River, where the fledgling military commander tried desperately to convince the Republic of Texas to team up with the Republic of the Rio Grande. President Mirabeau Lamar refused any alliance, but Canales convinced Col. Samuel W. Jordan, Col. Luis López, and Capt. John T. Price to lend support. They recaptured Laredo in late July. Jordan, López, and Juan Nepomuceno Molano then moved south from Rio Grande City to conquer Guerrero, Mier, and Camargo before turning into the Mexican interior, capturing Victoria, and heading for Saltillo. But López and Molano betrayed their comrades.

The Texans shot their way out of the trap and retreated toward Laredo, arriving in late October. By that time Canales had decided to embrace the Centralists. The Texans went home and the Republic of the Rio Grande went out of business on November 6. According to historian Jerry Thompson, it "lasted 283 violent, tumultuous days."

As Texas and Mexico quarreled over ownership of the Nueces Strip, Mexican outlaws made the territory their special marauding zone. To counter the turbulence, Texas organized additional rangers for fighting Indians and Mexicans. One of them was Jack "Coffee" Hays, who came to Texas from Tennessee after his parents died of yellow fever. He missed the Battle of San Jacinto by only a few days. But by early April 1841, he was marching on Laredo, clashing with strong Mexican military forces. At the Battle of San Ignacio, a ranch on the San Antonio-Laredo Road, a running fight extended to Laredo. The rangers captured it.

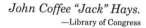

John Coffee "Jack" Hays.
—Library of Congress

Santos Benavides was Laredo's most famous citizen. Born in 1827, he became Laredo's mayor and then chief justice of Webb County. During the Civil War he commanded a company of Texas state troops that tangled with bandit and politician Juan Cortina. Benavides surprised Cortina sacking the tiny Texas community of Carrizo, and he drove the Mexican renegades south across the Rio Grande. The Confederacy later authorized a Benavides Regiment and promoted Benavides to brigadier general, the highest rank held by a Hispanic during the war. A joint session of the Texas legislature thanked Benavides for his defense of the border.

Meanwhile, Laredo had trouble getting its political house in order. The elite, a coalition of old but wealthy families, had retained political control for so long that they believed such powers were ordained. By the 1880s, a reform movement demanded change. The old guard, called the Botas (Boots), were

Santos Benavides.
—Eugene C. Barker Texas History Center, UT Austin

The Laredo City Hall and Market House with Mexican carts in front, circa 1890. —The Institute of Texan Cultures

politically opposed by the Guaraches (Sandals). The latter were poor, generally, but many of their leaders were disenchanted Botas.

According to Jerry D. Thompson in his *Warm Weather & Bad Whiskey*, the sanguinary bloodletting started during the elections of April 7, 1886. A victorious political parade and rally was meandering drunkenly through the center of town when shooting started from the roofs and streets. A cannon fired a couple salvos. The carnage ended with between sixteen and thirty dead. Fort McIntosh intervened to halt the bloodletting.

Francisco Madero, who later became president of Mexico, attempted to ignite the 1910 Mexican Revolution from across the Rio Grande in Nuevo Laredo (New Laredo) and failed. Laredo was second to El Paso in border importance during the 1910-20 Mexican Revolution. As a prominent border crossing and Mexican entry point, Laredo's railroads and imports attracted attention. Throughout the revolution, Laredo remained a focal point for intrigue and controversy.

The Laredo Army Air Field opened in November 1942 and had 14,000 personnel and 250 aircraft. A gunnery school operated there and closed in 1946. In 1950 the base merged with the Laredo Municipal Airport.

Laredo is presently known for its history, its underground gas discoveries, its irrigated farming, and its Mexican port of entry. Like most border towns, Laredo has invested heavily in tourism and the maquila industry.

Nobody visiting Laredo should miss the restored Fort McIntosh with its Nuevo Santander Museum. The Republic of the Rio Grande Building has been restored in Laredo. The San Augustine Church, built in 1772, is open to visits. Finally, the Texas-Mexican Railway (Tex-Mex Railway) has a scheduled 157-mile run to Corpus Christi and back.

Fort McIntosh opened as Camp Crawford on March 3, 1849, and received its present name on January 7, 1850. The new name honored Lt. Col. James McIntosh, killed during the Mexican War battle of Molino del Rey in 1847. The fort's first permanent buildings were constructed in 1868. During World War II the post trained mechanized infantry troops. The doors closed in 1946. Today the very fine and worthwhile Nuevo Santander Museum occupies some of the structures while others are educational buildings for the Laredo Junior College.

Eagle Pass

Eagle Pass is northwest of Laredo, near the junction of US 57 and US 277. Because Eagle Pass is just across the Rio Grande from Piedras Negras (Black Rocks), Coahuila, it is a significant Mexican port of entry with access to Saltillo, San Luis Potosi, and Mexico City.

This Texas village started in 1849 as Camp Eagle Pass, and it became Fort Duncan that same year. In 1850, Henry Matson opened a saloon in a borrowed tent outside the post doorway, and a surveyor named the subsequent town El Paso del Aguila (Eagle Pass).

Main Street in Eagle Pass, Texas, 1890. —The Institute of Texan Cultures

Fleeing slaves often crossed into Mexico from Eagle Pass, as did renegade Indians, especially Kickapoos. In 1855 Texas Ranger Capt. James Hughes Callahan led 115 men into Mexico. They claimed to be chasing Indians, although historians suspect they sought runaway slaves. A rising river blocked Callahan's retreat and he burned Piedras Negras as a diversion while he escaped. This clumsy escapade cost the United States $50,000 in claims.

During the Civil War, Eagle Pass was a gateway for Texas cotton. Huge wagons rumbled southeast to the Matamoros port of Bagdad.

When the Civil War ended, the last unsurrendered Confederate force, roughly a thousand men led by Gen. Joe Shelby, rode through Eagle Pass and entered Mexico, burying its rebel flag in the Rio Grande. The flag episode has since become known as the "grave of the Confederacy incident." The soldiers marched to Mexico City, where French Emperor Maximilian refused their services but did set aside the province of Carlotta for the homeless men to colonize.

The Eagle Pass Army Air Field opened in June 1942. It gave single-engine training to aviation cadets. The post was abandoned in 1945.

Downstream on the Mexican side about twenty-five miles is the village of Guerrero. During the early 1700s, Guerrero launched the Spanish occupation of Texas. The old Camino Real left the Rio Grande at Guerrero and carried the banners of empire across Texas. Guerrero laid the foundation for San Antonio and Nacogdoches.

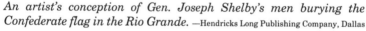

An artist's conception of Gen. Joseph Shelby's men burying the Confederate flag in the Rio Grande. —Hendricks Long Publishing Company, Dallas

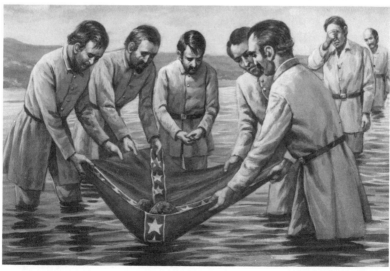

Kickapoo Indians

Eagle Pass is home to a unique people originating in Wisconsin during the 1840s, but who were gradually displaced to Illinois and then to the Sabine River. Following Texas independence, one group went north to the reservation in Indian Territory, while the others settled forty miles south of Eagle Pass at Morelos, Coahuila.

Until the 1870s, the Kickapoos not only guarded the Mexican border against American raiders (including Indians) coming south, but they repeatedly staged their own thrusts into Texas. One Texan described cattle raids by Kickapoos as "beyond belief."

All this ended when Col. Ranald Mackenzie charged across the Rio Grande in 1873. His forces destroyed Kickapoo villages and captured so many women and children that those Kickapoos escaping the army's onslaught packed up and voluntarily entered the reservation in Oklahoma. They had to just to see their families again.

Hundreds of Kickapoos gradually returned to Mexico, however, although by the 1940s they had again entered the United States. This time they were migrant workers.

The Kickapoos built a squatter settlement of wood and cardboard under the international bridge at Eagle Pass during the 1960s. Here their public plight was a dilemma for both countries. The Americans could not get them to return to Oklahoma reservations, and the Mexican government could not coax them to settle in Mexico.

Finally, in the 1980s, the U.S. government surrendered. The Texas Kickapoos obtained federal recognition during the 1980s, as well as a 125-acre reservation south of Eagle Pass on Farm-to-Market Road 1021. Even so, the reservation is primarily a summer home. The Kickapoos generally spend the winter in El Nacimiento, a village near the headwaters of the Rio Sabinas, eighty miles southwest of Eagle Pass.

Fort Duncan

This key border post was established on March 27, 1849. Most buildings were of native sandstone. Buffalo soldiers of the 9th Cavalry served here after the Civil War and were led in Mexican forays by Capt. John Bullis and Lt. Col. William Shafter. After the border troubles ceased, the post became an Eagle Pass city park and country club. Several buildings have been restored.

San Antonio—Zapata
201 miles

Poteet, Freer, Bustamante

Poteet is known as the "Strawberry Capital of Texas," and the town proudly displays a giant strawberry monument that is seven feet tall and weighs 1,600 pounds. Freer was once the most prosperous town in South Texas, primarily because in 1933 it had one of the largest oil fields in the United States. Bustamante started as a ranch headquarters for Don Pedro Bustamante in 1802, except that Don Pedro called his place "Las Comitas," named for a dark-skinned fruit similar to the persimmon. Comanches burned the ranch in 1820, but another structure replaced it. The building still stands.

Zapata

This village was settled about 1770 by residents of Guerrero, Mexico. They called the tiny village Carrizo because of the Carrizo Indians who originally lived here.

In honor of Col. Antonio Zapata, and because his descendants owned most of the land, Carrizo was renamed Zapata on May 2, 1901. The county name also became Zapata.

Antonio Zapata was born in poverty at Guerrero, but he eventually accumulated a fortune in sheep. He became a well-known businessman, a determined Indian fighter, and a Mexican Federalist who advocated a strong Mexican government as laid out by the 1824 constitution.

When Federalists attacked the Centralists in December 1837, it seemed northern Mexico might be freed from the Centralist yoke. Zapata was second in command to Antonio Canales, although Zapata was the more aggressive fighter. Canales consulted spirits and waited for the Centralists to run out of ammunition. Ironically, it was Zapata who ran out of ammunition. In March 1840, he and thirty men were trapped at Santa Rita de Morelos upriver from Laredo. The gallant Zapata surrendered, only to be told that he would be killed if he did not join the Centralists. Zapata refused. Then he was asked to refuse further cooperation with the Federalists. Again Zapata refused.

The army executed Zapata, severed his head, and floated it in a cask of brandy. The head was displayed in Laredo, then placed on a stake in Guerrero for three days as a warning not only to Zapata's family, but to other Federalists.

Two years later, Texas Gen. Alexander Somervell briefly occupied Carrizo while 300 other Texans crossed the river into Mexico, raided Guerrero, then confiscated boats at Carrizo and floated downriver to attack Mier. The raiders were captured and numerous executions followed. During a forced lottery, prisoners who drew black beans from a jar were summarily shot.

Thereafter the village drifted dreamily until 1953, when presidents Dwight D. Eisenhower and Adolfo Ruíz Cortines dedicated Falcon Dam. Washington had already relocated Zapata's 2,000 residents, along with the people of the villages of Falcon and Lopeno, plus twenty-four cemeteries, to higher ground. Workmen built a new Zapata, including a modern courthouse on a 846-acre site.

In 1954, Falcon Dam restrained the largest flood on record. Thundering waters rumbled out of the Devils and Pecos rivers, inundating Del Rio and Laredo. American boundary commissioner Joseph Friedkin described the devastation as sickening, but he was impressed and gratified when, from the air, Friedkin watched dark and muddy waters rolling to a standstill at Falcon Dam. Beyond that dam, the scene was tranquil.

I-37
San Antonio—Oakville
82 miles

Pleasanton, Three Rivers, Oakville

A statue in Pleasonton's city plaza proclaims the town as the birthplace of the cowboy. In 1858 the town was named for Col. John Pleasants, who served in the Texas war for independence. The town's other claim to fame is the Longhorn Museum. As for Three Rivers, it began as Hamiltonburg, but became Three Rivers in 1913 because the Atascosa, Frio, and Nueces rivers meet here. The town is rich in oil and uranium. Then there's Oakville. It was a junction for the San Antonio-Corpus Christi stage in 1879.

George West—Lower Rio Grande Valley

George West

In 1861, George Washington West bought 2,000 acres and created the George West Ranch. In 1912, after putting up $100,000 and encouraging the railroad to come through, he developed a town site known as George West. The community built a hotel and school, then added water, a sewer system, and a fire department. Two bridges crossed the Nueces. The railroad came through, and in 1919 George West became the county seat.

Incidentally, your chances of encountering a tornado near George West are pretty slim—next to nothing, the experts believe. But fifteen miles southwest of town, on US 59, on May 10, 1959, a tornado crossed the road. In doing so, it literally blew a 300-foot stretch of pavement off the highway.

Alice

The San Antonio & Aransas Pass Railroad built a depot here in 1888 and the resulting town was first called Bandana, then Kleberg. In 1904, the name changed to Alice in honor of Alice King Kleberg, daughter of Richard King of the King Ranch. Originally the town catered to livestock interests, and it thrived as the world's largest cattle shipping center in spite of a fire that destroyed the business section in 1909. By the early 1920s, Alice was better known for its melons and fruits. Then oil was discovered during the early 1930s, and Alice became a hub of the petroleum business.

Alice is now known for its scientific livestock breeding. The Beefmaster breed of cattle was developed here.

The South Texas Museum is in Alice.

Falfurrias

Falfurrias was founded in 1883 by developer Edward Lasater. He claimed the name meant "Land of Heart's Delight," the "Heart's Delight" referring to a prominent local desert flower. The town was a starting point for cattle drives along the Chisholm and Western trails. Lasater owned one of the world's largest herds of Jersey milk cows. In 1909 he opened a creamery that still produces high-quality milk and butter. He also entered politics, and in doing so fought with South Texas political bosses Manuel Guerra and Archie Parr. The echoes of those battles still extend across Texas.

Tom Lasater, one of Edward's descendants, wrote *The Lasater Philosophy of Cattle Raising*. It argues against most conventional ranching theories. Lasater eliminated the practices of implanting feedlot cattle with hormones and spraying livestock for flies. He also stopped dehorning cattle, using insecticides, and killing rattlesnakes, coyotes, prairie dogs, and locoweeds. Lasater's theory was that weak cattle would eliminate themselves. Livestock, left to their own resources, would be healthier and better for it. The *Lasater Philosophy* remains a best-selling book for Texas Western Press at the University of Texas at El Paso.

San Diego

This little brush country community is located ten miles west of Alice on Texas 44. The town was organized about 1858, but it is best known for the 1914 "Plan of San Diego," a scheme that still has historians arguing over its validity. A group of German agents plotted in San Diego, Texas, and supposedly called for a Hispanic uprising on February 20, 1915. Throughout South Texas, every Anglo male over sixteen would be assassinated. Mexico would be united in a "holy" war against the United States, and the "lost" territories of Texas, California, New Mexico, and Arizona would be regained. Shortly thereafter the "Zimmerman Note" revealed evidence of German efforts to involve Mexico and the United States in a conflict, thus diverting American attention from Europe. The San Diego "Plan," if it actually existed, never came to pass, although isolated border settlements and ranchers considered themselves in real danger.

Kingsville

This town is southeast of Alice on US 77. Kingsville has to be a patriotic, flag-waving, down-home place because it was established on July 4, 1904. It is the home of Texas A&I University as well as the Kingsville Naval Air Station. Richard King gave the town its name. He was a runaway who came to Texas in 1847 and operated a steamboat on the Rio Grande. During the Civil War he smuggled cotton into Mexico and brought out money and weapons for the Confederacy. When the war ended, Richard King was a wealthy man. He and his wife, Henrietta Chamberlain, daughter of a Presbyterian preacher, lived briefly in Brownsville, settling on Santa Gertrudis Creek.

In 1853 King purchased 15,500 acres of brush country for $300. When he died in 1885 you could drive a hundred miles in any direction and still be on King land. Today, the King empire comprises eleven million acres on five continents. King was a perfect name for an American of royal spirit, daring, and vision.

After Richard King's death, his wife, Henrietta, proved just as astute and tenacious as her husband. Along with attorney Robert Justus Kleberg, who became King's son-in-law, Henrietta implemented the King dream. They

Richard King. —The Institute of Texan Cultures

doubled the ranch's size, found underground water, and doubled the holdings again. The ranch, which had always been huge, became progressive as well by experimenting with cotton, grain, vegetables, and citrus.

The ranch stumbled after World War I. Drought and debt drove it to its financial knees, but the grandson, Bob Kleberg, returned it to ranching. According to writers Larry Hodge and Sally Victor, Kleberg already had the largest ranch in the world. Now he made it "the most famous." In doing so he brought in Humble Oil, which struck gas and oil.

The ranch developed the Santa Gertrudis cattle as a separate strain, a cross of three-eighths Brahman and five-eighths British Shorthorn. Kleberg also "created the first beef breed of cattle to be developed in America and then spread around the globe." Today, visitors can drive around a twelve-mile loop leading past the ranch headquarters and other points of interest. The King Ranch was designated a national historic landmark in 1961.

Henrietta Chamberlain King. —The Institute of Texan Cultures

San Antonio—Beeville
90 miles

Floresville, Panna Maria, Kenedy, Beeville

Floresville started during the 1820s and is the final resting place of the Canary Island colonists who settled San Antonio during its formative years. Panna Maria is east of Falls City on Texas Farm Road 81. America's first colony of Poles arrived there in December 1854. Kenedy was first known as "Kenedy Junction" in honor of Mifflin Kenedy, a partner with Richard King in the riverboat business. Since trains went through each day, cowboys at the local beanery fired weapons to amuse themselves and scare the passengers. The Irish settled Beeville in 1826. For a while, the village was called Maryville in honor of Mary Hefferman, the only survivor of a family murdered by Indians in 1853.

Lower Rio Grande Valley

The lower Rio Grande Valley of Texas is bound on the east by the Gulf of Mexico and Padre Island. The region's southern border is the Rio Grande. To the north is Farm Road 1017 and Texas 186. In the remote west lies Farm Road 755.

The lower Rio Grande Valley extends roughly 100 miles from east to west and 50 miles north and south, a plot of Brush Country formed three million years ago along with the Gulf Coast. The valley is a flat, tidal basin area. The Rio Grande over eons of time has meandered and laid down extensive deposits of delta and alluvial earth intermingled with salt from evaporating seas.

The valley matured as quasi-desert range land. The Spanish avoided it until the mid-1700s, when several towns formed on the present Mexican side of the Rio Grande. Brownsville, the first Texas village, was not even created until 1846 when Americans invaded Mexico from nearby Fort Brown.

Anglo-Americans started arriving about 1904, when the Missouri-Pacific chugged into Brownsville and essentially changed the lower valley forever. The rails brought eastern and northern farmers south to where a circuit-riding oblate father had a century or so earlier brought oranges into the valley. Seven trees grew from the seeds, and an orange and grapefruit industry eventually expanded that amazed the world. For a while fruit was produced only for personal consumption, but by 1912 John H. Shary, a land developer from Nebraska, built irrigation ditches across 16,000 acres of brushland near Mission. By 1920, the trains were hauling the produce north, about 70 percent of it being grapefruit.

Between 1914 and 1916, border troubles frequently roared out of control in the lower Rio Grande Valley. Most Americans are conditioned to think of Pancho Villa and his 1916 raid on Columbus, New Mexico, when we think of marauders along the international line. What people tend to forget, however, is that the pattern for such raids began in the lower Rio Grande Valley even though the problems themselves originated with chaotic conditions in the federal Mexican government, especially with the assassination of President Francisco Madero in 1914.

For a while, the valley was thinly protected by elements of the 3rd and 12th cavalries and the 6th Field Artillery. After Texas Governor James E. Ferguson hired rangers to protect the border, he also pleaded for more soldiers. However, Maj. Gen. Frederick Funston, from his command headquarters at Fort Sam Houston in San Antonio, refused additional forces, arguing that the outlaws were primarily Texas thieves. Even the Plan of San Diego—drafted in Monterrey, Mexico, but written by Victoriano Huerta's adherents in San Diego, Texas, in 1915—did not arouse much attention. Although the plan called for an uprising of Hispanics living in Texas and for the establishment of an independent republic to be later incorporated into Mexico, the U.S. Army treated the plan as a meaningless visionary scheme.

Funston started changing his mind in early 1915 when prominent valley residents appealed directly to the secretary of war. Angry and bewildered citizens took the law into their own hands. The Texas Rangers dealt out summary justice. A 12th Cavalry patrol captured documents that described the bandit raids as Mexican inspired and claimed 3,000 Hispanics had sworn allegiance to the Plan of San Diego. At least 500 marauders were reportedly preparing for an attack on Brownsville.

Funston accused Gen. Emiliano Nafarrate, commander of Venustiano Carranza's forces at Matamoros, of guiding and directing the raids. Funston demanded assistance from Washington, threatened northern Mexico with invasion, and sent two battalions of infantry to Brownsville. The concerned U.S. government in Washington also dispatched the 4th Infantry and the 6th Cavalry to Harlingen and split the 19th Infantry between Fort Sam Houston and Del Rio. Funston now had half the United States Army. There was talk of martial law in the four valley counties.

Hispanic families in the valley fled into Mexico. Anglos in isolated ranches and settlements sent their dependents to larger cities.

By now, Mexican desperados had derailed the St. Louis, Brownsville & Mexico train, robbing the passengers and killing two while wounding three. A pursuing posse captured the alleged raiders; they lynched four and shot six.

Fifty miles west of the train wreck at Ojo de Agua in Hidalgo County, outlaws attacked a sleeping sixteen-man cavalry patrol. Three soldiers died and eight were wounded. An infuriated Funston requested "no quarter" for the enemy, but Washington wisely refused to countenance it.

After late 1915, the raids tapered off. The United States recognized Venustiano Carranza as president of Mexico, and he made political changes along the border, especially at Matamoros. A company of *rurales*, organized in Reynosa, were as coldly efficient as the Texas Rangers. They drove out or killed Mexican outlaws along that section of the border. These changes, of course, did not end the outlawry, and in fact the raids continued for another two years. But 1915 was at least a beginning of the end.

Gradually the valley returned to farming and ranching. By 1940 one-hundred thousand acres were in fruit tree production.

Although the lower Rio Grande Valley is the southernmost citrus fruit production region in the United States, due to hard freezes during the 1940s the output dwindled. Other blows fell during the freezes of 1951 and 1962 when the valley lost a major portion of its white grapefruit. A majority of farmers switched to the new Ruby Red, a pink-fleshed fruit. By 1964, Ruby Reds had secured the market, and farmers planted even more trees per acre.

Thanks to unique weather/insect/taste research experiments going on at Texas A&M University, the future of produce in the valley is brighter than ever.

US 83

Rio Grande City (Fort Ringgold)—McAllen

35 miles

Fort Ringgold

Camp Ringgold was established in 1848 and became Ringgold Barracks in July 1849. Rio Grande City evolved around it. The post was named for Maj. Samuel Ringgold, the first American army officer killed (a Mexican cannonball severed his right leg) during the Battle of Palo Alto, the first engagement of the Mexican War.

Ringgold hosted black and white cavalry units and played a strong role in suppressing outlaws during the Cortina Wars of the mid-1800s. Fort Brown at Brownsville and Fort Ringgold at Rio Grande City anchored opposite ends of the valley. Soldiers at each fort were capable of driving south into Mexico and flanking Cortina, a threat keeping the wily outlaw chieftain from becoming an even greater menace.

In 1859 the post was abandoned, only to be reopened in 1861 and surrendered to the state of Texas. United States troops returned by 1869, this time to chase Comanches as well as outlaws and revolutionaries. It became Fort Ringgold in 1875 as the government started replacing the adobe and wood buildings with more permanent structures of brick.

Texas citizens ambushed a squad of black 9th Cavalry soldiers in 1875, and several men died in the brief fight. One of the suspects was tried in a civilian court but was acquitted. Murder indictments were then handed down against three troopers as well as their company commander. All five were eventually acquitted. The 9th Cavalry was transferred to New Mexico and replaced by the (white) 8th Cavalry.

Ringgold was scheduled for deactivation in 1912, but was enlarged in 1917 due to border disruptions caused by the Mexican Revolution. The post remained active until it was abandoned in 1944. In 1946 the Rio Grande School District absorbed it.

Rio Grande City

The city, a natural mooring site on the Rio Grande, was in 1753 a camp on the Garza Rancho, a portion of José Escandón's colonies. The locals called it "Carnestolendas." By 1847, Henry Clay Davis, an adventurer, acquired the Garza Rancho and it became "Davis Landing." Since ship traffic to and from the gulf generally ended here, a business district developed around the river wharfs.

When Fort Ringgold was established in 1848 the town was already called Rio Grande City. Cotton, travelers, and animal hides were shipped downriver to Brownsville and on to New Orleans or Europe. Boundary Commissioners John R. Bartlett and Maj. William Emory met at Rio Grande City in 1851 prior to leaving for Washington.

Camargo, across the Rio Grande from Rio Grande City, was established in 1749 and is one of the oldest towns in the Rio Grande Valley. The two cities played out an important bit of history when French imperialist forces met Mexican loyalists at Santa Gertrudis Ranch (inside today's Camargo) during the 1860s. While 25,000 United States troops waited at Ringgold in case Mexican forces should need them, Gen. Mariano Escobedo attacked French elements. When the day ended, the imperialists, with their Austrian and ex-Confederate mercenaries, had been defeated. French power had been destroyed in Mexico.

Later on when Porfirio Díaz came to power as dictator of Mexico, Gen. Mariano Escobedo entered the gunrunning business as a revolutionary. Maj. William Redwood Price, commander at Fort Ringgold, became suspicious of Escobedo. When the general showed a strong interest in the steamer *Ackley*, Price boarded the ship and confiscated eight cases of Remington breech-loading rifles not registered on the manifest but ordered by Escobedo. He arrested the general and fourteen officers, charging them with violations of American neutrality laws. United States Commissioner J. C. Eiret placed the accused on parole.

Throughout its history, Rio Grande City has undergone Indian raids, revolutionary activities, gunfights, and cattle rustling. On the plus side, Francoise La Borde, a French trader, finished construction of a Country French home in Rio Grande City in 1890. When he later committed suicide, the building passed through several hands and today is a restored, first-class hotel.

A new international bridge replaced the ferry in 1966, and irrigation water from the Falcon Reservoir opened up additional farmland. While Hurricane Beulah in 1967 dampened some spirits, the town recovered and continued its progression.

Tourist sites today include the Starr County Courthouse, the Immaculate Conception Church, and "Our Lady of Lourdes Grotto." The latter is a replica of the shrine in Lourdes, France.

Mission

As a town, Mission started about 1908, although it takes its name from the nearby La Lomita Mission of 1820s origin. The mission was an overnight rest stop for padres traveling between Brownsville and Roma. The town advertises itself as "Home of the Grapefruit," specifically the famed Texas Ruby Red. The Mission Packing Plant was the first modern industrial facility in the valley.

Near Mission is the Los Ebanos ("Ebony Trees") ferry, which operates daily on a hand-pulled basis. It crosses the Rio Grande between Los Ebanos and the Mexican village of Diaz Ordaz.

McAllen

McAllen is named for Scotsman John McAllen and his son John Ball McAllen. They built the McAllen Ranch near the railhead, and it is an agricultural area that the St. Louis, Brownsville & Mexico Railroad promoted in 1904. Farmers arrived a year later and fruit and vegetables were on their way to market by 1906. The town started expanding as a winter resort in 1941, when the construction of a suspension bridge across the Rio Grande provided a more convenient connection to the larger city of Reynosa, Mexico. McAllen is a major shopping center for the valley as well as northeastern Mexico. Winter visitors arrive primarily from the western as well as the north-central states. McAllen has a memorial library as well as the McAllen Botanical Gardens and McAllen International Museum. The Santa Anna National Wildlife Refuge is just sixteen miles southeast of McAllen.

McAllen—Brownsville

Hidalgo, Progreso, Santa Maria, La Paloma, Olmito, Pharr, Donna, Mercedes, San Benito, Los Fresnos

Hidalgo is the site of an ancient Rio Grande ford used by Indians as well as Spanish. The remaining towns form the heart of the lower Rio Grande Valley. As farming and canning communities, they date their existence after the turn of the century.

Fort Brown and Brownsville

Brownsville, the southernmost Texas city as well as the largest city in the lower Rio Grande Valley, began as Fort Brown. The post was activated in 1846 as a jumping-off site for the army of Gen. Zachary Taylor when he invaded Mexico. The May 8, 1846, Battle of Palo Alto was the first engagement of the Mexican War, and it occurred twelve miles northeast of Brownsville. Taylor won. In 1850 the post was abandoned and given to Brownsville, a town expanding outside the military gates and across the Rio Grande from Matamoros, Tamaulipas, Mexico.

Juan Cortina, the bandit, revolutionary leader, and eventual Tamaulipas governor, occupied Fort Brown and Brownsville on September 28, 1859. However, the residents pleaded with Mexican Gen. José Carvajal for assistance, and elements of the Mexican Army crossed the Rio Grande and protected Brownsville from Cortina, an unparalleled event in border relations. The Mexicans were relieved by United States Army Maj. Samuel Peter Heintzelman and the 2nd Cavalry as well as fifty-two rangers led by famed Texas Ranger John "Rip" Ford.

In November 1863, the Union Army occupied Fort Brown as well as Brownsville, dubbing the village "Dogtown" because of stray animals. However, Union forces were driven out within a brief time. The last battle of the Civil War, fought after the conflict had officially ended, took place twelve miles east of Brownsville at Palmito Ranch on May 11, 1865. The Confederates won.

Dr. William C. Gorgas, who later became surgeon general of the United States Army, was stationed at Fort Brown. His studies led to the eventual control of yellow fever. The hospital is today's administration building for the Texas Southernmost College, a municipal facility.

Fort Brown also was privy to one of the Southwest's great travesties. During the early 1900s, the fort was garrisoned by black infantry. Race relations between the military and white civilians were tenuous, made worse

Gen. Zachary Taylor led an American army across the Nueces Strip
and invaded Mexico in 1846. —National Archives

John S. "Rip" Ford, one of the most famous Texas Rangers of his time. He got the name "Rip" during the Civil War— when he wrote survivors to notify them of a soldier's death, he always scratched R.I.P. to terminate the correspondence.
—Texas State Archives

Fort Brown, Texas, circa 1861. —The Institute of Texan Cultures

Juan Cortina, terror of the Mexican border.
—National Archives

when a local white woman claimed a black soldier had raped her. Both factions were angry, confused, and uncertain of what to do next.

With no peacemakers in evidence, on the warm, humid night of August 13, 1906, several shots were fired by unknown parties. Reason quickly became a casualty of racism and poor leadership. The soldiers assumed a local mob was attacking. Civilians thought black soldiers were storming the town. A ten-minute shooting spree ended with a policeman wounded and a civilian dead. Nobody knew who fired the shots, but the blame fell on the infantry.

The gunfire probably originated from the fort, but if any black soldiers knew what happened, or who was involved, they refused to tell. As a result of this "conspiracy of silence," and a lack of Washington political backbone, the tragedy was compounded. Secretary of War William Howard Taft couldn't find anyone guilty, so he found them all guilty. Upon his recommendation, President Theodore Roosevelt, with no public hearings and nobody going to trial, summarily discharged three companies, 167 black soldiers, without honor.

Edmund Jackson Davis, district attorney for Brownsville and a Unionist. He tried to divide Texas into three states. As governor of Texas during the Reconstruction period, he was a dictator as well as an able, honest, and influential politician.
—Archives Division, Texas State Library

The Missouri Pacific and the Southern Pacific reached Brownsville, and today the city is a resort center as well as an agricultural, industrial, and trading crossroads.

On nearby Farm/Ranch Road 1419, a natural palm forest still exists. These trees gave the Rio Grande its initial name: River of Palms.

The Brazos Island State Park is not actually an island but a spit of land (Boca Chica, meaning "Small Mouth") just south of South Padre Island. The beaches are undeveloped. The city also has the Brownsville Art League Museum, the Brownsville Historical Museum, a tourist information center, and an excellent public library. Matamoros also has several quality museums and historic buildings.

Harlingen

Harlingen was founded in 1901 and named for a village in the Netherlands. Rangers and national guardsmen frequently kept the peace, and in popular parlance the town was called "Six-Shooter Junction."

Regardless of when a visitor arrives at Harlingen, a harvest is almost certain to be in progress. As a crossroads of the lower Rio Grande Valley, Harlingen is a thriving resort town as well as a trade and shipping center.

Harlingen Army Air Field, used primarily as a gunnery school, opened in 1941 and closed in 1946. Today the Confederate Air Force is based at Rebel Field. The original working model of the Iwo Jima War Memorial is on display at the Marine Military Academy.

The Confederate Air Force Flying Museum has World War II vintage military aircraft from the United States, Britain, Germany, and Japan. Among those on display are the P-40 Warhawk, P-38 Lightning, P-47 Thunderbolt, P-51 Mustang, P-63 King Cobra, PBY Catalina, P-82 Twin Mustang, F4F Wildcat, F6F Hellcat, F8F Bearcat, F4U Corsair, B-17 Flying Fortress, B-29 Superfortress, A-26 Invader, B-25 Mitchell, A-20 Havoc, C-47 Skytrain, British Supermarine Spitfire, and German Heinkel HE-111 and Junkers JU-52.

The Laguna Atascosa National Wildlife Refuge is near Harlingen. So is the Port of Harlingen barge facility on Arroyo Colorado and the Rio Grande Valley Museum.

SIX

Post Oak Savannah

*The Post Oak Savannah is a part of the true prairie
. . . grassland within a grassland climate that supports
isolated trees.*

Charles J. Scifres, *Brush Management*
(Texas A&M Press, 1980)

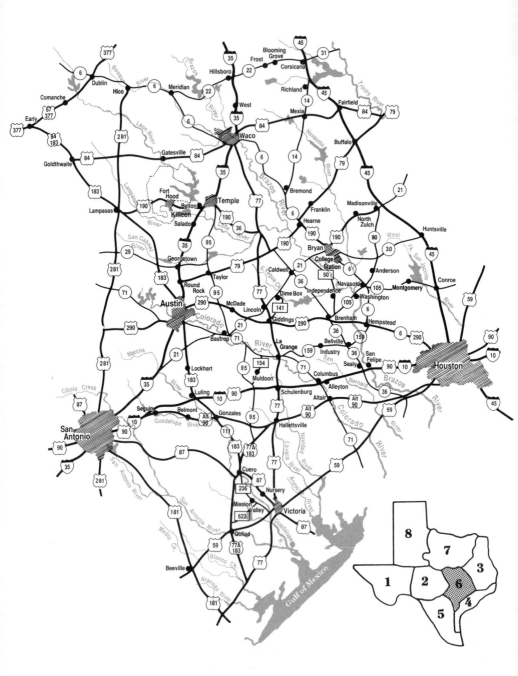

For our purposes, the Texas Post Oak Savannah runs a hundred miles east to west and two hundred north to south. It cuts an irregular northern boundary between Dallas and Waco by following Texas 22 west from Corsicana (SSE of Dallas) to Meridian, Texas 6 to Dublin, and US 67-377 southwest to Early. Its western border rumbles southeast from Early along US 183 to Austin, then heads south along I-35 to San Antonio, and finally jogs southeast on US 181 to Beeville. The southern boundary is marked by US 59 between Beeville and Houston. And the eastern border follows I-45 from Houston north to Corsicana. Because it is so large, the towns in this section are arranged under its northern, middle, and southern portions.

The post oak that lends its name to this region of Texas is a small broad-leaved, symmetrical tree, usually taking root in light, sandy soil. It generally grows in clumps or "islands" on Texas savannahs. In a land where trees are scarce, as they are on the western edge of the prairie, the presence of post oaks increases land values. Timber from the post oak is used in constructing buildings and fences.

Precisely defining the Post Oak Savannah is not simple. It encompasses the most diverse landscape of any region in the state. Parts of it belong to several more distinct geographic zones, and often it is simply called Central Texas. The savannah intrudes heavily upon the Brush Country as well as the Gulf Coast; it also reaches into the Pineywoods, encroaches upon plantation country, and is heavily influenced by the waxy blackland prairie. The northern portion of the savannah (north of Waco) includes a section of the tree-covered ridge known as Eastern Cross Timbers that extends south from Oklahoma and the Red River.

The Old South and the Old West blend together in the Post Oak Savannah. During the mid-1700s the savannah, along with the Gulf Coast, comprised most of the Spanish province of Texas. A hundred years later patriots in this area forged the Republic of Texas. Early locomotives chugged across the region, and the first cattle trails started here.Today, the Post Oak Savannah is the most recreational area in the state. Water sports are plentiful. Hunting is superb. And many state parks are located on the savannah.

General Vicente Filisola.
—The Institute of Texan Cultures

Prior to the turn of the nineteenth century, Comanches and Tonkawas ruled this land and posed a threat to early settlers. Later the Wichitas, often armed with French-made weapons, joined in repelling the newcomers. Indian-white tensions heightened following the successful 1836 war of independence as settlers flocked into the region. Other Indian groups such as the Cherokees, Delawares, Shawnees, and Kickapoos—recently removed to Texas from their homelands east of the Mississippi River—also resented the settlers. Their anxiety and indignation led these Indians to become allied with the Italian mercenary Gen. Vicente Filisola, who guarded Mexico's northern frontier and whom Santa Anna had placed in charge of recovering the lands under dispute north of the Rio Grande.

Filisola lacked sufficient military strength to reconquer Texas, so he recruited an auxiliary force of Indians and Mexican loyalists still living in the new republic. This contingent was commanded by Vicente Cordova of Nacogdoches. As soon as Mexican regulars poised on the border were ready, Filisola planned to ratchet the two armies together like a military pincer to crush the Texans.

But the so-called loyalist alliance had problems. The Mexican government was too busy defending Mexico City from political and revolutionary factions within the country to send any significant assistance to the northern frontier. Also, some of the Indians in the alliance did not advocate attacking the Texans, and those who did had little ammunition. Furthermore, communications between all parties, including Filisola and Cordova, were weak.

In May 1838 Cordova took a few loyalists and twenty-five Cherokee and Caddo warriors across the Rio Grande at Matamoros to confer with Filisola. Meanwhile, Thomas J. Rusk, a commander of the Texas militia, learned about the forces marshalling against him. He immediately issued a proclamation calling on all revolutionaries to disperse. The loyalists responded with their own proclamation, promising to "sustain their rights," but few things worked in their favor.

The Texans killed a loyalist courier and learned the details of Filisola's half-baked invasion plan, including Indian involvement. They quickly made an example of the Kickapoos, in particular, by smashing several of their villages in East Texas. The strategy worked by causing other Indian groups to doubt the strength, reliability, and vitality of the Mexican army against the Texans. Cordova, however, remained faithful to the pincer plan and continued fighting guerrilla-style near the upper Trinity River, trusting that Filisola would march north from the border.

But Filisola's government was undermining any hopes of recapturing Texas. As he fought to crush Mexican revolutionaries and Comanche uprisings in northern Mexico, higher powers in Mexico City sent Gen. Valentín Canalizo to replace him. The change in command disturbed Cordova, who took fifty-three loyalists, six Biloxi Indians, and five black men to again meet Filisola near the border. The travelers left a broad trail easily followed by Texas Col. Edward Burleson, who at first believed he was tracking Comanches. After a couple days, it became obvious he wasn't.

On March 29 Cordova paused at Mill Creek in a post oak grove. Only the village of Seguin lay between him and the border, and Cordova apparently planned to destroy the town. But Burleson's militia caught up with the Mexican and attacked his party late in the afternoon. For a while the battle seesawed, then a grass fire broke out and the fighting became confused. The conflict peaked when Texas marksman Dr. James Fentress wounded Cordova; after that, the loyalists galloped away as the battle sluggishly wound down. The Texans captured eighteen loyalists, but not Cordova. And even though the rebellion had not yet died, the Battle of Mill Creek, sometimes known as the Battlefield Prairie Fight, was over.

The Texans continued pursuing Cordova for several months and nearly caught him in August as his loyalist alliance camped on an island in the Angelina River. But as Texas forces closed in, the revolutionists scattered into Mexico. In the aftermath, numerous indictments for treason were returned in

Nacogdoches. But the threat to the Republic of Texas known as the Cordova Rebellion had ended.

New settlers rapidly populated the Post Oak Savannah. At the time of the 1836 revolution against Mexico, Texas had about 30,000 people. Within two years after its 1845 annexation into the Union, the figure soared to 100,000. By the time of the Civil War Texas boasted a half-million residents. The state had only sixteen counties in 1856; two years later it had thirty-five.

No military fighting occurred on the Post Oak Savannah during the Civil War, but postwar Reconstruction proved difficult. Although the countryside had not been invaded, conquered, and subdued, its residents suffered economically. By some estimates, 100,000 slaves had lived in Texas at the beginning of the Civil War. By the time the fighting ended, all were freed and some had received property. But there was little work and no money. With the government in chaos, restlessness and hatred stalked the land. In the Post Oak Savannah, that meant night riders, feudists, and relentless suppression by federal soldiers. Everybody lost.

Today, although the land is laden with heavy, complex thickets of woody plants that reduce its grazing potential, the savannah is still suited to livestock production. Unlike many rural areas in the country, small farms here are becoming more common. And the Post Oak Savannah carries the legacy of its historical past, with hardly a town lacking in revolutionary or Sam Houston stories.

NORTHERN POST OAK SAVANNAH

This subsection includes that portion of the Post Oak Savannah north of US 79 between Austin and Buffalo.

Texas 22
Corsicana—Meridian
61 miles

Corsicana

In 1849 postmaster Hampton McKinney established the McKinney Inn. Around it grew Corsicana, named for the Mediterranean isle of Corsica, which was the parental homeland of Texas revolutionary hero and statesman José Antonio Navarro.

In the early 1870s, John Wesley Hardin and his nineteen-year-old cousin Simp Dixon fled to this region after killing some black men elsewhere in the state. United States soldiers engaged the pair of outlaws in a brief battle near Richland Bottom, during which two soldiers died. The soldiers later killed Dixon in nearby Limestone County.

Cattle raising remained a primary occupation in and around Corsicana until 1895, when the Corsicana Oil and Development Company drilled a well producing two and one-half barrels a day. Other strikes quickly followed and Corsicana became the original oil boom town in Texas. Magnolia Oil, later named Mobile Oil Company, built the first refinery in Texas at Corsicana, and that city became the first in Texas to use natural gas for fuel and lighting.

By 1950, after the oil boom faded, Corsicana resumed raising cattle and farming the blackland prairie. Today Pioneer Village is one of the town's main tourist attractions. Another site visitors may want to see is the Collin Street Bakery, which has made and distributed the world-famous "Deluxe" fruitcake since 1896.

Blooming Grove, Frost

A village called Gradyville was established shortly after the Civil War. It was named Blooming Grove for the son of a nearby rancher, Blooming Davis, and for a grove of nearby trees. In 1881 the town moved a mile north to the Cotton Belt Railroad.

Frost began as "Cross Roads" because of its location among plantations and horse ranches. When the Cotton Belt Railroad went from Corsicana to Hillsboro in 1881, it did not build track through Cross Roads but created a station nearby and named it for Samuel R. Frost, a Corsicana lawyer and judge who became attorney for both the Cotton Belt and the Houston & Texas Central railroads. The merchants at Cross Roads moved to Frost, and the new town thrived. In 1930 a cyclone destroyed much of the town and killed twenty-two people, but the community gathered itself and rebuilt.

Hillsboro

This town began as a county seat with a log cabin courthouse in 1853. The present stone courthouse was built in 1890, and although it was called "a monstrosity" by the *Saturday Evening Post* and "an outstanding cathedral" by *Harper's*, the truth is that almost no one was indifferent and everyone still has an opinion. Architecturally, it is a combination of the Classical Revival, Italianate, and French Second Empire styles.

The streets are lined with restored Victorian homes, and tours are available. Those who visit the Confederate Research Center & Gun Museum will not be disappointed.

Meridian

Tawakoni Indians, who along with the Wacos belonged to the Wichita group, lived here prior to the middle 1800s. On July 4, 1854, the town of Meridian was established because of its location on the hundredth meridian.

The Horrell brothers, ranchers and feudists, were famous around Lampasas, Texas, as well as Lincoln County, New Mexico. The law arrested Martin and Thomas Horrell for robbing and murdering a Bosque County merchant in 1877. While confined at Meridian, a group of irate vigilantes broke into the jail and shot the brothers to death.

Today the 503-acre Meridian State Park and lake are popular recreation spots.

Hico

Hico, pronounced "HIGH-co" is one mile south of Texas 6 on US 281.

Dr. J. R. Alford founded Hico and named it for local Indians. The town was originally on Honey Creek, but when the Texas Central Railroad bypassed it in late 1880, the village moved several miles north. Every building was transferred with the exception of the J. G. Barbee limestone mill. Until it was demolished in 1940, the mill was a historical landmark.

Hico's present claim to fame is the grave of Olie "Brushy Bill" Roberts. During the 1970s he swore he was the original Billy the Kid. *Alias Billy the Kid* by C. L. Sonnichsen and William V. Morrison (University of New Mexico Press) remains the best-known book touting Brushy Bill as the Kid.

Dublin

Dublin started in 1854 and originally was spelled Doublin. The name meant "Double in," a reference to anticipated Indian raids. Like many regional towns, it moved four miles and relocated on the Texas Central Railroad.

Dublin—Early

Comanche

The county seat and the county were named for the Comanche Indians. The northern portion of the county lies in the Cross Timbers while the southern portion is in the Grand Prairie region. The town of Comanche has black, waxy, loamy soil. Post oak and mesquite grow in the southern and western parts of the county. This led to numerous farms and ranches even though the only wagon road was laid out by army engineers in 1850 so that supplies could be hauled from Fort Gates to Forts Griffin and Belknap.

Most early residents were from Arkansas, Tennessee, and Georgia, and the most exciting years for Comanche were the 1870s. By then you could reach Comanche from two directions: from the south via Fort Griffin and the Western Cattle Trail, and from the east along a single wagon road cut through deep woods and heavy sand.

Transportation didn't stop Joe Hardin, a black-haired, blue-eyed attorney, from bringing his wife and daughter to Comanche in 1871. Joe's parents and other family members followed. They were James G. "Preacher" Hardin, his wife, and several children. In April 1874, John Wesley Hardin, the final Hardin boy, rode in. He had slightly curly hair, gray eyes, and a fast gun. John Wesley Hardin was an outlaw and on the run for his part in several killings during the Sutton-Taylor Feud near Cuero, Texas. Hardin also brought a friend with him: Jim Taylor, wanted for murder.

Hardin loved to drink and race horses. In fact, he arranged a series of horse races in May 1874 and expected to run his own mount, Rondo. Up to a point, this was Hardin's lucky day. He won $3,000 in cash, a couple wagons, several head of cattle, and fifteen saddle horses. He also apparently won a lot of whiskey. During the rest of the afternoon, Hardin and his friends staggered from one "refreshment stand" to another, gambling and drinking.

Late in the afternoon, the intoxicated party entered the Jack Wright Saloon, where they encountered Charlie Webb, a Brown County deputy sheriff in town for the festivities. Hardin and Webb had words, with Hardin goading Webb. Who drew first isn't clear, but Hardin, Taylor, and another party began shooting at Webb, who never had a chance. His first shot grazed Hardin's leg.

By now, A. E. "Bill" Waller, captain of Company A of the Frontier Battalion of the Texas Rangers, had entered Comanche County and was making John Wesley and Jim Taylor the object of an intensive manhunt. It was not a successful one, although it did give vigilantes sufficient nerve to lynch two Hardin friends, the Dixon boys, as well as brother Joe Hardin, who was widely disliked for his suspect land deals.

John Wesley Hardin at age eighteen in Abilene, Texas. The Colt pistols were with him at the time of his death. —Bobby McNellis

John Wesley Hardin slipped through the dragnet and fled east, only to be captured on August 23, 1877. Ranger captains John Armstrong and Jack Duncan trapped him on board a train in Pensacola, Florida, clubbed him to the floor, chained him, and took him back to Texas, where a judge sentenced Hardin to twenty-five years in the Huntsville Penitentiary.

Today, Comanche is a trade center for surrounding ranches. It has a county historical museum. The courthouse, now the oldest one in Texas, has been relocated to the southwest corner of the Comanche town square.

US 84
Goldthwaite—Fairfield
154 miles

Goldthwaite

Goldthwaite is at the crossroads of US 84 and US 183, the latter being sometimes known as the Ports to Plains Highway. Goldthwaite is in an area once fought over by Comanches and Apaches, and as a town it did not originate until 1885. The town is a center for agricultural trade. The Mills County Historical Museum features exhibits on local history.

Gatesville

The central prairies collide with much rougher country at Gatesville, named for Fort Gates, which was five miles east. The post was established on the north bank of the Leon River in October 1849. The 8th Infantry was housed inside a stockade, a rare fortification in the West. The garrison was deactivated in 1852, the first Texas fort to outlive its usefulness. Of the fort's seventeen buildings, none are still standing.

The town of Gatesville started in 1854 and is best known for the Gatesville State School for Boys, which opened in 1889 with sixty-eight youths, all of whom were transferred to the school from penitentiaries.

Brazos River

The Rio Grande may be the longest river on the border of Texas, but the Brazos is the longest river *in* Texas and is renowned in history and folklore. Its swirling, muddy waters, treacherous with sand and meandering channels, almost halted the "Runaway Scrape" in 1836. The frightened settlers took three days to cross, and they did so just a couple jumps ahead of advancing Mexican troops.

The 840-mile-long Brazos rises in three branches: the Double Mountain, the Clear Fork, and the Salt Fork. Although its remote headwaters are in New Mexico, it is a Texas stream, rolling across the Great Plains, the Post Oak Savannah, and the coastal plains. The river is navigable for 250 miles above its mouth.

Caddo Indians called the river Tokonohono, and La Salle named it the Maligne. Early Spanish explorers called it Brazos de Dios (Arms of God). One legend claims that some of Francisco Coronado's men, lost and dying of thirst, were led by friendly Indians to this stream. The Europeans named the river after the Savior's benevolence. Another story claims an 1860s drought forced miners near San Saba to struggle north for water. Most died, but thanks to

285

The Brazos River near Washington-on-the-Brazos.

divine intervention, a few stragglers made it to the Brazos. Finally, there is the story of a Spanish ship off the Texas coast running out of drinking water and being saved after encountering fresh water from the Brazos pushing its way out to sea.

Texas magazine has another version, one having its roots in the Biblical story of Moses being saved at the Red Sea. It seems that Indians attacked a Texas mission and killed all the inhabitants except the priest and a small group of converts. They forded the Brazos with pursuers closing in. In midstream, a wall of water caught the onrushing attackers and destroyed them. The padre described the act as "divine intervention." His little group had been saved by the arms of God—*los brazos de Dios. Texas* magazine admitted the story was apocryphal and said a more logical explanation for the river's name is "its widespread tributaries [arms] that drain some 42,000 square miles of Texas."

Of course, the Spanish often confused the Brazos for the Colorado, and vice versa, as the names were frequently interchanged. The word "colorado" actually means red, or muddy, a description more applicable to the Brazos than the Colorado.

Although the Indians, French, and Spanish knew of the Brazos, the first permanent settlement was San Felipe de Austin, founded by John McFarland, one of the Old Three Hundred. San Felipe was the colonial capital of Texas, whereas Columbia and Washington-on-the-Brazos were seats of the Republic of Texas government. Since those early days, almost every bend in the Brazos has had its own name. Some honor the pioneers, while others refer to special features or activities.

Almost every cattle drive north had to cross the Brazos, and tales of those dirves abound. The same can be said for Indian fights along its banks.

Some of the wealthiest families in Texas lived along or near the Brazos in pre-Civil War days, their sugar and cotton plantations stretching for miles. Today the river is a source for power, irrigation, and recreation, as well as the subject of conservation and reclamation efforts. Canoeing on the Brazos is extremely popular.

Waco

The Waco (Hueco, Wéco, Wacco) Indians were part of a single group collectively known as Tahuacanos, or what modern anthropologists describe as a Caddoan-speaking branch of the Wichita tribes who entered Texas during the early 1800s and settled in a single village along the Brazos River near present-day Waco. When traveling, they used buffalo-hide tepees. But at home, they built shelters of wood and dried grass twenty-five feet high. Grass mats graced the floor, and a hole in the roof acted as a chimney. The Wacos were farmers as well as hunters. By 1843 they had made peace with the Republic of Texas but were driven out by the Cherokees and placed on the Brazos Indian Reservation, only to be removed across the Red River into Indian Territory (Oklahoma) in 1859.

A series of cold springs flowed near Waco, making the region perfect for settlement. The Mexican government granted the Waco village site to Thomas Chambers in 1832. The site attracted a battalion of Texas Rangers and the establishment of Fort Fisher followed in 1837. Fisher was abandoned after a few weeks, and Chambers sold the property in 1848 to John S. Snydor, former mayor of Galveston as well as operator of a slave market. Snydor, in cooperation with developer Jacob De Cordova and George B. Erath, a ranger at Fort Fisher, surveyed a site and sold land for $1 an acre. The founding fathers called their community "Lamartine," but Erath convinced his partners the name should be Waco, and the designation became official in 1856.

Practically no settlers arrived until statehood, and no heavy concentrations of immigrants until after the railroads. Lumber had to be imported by ox train from East Texas, one hundred miles distant.

Waco was a hub of Texas secession, the movement being financed by Deep South plantations and the sweat labor of slaves. The economics ensured Waco's position as one of the largest inland cotton markets in the world. Although the Civil War freed the slaves and shattered the Waco economy, growth continued because of the Chisholm and Shawnee (feeder) cattle trails jutting up from San Antonio and points south.

In 1857, William McCutcheon, from Bastrop County, and his sons, drove a herd past Waco to Illinois. Jesse Day tried the same thing from Hays County, Texas, but he drowned while swimming livestock across the Brazos at Waco. His boys buried him and then pushed the cattle on to St. Louis.

Cattle drives forded an amazing number of rivers: the Colorado, Brazos, and Red being three. Drovers L. D. Dan and George Taylor reached Waco and found the Brazos running full. "It was a wonderful sight to see a thousand steers swimming all at one time. All you could see was the tips of their horns and the ends of their noses as they went through the water," L. D. wrote.

Brazos floods southwest of Waco often delayed herd crossings for weeks. The greatest recorded loss occurred among a herd of longhorns bedded down and waiting for the river to drop. A sudden afternoon thunderstorm panicked the cattle and created a stampede. When the sun came up the next morning, 2,700 were twisted and lying in heaps throughout a ravine still referred to as Stampede Gully.

Captain Shapley P. Ross, a Kentuckian and former Texas Ranger, opened the first ferry across the Brazos at Waco in 1849. But cattle frequently bypassed the village and forded the river at a more shallow location. For a while Waco didn't object. Its cotton-based economy was sufficient in itself. But when that way of life stumbled after the Civil War, cattle supplemented the towns income. Trail herds dramatically increased, but when a few consistently bypassed Waco in search of lower and safer water, the Waco city council called for a bridge. Unfortunately, neither the city, the county, nor the state had sufficient funds.

A private Waco Bridge Company formed in 1866 and retained Thomas M. Griffith, a New York civil engineer, to supervise construction. The bridge footers went in first, followed by medieval towers containing 2.7 million bricks. Cables supported a wooden roadway, and the bridge was completed in December 1869. Neither horsemen nor livestock could proceed faster than a flat-footed walk.

The first tolls were collected on January 1, 1870. A chuck wagon cost fifty cents, but at least the food didn't get wet. Mounted riders paid ten cents. The longhorns were charged five cents a head. Not all drovers wanted to pay, however, so unless the water was unusually high, and until the bridge company purchased land containing access to fords, more steers still went under the bridge than went over it.

The Waco Suspension Bridge was the world's third longest, as well as the first bridge across the Brazos. Waco immediately became a major crossroads in the state. The structure's 475 feet of river span cost $144,000, and it was a source of controversy from the moment it opened. Some factions wanted a free bridge. In 1889 a disgusted Waco Bridge Company sold out to the county for $75,000. Shortly afterwards, the city purchased it from the county for a dollar.

It remained in use until 1971, when the city council officially retired it to the official status of a national monument. To this day, it remains one of the great engineering feats in Texas. It survived the May 11, 1953, tornado that destroyed most of downtown Waco. Griffith used the lessons he learned to assist with building the Brooklyn Bridge.

Waco has been called "Geyser City" for its artesian wells of hot mineral water. Pharmacist Charles Alderton invented Dr Pepper (no period after the Dr), and named the soft drink for the father of a young lady he courted. Since sugar was rationed during the war, the Dr Pepper company proved that ordinary workers had energy letdowns during work. The remedy was to drink a Dr Pepper three times a day. The War Rationing Board was convinced. Soft drink manufacturers received additional sugar and a slogan: "Drink a bite to eat at 10, 2 and 4 o'clock." It became a part of American folklore.

Residents have referred to Waco as the Athens of Texas. Its strength was Baylor University, the principal Baptist college in the South.

Back in 1841, Judge Robert E. B. Baylor organized an educational branch of the Texas Union Baptist Association. It established a school called Baptist University in 1846 at Independence, Texas. The first degree was granted in 1854. During the early 1880s, it consolidated with Waco University, moved to the Waco campus, and was rechartered as Baylor University at Waco in 1887.

Robert Emmett Bledsoe Baylor.
—The Institute of Texan Cultures

Toward the turn of the century, however, controversy centered around Baylor. It began with William Cowper Brann, editor and publisher of *The Iconoclast*, which originated in Austin but moved to Waco in 1895. Brann was a liberal who detested "organized virtue."

Brann offended religious people with his charges of hypocrisy and sanctimony. Tom E. Davis, a conservative, had strong ties to Baylor. On April Fool's Day, 1898, Davis shot Brann on Austin Avenue in the middle of downtown Waco. Brann whirled and emptied a revolver into his attacker. Both men died of wounds during the following day.

Since those controversial years, Baylor has emerged as one of the truly great national universities. Its Armstrong-Browning Library holds the world's largest collection of Robert and Elizabeth Browning writings. The building is an architectural masterpiece.

Baylor is also home to the Strecker Museum. In 1991, Bill Daniel, a former governor who was an attorney as well as a Baylor benefactor, transported twenty-three historic structures (tenant houses, stables, bars) from Plantation Ranch in Liberty County to Waco. They were the remnants of a river town on the Trinity, and these buildings are being restored at the Strecker Museum so people might understand what early-day Texas living was all about.

As for the Brazos, small steamboats plied its waters during the early days. The river has since been deepened to accommodate larger ships. The *Brazos Queen II* at Waco is a floating riverboat restaurant.

Finally, old Fort Fisher has been restored. It houses the Homer Garrison Memorial Texas Ranger Museum and Texas Ranger Hall of Fame. The fort is also headquarters for Company F of the present-day Texas Rangers.

Waco will probably long be rememberd for David Koresh and his group of religious followers generally called Branch Davidians. Numbering well over a hundred, they established a compound near Waco, stockpiling the structure with food, Bibles, and weapons. On February 28, 1993, agents from the U.S. Bureau of Alchohol, Tobacco and Firearms, determined to confiscate the illegal weapons, raided the compound. Four agents were slain and sixteen wounded in the gun battle that followed. At least one Davidian was killed and several wounded in the unsuccessful assault. The FBI took charge, and for fifty-one days the siege went on. David Koresh repeatedly joked with or harangued the agents as he negotiated, renegotiated, screamed, read religious tracts aloud for hours, threatened the Apocalypse, and referred to himself as the Messiah. A dozen or so Davidians left the compound, but most members remained. On April 19, 1993, at 6 A.M., agents warned the besieged Davidians to exit or the agents would use tear gas on them. When they refused to surrender, the government sent a converted M-60 tank to knock holes in the building and introduce the gas. A fire of dubious origin swept the compound. Within an hour the towering flames, fanned by a stiff prairie wind, dry wood, and stacks of Bibles, had consumed the building. David Koresh and approximately eighty men, women, and children perished.

West

The town of West is located seventeen miles north of Waco on I-35.

Named for T. M. West, who opened a store and hotel in 1856, West is today a Czech community. Its Czech food and Church of the Assumption is worth a stop. The newspaper *Vestnik and Czechoslovak* prints a directory of Texas Czechs.

Three and one-half miles south of West, and 16 miles north of Waco, one of the oddest events in Western history took place on September 15, 1896. Pundits call it the "Crash at Crush."

William George Crush, an employee of the Katy (Missouri-Kansas-Texas) Railroad, observed a truism that people always flock to a wreck scene. Therefore, his reasoning followed that they would pay to watch a spectacular, deliberate train crash between charging locomotives.

Katy advertised "The Great Train Wreck" all over the nation, and up to fourteen trains carried passengers to Crush near West at $2 for a round trip. Between 30,000 and 40,000 viewers watched the show from steep hills overlooking the tracks.

With two miles between them, and one practice run, two 35-ton locomotives, each pulling six empty boxcars, churned inexorably toward each other. Engineers opened the throttles and jumped.

At sixty miles per hour, the trains collided. The boilers exploded and debris rained upon the spectators. Three people were killed and dozens injured. The show was quite an event, but it has never deliberately been duplicated.

Mexia

Mexican Gen. Jorge Hammerking Mexia donated land for a townsite when the Houston & Texas Central Railroad built through in 1871. At first the village was barely more than a cattle and cotton community, but natural gas production in 1912, and an oil gusher in 1921, led to a population jump from 4,000 to 40,000. Along Mexia's "Golden Lane," massive amounts of oil flowed to market each month, and it wasn't until 1945 that production dropped below one million barrels a year.

The old Mexia Hotel, once called the Virginia House, catered to well-to-do travelers. The less affluent parked vehicles in the yard and rolled up in their blankets on the floor of the hotel's wagon house.

The Confederate Reunion Grounds is now a state park, the last reunion occurring in 1946. The Fort Parker State Park and Historic Site contains the restored Fort Parker. Cynthia Ann Parker was kidnapped from the stockade by Comanches in 1836. (See page 20 for Cynthia Parker's story.)

The nearby Tehuacana Hills and village of Tehuacana are the highest points between Houston and Dallas.

Fairfield

Planters called the town Mount Pleasant prior to 1850, but it was renamed by settlers from Fairfield, Alabama. The town was home to the Fairfield Female Academy, which opened in 1858 but closed in 1889.

The Freestone County Museum is housed in the century-old jail. It once allegedly imprisoned the notorious outlaw John Wesley Hardin.

The town square contains the famed "Valverde Cannon," one of six captured by Confederates at Valverde, New Mexico, as the South attempted to open an empire to the Pacific. The conquest failed, and the other five cannons are unaccounted for. The one in the town square was buried in Fairfield, only to be dug up during the exuberance following Grover Cleveland's election as president. The cannon has protected Fairfield ever since.

I-35
Waco—Round Rock
87 miles

Temple

Temple is more than one large medical facility. It was named for B. M. Temple, chief construction engineer for the Gulf, Colorado & Santa Fe Railroad, which started selling town lots on June 29, 1880. The community became a railroad division point and its large population attracted a professional class of lawyers, merchants, and physicians.

The Santa Fe Hospital was established in 1892, King's Daughters in 1897, and Scott-White in 1894. Following these came the Olin E. Teague Veterans Center and the Texas A&M University School of Medicine. Temple's hospital installations are worth hundreds of millions of dollars.

Temple has its Railroad and Pioneer Museum. There is also a Grove County Life Museum and a Czech Heritage Museum.

Belton

Belton began as Nolansville on Nolan Creek in 1850. A year later it became Belton. Saloons were whiskey barrels tipped upright under trees. Mary Hardin-Baylor College was once the oldest women's college (it's now co-educational) west of the Mississippi.

Spaniards searched the area south of Belton for gold and silver. Numerous shafts still dot the region.

The Chisholm Trail enhanced the city's rowdy reputation. In 1874, nine men were jailed and charged with horse theft. Vigilantes executed all nine in their cells.

Killeen

Killeen is eighteen miles west of Temple on US 190.

Originally called Palo Alto, the town was renamed for Santa Fe Railroad civil engineer Frank P. Killeen in 1882. For years it was an agricultural shipping point. The community's population has mushroomed from less than 600 people in 1950 to over a hundred thousand, thanks primarily to Killeen's access to Fort Hood.

On October 16, 1991, Killeen gained unwanted worldwide attention when derangned gunman George Hennard of Belton, Texas, killed twenty-three people at a Luby's Cafeteria. Hennard drove his pickup truck through a window and randomly opened fire with a semiautomatic pistol. It was the deadliest mass shooting in United States history. Hennard committed suicide as the police closed in.

Fort Hood

Fort Hood is the largest army post in the world. It supports 180,000 people, which includes military personnel, dependents, and civilian workers.

Texans naturally expect their military posts to date back to frontier times, but Fort Hood got its start in 1942 by training soldiers to destroy enemy tanks. It was named for Confederate Gen. John Bell Hood and was originally called Camp Hood. In 1950 the government designated it a permanent installation. Today it contains 217,000 acres and covers 339 square miles of Post Oak Savannah.

Fort Hood is the only two-division post in the army. The 1st Cavalry and 2nd Armored divisions are stationed there, the largest concentration of armored power and military population in the United States. The monthly payroll exceeds $35 million. The 1st Cavalry Division Museum displays 150 years of cavalry gear and history. The 2nd Armored Division Museum covers from 1940 to the present, but the emphasis is on World War II.

Salado

Salty Creek is responsible for the name Salado, which Texans usually pronounce "Suh-LAY-doe." The Tonkawa Indians thought the creek water had curative powers. The Laredo-to-Wichita Falls mail route came through here, as did a leg of the Chisholm Trail. Salado College, which failed in 1880, was established with the town on October 8, 1859. Local landowner Sterling Clack Robertson donated the land. In 1881 the state legislature debated whether to place a university in Salado.

A scenic mill with waterfall and the Stagecoach Inn are intact near Salado. During Chisholm Trail days, pioneers, cattlemen, politicians, and military officers signed the hotel ledger.

The twenty-two-room Robertson mansion still stands. Its outbuildings, slave quarters, and cemetery make it the only plantation still completely intact in Texas.

San Gabriel River

The river was named San Francisco Xavier in 1716 by Fray Isidro Felix de Espinosa and Domingo Ramón. Within a century, however, the name was changed to San Gabriel. It has three forks, North, Middle, and South, all of which converge at Georgetown. The stream flows northeast for fifty miles and empties into the Little River.

Georgetown

George Washington Glasscock, a businessman, contributed 172 acres of land for Georgetown in 1848. Less than a decade later, Lt. James O. Rice and a company of Texas Rangers attacked a gathering of Indians and Mexicans led by Manuel Flores along the San Gabriel River, nine miles west of Georgetown. Flores was slain, his men scattered, and his supplies captured. A letter in the baggage described the Cordova Rebellion.

The Victorian downtown has been preserved as part of the Main Street Project. The Elias Talbot home was an "underground tunnel" used by slaves fleeing to the North.

Southwestern University, a Methodist school, has its Mood Heritage Museum on campus.

Round Rock

This community started as "Brushy," for nearby Brushy Creek, but the name was changed to Round Rock in honor of an immense round rock in the channel of Brushy Creek. The Texas Santa Fe Expedition was organized here in 1840, and the Texas Archives War ended near here during the same decade. But this poem tells what made the town famous:

Sam Bass was born in Indiana, it was his native home;
And at the age of 17, young Sam began to roam.
Sam first came out to Texas, a cowboy for to be—
A kinder-hearted feller, you seldom ever see.

Show me an East Texas lad of a generation or so ago who could not repeat from memory the words to that stanza and I'll show you someone who thought the Alamo was a grocery store.

Bass raced horses and robbed stagecoaches and banks. One afternoon he and his two-man crew (Seaborn Barnes and Frank Jackson) selected Round Rock for the day's activities. However, the town was filled with rangers. As the outlaws strolled toward the bank, saddlebags slung over their arms as if anticipating a big withdrawal, Deputy Sheriff A. W. Grimes noticed a suspicious bulge under one of their coats. Sauntering over to Bass, he asked, "Say Mister, are you carrying a gun?" Those were his last words.

As the outlaws raced for their horses, Ranger Dick Ware shot Barnes in the head, killing him instantly. A storekeeper mangled Bass's hand with a wild bullet. As he and Jackson reached their horses, ranger Ware or George Herold shot Bass in the back. The outlaws hid that night in the cedar brakes while Jackson bandaged Sam's wounds before fleeing. The rangers found Bass lying under a tree the next morning.

In jail, Bass thought he might recover. Then his condition deteriorated. When told the worst, he said "Let me go." Sam Bass died on July 21, 1878, his birthday.

Sam met his fate at Round Rock, July the twenty-first;
They pierced poor Sam with rifle balls, and emptied out his purse.
Poor Sam he is a corpse now and six feet under clay;
And Jackson's in the bushes, trying to get away.

Sam Bass is buried near the river. His stone reads, "A brave man reposes in death here. Why was he not true?"

Be sure and visit the Palm House Museum.

US 79
Round Rock—Buffalo
125 miles

Taylor

Originally called Taylorsville in 1876, this town was named for Edward M. Taylor, an official of the Houston Belt & Terminal Railroad. Its population was originally German-Czech. The area contains black, waxy soil. Cotton is a principal crop. Tonkawas and Comanches once roamed the area, and the early Spanish made expeditions through the region. The Moody Museum is the restored Victorian birthplace of former Texas governor Dan Moody.

Hearne

S. W. Hearne started this town in 1854. By 1890 the farmers had 3,600 acres under cultivation. Hearne was a railroad junction point, and its founder, along with other Brazos Valley farmers, started the Hearne & Brazos Railroad Company, which built 16.42 miles of track in 1893. A branch of the Southern Pacific bought it a few years later. The Hearne depot has since been restored. Near a Brazos River rock formation known as Cannonball Shoals, attempts were made during the late 1800s to create locks so that the Brazos might be navigable farther upstream.

Franklin

Franklin started as "Morgan" and was named after a railroad official. However, the post office forced it to change names, so Morgan became Old Franklin and then Franklin. A stone courthouse was built in 1882. The nearby Mt. Pleasant Cemetery holds the remains of Walter Williams, the last surviving veteran of the Civil War. He was a Confederate, so maybe the South won after all.

Richland—Bremond

Richland

This tiny village straddling I-45 and Texas 14 actually began as Salt Branch, named for a nearby creek. It had an oil boom in 1895, and another in 1923, but it has remained a shipping point.

Just west of Richland, near the confluence of Richland and Pin Oak Creek, is Pisgah Ridge, the only broken country in the region. Newcomers in Pisgah were reportedly rolled downhill in a barrel while local rowdies fired at them. Survivors were welcomed.

Killings were common in this area. The ridge became a hideout for outlaws, one of whom was John Wesley Hardin, on the run for killing a freed slave. Hardin hid with relatives and even taught school. He also killed a soldier near Corsicana in early 1869 and fled back to Pisgah Ridge.

Bremond

This is a Polish town settled extensively in the 1870s. Three miles southwest is Wooten Wells, a famous health resort that burned in 1921. Mineral-water spas attracted three hotels, but none lasted.

MIDDLE POST OAK SAVANNAH

The middle portion of the Post Oak Savannah lies between US 79 on the north and I-10 on the south. The western and eastern borders, as before, are I-35 and I-45, respectively.

US 190
Madisonville—Bryan/College Station
36 miles

Madisonville

Sam Houston spoke against secession in Madisonville, doing so from the lawn of a castlelike courthouse having towers and gables. The town was named for James Madison. The Woodbine Hotel dates from 1904. It is restored and still in service.

North Zulch

When the Trinity & Brazos Valley Railroad bypassed Zulch, the village moved north to link up with the railroad, and changed its name in the process.

Nine miles north of North Zulch is Normangee, once known as "Roger's Store." Nearby is the ghost town of Navaroo, originally called Navaroo Crossing for its location on the Trinity River. The railroads put not only Navaroo out of business but also most other river towns.

Bryan/College Station

These two towns are virtually one city and will be discussed together. Bryan is something of an old plantation town because of the fertile Brazos bottomlands and because it was settled by Stephen F. Austin's colonists. William Joel Bryan, an early settler, donated land for the town in 1855. The Allen Academy opened in 1886 and, with the Villa Maria Ursuline Academy for Girls, which came along later, established Bryan as an educational center.

When the railroads arrived following Reconstruction, the cotton economy soared because blacks were still bound to the land, not as slaves but as sharecroppers or tenants. They purchased products through a company store or commissary, and therefore remained constantly in debt and obligated to an overseer.

Vagrants were additional sources of labor. They were removed from trains, fined by the courts, and forced to work off their sentences in the fields.

By the 1930s, Italian and Bohemian residents owned many Bryan homes. Cotton gave way to alfalfa.

College Station, a land-grant institution, began as the Agricultural and Mechanical College of Texas. Today it is proudly known as Texas A&M. All students originally took military training. The college opened in 1876 as the first school of higher learning in Texas. College Station referred to a station stop on the Houston & Central Railroad. As a legitimate town, it was not founded until sixty-two years later. Bryan and College Station are intertwining cities.

The school began with 2,614 acres. Today the main campus covers approximately one and one-half square miles. The school achieved university status in 1963. Today there are approximately 250 buildings and a population approaching 50,000 students, faculty, and staff.

Texas A&M has an excellent university press. College Station has Texas World Freeway, where top names in auto racing provide thrills. Bryan has the Brazos Valley Museum of Natural Science.

Texas A&M College,
Bryan, Texas, 1876.
—The Institute of Texan Cultures

The Texas State Penitentiary at Huntsville.

I-45
Huntsville—Conroe
30 miles

Huntsville

Huntsville intrudes upon several geographic zones. It qualifies as Central as well as East Texas, and it is Big Thicket as well as Post Oak country. It started as an Indian trading post during the year of Texas independence, 1836. Pleasant and Ephraim Gray named it after their hometown, Huntsville, Alabama. The town quickly acquired banks, churches, and newspapers.

In 1847 the legislature established the Texas State Penitentiary (commonly called "The Walls") at Huntsville. The first convict arrived on October 1, 1849. During the Civil War period, Union prisoners confined here produced 1,500,000 yards of cloth annually. The prison has housed a shoe factory, printing plant, machine shop, mattress factory, candy factory, and an automobile license plate plant. The electric chair executed many a luckless prisoner between 1924 and 1964, although the death process now is handled by injection. The Texas Prison Rodeo stadium still stands, but the rodeo was abolished in 1987.

John Wesley Hardin was a famous inmate at Huntsville. Hardin killed Charles Webb, a Brown County deputy sheriff, in 1874. The fugitive was captured by rangers three years later and sentenced to twenty-five years in prison. Behind bars, Hardin became captain of the debating team and head of the Sunday School class. He studied law and earned his degree. Governor James Hogg released him in 1894. He practiced law for a year in El Paso before Constable John Selman shot him dead.

The red hills near Huntsville reminded Sam Houston of his Virginia birthplace. After stepping aside as president of the republic in 1844, Houston purchased plantation land fourteen miles from Huntsville and called it Raven Hill. He also had another place closer to town he called his Woodland Home. Although it was little more than a dogtrot cabin, it was airy and Houston could sit there and whittle while he talked politics with his friends.

In 1859, Houston ran for governor on an anti-secessionist platform and won. However, in 1861, after Texas had voted to secede, Houston refused to abandon the Union. The citizens removed him as governor. Houston had by now sold Raven Hill as well as the Woodland Home in Huntsville. When he returned worn and dejected to Huntsville, he lived in an architectural oddity known as the Steamboat House, a home built by others to resemble a

Sam Houston Monument, Oakwood Cemetery, Huntsville.

Mississippi River Steamboat. There, living on the bounty of friends, he died on July 26, 1863. The last word he spoke was "Texas."

Houston is buried in the historic Oakwood Cemetery at Huntsville. Numerous other pioneers lie nearby.

The Texas Department of Corrections headquarters is in Huntsville. Sam Houston State University maintains a criminal justice (law enforcement education) center.

In addition to the Oakwood Cemetery, Houston has the Gibbs-Powell House Museum, the fifteen-acre Sam Houston Memorial Museum Complex, and the Texas Prison Museum.

Conroe

Isaac Conroe owned a thriving lumber mill on the western edge of the Big Thicket, a railroad at the crossroads known as "Conroe's Switch." Gas wells started production in 1931, and the Conroe Oil Field followed. It is still producing, and was for a while one of the largest oil fields in the nation. A simulated railroad depot serves as a tourist information center.

Texas 105
Conroe—Navasota
44 miles

Montgomery

Gen. Richard Montgomery was a Revolutionary War hero who named this town after himself in 1838. A primitive telegraph route once linked portions of East Texas, including Montgomery, on a trail known as the Old Wire Road. Lumbering, agriculture, and oil are today's primary industries.

Navasota River

The Spanish gave this river a variety of titles. Domingo Terán de los Rios named it San Cypriano. Fray Isidro Felix de Espinosa and the Marquis de Aguayo named it the San Buenaventura. Local Indians called it Nabatsoto. Pedro de Rivera in 1772 called it the Navasota, and the name has since stuck.

The river rises in the Hill Country and flows 125 miles southeast, emptying into the Brazos about six miles southwest of Navasota.

Navasota

The town Navasota, like the river, has a convoluted history in terms of names. Francis Holland, an 1822 settler, called the acreage Hollandale. David Arnold arrived ten years later, and he renamed the location Cross Roads. In 1852, James Nolan built a log cabin stage stop, so he naturally liked Nolanville. The post office intervened in 1856, however, and created Navasota.

A fire set by unpaid Confederate soldiers destroyed most of Navasota in 1865. Two years later a plague of yellow fever reduced the population by half. But better times were on the way, and by the mid-1880s a spate of railroads gave the village a degree of prosperity.

Many historians believe the French explorer La Salle died in this vicinity. A statue of him looms near downtown Navasota. The Navasota downtown, incidentally, is on the National Register of Historic Places.

Texas 90
Navasota—Anderson
9 miles

Anderson

Anderson began with construction of the Fanthorp Inn in 1834. Today the inn is a state historic site, and tours are available. The town was originally called Alta Mira (High Views), but the name was changed to honor Kenneth L. Anderson, a former vice president of the Republic of Texas. A munitions plant here assisted the Confederacy. According to a historical marker, the old stone courthouse, destroyed twice, hosted the trial of a member of the Clyde Barrow gang back in the 1930s. He consigned the court to hell.

The cabin of Tapley Holland still survives. According to legend, when William Travis drew his famous line in the sand at the Alamo, Holland was the first man to cross.

Anderson once had ten times its present population.

Independence Hall, where the Texas Declaration of Independence was signed at Washington-on-the-Brazos.

Navasota—Brenham

25 miles

Washington-on-the-Brazos

Andrew Robinson, the first settler of Stephen F. Austin's "Old Three Hundred," arrived in Texas in 1821 with his wife, Nancy, and their two children. By 1824 Robinson held title to 9,000 acres and had become cofounder of Washington, a tiny village named for Washington, Georgia. It sat astraddle the old Spanish (La Bahía) Road, between Goliad and East Texas, and was situated at the La Bahía Crossing on the Brazos River. Besides a livestock and farming business, Robinson operated a ferry.

Robinson sold the property to another settler, John Hall, in 1835. Hall organized the Washington Town Company. It sold lots near the ferry landing.

In 1835, the general council of the insurgent Texas government met in Washington and promoted the town as a site for a convention in early 1836.

The community probably became Washington-on-the-Brazos to distinguish it from Washington-on-the-Potomac.

Delegates from municipalities in Texas met in Washington on March 1, 1836. Forty-four arrived on time, fifteen straggled in by March 11, and two never appeared. William Fairfax Gray, a Virginia lawyer and land agent, called Washington "a disgusting place" with "not one decent house and only one well-defined street."

Sam Houston, "looking broken in appearance" but not forgetting his courtly manners, arrived a day early. Clerks, delegates, and over 200 soldiers put a strain on Washington's accommodations. Many slept on the ground.

George Campbell Childress called the meeting to order on March 1 in Independence Hall, an unfinished building costing $170 to rent for three months. Childress and a committee wrote a declaration of independence that was accepted after less than an hour's debate. Essentially, the delegates had come to declare Texas free and to organize a republic, establish its government, and frame its constitution. During these deliberations, messages kept arriving from William Travis, notes that momentarily lifted morale but then caused deep depression as the delegates realized the Alamo was doomed.

George Childress, author of the Texas Declaration of Independence.
—Archives Division, Texas State Library

Anson Jones, the architect of annexation to the United States. He was the last president of the Republic of Texas. —Gonzales Historical Museum

David Burnet was elected provisional president of the republic, and Sam Houston was appointed commander in chief of the army. Houston left the convention on March 7 to begin raising his forces.

By March 17, the delegates finished their deliberations, knowing that if they were caught by the Mexicans, they would be executed. Hearing that Mexican cavalry was sixty miles distant and closing, the Texans hastily packed and, according to Gray, "dispersed in all directions." Washington was left with little but wind blowing through the trees.

There were fifty-nine signers of the Texas Declaration of Independence, and their ages ranged from twenty-four to seventy. The average age was forty-three. Three were born in Europe, one in Mexico. Two signers were Hispanic. Eleven died violently, four by suicide. Two were slain at San Jacinto.

George Childress, next to Houston the most significant individual at the convention, designed the Lone Star symbol, the "single star of five points" that was adopted as the republic's emblem. Childress ultimately became a tragic figure. Despondent over family matters, he killed himself in 1841.

The center of Texas government moved to Harrisburg from Washington, and then shifted to Austin. In 1842, Houston transferred the capital back (until 1845) to Washington when Mexican armies threatened the republic.

Although lasting political fame passed it by, Washington-on-the-Brazos thereafter had a brief moment of economic life via the cotton trade. However, even that collapsed when the railroads bypassed the village during the 1850s. The Civil War further impoverished the community.

Meanwhile, Anson Jones, fourth and last president of the republic, purchased a quarter-league of land near Washington on property he called Barrington, named for his birthplace, Great Barrington, Massachusetts. After a series of physical ailments, political setbacks, and crop failures, he sold Barrington and moved to Houston. A month later, on January 9, 1858, Jones committed suicide. The state moved the Jones home to Washington-on-the-Brazos, where it was preserved and still exists.

In 1901, a group of citizens dedicated an independence monument alongside the restored Independence Hall. Fifteen years later, the state purchased the first of 165 acres and Washington-on-the-Brazos State Historical Park was opened. Attractions include the Anson Jones home, picnic areas, an amphitheater, and the Star of the Republic Museum. The park is open daily.

Independence

Independence is on Farm Road 50, nine miles north of Texas 105 and twelve miles north of Brenham. Sam Houston was baptized in the Baptist Church in 1853, and Houston's wife, Margaret, lies nearby with her mother, Nancy Moffette Lea. Several delegates met with Houston in Independence prior to traveling on to Washington.

Baylor University opened in Independence, and when it was coed, the males sat on the right side at church and the women on the left. After the college was segregated by sex, the university was reserved for men and the women attended Baylor Female College, now only a ruins. The town square was meant to contain a courthouse, but the county seat went to Brenham by two votes. Independence was originally known as Coles Settlement.

Brenham

Brenham started as a Mexican land grant when the area was a part of Coahuila y Texas. The town was named after Richard Fox Brenham, a former Kentuckian involved in several Texas military forays against Mexico. He was slain during the Battle of Salado in February 1843.

During the Reconstruction period following the Civil War, numerous Germans migrated into Brenham. Brenham became a federal military post. Due to rioting, the town was partially burned in 1867.

The world-famous Blue Bell Creamery, named for the wildflowers that blanket the Brenham area, opened in 1907. Today the factory produces twenty million gallons of ice cream per year. Plant tours are available.

College Station—Bastrop

Caldwell

Mathew Caldwell signed the Texas Declaration of Independence and later led several military expeditions against Indian and Mexican forces. During the 1840s, Caldwell, Texas, was named for him. It was built near the site of Fort Tenoxtitlán (the Aztec name for Mexico City), one of a chain of Mexican garrisons designed to Mexicanize Texas (prior to 1830) and prevent immigration from the United States.

Texas Camp Meetings started in Caldwell in 1841. The Burleson County Historical Museum displays relics of frontier life.

Old Dime Box

Old Dime Box, or Dime Box as it appears on most maps, is three miles southeast of Texas 21 on Farm Road 141. The name stemmed from dimes (left for postage) deposited in a box at Joseph Brown's Mill. In 1944, Senator Lyndon B. Johnson talked President Franklin D. Roosevelt into launching his March of Dimes drive from Old Dime Box, Texas.

Lincoln

Lincoln is best known as a home of William Preston Longley, better known as Bill Longley, perhaps the wildest outlaw the state of Texas ever knew. He killed a man in Lincoln, and Longley's murderous escapades thereafter led him all over the West.

Bastrop

Baron Felipe Enrique Neri de Bastrop has a vague early history. He claimed to have been born in Holland of noble parents. Recent historians say he was an imposter and embezzler born in Dutch Guiana with the name Philip Hendrik Nering Bogel. Regardless, he became a fascinating, important, and very influential man. The history of the United States might have been far different if this energetic, physically imposing "baron" had not lived. By 1795 he was selling land to colonists in Spanish Louisiana. When that territory passed to the United States, he migrated to Texas and settled in San Antonio, where he operated a freighting business while gradually gaining political influence.

Moses Austin.
—Archives Division,
Texas State Library

When Moses Austin sought permission to settle American colonists in Texas, he failed until Baron Bastrop intervened with local authorities. Even after Austin's death, Bastrop aided his son Stephen. Until his own death in 1827, Bastrop represented the Mexican state of Coahuila y Texas, was instrumental in establishing the port of Galveston, and stoutly supported the cause of Texas immigration and its American settlers. He died a pauper and is buried in Saltillo, Mexico.

The community of Bastrop is one of the oldest settlements in Texas. The first settlers arrived in 1829, establishing themselves in Stephen F. Austin's "Little Colony." Originally called Mina, it was incorporated and the name changed to Bastrop on December 18, 1837. Agriculture, cattle raising, brick making, lumbering, and shipping were principal industries. The 3,550-acre Bastrop State Park contains the "lost pines," an isolated area of stately pine trees far west of the pineywoods of East Texas. There is also the Bastrop Museum, Lock's Drug (medical) Museum, and the nearby Central Texas Museum of Automotive History.

Hempstead—Austin

Hempstead

Founded in 1857, Hempstead attracted the Houston & Texas Central Railroad before becoming a prominent Confederate troop and supply center.

One could write volumes about the violent history of Hempstead, but we'll limit this book to the story of what happened when the "drys" and "wets" argued over the virtues of, you guessed it, demon rum. The troubles started in April 1904 when Tucker Pinckney was shot and killed by mistake. Or so it was said.

His brother John, supported by the drys, was already serving in Congress. However, the wets still controlled the county, and wets were what was commonly known as the "courthouse crowd." Nevertheless, the town supported prohibition even if officials were not enforcing it. So over 200 drys signed a petition containing unflattering comments about the courthouse crowd. The petition called for a company of Texas Rangers to enforce the law.

One final meeting was called in April 1905 at the courthouse so that drys might properly dot the i's and cross the t's before sending off the petition. But in the heat of debate, shooting started. Four men were slain, including Mills and John Pinckney, both dry and dead. The slayers were acquitted, and historians still debate if the town stayed dry or turned wet.

One of the most interesting figures to come out of Hempstead was Norris Wright Cuney. Although born in plantation slave quarters, he studied law in 1859 at the Wiley Street School for Negroes. Cuney supported the Texas Union League and urged black political activity and Republican loyalty. After 1872 he emerged as leader of the Republican Party in Texas and attended national party conventions as chairman of the Texas delegation. In 1896, the party broke his Texas power when it refused to seat his delegation. Blacks were thus denied a significant voice in Texas politics until the 1960s. Cuney is buried in Galveston.

Giddings

J. D. Giddings, pioneer and stockholder of the Houston & Texas Central Railroad, created this town and named if for himself. The town was settled primarily by German Wendish Lutherans, who published the only Wendish newspaper in the United States, *Deutches Volksblatt*. Giddings once advertised itself as "the center of diversified farming and home of Texas's largest turkey-dressing plant." The notorious Wild Bill Longley was hanged at Giddings on October 11, 1878; a historical marker identifies his grave. The Lee County

Museum and the Serbin Community-Wendish Museum are both worth visiting.

McDade

Most towns along the road to Austin are tiny and peaceful and look alike: Manor, McDade, Butler, Elgin. Between McDade and Elgin is an area known as "the Knobs," three hills on the northeast horizon. They have silently observed an enormous amount of violence.

Right after the Civil War, rustlers and desperados moved into the Knobs. For entertainment, they lynched a black man in 1874. A year later, two white men met the same fate. When Bill Craddock, better known as Pea Eye, threatened to testify against some rustlers, he took twelve buckshot and was left dying on the floor of his wagon.

By 1876, John, Prentice, and Jim Oliver headed a powerful ranching family. They tried to scare off rustlers by bundling two of them inside the fresh hides of stolen cattle. Within weeks a gang of twenty attacked the Olive house. Several people died in the fight. Vigilante groups were formed, and additional lynchings started.

On June 27, 1877, the vigilantes raided a home where a dance was in progress. They left with four men, all of whom were later found dangling from the same tree limb.

In 1883, Deputy Sheriff Heffington was shot dead. On Christmas Eve, a group of masked men carrying Winchesters entered a saloon and left with three captives. The next morning several law officers cut down the frozen bodies. Jack and Asbury Beatty challenged the vigilantes from the street that same day, and died there.

As time passed, additional killings took place, but the town gradually became peaceful.

I-10
Houston—San Antonio
197 miles

San Felipe

The full name of this town is San Felipe de Austin. In 1823, Stephen F. Austin chose it as headquarters for his first group of colonists. The colony had no legal land limits. The property lay between the Lavaca and San Jacinto rivers, and between the Gulf of Mexico and the Old San Antonio Road. As unofficial capital of the first Anglo-American settlements, San Felipe occupied high prairie ground overlooking a bend of the Brazos. By 1836, San Felipe had four plazas, five stores, and perhaps thirty houses. The provisional government conventions of 1832 and 1833, and the Consultations of 1835, led to the Texas Declaration of Independence signed at Washington-on-the-Brazos in 1836.

Upon retreating from Santa Anna in 1836, Sam Houston's army burned San Felipe. Portions were rebuilt a year later. San Felipe was county seat of Austin County until 1846, when Bellville took it away. The railroads bypassed San Felipe and the town declined.

During its prime, however, many events happened in San Felipe. The Texas Rangers were organized. The first English-language newspaper in Texas (the *Gazette*, 1829) started, as did the Texas postal system.

An 1885 painting depicting the settlement of the Austin colony. The center figure is Stephen F. Austin. Also pictured are Baron de Bastrop and Samuel May Williams.
—The Institute of Texan Cultures

The Stephen F. Austin State Park contains 664-acres divided into two sections: historical and recreational. The historical portion includes a replica of Austin's home.

Sealy

During the late 1870s, San Felipe sold part of its land to the Gulf, Colorado & Santa Fe Railroad. In July 1899 a disastrous Brazos flood forced the railroad to move to Bellville. Other lines serviced Sealy. A 1900 storm also destroyed much of the town. Nevertheless, Sealy has retained an attractive downtown. It is home to the world-famous Sealy Mattress factory.

Bellville and Industry

Bellville is fifteen miles north of Sealy on Texas 36.

Named for Thomas Bell, one of the Old Three Hundred, Bellville had an abundance of pines and soft, limestone water. Early German immigrants came through here. The High Cotton Inn, a 1906 Victorian mansion, has been restored for visitors.

About ten miles west of Bellville on Texas 159 is Industry, founded in 1838 as the first German town in Texas. Since fine tobacco could be grown here, founder Friedrich Ernst planned to open a cigar factory. Most migrants used Industry as a way station from Galveston and Houston to the Texas interior.

Alleyton

At one time Alleyton, named for the Rawson Alley family, was the largest town in the county. Anglo-Americans settled here about 1824 on the site of prehistoric Indian villages. In 1860, Alleyton became the terminus for the Buffalo Bayou, Brazos & Colorado Railroad. Noted gunfighter Dallas Stoudenmire, slain in 1882 at El Paso, is buried in Alleyton, but his grave location is unknown.

Columbus

A gristmill, ferry, and saloon comprised Beason's Crossing before, tradition says, that name was changed by a resident of Columbus, Ohio, in 1836. An Indian village known as Montezuma occupied the site in prehistoric times. Baron de Bastrop assisted members of Austin's colony with Anglo settlement beginning in 1823. That makes Columbus the most continuously settled Anglo-American community in Texas.

Prior to the Civil War, steamboats sailed the Colorado to Columbus. The *Moccasin Belle* even left her anchor as a community decoration.

Stephen Austin recommended Columbus for the capital of his colony, but San Felipe had better navigational possibilities on the Brazos River. In 1836, Sam Houston burned Columbus and fell back to San Jacinto.

The Stafford Bank and Opera House in Columbus, Texas. Built in 1886 by millionaire cattleman R. E. Stafford, it seated 1,000 people. Lillian Russell and Harry Houdini were only two of many prominent entertainers who performed here. —Darrell Jepson

John Stafford's ranch house a few miles south of Columbus. It is vacant and close to being in ruins because heirs cannot agree on how it should be preserved. —Darrell Jepson

Often known as the City of Live Oaks, Columbus was a cotton and lumber shipping point. Today it is geared strongly toward tourism. There are several walking and driving tours past Victorian homes, plus the Old Water Tower/ United Daughters of the Confederacy Museum. Visitors can view the Alley Log Cabin, the Live Oak Art Club Center, the Senftenberg-Brandon House Museum, the old Stafford Opera House, and the courthouse.

Schulenburg

Germans, Czechs, and Austrians settled here about 1875. Louis Schulenburg donated land for the railroad and gave the town his name. Ernst Baumgarten, an earlier settler from Germany, designed a cottonseed crushing plant, the first in the United States. His son developed a process for refining cottonseed oil.

Schulenburg has a strong musical and cultural background. An incredible number of bands are in residence here, and festivals combining music with excellent German-Czech cooking are held with the flimsiest of excuses.

La Grange

La Grange is sixteen miles north of Schulenburg on US 77. An old buffalo trail that came to be known as La Bahía Road crossed the Colorado River near the confluence of Buckner's Creek. In 1819, a trading post went up, followed by a twin blockhouse in 1826. The blockhouse became Moore's Fort, and by 1831 a community had started. Settlers from Fayette County, Tennessee, named it for their hometown: La Grange. (The name is often spelled as one word.) A settlement known as Colorado City was established across the river, but it lasted less than a decade.

In September 1842, when Gen. Adrian Woll captured San Antonio, Nicholas Mosby Dawson led fifty-three men out of La Grange to reinforce the Texans. Upon approaching San Antonio, and seeking to link up with other Texas forces, Dawson's men were surrounded during the Battle of Salado by a unit of Mexican cavalry who killed several of the Texans with artillery. Most of the others surrendered, including Dawson, and were executed. Of the fifteen prisoners, only nine survived to return to Texas.

In 1848 the remains of forty-one of Dawson's men, plus the remains of those shot during the Black Bean Incident of the Mier Expedition, were buried at Monument Hill at La Grange. The Daughters of the Republic of Texas purchased the grave site, known as the Bluff, and the road leading up to it in 1905. The State of Texas erected a forty-eight-foot monument in 1936. Monument Hill is a state historic site.

La Grange has a number of antique shops and historic structures, including the 1841 Faison Home Museum.

Muldoon

To reach Muldoon, take Texas 95 north from I-10 and go seven miles north on Ranch Road 154. The town is named for Irishman Michael Muldoon, a chaplain to the last viceroy of Mexico and a priest for Stephen F. Austin's colony. He was political as well as religious, rescuing Austin and others from Mexican prisons. President Anson Jones wrote him a letter thanking him for his services on behalf of Texas. Muldoon disappeared, a forgotten man of Texas.

Luling

This town is at the crossroads of US 183 and Texas 80, one mile north of I-10. Luling was once the end of the freight road from Chihuahua. Established in 1874 as a terminus of the newly built Sunset Branch Railroad, it was a cattle and freight village. Oil was discovered in 1922 after cattle and railroads had passed the town by. Today many of the oil-well pumpjacks are dressed as cartoon characters. Palmetto State Park is nearby.

Lockhart

This town is fourteen miles north of Luling on US 183. It was originally called Plum Creek, but by 1848 the name had been changed to honor Byrd Lockhart. He was a surveyor and military man who received the Plum Tree lands for Mexican services in building roads during the early 1830s from Gonzales to Matagorda Bay and to San Felipe.

In the summer of 1840, Chief Buffalo Hump led Comanches down the Guadalupe River Valley in a rampage of death and destruction. After sacking Linnville they started retreating, but were unable to move quickly because of so much loot. Texas forces overtook the Indians at Plum Creek, and on August 11, 1840, the battle commenced.

John Jenkins described the Comanches as "arrayed in all the splendor of savage warriors, and finely mounted they bounded over the space between hostile lines, exhibiting feats of horsemanship and daring that none but a Comanche could perform."

When the two lines converged, a running battle lasted for fifteen miles. Over eighty Comanches were slain; the Texans lost one man. Late that evening, the Tonkawa Indians, allies of the Texans, ceremoniously roasted and ate portions of their Indian enemies. Although the Comanches continued their guerrilla tactics for two more decades, after Plum Creek they never again attacked a town.

The Dr. Eugene Clark Library is the oldest continuously used library in Texas. The Caldwell County Museum is worth visiting, and the Caldwell County Courthouse is ugly enough to be beautiful.

An engraving of Texas Rangers fighting Indians. —The Institute of Texan Cultures

Seguin

This city is named for Juan Seguin, a Mexican born in San Antonio who fought for Texas liberty. He escaped the Alamo when Travis sent him through Mexican lines for reinforcements. He later fought with Houston at San Jacinto, was mayor of San Antonio (and arranged the burial for the Alamo heroes), and died in Nuevo Laredo, Mexico, in 1889.

A company of Mathew Caldwell's Gonzales Rangers founded a site that they called Walnut Springs, then Ranger Oaks. In 1839 the community became Seguin. Heavy German immigration started. Since jails were expensive commodities, Seguin had its "Whipping Oak" as well as a three-inch iron ring that held prisoners while they were lashed.

Seguin has numerous historic homes and buildings, most of them Victorian and restored.

SOUTHERN POST OAK SAVANNAH

The southern portion of the Post Oak Savannah includes everything south of I-10 as it runs between San Antonio and Houston. The Post Oak Savannah, as outlined at the beginning of this section, abuts the Gulf Coast region along US 59 and US 77, stopping just north of Corpus Christi, and on its southwest it abuts Brush Country along US 181 between San Antonio and Sinton.

US Alt 90
Altair—Seguin
90 miles

Altair

This village started as a cattle-loading station known as Stafford's Ranch. Apparently there were legal disputes, and the community became Altair for the brightest star in the constellation Aquila. There are some who believe the town got its name because cowboys were "all on a tear."

Hallettsville

Named for Mrs. John Hallett, who donated land for a townsite, this community is on the Lavaca River and is an equal distance between Houston and San Antonio. It is also German and Czech territory, as are the surrounding villages.

Hallettsville represented the northern edge of the Sutton-Taylor Feud in 1870. Some of the Kellys lived on a ranch near a hamlet called "Sweet Home." A Sutton posse arrested William and Henry Kelly. Both were shot dead in a thicket a few miles distant. Twenty years later, W. A. Stubbs, a Hallettsville police officer, killed Bob Kelly at a dance, and was himself slain when the Kellys caught him sitting in a saloon window.

But Hallettsville survived the feud. Today the town is a shipping center. It sends cattle, turkeys, pecans, cotton, and other products to market.

Gonzales

This capital of Green C. DeWitt's Colony in 1825 was named after the Mexican patriot Rafael Gonzales, former governor of the joint state of Coahuila y Texas. The streets were named for saints. Indians burned the settlement the same year it was created, and Sam Houston burned it again eleven years later while retreating from Mexican forces.

Gonzales represented the westernmost point of Anglo-American penetration and colonization in Texas, and therefore much of the revolutionary activity centered around it. Gonzales probably paid a high price in terms of soldiers killed, because three revolutionary armies were raised there.

In 1831, Gonzales borrowed a cannon from the garrison at San Antonio and used it to frighten hostile Indians. Four years later the Mexican Army wanted it returned. When the request was refused (the colonists buried it in a peach orchard), one hundred Mexican regulars marched on the town. The defenders of Gonzales increased from 18 to 150. Commander John H. Moore dug up the cannon and on October 2, 1835, marched to meet incoming Mexican soldiers at the nearby Guadalupe River. Moore's battle flag contained a crude drawing of the cannon with the words "Come and Take It." One Mexican soldier was killed and the others retreated, ending what is often called the "Lexington of the Texas Revolution."

Stephen F. Austin assumed command of the army, and captured San Antonio. James Fannin then led some of these soldiers during a march on Matamoros, but the forces hesitated at Goliad and many were captured and executed by General Santa Anna. Meanwhile, thirty-two immortals left Gonzales to join Travis at the Alamo, the only reinforcements the Alamo ever received.

Sam Houston issued an evacuation order from Gonzales, and the Runaway Scrape commenced. Houston then burned Gonzales and, using the core of the Gonzales fighting men to assist him, he destroyed Santa Anna's army at San Jacinto in 1836.

A century later, the Texas Historical Commission created a library in memory of those Gonzales men who fell at the Alamo. Today it is called the Gonzales Memorial Museum. The town is filled with historical markers. Independence Park has a nine-hole golf course. One of the local historic sites is the 1887 jail complex, complete with hanging quarters and dungeon.

Visitors might also want to visit Pioneer Village, a twelve-acre plot holding restored buildings dating from 1830 to 1892. In 1863, the Confederates feared the Union might attack Texas with a thrust up the Guadalupe River. So the only Confederate fort ever to be commissioned west of the Mississippi River was built on a hill just north of Gonzales. It overlooked the junction of the Guadalupe and San Marcos rivers. It was called Fort Waul, for Thomas Neville Waul, a local plantation owner. Fort Waul never fired a shot, and its ruins stand at the entrance of Pioneer Village.

Gonzales today leads the state in poultry production and is an important cattle-raising center. The surrounding agricultural area sustains a wide variety of feed crops.

Belmont

Centerville, a stage stop halfway between Gonzales and Seguin, was the original name of this village. The state already had a town with that name, however, so the name became Belmont, supposedly after the Belmonts of racing fame.

US Alt 77 and US 183
Cuero—Goliad
31 miles

Cuero

The name is Spanish for cowhide, but Cuero was once the "Turkey Capital of the World." Cuero and Clinton (the latter along the Guadalupe River three miles southwest of Cuero) were the seat of the Sutton-Taylor Feud, the bloodiest in Texas.

Boiled down to its bare essentials, the feud involved the Taylor family, the Texas State Police, and Reconstruction. Although there were earlier killings, the feud basically started in Clinton on Christmas Eve 1868, when a Sutton-Taylor horse deal fell through and Buck Taylor and Dick Chisholm were shot dead in the streets.

Several other regional killings took place, and on April 1, 1873, the Taylors caught William Sutton in a saloon in Cuero and wounded him. More regional killings occurred until the Taylors besieged the Sutton faction in Cuero for a day and a night. The Taylors were then besieged in turn when help arrived for the Suttons. On March 11, 1874, Bill and Jim Taylor killed William Sutton on board a steamer in Indianola harbor.

Three Taylors were brought into Clinton, charged with cattle theft. On the night of June 14, 1874, they were taken to the courthouse and hanged. Shortly afterwards, Rube Taylor, the marshal at Cuero, was killed in a fight at Clinton. Jim Taylor and two of his friends also died.

By now the Texas Rangers had become involved. Since the leading participants were already dead, however, and most of the others in hiding, the feud gradually ceased. There had been enough killings.

Cuero is today an agricultural and recreational center. St. Mark's Lutheran Church is one of the most photographed churches in Texas. The DeWitt County Historical Museum is in a restored 1886 house with period furnishings.

Mission Valley

Mission Valley is located fifteen miles south of Cuero on Farm Road 236. The faint mission ruins are still visible (but are on private land). This mission-fortress was originally built at Matagorda Bay in 1689. The mission was Nuestra Señora del Espíritu Santo de Zuñiga, and the presidio was Nuestra Señora de Loreto. Thirty-six years later, the mission-fortress moved to Mission Valley and remained there a quarter-century. It catered to the Comanche and Karankawa Indians before transferring to Goliad.

Goliad

This is one of the three oldest municipalities in Texas. When the Mission Nuestra Señora del Espíritu Santo de Zuñiga and the Presidio (fort) Nuestra Señora de Loreto arrived here in 1749, they settled on the Aramana Indian village of Santa Dorotea. The settlement became known as La Bahía. It was a popular name for both the mission and the presidio, both of which underwent occupation in 1812 by the Gutiérrez-Magee Expedition. In June 1817, Henry Perry, a filibuster, attempted to overrun the presidio and committed suicide to escape capture. Four years later, filibuster James Long paused briefly at La Bahía.

In 1829, the Coahuila y Texas congress decided that La Bahía was no longer a mission-presidio settlement of Indians, priests, and soldiers. As a regular town, the name was changed to Goliad.

Six years later, Gen. Martín de Cós, the Mexican commander at Matamoros, landed on the Texas coast and entered Goliad on October 2. He then marched to San Antonio. As he left, a Texas company of forty-nine volunteers reached Goliad on October 10, 1835. Capt. George Collingsworth wrote, "I arrived here last night at 11 o'clock and marched into the fort by forcing the church doors;

320

La Bahía Presidio, Goliad, Texas. —The Institute of Texan Cultures

and after a small fight they surrendered with three officers and twenty-one soldiers, together with three wounded and one killed."

The 1835 capture of Goliad cut off supplies to Cós. It also made arms and supplies at Goliad available to the Texas army then surrounding San Antonio.

Meanwhile, James Fannin, a soldier of fortune elected commander in chief of the volunteer army of Texas, had gathered volunteers to invade Matamoros. They were on their way, but upon reaching Goliad they stopped, uncertain of what to do because Gen. Santa Anna had overrun the Alamo. Houston sent orders for Fannin to destroy Goliad and leave. Instead, as Mexican Gen. José Urrea closed in, Fannin prepared for a siege and even divided his forces. All of Fannin's soldiers were captured. The Texans were herded outside the presidio on Palm Sunday morning, separated into groups, marched for a brief distance, and on March 27, 1836, shot as they milled around or fled. Only a handful escaped, and over 350, including Fannin, were massacred.

James Walker Fannin. —Archives Division, Texas State Library

Following the slaughter, Goliad languished. In 1930, the city and county purchased the mission and deeded it to the state. Additional reconstruction started. Today the Presidio la Bahía welcomes tourists, and its chapel still handles religious services. Goliad State Park and the Market House Museum are open. The General Zaragoza State Historic Site contains the reconstructed birthplace and a statue of one of Mexico's great heroes. General Zaragoza was born in Goliad in 1829, and under President Benito Juárez in 1862 he defeated the French army and forced it from Mexico.

Two miles south of Goliad, a monument marks the grave of Col. James Walker Fannin, Jr., and his men.

SEVEN

North Central

*A world big enough to hold a rattlesnake and a purty
woman is big enough for all kinds of people.*

Old-time cowboy saying

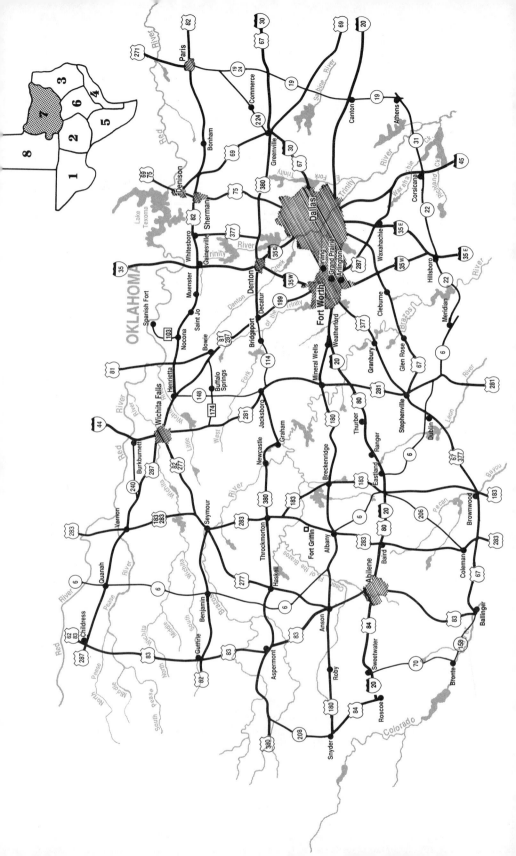

N orth Central Texas is bound on the north by the Red River; on the east by US 271 and Texas 19 as far as Athens; on the south by Texas highways 31, 22, and 6 between Athens and Dublin, then US 67 west to Ballinger; and on the west by US 83 north from Ballinger through Abilene and on to the Red River north of Childress.

The landscape in this part of Texas is marked by broad, spirited expanses of plains and broken prairie that grows few trees but makes up some of the richest farmland in North America. In earlier times an ocean of pale-colored, saddle-high grasses waved across this region. The Indians used the grass to thatch their dwellings. Indian, buffalo, and grama grasses still grow here, as do the big and little bluestem and numerous wildflowers. The black prairie is as deep as it is abundant, but it's rare on a world scale, occurring only here in North Central Texas and within a small region of Australia.

The fine-textured soil of North Central Texas is characteristically dark. It grows some of the world's finest cotton. When it gets overly damp, though, the sticky, plastic ground turns to glue and is especially adept at trapping farmers' pickup trucks. Even after the advent of mechanized farm machinery, they used to hook up animals to pull their plows. But the ground isn't always wet, and when the upper crust dries out, it cracks.

The Spanish paid scant attention to farming possibilities in this region. They generally ignored it, except when foreigners passed through. In 1769 Athanase de Mezieres, lieutenant governor in charge of the Red River Valley from the Louisiana district of Natchitoches, moved to suppress traffic in stolen horses and captives among the Taovaya Indian villages. This tribe moved into the region from Kansas and Nebraska, and lived in the upper Red River Valley near present-day Spanish Fort.

The Spanish regarded the Taovayas, like the Comanches, as one of the troublemaking "Nations of the North." In the vast company of Comanches a decade earlier, the Taovayas had participated in the infamous raid on Mission Santa Cruz de San Saba near present-day Menard (see Texas Hill Country) in 1758. With the mission in ruins, the Spanish launched a retaliatory expedition against the Indians the following year, but it was soundly repelled. The Spanish never rebuilt the mission and soon permanently abandoned the presidio.

The Taovaya traded with the English on the east and the Comanches on the High Plains, but peace came between them and the Spanish only after de Mezieres forged a settlement. Three-quarters of a century later, the Taovaya signed a treaty with the United States and settled peacefully in Indian Territory—Oklahoma.

The Wichitas also lived along the Texas side of the Red River. Like other Indians in the Caddo group, they lived in round thatched huts that resembled beehives. The more aggressive Kiowas and Comanches flanked the Wichitas on their north and west. They all hunted the massive herds of buffalo that roamed the plains, killing them usually with spears and arrows. The Wichitas accepted the same treaty as the Taovayas and also ended up in Oklahoma.

In the late 1830s and early 1840s, as Texas angled for statehood by trying to acquire citizens as rapidly as possible, the republic granted *empresario* contracts similar to agreements signed under the Spanish and Mexican regimes. The system called for vast areas to be designated as colonies, and only settlers committed to a colony could obtain land within its boundaries until the contract had been either completed or forfeited.

In one case, four agreements were signed between the Republic of Texas and a group of *empresario* associates representing the Peters Colony in 1841 and 1842. The *empresarios* called themselves the Texas Emigration and Land Company, and the "associates" were divided between the United States and Great Britain. Their grant encompassed 16,000 square miles and reached a hundred miles south of the Red River. But not all Texans thought *empresario* contracts were the best way to settle the country, which was mostly filling in just fine without using that system. American settlers were spilling to the frontier's edge in a restless grab for turf. They objected to premium parcels of public lands set aside for colonists who had not yet even arrived.

The Texas congress heard the clamor and, over President Sam Houston's veto, repealed all colonization contracts in early 1844. The Peters case went to adjudication and waited nearly forty years for the United States Supreme Court to settle the dispute. It denied the company compensation.

Meanwhile, settlers from Appalachia and other areas east of the Mississippi flocked into Texas. The North Central also attracted many German, Swedish, and Czech immigrants, most of whom became farmers of sorghum, cotton, corn, and wheat.

In spring 1843, nearly 150 Texans broke the monotony of their lives and volunteered for an expedition led by Joseph Snively. Texas in those days claimed most of New Mexico and Colorado and, on paper, had made Santa Fe the seat of Santa Fe County. Snively, an engineer, army officer, and sometimes diplomat, petitioned the Republic of Texas and received permission from it to capture rich Mexican caravans traveling from Missouri over the Santa Fe Trail to Santa Fe. A portion of the money or booty would go to the republic.

Snively's forces called themselves the Battalion of Invincibles. Most units were strategically placed to intercept the caravans by May 27, but dissension arose over the group's leadership and disposition of the anticipated plunder. The Mexican caravans, however, were few, and the difficulties in intercepting them were many. Within a month the quarreling Invincibles had split into bickering factions that had to be rounded up and disarmed by the United States Army. The remnants of Snively's expedition, dispirited and weary, slunk south of the Red River and on August 6 disbanded at Bird's Fort (Arlington) on the Trinity River.

In the midst of so much settlement occurring everywhere in Texas, Indians in the North Central region started feeling squeezed by new farmers, cattle drivers, and buffalo hunters on their lands. On February 16, 1852, the state belatedly recognized that the natives needed separate, secure lands. Two years later, in 1854, the legislature set aside twelve leagues to be surveyed, governed, and policed by the federal government. The Indian reservation would be divided into three square districts.

Under guidance from the U.S. War Department, Indian agent Robert Neighbors and Randolph B. Marcy, the former brigadier general who explored the Red River and established the Marcy Trail across North Texas, consulted with various tribes to persuade them to live on these reservations. The largest was the Brazos Indian Reservation, headquartered three miles east of present-day Graham and not far from Fort Belknap (now Newcastle). The reservation for Comanches lay forty miles west on the Clear Fork of the Brazos. And the third tract, intended for Mescalero and Lipan Apaches, adjoined the large Brazos reservation. But the Apaches shunned reservations, so Neighbors lumped that unused land onto the Brazos Reservation, making it eight leagues square. The federal government controlled and operated both of these reservations, as well as ten miles surrounding, to prevent the sale of liquor.

Approximately 2,000 Indians took up residence on the Brazos Reservation while some 450 Comanches entered the other one. The government allotted $80,000 annually for supplies, which included the weekly purchase of thirty-four head of livestock from stockmen.

Residents on the Brazos Reservation farmed 600 communal acres, making it an economic success. They grew corn, wheat, and melons. The Comanches showed little interest in raising crops. Furthermore, their tendency to jump the reservation and conduct raids aggravated the racial hatred that consumed many whites. By mid-1859, after several violent incidents, Neighbors realized that his charges had no future in Texas. The state reclaimed the reservation lands and Neighbors escorted the Indians across the Red River into Oklahoma, where the tribes blended among the reservation Wichitas in the Wichita Valley. Sadly, within a few months, a band of warring Comanches swept through the valley and slaughtered practically all the reservation inhabitants. There were no further reservation experiments in Texas until recent times.

Throughout the violence-prone period of the 1850s, Texas became a pivotal crossroads between the eastern United States and the goldfields of California.

The best-known overland routes to California—the Santa Fe Trail and the Hastings Cutoff of the Oregon Trail, which traced the Mormon Trail as far as Salt Lake and gained notoriety in 1846 from the ill-fated Donner party—lay to the north. In 1849, soldier, trailblazer, and mapmaker Randolph Barnes Marcy saw the need for a southern overland route through Texas. That year he escorted a party of emigrants from Fort Smith, Arkansas, to Santa Fe, and on his way back he blazed the Marcy Trail (often known as the California Road) across North Texas. His effort began at the little village of Dona Ana, New Mexico, fifty miles north of El Paso. Traveling east, he marked a course through Pecos and across the Pecos River at a ford called Emigrant Crossing, then circled a few miles north of Odessa and Midland and dipped through Big Spring. In North Central Texas, Throckmorton became a trail stopover. From there, Marcy roughly followed the present route of Texas 79 up to Archer City, where he turned due east to Buffalo Springs and on toward Fort Smith along already-established trails. A decade later the Butterfield Overland Mail followed much of Marcy's route to California.

A lesser-known trail ran west from Dallas across the Trinity, Brazos, and Colorado rivers in North Central Texas. It was used mostly by people from Louisiana or northeastern Texas. Those from Louisiana traveled by flatboat up the Red River to Shreveport, then followed the Arkansas River to Pine Bluff and on into Texas.

From 1858 to 1860 the Butterfield Overland Mail stage crossed the Red River to enter or exit North Central Texas by way of Colbert's Ferry, fifteen miles north of Sherman. The entire route from Tipton, Missouri, to San Francisco took twenty-five days, and the mail went through almost without exception. From Sherman the stage traveled west through Whitesboro, Gainesville, Earhart, Jacksboro, Graham, Fort Belknap, Fort Phantom Hill, Fort Chadbourne, Carlsbad, and across the Pecos, heading west. Most passengers endured the trip without rest, for the coach traveled day and night. If a traveler laid over, he forfeited his seat.

Emigrants frequently left messages attached to trees or bushes along the 2,000-mile trail for relatives or friends following behind. The letters told of water locations and hardships, including Indian scares and deaths. There wasn't much humor.

Railroads brought farmers to this broad, almost treeless prairie. The Houston & Texas Central opened the North Central portion of the state in 1873, when it entered Dallas from the south and surged on toward the Red River. The railroad had another line that reached Dallas from Texarkana. The farmers were quick to use the rails for shipping their cotton to market. For seventy years or so, from the Civil War until the 1930s, the North Central grew cotton almost exclusively. Since then the farming has diversified.

North Central Texas today is rich not only in farms and ranches but in cities as well. Dallas is the second-largest metropolis in Texas, and to many people all over the world who tuned into the popular television series of the same name, Dallas is Texas. The Southfork Ranch, where "J.R. Ewing" wheeled and dealed on the show, lies on Farm Road 2551 northeast of Dallas, but willing visitors should first check with the local chamber of commerce to verify whether it is open to the public.

Red River

The Texas-Oklahoma border runs about 350 miles along the Red River as the crow flies, but the meandering river's bank adds nearly 200 miles to that figure. From its source in the Texas panhandle to its confluence with the Mississippi River northwest of Baton Rouge, the Red flows a total of 1,360 miles. The river also forms a portion of the boundary between Texas and Arkansas. It got its name from the color of the sediments it carries. In times past it has been called Rio Roxo, Red River of Natchitoches, and the Red River of Cadodacho.

Francisco Coronado's expedition in 1541 explored the upper reaches of the Red River. The following year Luis de Moscoso led an expedition from Louisiana that crossed the river and penetrated East Texas. A century and a half later, in 1690, explorer Domingo Terán de los Rios ascended the Red River to a point near the Caddo settlements. The French ascended farther still and, early in the eighteenth century, flew their flag at several Taovaya villages near Spanish Fort, between modern highways US 81 and I-35.

Of the Red River's main headwater branches, the longest is Prairie Dog Town Fork, which rises southeast of Amarillo and carved Palo Duro Canyon some three million years ago. The Salt Fork of the Red and the North Fork of the Red also originate in the Texas panhandle, but they course into Oklahoma before flowing into the main channel.

Before 1762, the Red River formed the boundary between French and Spanish holdings. Then Spain acquired the French province of Louisiana and held all the land on both sides of the river, but Napolean persuaded Spain to return the province to France in 1800. Three years later, the United States purchased Louisiana from France for $15 million. In 1804-1805, William Durbar explored the river to the mouth of the Washita (now Lake Texoma), and after his return Dr. John Sibley provided the United States a detailed description of Durbar's findings. The Red defined the northern and eastern boundaries of the Spanish province of Texas. When Congress ratified the Adams-Onís Treaty in 1819, in which the U.S. relinquished any claim to Texas in exchange for acquiring Florida, the Red remained the northern boundary of Spanish Texas, but the eastern boundary moved west to the Sabine River.

The Republic of Texas recognized the Red River as its northern boundary on December 19, 1836. Of course, since rivers sometimes carve new channels during flood season and may choke up with silt during dry periods, they make poor boundaries. In time, the precise northern border of Texas was called into question. Did the legal boundary exist where the river ran in 1836, or in 1845

331

when Texas entered the Union, or did it change from year to year as the river eroded into different channels? In 1918 this became a pressing issue because of recent oil discoveries. Five years later the United States Supreme Court ruled that Texas owned the portion of the river up to the margin of the sand bed on its south bank, Oklahoma owned the coordinate portion on the north bank, and the United States owned the sand bed in the middle of the river.

In the mid-1800s, trading posts sprang up at principal fords along the river. One was in Grayson County at a place called Colbert's Ferry. After storming out of Missouri, the Butterfield Overland Mail stage entered Texas there and barreled west for El Paso.

During the Red River Campaign of the Civil War in 1864, the Union planned to invade Texas by way of the river. But Confederate troops stalled the Northern army during two battles along the river in Louisiana, and the Union made no further attempts to enter Texas by way of the Red River.

A series of campaigns called the Red River Indian War raged a decade later. Gen. Ranald Mackenzie led the charge against Indians who had left their reservations in Indian Territory (Oklahoma) to hunt buffalo. But they also raided settlers in Texas and were soon defeated by Mackenzie's force.

When cattle drives bound for railheads in Kansas and Nebraska started moving out of Texas, the drovers dubbed fording areas with such names as Ringgold, Red River Station, and Doan's Crossing. Just north of Vernon, Doan's Crossing saw an estimated six million cattle and one million horses ford the river between 1876 and 1895.

The Red drains 31,000 square miles in Texas. Its principal Texas tributaries are the Sulphur, Wichita, and Pease rivers. Eighty miles east of Wichita Falls, the river flows into Lake Texoma, the tenth-largest lake in the United States.

US 82
Paris—Wichita Falls
178 miles

Bonham

Bonham was established as Bois d'Arc (a fence-hedge seed) in 1837 and grew up around a log blockhouse called Fort Inglish. The village became Bonham in 1843. It was named for James Butler Bonham, a South Carolina attorney who twice slipped through Mexican lines to seek assistance for the Alamo. He returned and died with his friends.

The greatest gunfighter of all time, John Wesley Hardin, was born in Bonham on May 26, 1853. His father was J. G. Hardin, a Methodist preacher and circuit rider. John left home at an early age.

Community growth languished until the Texas & Pacific arrived in 1873. Sam Rayburn, a congressman for forty-eight years and Speaker of the House for seventeen years, willed his home and library to the people of Bonham. The home was built in 1916 and remodeled in 1934. The Sam Rayburn Library was dedicated October 9, 1957.

James Butler Bonham, an attorney who joined Travis at the Alamo. He left the Alamo twice to seek assistance, but returned to die with his comrades. —Archives Division, Texas State Library

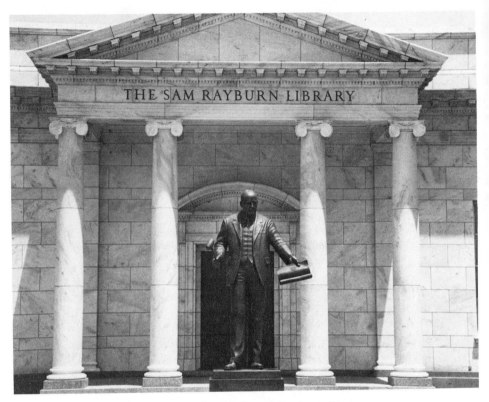

The Sam Rayburn Library, Bonham, Texas.

Bonham also has its Fort Inglish Park with a replica of an 1837 log blockhouse and stockade. The Fannin County Museum is open three days a week.

Sherman

John Selman, the man who killed John Wesley Hardin in El Paso in 1895, spent some of his formative years in the Grayson County town of Sherman. Perhaps Selman and Hardin knew and disliked each other at an early age.

The town was laid out in 1846, but in the quest for adequate wood and water, it moved to its present location in 1848. The townspeople named it for Sidney Sherman, a Massachusetts native who raised funds as well as armies and fought at the battle of San Jacinto. Sherman was credited with coining the San Jacinto battle cry, "Remember the Alamo."

The Butterfield Overland Mail route passed through Sherman in 1858. A downtown fire in 1875 cleared the way for the construction of brick structures. Austin College was founded in 1846, and today sprawls across sixty acres.

One of the West's more poignant episodes came to a conclusion in Sherman. In 1851 the Royse Oatman family left New York for California. Eighty miles west of Yuma, Arizona, their caravan was attacked by a party of Yavapais, who captured two of the Oatman children, Olive and Mary Ann, and sold them to the Mohaves. Mary Ann died in 1853, but the tribe adopted thirteen-year-old Olive and tattooed her face. Five years later, after being rescued and recovering from her ordeal, she became a national celebrity. When Olive was twenty-eight, in 1865, she married John B. Fairchild at Rochester, New York, lived in Michigan for seven years, and then moved with her husband and children to Sherman, Texas, where Fairchild founded the City Bank. Olive Oatman Fairchild died there on March 20, 1903, and is buried in the West Hill Cemetery.

By the mid-1920s Sherman had become the fifth industrial city in Texas, and it is still an industrial center with one of the higher per-capita incomes in the state. It remains the major commercial market between Dallas and Tulsa. The Sherman Historical Museum boasts some interesting murals from the Great Depression. Also, the first Confederate monument in Texas was erected in the Sherman courthouse square.

Ten miles south of Sherman on US 75 is Van Alstyne, which partially grew out of the old Mantua settlement. It was named for Marie Van Alstyne, a major stockholder of the Houston & Texas Central Railroad. Its museum houses horse-drawn buggies and early family memorabilia as well as caskets, grave-liners, cooling boards, and other equipment used by frontier undertakers.

Denison

Fifteen miles north of Sherman, on US 75, is Denison, a stop on the Butterfield Overland Stage route in 1857. The town was named for George Denison, director of the Missouri, Kansas & Texas Railroad, which arrived in 1872 and created a railroad and industrial center. A strike of railroad workers led to martial law in 1922. Dwight Eisenhower, General of the Armies and 34th president of the United States, was born here on October 14, 1890. His home at 208 Day Street was opened to the public after World War II.

The "Red River Bridge War" caused a stir in 1931, after Texas had built a free bridge (a half-mile east of the toll bridge) across the Red River at Denison. The Red River Bridge Company of Texas, which owned the toll bridge, agreed to permit construction for $60,000 and other considerations. But a few days before the scheduled July 1931 opening, the bridge company demanded $150,000. The state of Texas offered no more than $80,000. On July 16, Oklahoma Governor William H. "Alfalfa Bill" Murray ordered the Oklahoma Highway Patrol to tear down the barricades on the Texas end of the free bridge. The traffic rolled unimpeded until the Texas Rangers arrived at midnight and securely shut down all access. The toll bridge then started charging 75 cents to cross one way and a dollar per round-trip. A furious

Governor Murray ordered his state highway department to plow up the road on the Oklahoma end of the toll bridge. But the dispute ended happily on July 25 when the Texas legislature, after twelve minutes of furious debate, voted to pay the bridge company its price.

Five miles south of Denison is the gateway to Lake Texoma. The water covers Coffee's Station, sometimes known as Lower Station. It was a trading post built by Holland Coffee in 1837 on the south bank of the Red River, a popular gathering place for Indians and settlers. A village called Preston grew up around it and was often called Preston's Crossing or Preston Point. Preston was a longhorn crossing point for the Shawnee Trail, which veered toward Sedalia, Missouri.

Coffee had married Sophie Porter, and one winter during the Civil War she waded the icy Red River to warn Col. James Bourland that federal scouts were approaching. This act made her the Texas female equivalent to Paul Revere.

Whitesboro

The Texas & Pacific and the Missouri, Kansas & Texas railroads formed a junction here in 1861. The town was named for Ambrose B. White, an Ohioan who settled in Grayson County and raised a frontier company to provide protection along the Red River during the Civil War.

Gainesville

Travelers trekking west over the Marcy (California) Trail decided they had gone far enough in 1850. They selected a site on Elm Creek and called it Gainesville after Edmund Pendleton Gaines. He was a Virginian, a soldier who arrested Aaron Burr in 1807 and appeared as a witness at his trial. Gaines afterwards rose to general, was a Mexican War veteran, and died at New Orleans in 1849.

Gainesville suffered through severe Indian raids before becoming a prosperous cattle center in the late 1860s. Cotton took over after the 1893 depression, and several oil fields picked up the slack during the early 1900s.

During the Civil War, the Texas legislature created thirty-three brigade districts to ensure security in the Confederate state. Nevertheless, rumors reached authorities of a "Peace Party Conspiracy" operating out of Gainesville. The secret organization was said to number several hundred men, and on October 1, 1862, the army took between sixty and seventy alleged plotters into custody in Cooke County and incarcerated them at the county seat of Gainesville. They were charged with "conspiracy and insurrection, disloyalty and treason." A "citizens court" composed of five men listened to the evidence and sentenced thirty-nine suspects to hang. The sentences were carried out in Gainesville. Three other accused were tried by military court martial and also hanged. The hanging elm was on the bank of Pecan Creek at today's California Street, near the entrance to Leonard Park.

Monument to the Confederate Soldier, courthouse lawn, Gainesville. The inscription reads: "God holds the scales of justice; He will measure praise and blame; And the South will stand the verdict; And will stand it without shame."

In 1875, Henry B. Sanborn, a barbed-wire salesman, arrived in Gainesville. Sanborn sold the first ten reels of wire ever peddled in Texas.

The third-largest circus in the world once operated out of Gainesville. Entertainers served without pay in this nonprofit, community-wide hobby. They appeared on cue at the Cotton Bowl in 1936. During 1947 they performed before 120,000 circus fans. The show terminated when an early morning fire destroyed the circus in 1954.

Frank "Bring Them Back Alive" Buck was born in Gainesville in 1884. The Frank Buck Zoo honors his memory. There is a historic homes tour in Gainesville, as well as the Morton Museum of Cooke County and the Gainesville State School for Girls.

Nearby, Farm Road 372 gently curves over hills and through the woods of the eastern Cross Timbers. The dense, narrow band of blackland and post oak woodlands marked the western edge of the frontier until 1870.

Muenster

German Catholics Emil and Carl Flusche established this town in 1889 and named it for Muenster, Germany. The Sacred Heart Church is one of the purest examples of Gothic architecture in Texas.

Saint Jo

The first settlers took up land in 1856 along the Elm Fork of the Trinity and called the resultant settlement "Head of the Elm." By 1870, herds of cattle passed along the nearby Chisholm Trail, so Joe Howells and I. H. Boggers laid out a village named Joe. Four miles to the east lay the Devil's Backbone, a ridge used by Indians for a lookout. By 1874, Joe was flourishing with two saloons, several residences, and a general store. However, this "sinful" prosperity upset city father Joe Howells. He was a moral man displeased with the sale of liquor, so he exerted civic pressure to ban alcohol. As a result, the village became "Saint Jo."

The Stonewall Saloon Museum is an authentically restored saloon. It did not disintegrate with time because it did not get much use.

Nocona

Peta Nocona was a Comanche leader, the husband of Cynthia Ann Parker. He commanded Indians at the battle of Antelope Hills in 1858 and was reportedly slain at Pease River in December 1860. Soon thereafter, ranchers William Broaddus and D. C. Jordan brought 15,000 cattle to this area and established a ranch headquarters that became Nocona. By 1881 Nocona sprouted the Virginia Hotel, and it catered to drovers on the Chisholm Trail, five miles east. Joe Justin opened a cowboy boot and leather shop during the early 1880s, generating Nacona's reputation as a "Leathergoods Center of the Southwest." The reputation still exists.

Twenty miles south of Nocona, on Ranch Road 175 and then 59, lies the former Chisholm Trail town of Bowie. It was named for James Bowie, the Alamo hero. Its Old West Museum has pioneer and Indian exhibits.

Spanish Fort

To reach Spanish Fort, take Farm Road 103 north from US 82 (at Nocona) for seventeen miles.

The Taovaya Indians had difficulty surviving in a sea of hostile Indian neighbors, so in exchange for trade privileges the French furnished weapons and built a crude stockade and moat in 1719. Evidently this assistance was effective, because the Indians and their French allies defeated a Spanish expedition led by Diego Ortiz Parrilla in 1759. That battle marked the beginning of the end of Spanish colonization in northeast Texas.

Within nineteen years the French vanished too, so the Spanish explorer Athanase de Mezieres named the village San Teodoro in honor of Teodoro de Croix, commanding general of upper Mexico. By 1812, smallpox had slain most of the Indians, and Americans emerging from the forests found only traces of Indian, Spanish, and French structures. They shrugged and referred to the site as simply the old Spanish fort.

Anglo-Americans never entered the region in large numbers until the 1870s. Their village became Burlington, a supply point for ranchers and traders. The Chisholm Trail also surged through until the railroads forced out the drovers. As the village declined, Burlington became "Spanish Fort." Not much remains today.

A major crossing of the Chisholm Trail known as the Red River Crossing existed three miles west of Spanish Fort. By some accounts, over 600,000 longhorns forded the river between 1860 and 1885 while being driven to the railhead at Abilene, Kansas.

Henrietta

In 1860, a group of settlers named this village Henrietta for the wife of Kentuckian Henry Clay. Indian uprisings overwhelmed the population during the Civil War. After most of the townspeople fled, a Dr. Elderidge brought in ten families from Illinois. They lived in houses abandoned by previous residents. Eventually the Indians drove them out too.

By 1873, with the Indians largely gone, additional colonists migrated in. This time they remained, and Henrietta went on to become a chief trading center for Fort Sill, Oklahoma.

Roughly twenty miles south of Henrietta on Texas 148, with a four-mile jaunt east on Ranch Road 174, is Buffalo Springs, only a mile or so from a ghost town of the same name. Over a century ago, emigrant trains out of Fort Smith camped here at Buffalo Springs on their way to California. The springs were a cornerstone of the Marcy Trail, a jumping off point for the West Coast.

Wichita River

The early Spanish called this waterway Rio del Fierro (River of Iron). That didn't make much sense, so later the stream was renamed for the Wichita Indians living on the riverbanks when the first European travelers arrived. The Wichita rises in three branches (North, South, and Middle forks) and empties, after a short distance, into the Red River.

Wichita Falls

Once upon a time there were waterfalls five-feet high in the Wichita River. That's how Wichita Falls got its name. The falls vanished over a century ago when the first dams were constructed on the river.

Morris Sheppard, U.S. senator from Texas who introduced the law that became the 18th Amendment. Sheppard Air Force Base at Wichita Falls is named for him. —Archives Division, Texas State Library

Early hunter Tom Buntin used to haul buffalo hides to Sherman to eke out his modest living. Otherwise, Mississippian J. A. Scott owned the area, but it wasn't until he died and his descendants had surveyed and mapped out lots in 1876 that a village came into existence. It was a crude settlement of buffalo-hide tents, dugouts, and shacks slouching alongside the Wichita River. By 1881, eight families lived here.

When the Fort Worth & Denver Railroad moved west from Fort Worth, the town of Wichita Falls offered half the necessary land if the rails would come through. The train arrived in 1882, and as usual there was a prompt sale of town lots. The village became a terminus for freight lines hauling buffalo bones. The wheat acreage became an economic mainstay. A building boom started with the traditional saloons and mercantile structures. The town was nicknamed "Whiskey Falls." Other rail lines developed Wichita Falls into a milling and supply center for northwest Texas and southern Oklahoma. Indians from Fort Sill often visited Wichita Falls when ordering supplies.

The discovery of crude in 1911 turned the town into an oil and machinery supply center. During a subsequent population boom, hotel guests slept in shifts or relays. Stock exchanges sprouted on the sidewalks. In the carnival atmosphere, it took nearly two dozen rangers to restore order. Still, when the community celebrated its 50th birthday in 1932, it dubbed itself the "City That Faith Built." Today, it prefers the nickname "Buckle on the Sun Belt."

Sheppard Field started in 1941 and continues today as Sheppard Air Force Base. It is a technical training center, one of the five largest in the United States. It also trains NATO pilots.

The Country Club Estates offers row after row of residences comparable to Houston's River Oaks and Dallas's prestigious Highland Park. Wichita Falls has the Museum and Art Center as well as the Wichita Falls Fire and Police Museum. The restored Kell House is interesting. Several lakes and parks dot the region. Those wishing to test their physical durability, or just observe others doing it, might consider the annual August "Texas Ranch Roundup" as well as the "Hotter'N Hell Hundred," a bicycle marathon.

I-44
Wichita Falls—Red River
15 miles

Burkburnett

Burkburnett is fourteen miles north of Wichita Falls, near the intersection of I-44 and Texas 240.

Samuel Burk Burnett, from Missouri, went up the Chisholm Trail for the first time in 1856. In 1867, he allegedly drew four sixes while playing poker, and 6666 became his brand in 1874 when he moved his ranching operations north of present Wichita Falls. Burnett's "Four Sixes" ranch eventually expanded across the Red River into Indian Territory.

During the 1870s, a small community grabbed a foothold on the Four Sixes, and the cowboys derisively dubbed it Nesterville. In 1879 it became Gilbert, named for its first settler, Mabel Gilbert. When the Wichita Falls & Northwestern Railroad chugged through in 1907, Gilbert moved one mile to the railroad.

Theodore Roosevelt was Burnett's guest during a 1905 wolf hunt. Roosevelt had such a bully time that he ordered the U.S. Postal Service to change Gilbert's name to Burkburnett. The town thus became the only Texas community in history to be named by a presidential edict. The Four Sixes ceased operation in 1910.

The Schmoker #1 gushed forth in 1912, but after initial activity and speculation, the area quieted until 1916, when another well came in. Again, things soon returned to normal. Then, on July 29, 1918, Fowler's Folly #1 blew in and brought with it the wildest oil boom in Texas. Over fifty oil rigs pumped frantically within Burkburnett as one gusher followed another.

President Theodore Roosevelt and a group of West Texans on a wolf hunt, May 1906. Standing, left to right: Lee Bivens, Capt. Bill McDonald, Jack Abernathy, Maj. S. B. Young, Capt. S. Burk Burnett, Roosevelt, E. M. Gillis. Sitting: two soldiers, unknown, Bonnie More, Chief Quanah Parker (kneeling), Cecil Lyons, Dr. Lambert, D. P. "Phy" Taylor. —Panhandle Plains Museum

In terms of total oil production, Burkburnett was never a major field. But in terms of excitement, glamor, color, investments, and wild, high living, Burkburnett took its place among the rip-roaring oil towns. Burkburnett was also partly responsible for the dramatic growth of Wichita Falls.

US 287
Wichita Falls—Quanah
90 miles

Vernon

This county seat began on the Waggoner Ranch (Three D brand) as Eagle Flat. Numerous eagles nested in the vicinity. The Western (Dodge) Trail cut through Eagle Flat, and travelers used the town as a final roundup ground prior to entering Oklahoma. Stores in Eagle Flat carried large stocks of merchandise, since upon leaving the river the cattle crossed 250 miles of relatively barren no man's land before emerging at Camp Supply on the

Canadian River. Sixteen to eighteen days were spent on the trip, and provisions for fifteen or more cowboys had to be purchased.

During the 1870s Eagle Flat changed its name to Vernon in honor of President George Washington's home, Mount Vernon. An army air force base named Victory Field was established near Vernon in 1941. It taught primary flight training but was phased out in 1944. The buildings were converted in 1950 into a rest home for aged patients from the Wichita Falls State Hospital.

Doan's Crossing, seventeen miles north of Vernon on today's US 283, was the principal ford on the Red River. An estimated 6 million longhorns crossed at Doan's, and Ohioan Corwin F. Doan supervised a settlement of twenty people, twelve houses, a wagon yard, and a hotel called the Bat Cave.

In 1883, cattlemen watching the demise of the open range proposed a Great National Trail beginning at Doan's Crossing (on the Oklahoma side) and extending to Canada. The three-mile-wide trail would guarantee access for cattle drives and contain bridges, water tanks, and feedlots. Congress rejected the idea.

Quanah

This town is named for Quanah Parker, son of the famous Comanche captive Cynthia Ann Parker and the last chief of the Comanche people. The Fort Worth & Denver Railroad surveyed the land here and auctioned lots in December 1886. Even in those days, the town appeared more midwestern than Texan.

Twelve miles south of Quanah, on Texas 6, is Copper Breaks State Park. It is best known for the battle of Pease River, which involved Quanah Parker. Cynthia Ann Parker and her daughter, Prairie Flower, were recaptured from the Comanches here in 1860. The two females died after a relatively brief period, but Quanah, as a Comanche chieftain, fought on for several years before making peace.

US 82
Wichita Falls—Benjamin
80 miles

Seymour

From 1876 to 1887 the Western Trail was the principal pathway from Texas to Kansas. It superseded the Chisholm Trail after Dodge City replaced Abilene as the primary northern beef market. The Western passed a half-mile east of Seymour, as did a fork of the old California (Immigrant) Road going west. The first settlers were from Oregon, which seems like reverse migration, but they thought enough of their former state to call this new town Oregon City. The post office rejected it on account of duplicate names, so in 1878 the village became Seymour, after Seymour Munday, a local cowboy posted on a nearby line camp.

Farmers and cattlemen struggled for supremacy, and the cowboys won when cattle trampled the crops. The town then built a two-story stone hotel

Quanah Parker, Comanche chief. —Gibbs Memorial Library

in 1880 to cater to drovers and immigrants. The stone of Seymour's courthouse walls prevented passing cowboys from recklessly firing into the structure and injuring or killing the judges.

The Wichita Valley Railroad arrived in 1890, and for several years Seymour was a western terminus for railroad freighting and stagecoach business. In 1906, oil was discovered.

The temperature in Seymour reached 120 degrees in 1936, setting a Texas record that still stands.

Benjamin

Hilory G. Bedford subdivided a section of land into home sites and named the community for his son, Benjamin. Wichita Falls shipped sufficient lumber for twelve homes in 1884, and the town became a cattlemen's center.

The town separates two major watersheds: the South Wichita and Brazos rivers. The Knox County Museum features local relics.

US 380
Greenville—Haskell
214 miles

Greenville

Gen. Thomas Jefferson Green of North Carolina was a Texas colonizer before serving in the congress of the republic. As second in command of the Mier Expedition, he helped lead his men to disaster. But he also escaped from the Perote Prison in Mexico. Greenville was named for him in 1846.

The town became a railroad complex, and today it's the center of a rich agricultural and industrial region. Audie Murphy, movie star and World War II's most decorated veteran, was born just a few miles north of Greenville. The public library dedicated a room in his memory.

The Puddin' Hill Bakery is world famous. The Hunt County Museum concentrates on cotton memorabilia and celebrity mementos.

Fourteen miles northeast of Greenville, on Ranch Road 224, is Commerce, Texas. Its main features are East Texas State University and the 1890 birthplace of Gen. Claire Chennault. The general commanded the famed Flying Tigers and was a close adviser to Generalissimo Chiang Kai-shek in China during World War II.

Denton

*The last time you experienced anything like Denton,
Texas . . . you probably asked her to marry you!*

Ad purchased in *Fortune Magazine*
by Denton Chamber of Commerce

This education, livestock, and manufacturing center originated on the eastern edge of the Grand Prairie portion of the Central Plains, a region of low hills and broad valleys, in 1857. It was named for John B. Denton, a Tennessee minister and lawyer killed during a battle with Indians at Village Creek, six

John Chisum, a Texas cowboy before he moved to New Mexico in search of more room. —El Paso Public Library

hills and broad valleys, in 1857. It was named for John B. Denton, a Tennessee minister and lawyer killed during a battle with Indians at Village Creek, six miles east of Fort Worth, in 1841. John Denton was initially buried in an unmarked grave near Oliver Creek, but cattleman John Chisum disinterred the remains and reburied them in his yard near Bolivar. In 1901, the remains were again removed and placed in the southeast corner of the Denton County courthouse lawn.

Denton, progressive and expansive, is generally considered a college town. Texas Normal College, which opened in 1890, evolved into the University of North Texas. Nearby, Texas Women's University became the largest university for women in the nation.

The Fighting Air Command Flying Museum is at Hartlee Field, a World War II training base. For those with other interests, the Victorian homes on West Oak Street, popularly called Silk Stocking Row, are worth the tour. And the Denton County Historical Museum offers a variety of exhibits.

Decatur

This little town began as Bishop's Hill in 1857 when Absolom Bishop surveyed the lots. Afterwards, for a few months, it was called Taylorsville, for Zachary Taylor. Before year's end it had become Decatur to honor Commodore Stephen Decatur.

The Butterfield Overland Mail passed through in 1858, but the "real" excitement arrived in 1862. The Peace Party Conspiracy, which defined itself as the "Loyal League," pledged to support the North. They used passwords, secret signs, and hand grips. Their objective was to resist the Confederate draft and maintain a spy system for the Union Army. In 1865, five leaders were tried at the Confederate arsenal in Decatur and hanged. Others were inducted into the Confederate Army (see Gainesville).

Racial tensions remained high in Decatur after the war. During Reconstruction, black soldiers from Fort Richardson frequently restored order.

The pink limestone courthouse, built in 1895, is a must for camera buffs. The Wise County Heritage Museum recalls the trail days, whereas the Dan Waggoner Mansion is a unique Victorian showpiece.

Bridgeport

W. H. Hunt negotiated with the Butterfield Overland Stage Company and obtained a charter to bridge the West Fork of the Trinity River in 1860. Out of this arose Bridgeport. Of course, the town didn't arise for very long because during that same year the bridge collapsed. Then the mail route was abandoned as the Civil War loomed. By 1873, however, a new bridge was constructed, making travel easier between Denison and Fort Richardson.

Jacksboro

This town went through two names (Lost Creek and Mesquiteville) before it became Jacksboro in 1858. The settlers were William H. and Patrick C. Jack. However, the village never prospered until Col. Samuel H. Starr brought in the 6th Cavalry in 1866 and created Fort Richardson on Lost Creek, the post farthest north in Texas. The post was named for Israel B. Richardson, slain during the battle of Antietam in 1862, and was considered necessary to keep the Kiowa, Comanches, and Kiowa-Apaches in check. In July 1870, at the bloody fight at the Little Wichita River, Capt. Curwen B. McLellan and fifty-six men were attacked by nearly 100 Kiowas. Thirteen Medals of Honor were awarded for gallantry in that action.

Gen. James Oakes and Ranald Mackenzie commanded here. Gen. William T. Sherman was visiting in 1871 when the Salt Creek Massacre (see Graham) happened twenty miles to the west. Seven teamsters were slain. Mackenzie lost the Kiowa trail in a rainstorm, only to learn later that the Indians had surrendered at Fort Sill, Oklahoma.

The rebellious chiefs were identified as Satank, Satana, and Big Tree, all of whom were returned to Texas for court appearances. During the trip, Satank committed suicide by attacking his guards. The remaining two sat through the first Indian trial in the United States, the proceedings taking place in Fort Richardson before the case was transferred to Jacksboro. Both Indians were found guilty of murder and sentenced to hang in Jacksboro on September 1, 1871. However, nationwide sentiment called for mercy, so a month prior to the execution date both entered the Huntsville Penitentiary, sentenced to life in prison.

In late 1873, after the tribes promised to remain on reservations and make war no longer, Satanta and Big Tree were released. The Red River War of 1874-75 was the immediate result.

In mid-1875, the Kiowas were again corralled. Satanta returned to prison in Huntsville, where he committed suicide on October 11, 1878, by plunging through a second-story window. Big Tree was arrested and released on the request of federal authorities. He settled on an Oklahoma farm, joined the Rainy Mountain Baptist Church, became a deacon and Sunday school teacher, and died at age eighty on November 13, 1932.

Fort Richardson was abandoned in May 1878, but it was reoccupied in November 1940 by the 2nd Battalion, 131st Field Artillery, 36th Division of the Texas National Guard. At sea when the Japanese bombed Pearl Harbor, the unit landed at Java and surrendered in March 1942. Many prisoners died while building the Burma-Siam railroad, and the remainder were not released until three years later when the Japanese surrendered. The restored military buildings are part of Fort Richardson State Park.

The Jack County Museum is located in the oldest house in the county.

Big Tree, famous Kiowa chief. —Eugene C. Barker Texas History Center, UT Austin

Graham

Before a town existed here, portions of what would become Graham served as a northern boundary of the Brazos Indian Reservation. (Fort Belknap is just eleven miles west of Graham on Farm Road 61.) The Indians lived in log houses and numerous circular dwellings of grass. These Anadarko, Caddo, Tehuacana, Tonkawa, Waco, Cherokee, Choctaw, Delaware, and Shawnee Indians, numbering 2,000, remained here until 1859, when they were removed to Indian Territory (see North Central introduction).

349

The Salt Creek Massacre occurred nearby on May 17, 1871. Roughly 100 Kiowas and Comanches attacked a wagon train led by Capt. Henry Warren, a government contractor, while the procession was traveling between Forts Griffin and Richardson. One wagon master and six teamsters were slain, one of them tied to a wagon wheel and burned after being scalped. The guilty Indian leaders were later tried for murder (see Jacksboro).

In 1872 the brothers Gustavus and Edwin S. Graham founded the town of Graham along Salt Creek, a tributary of the Brazos River. Five years later, forty cattlemen met under a huge oak tree near the courthouse to organize the Cattle Raisers Association of Texas.

Oil was discovered in 1917. Today the city calls itself "The Land of Lakes and Opportunity." Historical restoration has taken place all over the community, especially near the courthouse square. Graham is a gateway to Possum Kingdom State Park.

Newcastle and Fort Belknap

Newcastle, England, gave this town its name in 1908. Both communities had iron and coal mines, but the English city thrived while the Texas city struggled.

As the frontier moved farther west, the U.S. Army expanded its defense system. One post was Belknap, two miles south of Newcastle on what is now Texas 251. It was the first fort on the new frontier line, and it pushed into Indian country. Gen. William G. Belknap, a Mexican War veteran, led his men to this spot near the junction of the Salt Fork and the Clear Fork of the Brazos River in May 1851. He died in November, and the post adopted his name.

The first buildings were of logs, but stone structures followed. A 29-foot well was dug by candlelight because of the intense daytime heat. The opposite extremes prevailed on December 27, 1856, when the 2nd Cavalry rode in. A raging blizzard blinded the men. The temperature dropped to below zero, ice formed six inches thick on the Brazos River, and horses froze to death on the picket line. Robert E. Lee and his 2nd Cavalry were stationed at Fort Belknap, as were numerous officers who made reputations during the Civil War.

A civilian settlement named Belknap sprang up around the fort, and Belknap was a junction point for stages. The town survived the abandonment of Fort Belknap in 1857 when the troops, discouraged by the poor quality of water, transferred out. Ten years later Col. Samuel Starr and the 6th Cavalry tried to resurrect the post. They found blowing sand, desolation, and a dead buffalo lying on the parade ground. After five months, Starr gave up and took his troopers to Fort Griffin. The remains of thirty soldiers were disinterred and moved to the national cemetery at San Antonio in early 1907.

Meanwhile, Robert Simpson Neighbors, who had almost single-handedly brought the trans-Pecos region into Texas, won controversial fame as a Texas Indian agent. To save the Indians from white destruction, Neighbors gathered

Comanches and others and placed them on a Texas reservation near Fort Belknap (see Throckmorton and North Central introduction). This infuriated numerous whites, most of whom insisted on Indian extermination rather than preservation. As it turned out, even the Texas reservations weren't safe. Neighbors transferred over 2,000 Indians to reservations in Indian Territory (Oklahoma) in August 1859.

Upon returning to the village of Belknap, Neighbors was engaged in street conversation when someone shot him in the back. He lies in an unmarked grave in the civilian cemetery. A state historical marker in his memory stands at the old military cemetery, a half-mile distant.

Fort Belknap was reoccupied by federal troops in 1867, but they retired to Fort Griffin shortly thereafter. Some buildings were restored for the centennial in 1936, and today the old fort is a county park. The former commissary building is now a museum.

Throckmorton

Every settlement in Throckmorton County began with Camp Cooper on the north bank of the Clear Fork of the Brazos, seventeen miles south of Throckmorton on what is now Ranch Road 2528. In 1855, Indian Agent Robert Neighbors and Capt. Randolph Marcy established two federal Indian reservations in Texas. The Brazos reservation was on the Brazos River, twelve miles south of Fort Belknap (see Fort Belknap and North Central introduction), and it contained individuals from the Waco, Wichita, Anadarko, Caddo, and Tonkawa tribes. The Comanche Indian reservation, under Chief Ketumse, was located on the Clear Fork of the Brazos, near what is now Throckmorton.

In order to prevent clashes between Indians and whites, Camp Cooper was established by Col. Albert Sidney Johnston in January 1856. Col. Robert E. Lee relieved him a year later.

The reservation experiment never succeeded in Texas. The whites ambushed Indians, and the Indians constantly slipped off the reservation to raid. As a result, when Neighbors removed his charges to Indian Territory in August 1859, there was no further need for Camp Cooper. It reverted to private property, and only a granite marker identifies the site of the Indian reservation.

Throckmorton is a ranching and farming center today.

Haskell

In prehistoric times, Comanches, Kiowas, and Kickapoos camped in this region. Buffalo hunters and gold seekers relaxed at Willow Springs. A settler named Thomas Tucker, who arrived in 1879, called it Rice Springs for Rice Durrett, a Reynolds and Matthews Cattle Company employee. In 1885, when the first post office was established, the name became Haskell, honoring Charles Haskell, killed during the Goliad Massacre. A local saloon catered to cowboys and dubbed itself "The Road to Ruin." It doubled as the town's only church.

Wild mustangs populated the area because of numerous springs, and mustangers worked their trade until the army no longer needed mounts. Visitors are reminded of these horses today when they see such landmarks as Wild Horse Mesa, Wild Horse Knob, Mustang Spring, Mustang Crossing, Mustang Hollow, and Wild Horse Tree.

South of Haskell, numerous Indian fights occurred. Double Mountain, Paint Creek, Lipan Point, and California Creek were but a few locations.

The J. U. and Florence B. Fields Museum of Fine Living has exhibits of glass, rugs, and furniture.

I-20

Canton—Fort Worth

80 miles

Canton

Settlers came here from Old Canton in Smith County in 1850, established a county seat, and hung on until 1872 when the Texas & Pacific Railroad arrived. Unfortunately, the railroad missed Canton by ten miles, and Wills Point, which wasn't all that far away, got the county seat. This angered the citizens of Canton. They armed and marched on Wills Point, intent on recovering the archival records. Governor Richard B. Hubbard dispatched the state militia to restore calm, and in the meantime the Supreme Court of Texas ruled in favor of Canton. The town still needed a railroad, however, and unwilling to use Wills Point, it established a village called Edgewood, ten miles north and on the railroad.

With plantation farming unprofitable in Van Zandt County, the slave population declined. Sidney S. Johnson of the *Canton Times* quoted a slave seller as saying he would just as soon hold his sales in a free (Union) state as bring his slaves to Van Zandt County. As a pun, Johnson coined the phrase "Free State of Van Zandt."

Canton is now a farming and livestock center. Its Brewer's Bells Museum has 3,200 bells, many rare and exotic. The Toy Museum displays favorite and unique toys of yesterday.

Dallas

Dallas rises from the rolling prairies of North Central Texas and sits in the geographical center of Dallas County. The Trinity River separates the main business district. Oak Cliff, a residential area, is south and west of the Trinity.

John Neely Bryan, farmer, lawyer, and Indian trader, was the first settler, arriving in 1841 and building a cabin in what is now the western end of the downtown area, today's county government region. Bryan dressed in buckskins, plowed with a broken tree fork, and crossed the Trinity River in a cottonwood dugout.

The Mabel Gilbert and James J. Beeman families joined him a year later, and the fledgling village became Dallas, probably named for George Mifflin Dallas, vice president of the United States from 1845 to 1849. However, it could also have been named for his brother, Commodore A. J. Dallas, of the U.S. Navy; or their father, Alexander James Dallas, secretary of the treasury; Joseph Dallas, a settler near the new town; or any of the brothers James R., Walter R., or Alexander James Dallas, all of whom served with the Army of the Republic.

Apparently the little village attracted interest, not all of it flattering. When John Billingsley arrived from Missouri in 1844, his journal recorded the following:

We soon reached the place we had heard of so often; but the town, where was it? Two small log cabins—this was the town of Dallas, and two families of ten to twelve souls was its population.

Dallas County was created in 1846 with Dallas as the county seat. By 1849 Dallas had sufficient people to attract the *Dallas Herald*. The *Dallas Morning News* absorbed it in 1885.

Bryan sold his town-site interests in 1852 to Alexander and Sarah Cockrell. Sarah promptly built a three-story hotel, and soon owned the ferry and toll bridge.

Francois Cantagrel, leader of French, Belgian, American, and Swiss socialists, formed a utopian society called La Réunion, establishing it on bluffs overlooking the West Fork of the Trinity a few miles west of Dallas. Approximately 300 colonists migrated to this settlement in 1855-56, but the soil was thin, there were insufficient houses, and colony finances were haphazardly administered. When this planned perfect city fell short of soaring expectations and ideals, most of the scientists, artists, musicians, and writers moved to Dallas. Several returned to France or New Orleans. Those Europeans who remained in Dallas gave the community a cultured, sophisticated, and cosmopolitan flavor, a quality encouraged and continuously enriched to this day.

By 1850, Dallas had nearly a thousand people, plus shops and factories, a stage line, two private schools, and congregations of Methodists and Presbyterians. The town was incorporated in 1856.

Francois Cantagrel of the La Réunion Colony. —The Institute of Texan Cultures

Dallas had very few Indian attacks, but it had numerous scares. Generally the tribes camped peacefully nearby, as in 1845 when a thousand Delawares pitched their tepees.

The Civil War barely touched Dallas, although the town was a Confederate administrative center. However, those were the days of slave-rebellion fears, when rampant rumors darkly described poisoned water wells and murdered masters. When the 1860 "great" fire destroyed most of Dallas, an informal jury of fifty-two men declared it a slave plot. The town lynched three blacks.

Immigrants poured into Dallas after the Civil War. Cattlemen used the town as a stopover, a way station for drives to Kansas and Missouri. The buffalo-hide industry adopted Dallas as a trade center.

Strangely, frontier violence rarely flared in Dallas. Most troubles amounted to little more than cattle and horse thefts.

Dallas was no natural gateway like El Paso, and it had no seaport, as did Houston and Galveston. Dallas was located at the forks of the Trinity, but this was not a navigable stream. However, Dallas was nevertheless destined to become a transportation hub and distribution center. The town had to have railroads and banks.

The Houston & Texas Central steamed into Dallas in 1872. The citizens contributed $5,000 in property and cash for a right-of-way and donated an additional 115 acres of prime land. The railroad provided Dallas with a north-south line.

When the Texas & Pacific arrived, the Texas legislature required the railroad to come within one mile of Browder Springs, where Dallas drew most of its water. The politicians then put together a $100,000 bond issue, got it approved in 1872, and used the money as a cash inducement for enticing the Texas & Pacific into downtown Dallas. An undisclosed amount of right-of-way land sweetened the deal. Dallas later constructed the $6 million Union Station, which serviced over a hundred trains per day.

Dallas County Courthouse, 1869. —The Institute of Texan Cultures

The telegraph arrived, newspapers received wire copy, and Dallas received national and international news on a daily basis.

Seven thousand people lived in Dallas in 1873. Over 700 buildings were constructed that year. Swiss and German immigrants settled along Swiss Avenue and Germania (Liberty since 1917) streets. Entertainment figures such as Edwin Booth, Sarah Bernhardt, and Lily Langtry played in Dallas. The North Texas Building became the city's first skyscraper. It went up in 1888, and so did the four-story Dallas Club for Gentlemen.

Dallas was the biggest inland cotton market in the world. It operated the largest publishing center south of St. Louis.

After a Trinity River flood in 1908 severed contacts with Oak Cliff, Dallas constructed five concrete and steel viaducts. They connected the east and west sections of the city and, because of the levee, created an industrial district meandering alongside the old riverbed.

Of course, Dallas had its competitors. Capt. William H. Gaston, a pioneer banker, established East Dallas in 1871, a forty-one-acre tract east of the Dallas central business district. It incorporated in 1882 and had good water as well as modern streets and schools. Educational institutions included St. Mary's College, St. Matthew's School, and Ursuline Academy.

East Dallas had 6,000 residents and more land area than Dallas. It did so well that historians still do not understand why it merged into Dallas. The annexation election passed easily in 1890.

The annexation of Oak Cliff was tougher and more controversial. This community began as Hord's Ridge on the west bank of the Trinity in 1845. William H. Hord, a Tennessean, founded it. By 1890, with Dallas threatening annexation, Hord's Ridge changed its name to Oak Cliff and incorporated with 2,500 residents. For the next ten years, Dallas plotted and Oak Cliff worried. An annexation proposal was defeated at the ballot box. But three years later, in 1904, with tough economic times befalling Oak Cliff, an annexation measure passed by eighteen votes.

Oak Lawn, on the Dallas south side, also fell. Its 1,000 acres achieved village status in 1874, and by 1906 it had become the exclusive residential site for wealthy Dallas residents. The city needed the tax rolls, however, and it also needed the expansion room, so Oak Lawn disappeared into Dallas.

Oak Lawn Park, ten acres in size, had been laid out by the street railway system so that riders might be lured to the countryside for picnics. Old-timers still talk about boat rides on the small lake and the free outdoor movies.

During the 1920s, the Dallas Southern Memorial Association campaigned for a suitable tribute to Gen. Robert E. Lee. The group raised $50,000 and hired noted sculptor A. Phemister Proctor to create a heroic bronze equestrian statue of Lee and place it in Oak Lawn Park. The remaining money went into a Robert E. Lee memorial scholarship fund, which still sends students to Southern Methodist University each year.

The Dallas park board changed the name of Oak Lawn Park to Lee Park. They built a replica of Lee's home in Arlington, Virginia, and furnished it antebellum style. A memorial honoring Southern heroes of all wars was designed as a fountain floating on the lake's surface in 1966.

This essentially left only Highland Park on the list for annexation. But it never happened. Highland Park, like its neighboring suburb, University Park (which began with the opening of Southern Methodist University), remained a separate community even while Dallas encircled it. Because so many prominent Dallasites live there, the possibility of future annexation, while threatening, is questionable.

The other town existing within the present limits of Dallas is Cockrell, which began as Cockrell Hill in 1853. The satellite cities of Dallas (and Fort Worth) are Grapevine, Farmer's Branch, Arlington, Duncanville, Culess, Hurst, Plano, Garland, Grand Prairie, Irving, Mesquite, Carrollton, and Richardson. Dallas and Fort Worth are a metroplex of 3 million residents.

Other than annexations and the arrival railroads, two additional events gave Dallas a major shove toward greatness. The town fought for and received a federal reserve bank, skillfully pulling it through the outstretched, anticipating fingers of Houston. Since its construction, the Eleventh District Federal Reserve Bank has attracted more than a hundred banks to the Dallas metropolitan area.

Dallas became the Texas centennial celebration city in 1936. Although Dallas had not even existed in 1836, it defeated all other applicants by bidding $10 million and putting up 242 acres of land. Celebrity visitors included President Franklin D. Roosevelt, scientist George Washington Carver, movie actors Ginger Rogers, Clark Gable, Robert Taylor, and Shirley Temple, singer Rudy Vallee, world heavyweight champion Jack Dempsey, and famous radio reporter Walter Winchell. Over 177,000 people crowded the midway on opening day. A year later, the centennial center became the site of the 1937 Pan American Exposition. Over 13 million visitors came to Dallas during those two events, and Dallas therefore became not only a place to be, but a place to be seen.

Defense industries started arriving in Dallas during World War II, and the city began manufacturing electrical equipment, aircraft, and missile parts. The population jumped to more than a million between 1940 and 1970.

The town passed a $175 million bond issue entitled "Goals for Dallas" in 1967. The Dallas-Fort Worth Airport was a reality soon afterwards.

But Dallas was a place of tragedy, too. Many people still equate Dallas with the assassination of President John F. Kennedy on November 22, 1963. Lee Harvey Oswald fired rifle shots from the sixth floor of the Texas School Book Depository Building at the corner of Elm and Houston streets. Vice President Lyndon B. Johnson took the presidential oath of office at Love Field in Dallas.

Southern Methodist University is the largest and oldest such institution in Dallas. The Dallas Theater center is the only theater designed by the famous

American architect Frank Lloyd Wright. Dallas has a civic opera, and the New York Metropolitan Opera visits annually.

The Dallas Cowboys of the National Football League play at Texas Stadium in Irving. The stadium seats 65,000 people. A few miles west in Arlington, between Fort Worth and Dallas, the Texas Rangers of baseball's American League play at The Ballpark in Arlington. Other professional sports teams in Dallas include the Dallas Mavericks (basketball) and Dallas Sidekicks (soccer). The Cotton Bowl game originated in Dallas, and every New Year's Day it features two of the nation's outstanding college football teams.

The fifty-two story First National Bank Building is the tallest structure in Dallas. Nearby is the famous Neiman-Marcus department store and a Memorial Auditorium Convention Center. County government occupies the west end of downtown, and city government occupies the east end. Warehouses, office buildings, and small industries claim the Trinity Industrial District, which adjoins the downtown. Dallas is 512 feet above sea level, gets thirty-four inches of rain annually, has a population of one million, and retains a council-manager form of government.

Dallas is the second-biggest city in Texas. Only Houston is larger. Yet, Dallas is the Southwest's largest banking center. It is second in the nation in

The original Neiman-Marcus Store in Dallas, 1907. —The Institute of Texan Cultures

insurance company home offices and is one of the country's top three fashion markets. Four Dallas churches are among the nation's largest in their respective denominations: First Baptist, Highland Park Methodist, East Dallas Christian, and Highland Park Presbyterian. The residents justly call their city "Big D."

Irving

Irving is essentially "Dallas Northwest." It was originally known as Gorbett, but Gorbett disappeared when the residents moved a few miles away to Kit after learning that the Chicago, Rock Island & Gulf Railroad was going that way. However, the railroad changed its mind and headed for Irving, which wasn't much more than a watermelon farm. Then Kit disappeared as everybody raced to Irving. Irving is today best known as home to the Dallas Cowboys and Texas Stadium. It is also the home of the National Museum of Communications, a dandy. The Dallas-Fort Worth International Airport is practically in Irving's front yard.

Grand Prairie

After the Civil War this little community started as Deckman, named for its founder, Alexander Deckman. In 1873, the Texas & Pacific Railroad renamed the village Grand Prairie for its location on the eastern edge of the Grand Prairie region.

Hensley Field, a training base for reserve pilots, was named after Maj. William N. Hensley, who crossed the Atlantic in a dirigible in 1919. By late December 1941, Hensley Field had become Midwest Area headquarters for the Air Corps Ferrying Command.

Numerous defense plants moved into Grand Prairie during World War II. Today the town has an amusement park called Clown Around, an International Wildlife Park, and a Palace of Wax & Ripley's Believe It or Not. A huge flea market called Traders Village caters to all kinds of tastes.

Arlington

Arlington grew out of a settlement called Johnson's Station in 1842. In 1876, a railroad survey went three miles south, so the village moved to the tracks and became Arlington. The area thrived on livestock raising, plus a budding health industry tied in with a deep mineral spring. Rose production added additional opportunities.

Jonathan Bird's fort was seven miles north of Arlington, and it protected the military road from the Red River to Austin. On September 29, 1843, Republic of Texas officials and Indian leaders met at Fort Bird and signed a treaty drawing a line between white settlements and native Americans. The Texas senate ratified it on January 31, 1844. Remnants of the Snively

Expedition (see North Central introduction) disbanded here in 1843. Bird's Fort disappeared by 1850, but a nearby village took the name of Birdville.

Arlington State College was founded in 1895 and became the University of Texas at Arlington in 1965. Arlington is famous for its Six Flags Over Texas, a 200-acre theme park. Otherwise, there is the Caelum Moor Sculpture Park, the Johnson Plantation Cemetery/Park, and the Fielder and Sewing Machine museums.

Fort Worth

In 1849, Maj. Ripley A. Arnold established a military post on June 6 in honor of Gen. William Jenkins Worth. Fort Worth thus began as Camp Worth on the Clear Fork of the Trinity River. Because of flooding, the post was moved to a bluff on the south side of the river where its name became Fort Worth in November 1849.

General Worth had fought in the War of 1812, had served bravely in the Florida Seminole Indian Wars, and had participated in the storming of Monterrey, Mexico, in 1847. He died of cholera at San Antonio on May 7, 1849.

The first settler in the area was John Press Farmer. He erected a tent at the river crossing in 1849, and likely operated a ferry. Other homesteaders arrived, living under the protection of fort guns. John Peter Smith, a local schoolteacher, surveyor, lawyer, Texas Ranger, and latter-day mayor, was so active in the town's creation that historians have dubbed him the "Father of Fort Worth." A stage line hooked Fort Worth to Yuma in 1850. By 1856, Fort Worth had a flour mill.

When Comanche leader Jim Ned planned an assault on Fort Worth in 1850, the soldiers knew about it and waited in ambush. The Indians were defeated along the Trinity River, and thus passed the last Indian fight in this area.

Incidentally, treaties during this period were generally conducted with individual Indian chiefs, except for Comanches. One treaty stipulated that Indians would remain *west* of a line drawn through what would become Fort Worth. That's how the expression "out where the West begins" got started. It also explains in part why the people of Fort Worth think of themselves as "West Texans" instead of "North Central Texans."

The army abandoned its log fort and transferred to Fort Belknap in 1853. Settlers occupied the empty buildings and barracks. An old stable became the city's first hotel. Seven years later, the state created Tarrant County and Fort Worth became the county seat. The town then had 500 residents.

Auctioneers bought and sold black people almost daily on the streets of Fort Worth, with men going for $200 to $300 and women averaging $150 each. Like Dallas, Fort Worth also heard whispers of impending slave revolts. Abolitionists were lynched from pecan trees.

Gen. William J. Worth. Historically, he is little known, but he gave Fort Worth its name.
—National Archives

The Civil War, which missed Fort Worth in terms of fighting, nevertheless had its crushing economic effects. Maj. K. M. Van Zandt, a returning Confederate veteran, described the town:

Fort Worth, as I first saw it late on an August afternoon in 1865, presented a sad and gloomy picture. The town had been laid out according to the general style, with a square in the center with stores surrounding it. A courthouse had been started in 1860. The rock walls had been built up as high as the first story, and there there the work had stopped. The very look of these walls accentuated the picture of desolation. The deserted officers quarters were still standing on

The Yuma stage leaving Fort Worth. —The Institute of Texan Cultures

the northeast side of the square, and the parade ground was still to be seen. On the south and west side of the square there were a few business houses, some of them stone or brick and two stories high. All of them had the shelves empty and the doors locked.

Van Zandt opened a mercantile store and purchased a city block for $300. As life and commerce returned, Fort Worth thrived in the cattle business. Texans had pointed their longhorns east after the war, and when that market closed or showed less than modest results, the drovers turned their herds north toward the railheads in Abilene and Dodge City, Kansas, in 1867.

When ranchers moving out of the Nueces and Rio Grande bottomlands reached the prairies south of Fort Worth, the trails merged into a recognizable track. The Chisholm slashed between Dallas and Fort Worth. The Western Trail lunged between Fort Worth and Fort Griffin. At any given moment a hundred thousand head of livestock might be grazing on the surrounding grasslands.

Henry Sinclair Drago, in his *Great American Cattle Trails,* described early Fort Worth as "just a miserable collection of saloons, dance halls and gamblers, either ankle-deep in dust or wallowing in mud, depending upon the season." At that point Fort Worth obviously had no grandiose vision of itself as anything other than what it was: a cowtown.

Fort Worth, locked in a bitter struggle with Fort Griffin on the west and Dallas on the east for dominance in the cattle trade, gradually took charge and grew as an outfitting and supply point. The town represented a last opportunity to repair wagons, to restock weapons and whiskey, and to purchase flour, bacon, beans, and coffee. When those same cowhands returned home, they again passed through Fort Worth, reoutfitting and purchasing gifts for those who stayed behind.

The great buffalo slaughter attracted outfitters to Fort Worth, the center for hide and bone sales as well as a rest and recovery location for rambunctious skinners, hunters, and suppliers. Up to 200,000 hides in a single season were shipped through Fort Worth. Hunters generally received a dollar for each.

The Civil War delayed construction of a courthouse, but the building was completed by 1870. A fire destroyed it in 1873.

Terrant County Courthouse in the 1870s. —The Institute of Texan Cultures

Nevertheless, 1873 was a good year for Fort Worth. The town incorporated. The Texas & Pacific Railroad drove to within twenty-six miles of Fort Worth but never arrived until 1876 due to the Panic of 1873. Even so, it cost the city 320 acres of prime land, property the city fathers promptly pledged. When the railroad steamed in on July 19, 1876, one of the speakers became so emotional that he predicted an eventual population of 5,000 people.

In May of 1880, the Missouri-Kansas-Texas Railroad arrived. This cost the town $75,000, and the sum was quickly raised.

By now the great cattle drives were ending. Barbed wire, the Texas tick, and irate farmers were shutting down the trails. Even the railroads contributed. Why spend months pushing livestock to Kansas and other such ports when cattle could be shipped by railroad east to market directly from Texas?

Railroads even revolutionized stock breeding. Ranchers commenced raising livestock with additional meat on their bones. The cattle became "shorthorns" rather than "longhorns," but unlike the longhorns, the shorthorns rarely walked over five miles in their life. Besides, more shorthorns could be jammed into railroad cars because they no longer needed so much room to swing their heads.

As railroads encroached deeper into Texas, Fort Worth took advantage of its opportunities. Its prime location near the state's geographical center made it a logical distribution point for beef processing.

By 1890, the Union Stock Yards were operating in Fort Worth. Three years later, Boston capitalist Greenlief W. Simpson purchased the Union and renamed it the Fort Worth Stockyards. Louville Veranus Niles, another Boston capitalist, reorganized the Fort Worth Packing Company.

In 1902, with America consuming a per capita average of sixty pounds of beef a year, Swift and Armour, two nationally known packing companies, built processing plants complete with pens, sheds, barns, and cold-storage facilities on the north side of Fort Worth. Overnight the Fort Worth Stockyards ranked fifth in the nation, behind Chicago and Kansas City but almost equal to St. Louis and Omaha. Sixteen million head of cattle passed through during the subsequent decade. The Fort Worth Stockyards Belt Railway provided servicing and transportation facilities. The town zoomed from a population of 27,000 in 1900 to 73,000 in 1910. By 1920 there were 105,000 people in Fort Worth.

In 1911, Niles also created and incorporated Niles City, a fledgling village one and one-half mile square in size and three miles north of Fort Worth. It absorbed the entire Fort Worth Stockyards District, which included major meat-packing firms, grain elevators, a cottonseed oil company, a petroleum refinery, and a pipeline products plant. Although smaller than Fort Worth, Niles had a $30 million tax base and rightfully enjoyed its reputation as the "Richest Little Town in the World." Fort Worth annexed it in 1922.

But the time of the stockyards was already winding down. The year 1917 marked a high point when 10,000 head of livestock passed through in a day. The twenties stayed relatively prosperous too, but the thirties brought a drought. Shortages started in the forties, and the stockyards began to grow obsolete in the fifties. By the sixties the battle had been lost to the feedlots. Cattle were no longer trucked in, and the auctions were moving west. The Exchange Building lobby, which led the nation in livestock trading, was as empty as the yards.

Today the Fort Worth Stockyards are a major tourist attraction. The Livestock Exchange, with its Spanish-style architecture, was built in 1903 and renovated in 1978. Cattle dealers, attorneys, and architects have offices there. Art shows have proliferated. The gigantic Billy Bob's Texas honky-tonk is still there, as are numerous restaurants, gift shops, boutiques, travel agencies, saloons, Western wear and saddle shops, and even an array of wild gunfights (not real, just for fun). For the last hundred years nobody has ever walked away from the Fort Worth Stockyards saying he or she was bored.

The Cowtown Coliseum, with its mission-style architecture, was built in 1908 and for many years was the largest show arena of its kind. Fort Worth purchased it in 1936 for the Cowtown Rodeo, an event occurring every Saturday night during the spring and fall.

But a community like Fort Worth paid a price for being a cowtown, a buffalo-hunters' town, a railroad town, a military town, and a frontier town. Obviously, there were more rowdy characters wandering the muddy streets than there were preachers, schoolteachers, and tax investors. And just as obviously, since these denizens law enforcement needed a certain built-in laxity. As Leonard Sanders wrote in his entertaining *How Fort Worth Became the Texas-most City*, the merchants believed the marshal "should keep the blood from flowing but not the liquor."

For a town of 7,000 people in 1880, Fort Worth had a variety of colorful saloons: the Headlight Bar, Occidental, Waco Tap, Cattle Exchange, White Elephant, and Red Light, just to mention a few. Historian Richard F. Selcer's 1991 book calls the district, "Hell's Half Acre."

In 1876, the town elected Timothy Isaiah "Long-Haired" Jim Courtright as marshal. Jim was lean and lanky, usually sporting a vest with the marshal's badge pinned alongside his Masonic pin. He was six feet tall, smiled through a handlebar mustache, and wore his hat at a jaunty angle. His famous nickname of "Long-Haired Jim" isn't quite borne out by his picture. A Fort Worth photo shows blond hair swept back and not quite covering the ears, meaning he wasn't all that long-haired, even if one considers the time, place, and barbers. Most accounts of Courtright refer to his ever-present six-shooters with the butts pointing forward.

Courtright was from Iowa. He served as a drummer boy during the Civil War, then worked as an army scout before getting married and by some accounts going on the road with Buffalo Bill's Wild West Show.

He was a very dangerous man, an alleged murderer but an adequate marshal if one ignores shakedowns. By 1880 he had exchanged his Fort Worth marshal's badge for one in Lake Valley, New Mexico. However, he left Lake

Valley in 1883 with indictments for murder out against him. By 1884 he was back in Fort Worth operating a private detective agency. In 1886, New Mexico dropped the muder charges against him.

Courtright aligned himself with the railroads during a bitter dispute with the Knights of Labor. The government appointed him acting United States marshal, and in 1886 he and five law officers moved a freight train out of the yards. Rifle fire caught the lawmen out in the open, and Tarrant County Deputy Sheriff Dick Townsend was slain. The fight was widely referred to as the "Fort Worth Massacre," and the *Fort Worth Gazette* described the ensuing atmosphere of the city in this manner:

Nearly every male citizen of the town is armed and prepared for trouble. It was reported that the strikers intended to raid the gun stores and burn the Union

"Long-Haired Jim" Courtright, a dangerous man with a gun until he met Luke Short. —Texas State Archives

Depot. It is also said that they threatened to clear the city of scabs within three days. Sheriff Maddox has arranged to give three taps continuously on the fire bell as a danger signal. The strikers use the Santa Fe switch engine for the same purpose. It is safe to say that two thousand citizens are now bearing arms, and if another collision occurs it will, in all probability, result in a more serious loss of life than that of yesterday.

Governor John "Ox Cart" Ireland soothed the situation. He ordered several companies of Texas Rangers to restore order in Fort Worth.

Courtright returned to operating his detective agency and promptly ran afoul of Luke Short, who owned an interest in the White Elephant Saloon at 308-310 Main Street. Short was a professional gambler from Arkansas and claimed friendship with Wyatt Earp and Bat Masterson. The gambler had

Luke Short was more of a gambler than a gunfighter, although he is remembered primarily for killing Long-Haired Jim Courtright in a classic gun duel. —Texas State Archives

killed men in quarrels, but now he was in Fort Worth and against the best in Jim Courtright.

Some stories say Courtright was shaking down gamblers and the fastidiously dressed Short refused to pay. Other versions suggest Short cheated too many cowboys, and a group of wealthy merchants had retained Courtright to put a stop to it.

Whatever, on February 8, 1887, the two men quarreled in front of the White Elephant, and suddenly the gunfire commenced. With a wild, lucky shot, Short blew off Courtright's "hammer thumb," and then put three bullets into more critical areas of the body. The former marshal went down, dying almost immediately and never getting a shot off.

Luke was never indicted. He died of dropsy in 1893 and is buried in the Fort Worth Oakwood Cemetery within a few hundred yards of Long-Haired Jim Courtright.

A decade later, in 1898 to be exact, a new crowd of colorful citizens drifted into town. They were the Wild Bunch.

George Leroy Parker, alias Butch Cassidy, from Circle Valley, Utah, headed this group. They were sometimes known as the Hole in the Wall Gang, but they used as many aliases as they did hideouts. The gang robbed trains and banks, stole horses, and in 1898 tried to let things cool by visiting Fort Worth, where they were unknown. Or so they thought.

Their plan didn't work because Cassidy, the Sundance Kid, and the others couldn't resist having their picture taken. The photographer liked his handiwork so well that he placed the photo in his shop window. Early one morning a strolling Pinkerton detective passed by and nearly dropped his bowler. There, in all their resplendent glory, posed the Wild Bunch. Up until that time, some of them had not even been identified. With law officers now seriously searching Fort Worth, the gang fled to South America where, by some accounts, they were slain.

In the meantime, even the Comanches had become tranquil. Instead of lifting scalps, they negotiated leases on grazing lands. Chief Quanah Parker, son of the Comanche white female captive Cynthia Ann Parker, frequently visited Fort Worth on business. On one occasion he and his uncle, Yellow Bear, registered at the Pickwick Hotel, a modern, classy accommodation. One of them blew out the gas lamp prior to retiring. Yellow Bear died, and Parker came very close to it.

But not only had the Indians become quiet, the Chisholm Trail was practically deserted by 1884. Still, traditions had been established, and whereas Houston, Austin, and Dallas had forsaken their cowboy heritage and moved on toward culturally uplifting and economically prestigious goals, Fort Worth had remained "Cowtown," headquarters for West Texas cattlemen. The *Live Stock Journal* began, and its influence created the Cattle Raisers Association of Texas, the most prestigious such organization in the West. One of the great events in the country still remains the Southwestern Exposition and Livestock Show, which takes place annually in January and opens with the nation's largest all-western parade through downtown Fort Worth.

The rough edges of Fort Worth gradually yielded as men and women built expensive mansions and turned their attention to cultural pursuits such as art museums, ballet, symphonies, and theater. A property tax of .5 to 1 percent ushered in an era of improved public education. Water, gas, electricity, sewers, and streetcars came to town. The Fort Worth Spring Palace opened in 1889, a cross-shaped structure depicting typical Texas scenes. It burned two years later.

Horseless carriages arrived in 1902 and were treated as curiosities as well as nuisances. Barnstormers reached town in 1911. One pilot, Calbraith Perry Rogers, flew in the wrong direction upon departing. When he realized his mistake he returned to Fort Worth, only to find onlookers jamming the field. Rogers couldn't set the craft down without striking people, so he made everyone think he was landing at the opposite end of the pasture. As the crowd surged in that direction, he gunned the motor, roared over their heads, and put the tires down where the crowd had just left.

During this same period, Fort Worth constructed a dam on the West Fork of the Brazos, thus creating Lake Worth and ensuring a water supply. Oil was also discovered in nearby counties, and Fort Worth blossomed as a major headquarters for oil companies as well as a shipping and supply point.

The Canadian government established three air-training fields near Fort Worth in 1914, but Washington absorbed them in 1917 for the training of its own pilots. The flying fields were abandoned following World War I, and Tarrant Field was established. It became Carswell Air Force Base in 1948.

General Dynamics and Bell Helicopter, in cooperation with Consolidated Aircraft Corporation, opened factories for the design and construction of airplanes, a business providing Fort Worth with a significant defense industry anchor. In the process, Fort Worth became an educational center. Texas Christian University arose, as did Texas Wesleyan University and the Southwestern Baptist Theologial Seminary.

Amon G. Carter had been an advertising man until buying out the *Fort Worth Star*, which later merged into the *Star-Telegram*. However, Carter is best remembered as the progressive dynamo behind the Amon Carter Museum of Western Art. The Museum opened in January 1961 primarily as a repository for the paintings and sculpture masterpieces of Charles M. Russell and Frederick Remington. Today the facility not only has an enormous collection of pioneer photographs but also has broadened its original intent to include the works of many western artists.

Today, in the 1990s, Fort Worth is still called "Cowtown." That's quite a tribute to a dynamic community.

B-24 Liberators in Fort Worth's General Dynamics plant, circa 1940s. —The Institute of
Texan Cultures

The Main Building of Texas Christian University in Fort Worth. —Eugene C. Barker
Texas History Center, UT Austin

Dallas—Hillsboro
65 miles

Waxahachie

This town's name comes from an Indian word meaning "cow creek" or "buffalo creek." The first settler put a plow into the prairie here in 1846. Later on, the Confederates operated a powder mill, but its usefulness ended in 1863 when it exploded.

Although the town sat squarely on the Chisholm Trail, Waxahachie thought of itself as a cotton market first and a cattle town second. The courthouse, built in 1895 of red sandstone and granite, remains an architectural gem. The Ellis County Museum and the Chautauqua Auditorium are worth visiting. So are the numerous Victorian homes with their gingerbread trim.

Dallas—Stephenville
100 miles

Cleburne

The first house went up in 1854, and the resultant community was named for Confederate Gen. Pat Cleburne. The Gulf, Colorado & Santa Fe Railroad arrived from Galveston and Fort Worth in 1881.

While few Americans have heard of the Chaparral automobile, Cleburne manufactured nine in 1911 and 1912. One is on display at Six Flags Over Texas in Arlington. Cleburne State Park and the Layland Museum are strong local attractions.

Glen Rose

This place started in 1849 as a trading post called Barnard's Mills. Settler Thomas Jordan purchased the mills in 1870 and renamed the town Glen Rose. Dinosaur tracks, the best preserved in Texas, have been found in the limestone beds. The town is often called the Petrified City because so much petrified stone was used in local construction. Sulphur springs were discovered before the turn of the century, and the town rapidly became a health and recreation center.

John Wilkes Booth.
—Library of Congress

A settler named John St. Helen believed himself dying in the 1870s, so he confessed to being John Wilkes Booth, the assassin of President Abraham Lincoln. He recovered, however, only to commit suicide later. Marks on his body were allegedly consistent with Booth's prior injuries.

Nobody should miss the Dinosaur Valley State Park.

Stephenville

The Stephens brothers, John and William, settled this area in 1854. Since then the region has prospered with nurseries and dairies. The Historical House Museum Complex is open every day except Monday.

Fort Worth—Stephenville
70 miles

Granbury

Thomas Lambert arrived here in 1854. A nearby settlement was called Stockton, and when that community grew to include Lambert's place, they became Granbury in honor of Gen. Hiram B. Granberry (the spellings are inconsistent), commander of the famous Civil War Texas Brigade, who was killed at Franklin, Tennessee.

Ashley W. Crockett, a grandson of Davy Crockett, published the *Hood County Tablet* in 1939. Elizabeth Crockett, the second wife of Davy Crockett, is buried in Granbury. The Granbury Square is on the National Register of Historic Places. The Granbury Queen offers tours on Lake Granbury. The Nutt House, a historic inn, is open for business on the downtown square, while the Hood County Jail is now a museum and visitors center complete with hanging tower.

Fort Worth—Anson
160 miles

Weatherford

Texas set aside 320 acres of vacant land as a county seat in 1856. The resultant town was named for Jefferson Weatherford, a Confederate veteran as well as a member of the Texas senate. A rough lumber courthouse went up that same year, to be followed in 1858 by a brick building. Both structures burned.

As the last settlement on the Texas frontier for many years, Weatherford wagon trains operated between Fort Worth and Fort Belknap. Much of that traffic ended, however, when the Texas & Pacific arrived in May 1880. The 1904 St. Louis World's Fair put Weatherford on the map when twelve of its watermelons took top prizes.

Two famous people came out of Weatherford. One was Mary Martin, who created the role of Peter Pan on Broadway. A bronze statue in front of the library honors her.

Oliver Loving, trail driver and cattleman. He pioneered the Shawnee Trail from Texas to Chicago and the Western Trail from Texas to Denver. He is best known for the Goodnight-Loving Trail, which extended from Fort Belknap, Texas, to Fort Sumner, New Mexico, and on to Denver.
—Nita Stewart Haley Memorial Library

The other was Oliver Loving, the first man to drive a cattle herd to market from Texas to Chicago. He created the Shawnee Trail. Another drive in 1859 helped instigate the Dodge or Western Trail. Finally, Loving and Charles Goodnight put together the Goodnight-Loving Trail. In 1867, when Loving died of gangrene in Fort Sumner, New Mexico, Goodnight brought the body back to Texas and buried it at Weatherford. Loving lies in Greenwood Cemetery.

The 1909 Santa Fe Depot is a restored brick structure open for visitors.

Mineral Wells

When Judge J. W. Lynch dug a well in 1877 and found abundant but unfit-to-drink water under his cabin, he then checked it for medicinal qualities. There were plenty. A town site named Mineral Wells was established in 1881.

The "Crazy Well" in 1885 revealed water reported to cure "hysterical manias." By 1900, at least 400 mineral wells catered to health visitors, most of whom resided in the Hexagon House Hotel. Today the town still attracts health seekers, but there is also a lively tourist trade in recreation.

Breckenridge

Former United States Senator (and vice president under James Buchanan) John C. Breckenridge of Kentucky gave this community his name in 1858. Public land was sold at auction and the village was established. Until after the turn of the century Breckenridge was little more than a trading post.

In 1918 the Breckenridge Oil Field started producing. By 1921, the boom was substantially over. In five years the population had jumped from 2,000 to 30,000 and then tumbled nearly all the way back down again.

Breckenridge is now mostly a center for ranching and petroleum activities. Possum Kingdom State Park is nearby. There is also a Breckenridge Aviation Museum as well as a Swenson Memorial Museum & J. D. Sandefer Oil Annex. Both are excellent.

Albany and Fort Griffin

Henry C. Jacobs, the first sheriff of Shackelford County, donated land for a town site in 1874. William C. Cruger, a deputy and later sheriff, named the village for his hometown, Albany, Georgia. Drovers heading for Dodge City on the Western Trail utilized Albany as a supply point.

Fort Griffin, on "Government Hill" overlooking the Clear Fork of the Brazos River, was twelve miles north of Albany on what is now US 283. The post was established in 1867. Initially called Camp Wilson, the fort was renamed for Maj. Gen. Charles Griffin. The first buildings were log barracks quartering four to six men in a space that averaged fourteen feet by eight feet. The post's mission involved escorting surveyors as well as the U.S. Mail and cattle drivers. Black "buffalo soldiers" (9th and 10th Cavalry and 24th Infantry) pursued and punished marauding Indians. Nearby Tonkawa Indians served as scouts.

A town also named Fort Griffin, but usually called "the Flats" (or occasionally "Hidetown"), sprang up on a broad valley between the fort and the river. It catered to off-duty soldiers, cattlemen, desperados, gamblers, prostitutes, and buffalo hunters, the latter's hides sometimes being stacked higher than a two-story building while awaiting shipment east. An advertisement in the *Frontier Echo* of November 16, 1877, stated, "Teams wanted to haul 200,000 pounds of buffalo hides to Dallas."

The Flats were notorious for lawlessness, especially cattle rustling. A secret vigilante committee formed, calling itself the "OLM," or "Old Law Mob." It lynched suspected horse thieves and other undesirables, leaving notes pinned to their clothing. Gamblers, thieves, and ladies of doubtful virtue started leaving town.

Rancher John Larn, who had married into the prominent Matthews family (a union of John Alexander Matthews and Sallie Ann Reynolds, which created the famed Lambshead Ranch), was elected sheriff to stop the murders and cattle thefts. Larn built a ranch at Camp Cooper on the north bank of the Clear

Fork of the Brazos. The post had been abandoned in 1861 when Comanche Indians from the nearby reservation were transferred to Oklahoma.

Killings and rustling grew worse under Larn, and he and his deputy, John Selman, who owned a ranch two miles distant, came under suspicion as instigators. On June 22, 1878, vigilantes took Larn into custody, escorted him to his own jail in Albany, and shot him while he stood behind bars. Selman fled the country after being warned by Hurricane Minnie Martin, a Fort Griffin prostitute. He surfaced in El Paso seventeen years later.

Fort Griffin was abandoned in 1881, and since 1938 the site has been a state park. Among the ruins is a large herd of longhorns, once fewer in number than the buffalo. They were saved and placed here through the efforts of Texas author J. Frank Dobie. A museum is on the Fort Griffin premises.

Meanwhile, the Texas Central Railroad arrived at Albany in 1881, and the town became a cattle shipping point. The Flats did not get a railroad, so the townspeople found other places to flaunt their vices.

The Georgia Monument is a stone marker and fountain near the Albany Chamber of Commerce. It was erected in 1976 to honor the Georgia Battalion, a group of volunteers in the Texas Revolution.

The restored Ledbetter Picket House in Albany is a visitor's delight, as is the South Texas Museum. The handsome limestone facade of the old Albany jail (behind the Shackelford County Courthouse) is now the Old Jail Art Center, featuring not only beautiful pieces of sculpture but works of art extending back to pre-Columbian periods. The Fort Griffin Fandangle is held during the last two weekends in June each year. Don't miss it.

Anson

This village started as the county seat of Jones County, so named in honor of former Texas President Anson Jones. It was originally Jones City. However, since Texas already had a town named Jones, the moniker changed to Anson.

In 1893, a fire destroyed over half the business district, which rebuilt immediately and became a cotton-shipping center. Today, the Cowboys' Christmas Ball is held annually. The ball originated in the Morning Star Hotel, which burned in 1890. The ball faded away for awhile, but now is staged in Pioneer Hall.

Seventeen miles north of Anson on US 277 is Stamford. The Texas Central Railroad arrived in 1899 and named the village Stamford after the hometown of the railroad president.

Swedish-born "Swen" Magnus Swenson came to Texas before the Civil War and entered the mercantile business. Although he introduced the Colt revolver to the Texas army and navy, he refused to live under the Confederacy and fled to Mexico until the war ended. He returned to create the SMS Flat Top Ranch, named for Flat Top Mountain just west of Stamford. It occupied portions of twelve counties (over 300,000 acres) and was so named for the

Svante "Swen" Magnus Swenson and his wife. —The Institute of Texan Cultures

A Swedish immigrant ship leaving Gotesberg, Sweden, for Texas. —The Institute of Texan Cultures

initials of the founder. Swenson is believed to be the first Swedish immigrant into Texas, and he operated an informal immigration bureau consisting of himself, an uncle in Austin, and a brother in Sweden. Through his efforts, hundreds of his countrymen migrated to Texas.

The town is widely known for the Texas Cowboy Reunion held for three days around each Fourth of July. The fair started in 1930, and it sponsors the greatest cowboy amateur rodeo in the world.

A Mackenzie Trail Monument is nearby, as is the Texas Cowboy Museum.

I-20
Fort Worth—Sweetwater
192 miles

Thurber

Thurber is the type of community you don't see much of in Texas. It was a coal-mining town wholly owned and opened by the Johnson Coal Company in 1886. In 1888, the Texas & Pacific Coal Company bought out the owners and the camp became Thurber. Fourteen mines and nearly 3,000 workers dug coal that fueled the western railroads. Over 10,000 people lived in Thurber, and they represented at least twenty nationalities. The miners frequently went on strike, and their wages rarely exceeded $55 a month. In 1888-89, a work stoppage brought in the Texas Rangers to restore order. A more successful strike in 1903 forced the company to create a 100 percent union town.

When oil blew in at Ranger in 1917, the firm changed its name to the Texas & Pacific Coal and Oil Company. Thurber thrived. The Snake Saloon had the largest horseshoe bar between Fort Worth and El Paso. However, the oil business now dominated the coal interests, especially since the Texas & Pacific Coal and Oil Company sold oil as a locomotive fuel. In 1921, the company broke its coal-mining contract and unsuccessfully operated the mines on a nonunion basis. Most of the mines closed.

In 1930, fire swept the town. By 1933 Thurber was abandoned. The buildings were wrecked, and over 3,000 frame houses sold for as little as $35 each. Electric poles and even sewer lines were dismantled and transferred to other locations. The company moved its offices to Fort Worth in 1934. Most of the land, with reserves of bituminous coal estimated at 100 million tons, was leased to nearby ranchers. Not much remains except a few scraggly foundations, an electric company smokestack, and a cemetery.

Ranger

A Texas Ranger camp gave a tent community the title of "Ranger Camp Valley." In 1883, the "Camp Valley" portion was dropped and only Ranger remained.

Ranger was just a cotton, ranching, agricultural village until oil was discovered in October 1917. The McClesky #1, a 1,700-barrel producer, came roaring in. The population soared from 1,000 to 30,000. The Texas & Pacific Coal and Oil Company leased practically the entire field as gusher after gusher made millionaires overnight. No oil field since Spindletop at Beaumont had been more speculative. Heavyweight champion Jess Willard came to town. So did fight promoter Tex Rickard, author Rex Beach, circus boss John Ringling, and oil man Harry Sinclair. By 1919, the field had produced nearly four million barrels of oil; then it peaked out.

Trains arriving at Ranger, Texas, 1905. —The Institute of Texan Cultures

A series of bank failures and a disastrous fire within the next four years ended the Ranger boom. The Roaring Ranger Museum will tell you all about it. A granite monument stands on the site of McClesky #1.

Eastland

Eastland essentially started with its rock courthouse in 1875. When the fourth courthouse was built in 1897, a horned frog known as "Old Rip" was placed in a cornerstone. He was still there and reportedly alive when the next courthouse was constructed in 1928. Old Rip remains on display, but not alive, in the courthouse.

Eastland has a Kendrick Religious Museum. Sixteen dioramas with sound and lighting explain the life of Christ.

Baird

The Texas & Pacific established Baird in 1880 when the railroad installed repair shops. A fire destroyed the town in 1883, but it quickly bounced back. The Callahan County Pioneer Museum is a community asset.

Abilene

Abilene owes its existence to Buffalo Gap, ten miles south of today's Abilene. The gap was a well-defined geologic slash in the Callahan Divide where migrating buffalo went south in the fall to forage in a warmer climate, returning north each spring to the Texas high plains. For years hunters met them coming and going at the gap, killing thousands and harvesting the hides.

The live oak trees provided a scenic and comfortable winter habitation for Comanches. Because ranchers drove longhorns through the gap, using it to link up with the Western Trail, a small settlement called Buffalo Gap started. In 1878 it became the county seat, and J. W. Carter, who owned the first saloon, became the first sheriff. Because he had no jail for several months, he ordered six pairs of handcuffs and three pairs of shackles. Prisoners were chained to trees until they could be transported to a "real" jail in Coleman City.

In the meantime, Fort Phantom Hill, originally called the "Post on the Clear Fork of the Brazos," although it was actually on Elm Creek, which was usually dry, was established fourteen miles north of present Abilene in 1851. The fort took its name "Phantom Hill" from the rise on which it sat, an eerie, ghostly, hazy hill when observed from a distance.

Its 500 soldiers of the 5th U.S. Infantry provided a link in the chain of frontier defenses reaching from the Red River to the Rio Grande. The soldiers kept hostile Indians away from settlements and suffered from hardship and loneliness. The water was awful, and timber had to be hauled forty miles. The post was abandoned in 1854 and burned by unknown parties within hours after the troops departed.

In 1871, Fort Phantom Hill had risen like a phoenix to become a satellite post of Fort Griffin. A town called Phantom Hill sprang up, its 546 residents living primarily by buying and shipping buffalo hides. However, by 1881, all traces of the town Phantom Hill had disappeared. Only the quiet, windswept military ruins remained.

Abilene, Texas, arose between Fort Phantom Hill and Buffalo Gap and was named for Abilene, Kansas, destination point for the old Chisholm Trail. Abilene had no sooner started, however, than the Texas & Pacific arrived in 1881.

The railroad steamed in alongside a collection of tents and sheltering saloons. Buffalo hunters, farmers, and construction workers were already there, but because of the railroads Abilene became a destination point as much as a way station. From then until 1885, when Abilene changed to an agricultural shipping center, the number of buffalo hides and bones heading for market almost equaled the number of cattle being moved out. Later, although no big oil strikes occurred near Abilene, the town became an oil- servicing depot.

The Sweetwater Baptist Association opened Hardin-Simmons College in 1892, and it achieved university status in 1935. The Cowboy Band of Hardin-Simmons had an international musical reputation. Not to be outdone, the Church of Christ created Abilene Christian College in 1906. The Northwest Texas Conference of the Methodist Church founded McMurry College in 1923.

Abilene has its Fine Arts Museum, a state park, a zoo, and Dyess Air Force Base, an arm of the Strategic Air Command. There is also a Phantom Squadron, a West Texas Wing of the Confederate Air Force. Don't ignore the Buffalo Gap Historic Village.

Sweetwater

Buffalo hunters needed a place to shop in 1877, so Billy Knight built a dugout store on the banks of Sweetwater Creek. When sufficient wood arrived for a building, the residents recognized their priorities and constructed a saloon. Two saloon keepers even acted as bankers for stockmen. By 1879 nesters and cattlemen had moved in, and the resultant village was called Sweetwater. The town became the temporary county seat in 1881 and moved two miles northwest to the Texas & Pacific Railroad in 1882.

Although the community was incorporated in 1884, when the disastrous "Big Blizzard" struck a year later, and the "Great Drought" visited in 1886-87, economic conditions forced the town to disincorporate. It did not recover until 1897. (*The Wind*, Dorothy Scarborough's novel, describes that devastating drought.) Then the incoming Colorado Valley Railroad Company lost its financing because of the Spanish-American War, so residents pooled their resources and combined the Colorado Valley Railroad Company with the

Kansas City, Mexico & Orient Railroad to be built from San Angelo through Sweetwater to Wichita, Kansas, in 1908.

The community also constructed a waterworks, and during that same year of 1908 Sweetwater began to grow. Sheep and cotton were strong products by the mid-1930s. By then the county had so many Hereford cattle that Sweetwater was often called Herefordshire.

Sweetwater Army Air Field opened during World War II, and women pilots trained there. A statue of Walt Disney's "Fifinella," a mascot of these female pilots, is on display in the courthouse building. The field closed in 1945 and became a municipal airport in 1950.

The world's largest Rattlesnake Roundup started at Sweetwater in 1958. It occurs every year in March. Substantial prizes are awarded. History buffs will enjoy the Pioneer City-County Museum.

Anita Locklear stands on the wing of a PT19A trainer at Avenger Field in Sweetwater, Texas, 1944. Locklear was a trainee. —The Institute of Texan Cultures

Baird—Coleman

Coleman

A site for the Coleman county seat was selected in 1876. People camping up and down Hord's Creek then moved in and bid for 160 acres of lots currently on the auction block. The courthouse, originally built of rawhide lumber from elm trees, served as a bachelors residence as well as a meeting hall for religious services. A cemetery started when a couple of cowboys shot it out. The streets were made sufficiently wide so that an ox team could turn without backing. Coleman is in the geographical center of Texas and today is primarily devoted to ranching. The Warbird Museum specializes in airplane restorations.

Camp Colorado was ten miles north of Coleman on Texas 206, a 2nd Cavalry post that opened in 1857 and closed in 1861. A telegraph line connected it with San Antonio. A few Texas Rangers were stationed there during the Civil War, but regular units never returned after the war. A replica of Camp Colorado has stood in the Coleman City Park since 1936.

EIGHT

Panhandle-Plains

A Fable: It was one of those days when God was creating the earth. He was working on Texas as darkness fell, and He had to quit. He gave the Great Plains of West Texas a smoothing stroke and said to Himself, "In the morning, I'll come back and make it pretty like the rest of the world, with lakes and streams and mountains and trees." But the next morning when He returned, it had hardened like concrete. As He considered having to tear it all out, He had a happy thought. "I know what I'll do," He said. "I'll just make some inhabitants who have appreciation for this style." And that is how it came about that the people who live in the Panhandle like it this way.

George Autry, *Texas Highways* magazine
(September 1990)

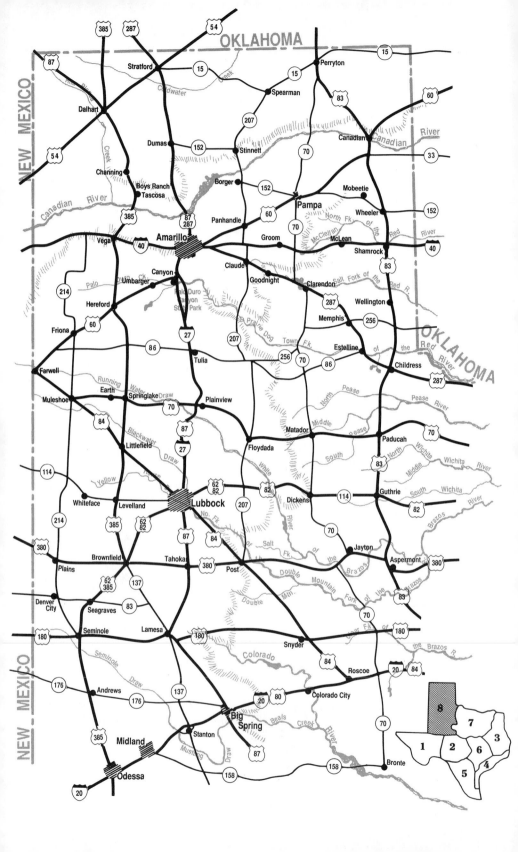

The early Spaniards who visited this land called it Llano Estacado, or the "Staked Plains." But nobody knows for sure exactly what they meant. Llano means plains. That's simple enough. Estacado, however, could mean staked or enclosed with stakes, or possibly palisaded or stockaded. Probably it refers to stakes the early explorers apparently drove into the ground. One account says the Spaniards tied their horses to the stakes. Another says they used the stakes (or rocks or buffalo chips piled to unnatural heights) as landmarks to find their way across the featureless shallow sea of grass.

For our purpose, the Panhandle-Plains are bound on the west by New Mexico and on the north by Oklahoma. Oklahoma also makes up the northern portion of the eastern border, which then jumps over to US 83 at Childress and continues on to US 380 at Aspermont, where it again turns south on Texas 70 down to Bronte. On the south the Panhandle-Plains are marked between Bronte and the New Mexico border by Texas 158, I-20, US 385, and Texas 176.

The wind blows steadily in this region, averaging twenty miles per hour 20 percent of the time—the windiest in the United States. (The second windiest area, in northwestern Minnesota, averages only twelve miles per hour.)

Commonly called the "Llano," this particular plain in the panhandle of Texas started taking shape some ten million years ago. As tectonic pressure forced the Rocky Mountains higher than the flatlands to the east, layer upon layer of waterborne sediment flowed and settled across 25,610 square miles of eastern New Mexico and the Texas panhandle. This process of sediment accumulation on the Llano continued until about two million years ago, according to Darwin Spearing in his *Roadside Geology of Texas*. Then the channel that became the Pecos River sliced a new, southward-coursing path near the mountains, severing the flow of sediment from the Rockies onto the Llano. Today the Pecos continues washing away mountain sediments and the Llano is an isolated plateau standing between 300 and 1,000 feet above adjacent lands along the Texas escarpment.

The Llano stretches from the Pecos River on the west to the escarpment on the east; from the Edwards Plateau on the south to the Canadian River on the north. This plain is the southern portion of a vast tableland that continues far north along the eastern slope of the Rockies commonly and collectively known as the High Plains.

Nine thousand years before the rise of the Roman Empire, humans worked and lived on the Llano. Paleo-Indians fashioned tools and weapons from flint in a tradition that continued for many centuries. Seven to nine thousand years ago, the people of cultures we identify as Clovis, Folsom, and Plainview roamed this region while hunting mammoths and other plains grazers. Five thousand years ago, when the present climatic conditions set in, the hunter-gatherers started making pottery and cultivating some crops. They still hunted buffalo on the massive grasslands.

Old World explorers wearing beards and armor found their way onto the Llano nearly five hundred years ago. After being shipwrecked on the Gulf Coast, Alvar Núñez Cabeza de Vaca wandered across Texas for nine years, and by 1536 he had seen the southern extremities of the Staked Plains. In 1540, Francisco Coronado led an expedition onto the Llano searching for the fantastic golden cities reported by Cabeza de Vaca. Coronado found only windswept loneliness—and buffalo. He was probably the first European to see the beast that dominated Plains Indian life, and he is generally credited with describing this region as Llano Estacado. Two years later an expedition led by Frenchman Hernando de Soto approached the Llano from the east. Although de Soto died of fever and was put to rest in the Mississippi River, remnants of his factious expedition reached the eastern periphery of the Llano before turning back.

Alvar Núñez Cabeza de Vaca and his comrades build crude boats to sail along the Gulf Coast, 1528. After being shipwrecked, Cabeza de Vaca and three other survivors embarked on an epic overland journey across Texas. —Hendricks Long Publishing Company, Dallas

An artist's version of Coronado's expedition camp. —The Institute of Texan Cultures

Both the Coronado and de Soto expeditions dreaded and feared crossing the Llano Estacado. Its harsh and desolate landscape did not invite them, and they thought only Indians could live on the Llano.

Finally, in 1601, Juan de Oñate, who had brought colonists north from Mexico in 1598, led a futile expedition across the panhandle toward the fabled Quivira, allegedly the most wealthy of the golden cities. With that failure, the Spanish decided to end further explorations of the region.

Two centuries later Mexican *ciboleros* (buffalo hunters) began making regular trips north. In the fall of each year they killed approximately 10,000 to 12,000 buffalo prior to 1874. Some of them doubled as Comancheros (Indian traders), who were generally not as vicious as some historians contend and were fairly common during the 1840s. After peaking in number during the Civil War, by the 1880s they had virtually disappeared. The Comancheros bartered trinkets and sundries, guns, ammunition, liquor, pots and pans, and oftentimes, captives.

On October 4, 1776, as the Americans in the East fought for independence from Great Britain, Spanish frontiersman Pedro Vial set out from San Antonio to blaze a direct route to Sante Fe. He crossed the panhandle and reached his destination on May 26, 1777. José Mares, a corporal with the Vial expedition, made a return trek to San Antonio in record time—only ten weeks, at an average of 17.6 miles per day. Vial later marked a path from Santa Fe to St Louis, which eventually became the well-known Santa Fe Trail.

Even though the Spanish never built any settlements in the Panhandle-Plains, some of the labels they hung on the land—Llano Estacado, Amarillo, Tierra Blanco, Palo Duro, Tascosa, and Bonito—remain intact.

By the 1820s Americans began finding their way to the Panhandle-Plains, but rarely to stay. At the beginning of the decade, Maj. Stephen H. Long led a twenty-man expedition to explore the region. He declared the entire Great Plains, including the Llano, the Great American Desert and pronounced it uninhabitable. His perception lasted for decades.

Josiah Gregg, who wrote the American classic *Commerce of the Prairies*, cut a trade route across the panhandle in 1840 as he sought a direct route between Santa Fe and the eastern United States. His trail passed through what later became Amarillo's "Old Town," then cut north to the Canadian River near Borger, and it eventually emerged at Fort Smith, Arkansas. A decade later, forty-niners followed Gregg's path en route to the California goldfields.

In 1841 more than 300 Texas volunteers jammed twenty-one wagons with merchandise and weapons and left Austin bound for Santa Fe. Historians still don't agree on whether this so-called Santa Fe Expedition constituted a military or trading operation. But while crossing the Llano near New Mexico, the travelers became confused, then lost, and had begun starving when the Mexican Army happened along, took them captive, and brutally herded them south through El Paso toward Mexico City.

Capt. Randolph B. Marcy—best known for establishing the Marcy Trail from Fort Smith, Arkansas, to Dona Ana, New Mexico—explored the central panhandle in 1849, and this is what he had to say about it:

> a view presented itself as boundless as the ocean. Not a tree or shrub . . . relieved the dreary monotony; . . . it was a vast illimitable expanse of desert prairie, a land where no man, either savage or civilized, permanently abides; it spreads into a treeless, desolate waste of uninhabited solitude, which always has been, and must continue, uninhabited forever.

The same year Marcy visited this region, Lt. Amiel Weeks Whipple of the United States Corps of Topographical Engineers charted a transcontinental railroad strip across the panhandle. Although the Civil War would be another dozen years in coming, its imminence kept the railroads from building along the route Whipple plotted.

From obscure camps on the trackless plains, the Comanches had developed a complex and varied culture and lived practically unmolested for generations. For a while, especially during periods when the United States was distracted by war, perhaps the Comanches thought the good times might never end. But that view was shattered soon after the end of the Civil War. Through the late 1860s and 1870s, white society trounced the Indians' way of life in Texas.

In 1869 the army established Fort Sill in Indian Territory (Oklahoma), primarily to keep the panhandle Indians under control. The first commissioner of Indian Affairs, Ely Samuel Parker, appointed Quakers as Indian agents, and their style of administration became known as the "peace policy." Indians largely ignored the first agents, and Americans snickered at them. Little changed until Col. Ranald Mackenzie relentlessly pursued Comanches and Kiowas from one panhandle stronghold to another and forced them on to reservations. Despite the imperiousness of this action, the reservations were the only place the Indians could survive as a people and a race.

With the Indians no longer a threat and hardly any buffalo left to graze the prairie, the first settlers on the Panhandle-Plains were sheepherders from New Mexico. Ruins of their rock houses still dot the Canadian River country, and they lived largely unmolested. Then came the cattlemen.

Charles Goodnight arrived in 1875 and claimed Palo Duro Canyon as his ranch. This was the first cattle ranch in the Texas panhandle. In all, Goodnight blazed five cattle trails north, the last of which ran from Palo Duro to Dodge City. Goodnight didn't always make friends easily, but he kept the good ones, such as Oliver Loving, for life. Another of Goodnight's friends was Bose Ikard, a former slave. Bose was nineteen when he started working for Goodnight in 1866. Goodnight always appreciated Ikard's dignity, cleanliness, and reliability, and when his friend died at age eighty-one in 1929, Goodnight recommended him to God through a marker on Bose's grave in Weatherford, Texas:

> BOSE IKARD . . . Served with me four years on the Goodnight-Loving Trail, never shirked a duty or disobeyed an order, rode with me in many stampedes, participated with me in three engagements with Comanches, splendid behavior.
>
> —C. Goodnight

Other Texas ranchers quickly moved up to the panhandle and staked out their own empires in the mostly vacant land. Thomas Bugbee, George Littlefield, Alfred Rowe, Lucien Scott, and R. B. Masterson were among them. Texas-sized ranches sprang up almost overnight, and by 1881 foreign corporations, especially from Great Britain, started arriving. One, a Scottish syndicate called the Prairie Land and Cattle Company, purchased Littlefield's LIT brand.

The Texas constitution of 1876 authorized the division of unorganized counties in the unpopulated (fewer than 150 qualified male voters) portions of West Texas, and authorities named them after signers of the Texas Declaration of Independence or other state heroes. Unorganized counties had no governmental bodies of their own, so they were attached for administrative and judicial purposes to the organized counties most convenient to their location. County seats had to be established within five miles of the geographical center of the county.

The first primitive roads were generally marked by plowing furrows in the virgin prairie to keep travelers from getting lost in the openness. Landmarks were so scarce that one giant cottonwood tree a few miles north of Amarillo soon became known by every cowboy in the panhandle.

By the early 1900s, the era of big ranches was drawing to a close. Extreme weather conditions, economic recessions, and plummeting beef prices (from $9.35 per hundred pounds to just $1.90) caused the largest ranches to trim their holdings. Farmers and small ranchers acquired the panhandle's best known brands: LS, XIT, 6666, Turkey Tracks, and Frying Pan. After the turn of the century the panhandle started becoming as well known for its farms as it had been for its ranches.

At first, the Panhandle-Plains seemed unsuitable for large-scale farming. The Llano had scarce surface water and received little rain. The hard crust of topsoil gave no hint that an immense reservoir of water lay underground. But farmers wasted no time in tapping its reserves, and agriculture throughout the Great Plains, including the Texas panhandle, owes its success to the Ogallala aquifer. In Texas, the peak land-boom years lasted from 1905 to 1910. The question then remains the question today: how long will the water last?

Towns took root to serve the farmers' needs. Mobeetie, Tascosa, and Clarendon were among the first during the mid-1870s in the Panhandle-Plains. Today Mobeetie and Tascosa are ghost towns. Most other panhandle villages got their start with the building of the railroads. The Fort Worth & Denver City railroad came through in 1887, as did the Santa Fe; the Rock Island appeared in 1901-02.

The oil business in the panhandle began in 1926, but within a few years the Great Depression put a hold on new development. Shortly thereafter the valuable topsoil, broken loose by plows from the prairie sod to grow farmers' crops, began blowing high into the air in thick clouds during the Dust Bowl of the 1930s. Black dusters added a sense of desperation to life in the panhandle. Gradually, the weather and the economy stabilized. Deep-well irrigation and the Second World War ended the slump. By the 1970s and 1980s the dust had settled, and the new treasure of the Panhandle-Plains is wheat, which, along with cotton and grain sorghum, is now counted among the top Texas cash crops.

Modern activity in the panhandle is diverse. The region boasts varied recreational areas and business zones, ranches and farms, and industry. But the land remains flat, and at times people on the plains can see forever. It's quite a view.

Oklahoma State Line—Amarillo

Shamrock

The Chicago, Rock Island & Gulf Railroad built a line across Wheeler County in 1902. The little town of Wheeler held a barbecue the day the railroad auctioned off town lots. Frank Exum, who owned a general store, applied for a post office, then changed the town's name from Wheeler to Exum. But in 1903 the railroad wielded its power to change the name to Shamrock in honor of George Nichols, an Irish sheep rancher who had lived in a dugout six miles north of town since 1890.

Oil was discovered in 1926, and today Shamrock contains some of the largest gas reserves in the nation. The town makes the most of its name, which is painted in bright green letters on the local water tower—the highest in Texas, incidentally. The high school adopted green and white as its colors, and the football team calls itself the Fighting Irish. Shamrock's official anthem is "My Wild Irish Rose," and the beauty queen is dubbed "Miss Irish Rose." Every St. Patrick's Day shamrocks are flown in from Ireland, and the town is proud of its fragment of the Blarney Stone taken from ruins of the Blarney Castle in County Cork, Ireland.

Twenty rooms of the Pioneer West Museum are filled with exhibits ranging from the Plains Indian to landings on the moon.

McLean

The Choctaw, Oklahoma & Texas Railroad Company dug a well here in 1901, and the community that sprung forth called itself McLean, for W. P. McLean of the Texas Railroad Commission. A local ladies undergarment factory led to McLean being called "uplift city." McLean had a German prisoner of war camp during World War II. If you want to know more about the local history, visit the Alanreed-McLean Area Museum.

Two remarkable Indian battles occurred in this area. The first fight took place on September 7, 1874. Lt. Frank D. Baldwin and three scouts were en route to deliver dispatches to Fort Supply in Indian Territory, Oklahoma. As they approached White Fish Creek in northern Donley County, they encountered and killed three Indians. Suddenly the white men found themselves surrounded by about 250 Indians. They shot their way out, but twice more they were surrounded and twice more they escaped the siege. After the Indians withdrew, the soldiers encountered a redheaded white youth called Tehan, meaning Texan. Kiowas had captured Tehan years earlier during a Texas raid, and he had been adopted by a Kiowa medicine man named Mamanti. On this day, Tehan was rounding up Indian livestock when Baldwin and the scouts "rescued" him.

The second engagement took place about six miles west of McLean and a few miles north on Ranch Road 291, on November 8, 1874, and it, too, involved Baldwin. The lieutenant and 125 soldiers escorting twenty-three empty supply wagons left the Prairie Dog Town Fork of the Red River the day before and had camped in a cottonwood grove on North McClellan Creek. Early the next morning, a scout reported seeing a Cheyenne village of 110 lodges and 500 warriors just over the next ridge.

Baldwin concocted a clever, if unorthodox, scheme. He ordered infantrymen into the twenty-three empty wagons and formed it into a double column. With a howitzer cannon in front and a single line of cavalry on each side of the wagons, Baldwin charged the unsuspecting Cheyennes. Stunned and confused, the Indians fled, and Baldwin thus earned his second Congressional Medal of Honor.

Groom

English widower and rancher Col. B. B. B. B. Groom managed the syndicated Francklyn Land and Cattle Company, and that made him particularly interested in leasing rights to panhandle grass. Because of his prominence here, when the Chicago, Rock Island & Gulf Railroad came through in 1903, it chose to call the new siding Groom.

Amarillo

Before there was a town called Amarillo, there was Juan de Padilla, the first Christian martyr in Texas. As a soldier in 1540, he had traveled to the Llano with Coronado. Upon their return to Mexico, Padilla became a Franciscan monk. Then, in 1542, he returned to the panhandle in the company of several companions and numerous Indian converts, but on November 30, 1544, Padilla was slain near Amarillo by Indians who weren't converts. Today a monument at Ellwood Park in Amarillo commemorates him.

Since the time of its beginnings as a supply depot and shipping point for hunters sweeping the last of the buffalo from the plains, Amarillo has always been a center for commerce in Texas. Within fifty years, "Ragtown" had grown from a collection of hide huts on a khaki-colored prairie into a metropolis. Buffalo hunters and bone gatherers may have sired Amarillo, but it was the Fort Worth & Denver City Railroad that actually created the town in 1887. Henry B. Sanborn, of the Frying Pan Ranch, laid out a town site for a place he called Oneida alongside Ragtown, and out of this unlikely conglomeration sprang Amarillo.

Before the Texas panhandle had a commercial center, the Santa Fe Railroad wanted to develop Panhandle City. The Fort Worth & Denver City

An engraving of Amarillo, Texas, as sketched from the depot, late 1880s.
—The Institute of Texan Cultures

Railroad favored Washburn. As it turned out, the businessmen of Colorado City, Texas, carried the most influence, and they wanted a town that could serve customers working in the vicinity of Yellow House (Lubbock). So they sent developer J. T. Berry north to locate a likely place, and he selected a well-watered site near today's Old Town in Amarillo.

Meanwhile, with the Fort Worth & Denver City Railroad on its way, new settlers had begun inundating the community of Oneida. They lived in shacks, tents, wagons, dugouts, or wherever they could find an empty space. The bulging population needed a governing body, so in 1887 a county was organized and Oneida became the county seat, but its name was immediately changed to Amarillo. In Spanish, *amarillo* means "yellow," and that's the color Sanborn painted every building in town. It took a dozen years for Amarillo to develop an administration, so in the meantime the county commissioners and Texas Rangers handled all legal and criminal chores.

On May 29, 1888, town lots were auctioned off for an average price of $50 to $100. Excursion trains hauled in prospects. Colorado City investors created a business district at Third and Parker streets, and one of the first buildings to go up was the twenty-five-room Champion Hotel. It served beef, canned goods, and wild game (when available) to guests, and a pile of empty cans marked the rear of eating establishments just as conspicuously as the sign out front. Soon a weekly newspaper, the *Amarillo Champion*, started operation, and rows of cow ponies stood tied to splintery wooden hitching rails on Main Street.

Amarillo became one of the nation's largest shipping points for cattle as huge herds from eastern New Mexico and the southern plains gathered at the railhead. Over 100,000 head shipped out each year from Amarillo. But, as Pauline and R. L. Robertson pointed out in *Panhandle Pilgrimage,* the railroads were unable to keep enough cattle cars on hand, requiring the stock to be held an average of about two weeks. The Frying Pan Ranch northwest of Amarillo set aside twelve sections of land to hold the transient stock. Another pasture lay southeast of Amarillo.

All those cattle constantly moving through contributed mightily to messy streets. Every time it rained the whole town groped through mud. Henry Sanborn considered Amarillo little more than a buffalo wallow. He argued for relocating the settlement one mile east, to higher and drier ground, and he was willing to pay up to $100,000 for the move, if necessary. At first, few residents endorsed the move. Then the monsoonal showers of 1889 hit, and the resulting quagmire shifted support in favor of relocating. Sanborn donated land for churches, and he gave a block of property to the *Amarillo Champion.* He even spent $40,000 constructing the new forty-room, two-story Amarillo Hotel, which ranchers and cattle buyers adopted as their headquarters and much of the town used as a social center. By law, the courthouse could not be moved for five years.

After area farms started producing cotton, Amarillo became a ginning and cottonseed-oil center. In 1901 the growing town built a two-story hospital, the first in the panhandle. Later, the discovery of oil brought refineries to the region and improved the railroad shipping facilities. During World War II, the Amarillo Army Airfield opened as a pilot-training school.

Meanwhile, a seemingly insignificant event destroyed the distant Fort Worth stockyards and revolutionized the Panhandle-Plains. Few people saw the change coming, and almost no one recognized it when it arrived. In 1883, farmers near Hereford tapped the Ogallala aquifer. Over the next few decades, that water changed the panhandle's landscape from grazing country to farm country. The grain farmers grew could fatten a yearling bovine to its preferred slaughter weight of 1,100 pounds in one-sixth the time it took for the same thing to happen with grass. Why ship cattle to the stockyards at Fort Worth when Amarillo feedlots were right in the middle of grain-production country? The panhandle soon became one of the nation's most abundant grain producers, and, by the end of the Second World War, 85 percent of the state's cattle were being trucked to auction in the panhandle.

Today Amarillo is the world's leading producer of helium, and its air quality has been rated among the highest in the nation. Amarillo is headquarters for the American Quarter Horse Association, the famous Cowboy Morning breakfast (spring through fall), and the World's Largest Livestock Auction every Monday and Tuesday. Other attractions in the area include Storyland Zoo, Wonderland Park, and an art and garden center. The unique and astoundingly beautiful Llano Cemetery is not only a final resting ground for

40,000 souls, it was the first Texas cemetery to be placed on the National Register of Historic Places. Amarillo is a gateway to Palo Duro Canyon and the annual summertime Texas Pageant.

Perryton—Guthrie
202 miles

Perryton

George M. Perry was an early settler and county judge, and so this village, eight miles from the Oklahoma line, was named for him. The Panhandle & Santa Fe Railroad created it, and residents from nearby Ochiltree, Texas, and Gray, Oklahoma, populated it when it became the most northern county seat in Texas in 1919. Perryton calls itself the Wheatheart of the Nation. Its Museum of the Plains is one of the best anywhere.

South of Perryton, across Wolf Creek, a legend exists of a white bull buffalo that once roamed this country. Hunters couldn't kill him, and the Indians wouldn't touch him. The story goes that as the buffalo herds thinned out, the white buffalo led one last stampede into a howling norther. He hasn't been reliably seen since.

Canadian River

The river rises in the Raton Pass of northern New Mexico and flows south to enter Texas by way of Oldham County. It then meanders eastward and northeastward across the panhandle and passes through Oklahoma before merging into the Arkansas River.

Pueblo Indians lived and camped along the banks of the Canadian River for centuries, and its canyons are dotted with numerous archaeological sites. Some historians believe the fabled city of Quivira sought by Coronado existed somewhere along the Canadian. Comanches took refuge here during the Indian Wars. Sheepherders constructed plazas (villages), and Comancheros and American traders found the Canadian River Valley a pleasant, scenic area to conduct business. Lt. J. W. Abert of the Corps of Topographical Engineers explored the river in 1845.

At 16,504 acres, Lake Meredith, which was created in 1926 by the United States Bureau of Reclamation, is the largest reservoir in the panhandle.

Today the Lake Meredith Recreation Area and its eight parks are managed by the National Park Service.

Canadian

The Panhandle & Santa Fe Railroad created this town on the Canadian River as the county seat of Hemphill County in 1887, even though the area had been established and settled before the railroad came through. As a trading center for ranching country, Canadian was originally known as Hogtown and later as Desperado City. It's public library remains the only one in America built and owned by the Women's Christian Temperance Union.

Extensive gas and oil discoveries were made near Canadian, although the town remains primarily an agricultural center. The Black Kettle National Grasslands lie immediately north of Canadian. The Canadian River Valley Pioneer Museum is strong on local history.

On September 9-14, 1874, Kiowas and Comanches raided Capt. Wyllys Lyman's wagon train about thirty-five miles south and east of Canadian, near the junction of Texas 33 and Ranch Road 2654. Historians call it the Battle of the Upper Washita, and it was the most prolonged Indian fight in panhandle history.

The battle started as Lyman and 104 men were hauling supplies in thirty-six wagons to Col. Nelson A. Miles. The reason it lasted so long was because the Indians wanted the white child they had named Tehan returned to them (see McLean). He had recently been recovered by an army officer and was traveling with Lyman's wagon train as it approached the divide between the Canadian and Washita rivers.

For five days approximately 400 Indians besieged the wagon train but were unable to overrun it. Many of the soldiers were in agony from wounds while all were dying of thirst. A scout finally broke through Indian lines and brought a relief force. Thirteen soldiers earned the Congressional Medal of Honor.

During the second day of the Battle of the Upper Washita, another party of Kiowas and Comanches about ten miles to the south engaged government scout Billy Dixon and five companions in a fight that came to be known as the Battle of Buffalo Wallow.

Dixon was carrying dispatches to Fort Supply on September 10 when the Indians attacked. After a brief stand with only one man killed and four wounded, plus the horses stampeded, Dixon's band took refuge in a buffalo wallow. All day long they defended their position and tried to patch their wounds as their ammunition dwindled. In the afternoon a hard rain fell, and, although it quenched their maddening thirst, it did nothing to improve the condition of their refuge.

By morning the Indians had left, so Dixon went for assistance. He found a cavalry column, but it could spare no ammunition to the wounded men; it did, however, leave some buffalo meat with the survivors and promise to notify higher command of their plight. Help finally arrived late that afternoon. The dead man was wrapped in a blanket and buried in the buffalo wallow.

Wheeler

After the army abandoned Fort Elliott in 1890 and a storm destroyed Mobeetie eight years later, a tiny village in the middle of the county gained favor as the new county seat. In 1886, five families living in dugouts within a two-mile radius formed a township. They named it Wheeler in honor of Royal T. Wheeler, a Vermont lawyer who became chief justice of the Texas Supreme Court in 1857. Today Wheeler is an agricultural center with extensive cattle feedlot operations.

A site near Kellerville, twenty miles southwest of Wheeler on Ranch Road 2473, marks the November 8, 1874, Indian engagement of Col. John W. "Blackjack" Davidson. En route from Fort Sill, Davidson's command struck a camp of Cheyennes and destroyed seventy-five lodges. The army chased the camp's refugees ninety miles before icy weather disabled the column and 100 cavalry horses froze to death.

Mobeetie

Mobeetie is eleven miles northwest of Wheeler on Texas 152. The town began in June 1875 as Fort Elliott near the head of Sweetwater Creek. The fort was named for a major of Custer's 7th Cavalry, Joel Elliott, who died during the dubious battle with Cheyennes on the Washita River on November 27, 1868. Both black and white soldiers served at Elliott, although never in numbers exceeding 500. The post was abandoned in 1890, and only a historical monument remains.

Mobeetie's first name was Sweetwater, but the post office rejected it because of a duplication. So the residents named the town Mobeetie, after an Indian word meaning "sweet water." It became the "Mother City of the Panhandle" and had two banks to service the community. "Hidetown" was an auxiliary of Fort Elliott where buffalo hides dried before traders hauled them to Dodge City via the 135-mile Jones-Plummer Trail. The huge local general store that bought and sold buffalo hides handled $100,000 in annual trade at its peak.

Buffalo hunters were rowdy enough, but the town also attracted desperados, soldiers, gamblers, prostitutes, gunmen, and hundreds of cowboys. Granger Dyer, Charles Goodnight's brother-in-law, died while quarreling with John McCabe. Bat Masterson, a renowned gambler as well as the Mobeetie surveyor, shot it out with a Fort Sill soldier named King for the affections of Mollie Bennon, a lady of soiled virtue. King and Mollie were both slain, and Masterson received a bullet in the stomach.

But law and order did arrive. Sam Houston's son Temple was district attorney. And Capt. George W. Arrington, a Texas Ranger, put fear into the

399

rowdies. J. M. "Honest Jim" Browning, another district attorney, gathered indictments against gamblers, many of whom decided to try their luck in Tascosa, 120 miles west of Mobeetie. Those who stayed and broke the law eventually ended up in a jail built of rock, complete with hangman's device. Today it is the Rock Jail Museum, a delightful place to visit.

Religious revivals made a difference in the 1890s. Before long there were as many churches in Mobeetie as saloons, marking an end to the town's rowdy days. But its future was doomed for other reasons. The railroads ignored Mobeetie, and when the Indian lands of Oklahoma were opened to white settlers, several Mobeetie residents opted to settle there. The army's abandonment of Fort Elliott didn't help either. But the crowning crush came on May 1, 1898, when a devastating storm killed six persons, injured dozens, and destroyed nearly every building in town except the jail. The county seat moved to Wheeler, and Mobeetie slid into its destiny as a ghost town. Since the 1970s, there have been numerous efforts to restore the town. Mobeetie may yet arise from the grave.

Wellington

John and Wiley Dickinson came to Collingsworth County in 1880 with 2,000 cattle and started the Rocking Chair Ranch. Their rocking-chair brand became one of the most famous in the West, and the ranch changed hands several times within only three or four years.

In 1887 an English syndicate bought the 235-square-mile outfit and it became the Rocking Chair Ranche Company, Limited. The principal owners were Sir Dudley Coutts Majoribanks, first baron of Tweedmouth, and John Campbell Hamilton Golden, the earl of Aberdeen. Another Englishman, John Drew, handled the transaction and returned to the ranch as its general manager.

Edward Majoribanks, Sir Dudley's brother, reported the ranch's affairs to the syndicate with meticulous accuracy—and not all of the news was good. Among the ranch's 15,000 cattle stood estates of various Englishmen who became fond of sending their sons there to gain exposure to the wild and wooly West. Local cowboys derisively dubbed the spread "Nobility Ranch," or "The Kingdom of Remittance Men." But the scions of nobility proved poor cattlemen; they were unable to cope with cowboy contempt and systematic stealing.

Drew lost his job as manager and the owners hired George W. Arrington, a captain in the Texas Rangers who had served from the Mexican border to Fort Griffin. Three years earlier he had investigated depredations on Charles Goodnight's ranch. In 1882 he resigned from the rangers to become manager of the Rocking Chair. Almost immediately, however, he went on to become sheriff of Wheeler County (1882-1890) and the fourteen unorganized counties attached to it.

Wellington, a town that sprang up on the ranch, was named for the duke of Wellington. The town of Pearl, two miles north, was expected to become the county seat in 1890, but the Rocking Chair foreman moved sufficient cowboys into the right precincts to give the vote to Wellington, 56 to 32.

On December 22, 1896, the Rocking Chair was sold to William E. Hughes's Continental Land and Cattle Company. Hughes, a sheepherder, lawyer, and banker, quickly subdivided his investment and sold the parcels. The Englishmen abandoned Texas but left some names that endure still: Wellington, Tweedy, Shamrock, Clarendon, and Aberdeen. Wellington's modern economy is based on agriculture, grain elevators, and small businesses.

Childress

George C. Childress, author of the Texas Declaration of Independence, gave this town his name when the Fort Worth & Denver Railroad came through. At that time Childress was part of the OX Ranch. Outlaws Jesse and Frank James allegedly hid out here. Nowadays the town is best known for cotton, grain, and livestock. The Childress County Heritage Museum is worthwhile.

Walter P. Chrysler, founder of the Chrysler Motor Corporation, brought his wife and first child to live in Childress during the fall of 1905. He worked briefly as general foreman of the Fort Worth & Denver Railroad shops before returning north.

Paducah

Sixteen votes in 1892 made Paducah a county seat, and most of those votes came about because promoters gave away sixteen town lots. The name stemmed from Paducah, Kentucky. The massive county courthouse resembles an Egyptian temple. The industry is mostly agriculture.

Guthrie

The Louisiana Land and Cattle Company had holdings in this area, so in 1891 it created a town and named it for W. H. Guthrie of Kentucky, a stockholder in the firm. Guthrie lies in the heart of the Four Sixes Ranch, one of the largest in the state. The local rock calaboose was called the "Friday Night Jail" because so many cowboys wound up there on Friday nights. Until the late 1930s, Guthrie didn't have a newspaper and was forty miles from a barber or a preacher. Zane Grey used this locale as a setting for his book *Thundering Herd*.

Thirteen miles west of Guthrie on US 82 is the Pitchfork Ranch headquarters. The ranch encompassed 120,000 acres and was owned by the Pitchfork Land and Cattle Company of St. Louis.

401

Pampa—Amarillo

Pampa

In 1887, a failed cattle ranch in the central panhandle caused the English-owned Francklyn Land and Cattle Company to go broke. A new English corporation called White Deer Lands assumed title, and general manager George Tyng leased the land to people who understood livestock raising.

The Santa Fe Railroad launched this community in 1888 as an agricultural and cattle center. Tyng founded Pampa in 1892 and named it after the South American Spanish term for a grass-covered plain. The area around here resembles the Argentinean pampas. After the turn of the century it became an oil-field supply point. In December 1942 the Pampa Army Air Field opened as a training site for twin-engine planes. The field closed in August 1946. The Pampa White Deer Land Museum is open most afternoons for those who want to savor the community's past.

Before the southern Plains Indians accepted their fate on reservations, they struck out at the growing numbers of emigrants moving onto their lands. An attack by Cheyennes on a German family crossing Kansas in September 1874 resulted in swarms of military units combing the Texas panhandle, looking for the four sisters who were taken captive. The Indians had killed their father, mother, brother, and older sister.

To evade the troops, the Cheyennes separated into smaller groups. The two older girls, sixteen-year-old Catherine and fifteen-year-old Sophia, vanished in one direction, while their younger sisters, seven-year-old Julia and five-year-old Adelaide, went in another.

By chance, Lt. Frank D. Baldwin encountered a large Indian camp on November 8 (see McLean). He charged and the Indians fled, leaving Julia and Adelaide behind. The girls hid in terror beneath a pile of buffalo robes, nearly naked and emaciated from weeks of mistreatment.

The older girls were with a Cheyenne leader named Stone Calf, who continued to evade capture through the winter. But in the spring, on March 6, 1875, he and about 820 of his people surrendered to white authorities in Indian Territory. Catherine and Sophia were turned over to soldiers and asked to identify the individual Indians who murdered their family and raped and abused them during their captivity. Thirty-one Cheyennes were placed in irons and sent to Fort Marion, Florida.

Congress diverted $10,000 from annuities for the Cheyennes and set it aside as an endowment for the four girls. Each received $2,500 upon reaching adulthood. They all married and lived long lives.

Panhandle

Commonly known as Panhandle City, this town got its name from its location. It began in 1887 as a switch point for the Panhandle & Santa Fe Railroad. A year later settler Thomas Cree planted the first tree, a bois d'arc, that broke the monotony of the flat, grassy plains. Unfortunately, agricultural chemicals killed the tree in 1969. The Square House Museum is one the best in the state.

Texas 207
Spearman—Borger
41 miles

Spearman

As panhandle towns go, this one got a late start. The North Texas & Santa Fe Railroad came through in the early 1920s, and railroad executive Thomas C. Spearman became the town's namesake. Today, grain storage and cattle are the principal enterprises in Spearman.

Stinnett

The Colorado, Rock Island & Gulf Railroad created this town in 1901 and named it for A. S. Stinnett of Amarillo. Like most panhandle towns, Stinnett was and is a grain-raising, livestock-producing, and shipping community.

Stinnett's major claim to historical fame, which it shares with Borger and Spearman, is its nearness to Adobe Walls. Two of the most dramatic Indian fights in western history occurred there, roughly twenty-eight miles east of Stinnett on the isolated south bank of the Canadian River. William Bent, a partner in a St. Louis trading company and owner of Bent's Fort on the Arkansas River, built an adobe post on the north bank of the Canadian River. Within five years the Indians became unfriendly, so Bent abandoned the post and it subsequently became a regional landmark known as Adobe Walls.

The first battle of Adobe Walls occurred in November 1864. Col. Kit Carson and a regiment of Union cavalry were hunting Indians when they became the hunted. The troops sought shelter inside the ruins, and Carson estimated that perhaps 5,000 to 6,000 Comanches and Kiowas showed up to conquer the soldiers, who finally abandoned those walls and beat a fighting retreat for many miles until the Indians broke off.

Ten years later, in 1874, traders built a new Adobe Walls a mile and a half distant from the original structure. The new trading center, simply a few business houses surrounded by a small stockade, catered to buffalo hunters. On Friday night, June 26, twenty buffalo hunters and freighters, one woman, and eight merchants occupied Adobe Walls. Among the buffalo hunters were Bat Masterson, who could also be classified as a gambler, and young Billy Dixon.

Seven years earlier, the Medicine Lodge Treaty had been signed in Kansas between leaders of the Plains Indians, except Comanches, and the United States government. The Indians agreed to settle on reservations in Indian Territory with a stipulation that they could continue to hunt buffalo seasonally on the southern plains without being molested by whites. (Worth noting is the fact that Texas had no federal public lands, so the federal government had no authority over lands in the Texas panhandle.) On this particular night in Adobe Walls, the white residents were celebrating their decision to remain in "forbidden territory." And, because most of the men there were buffalo hunters who, with good equipment and capable skinners, might rake in up to $300 or $400 a day for hides delivered in Dodge City, there was a lot of money at stake in Adobe Walls.

Saturday morning, a bugle sounded and about 700 Comanches, Cheyennes, and Arapahos attacked. Apparently a black deserter from the army had joined the Indian force and brought his bugle to sound the charge on Adobe Walls. The Indians, led by Chief Quanah Parker, swarmed into the encampment, firing through windows, shooting into doors, climbing up onto the roofs, and even stealing wagons. Two brothers named Shadler were killed, but the rest of the whites barricaded themselves inside four adobe buildings. Waves of attacks lasted throughout the morning; however, since each assault commenced with bugle calls and the whites understood the signals, they knew when to brace themselves for another charge. Late that afternoon, the Indians ceased attacking but did not leave.

William Olds, a hide hunter, accidently killed himself with his own rifle while climbing down from a roof tower. His wife, the only woman at Adobe Walls, resisted panic to continue assisting the defenders.

The Indians continued the siege several days. The defenders could not flee because all the horses had been killed or driven off. Inside the compound, dead Indians and horses lay twisted and scattered everywhere. The stench became unbearable, so at night the hunters slipped outside and rolled bodies of animals and men onto buffalo hides, then dragged the cadavers out of smelling range.

On the fourth day, a small group of mounted Indians appeared on a distant butte. Dixon raised his .50 caliber Sharps rifle and fired. His tiny target, 1,538 yards (seven-eights of a mile) away, reeled and fell off his horse. In what some people have called "the shot of the century," Billy Dixon killed an Indian leader and sent the others scurrying for cover. That broke the back of the siege.

Two months later, Col. Nelson A. Miles, with Billy Dixon and Bat Masterson as scouts (neither ever returned to hunting buffalo), were at Adobe Walls when Indians attacked two plum hunters, killing one. This incident has sometimes been referred to as the third battle of Adobe Walls.

The battles at Adobe Walls ended Indian dominance on the plains. The federal government abandoned the so-called peace policy administered by Quaker Indian agents, and thus began the Red River War of 1874 and 1875. When it ended, all surviving panhandle Indians were solidly on reservations.

Panhandle Oil Field

A group of Amarillo businessmen in 1916 formed the Amarillo Oil Company. Their explorations for oil fields in Carson County proved fruitful in April 1920. Their find turned out to be an extensive field underlying Wheeler, Gray, Carson, Hutchinson, Potter, and Moore counties. For a while it was the world's richest single field. During its first big year, in 1926, it produced nearly twenty-six million barrels of oil. Production nearly doubled as the rich Borger and South Pampa fields were developed.

Borger

This thriving community was a late starter compared to most other panhandle settlements. After discovery of the Panhandle Oil Field in 1926, developer A. P. Borger purchased 240 acres on the Canadian River. The lure of oil plus sensational advertising brought 45,000 people here within eight months. Oil-field shanties lined a three-mile-long street. In 1929 the state militia had to be called in to deal with the undesirable elements that threatened the honest workers. By the 1960s, Borger had become one of the nation's largest centers for oil, carbon black, and petrochemical production. The Hutchinson County Historical Museum has displays ranging in subject from Coronado to the oil fields.

US 287
Stratford—Amarillo
83 miles

Stratford

Stratford-on-Avon, that's what Walter Colton, an Englishman, named this settlement in 1885. In 1900, the site became a shipping point for the Chicago, Rock Island & Gulf Railroad. When the county seat passed from Coldwater to

Stratford in 1901, Coldwater sought an injunction. Stratford residents took the county records at gunpoint and guarded them in a tent until things quieted down.

Today, the Stratford skyline is made up of wheat elevators. Many Stratford residents will always remember the May 1978 storm that dumped twelve inches of snow on their town. The next day a tornado came through and three inches of hail fell.

Dumas

Louis Dumas was president of a town-site company that founded this county seat in 1892. That same year, grasshoppers swept through in such numbers that almost every resident left. Although ranching gave rise to the town's economy and farming sustained it through many years, it is natural gas that keeps it thriving today. Two-thirds of the nation's helium is produced here. The Moore County Historical Museum is a good one.

US 385

Dalhart—I-40

66 miles

Dalhart

A little town called Twist came into existence when the Chicago, Rock Island & Pacific Railroad intersected the Fort Worth & Denver City Railroad in early 1901. Folks then changed their town's name to Twist Junction. Later they wanted to call it Denrock, but postal authorities objected, so the residents combined the first syllables of the twin counties (Dallam and Hartley), and Dalhart came into existence. Its main street was called Rag Avenue because of the double row of combination canvas-wooden shacks interspersed with sod dugouts that originally lined the street. At that time it was a real cowboy town, complete with wooden boardwalks. A blizzard that struck in 1912 blew snow into drifts ten feet deep. Cattle died by the thousands.

During the 1920s farmers plowed thousands of acres of rangeland to plant grain. They harvested bumper crops until a series of droughts dried the soil to dust and windstorms blew tons of it away.

An empty-saddle monument is at the north end of Dalhart's V-shaped underpass. A widow asked that a horse bearing an empty saddle appear in the annual XIT reunion parade. The Dallam-Hartley Counties Historical Museum has strong western and cowboy themes. There is also an XIT Museum in Dalhart.

Channing and XIT Ranch

To see Channing is to see the XIT Ranch, for this little community is XIT headquarters. It was named for George Channing Rivers, a paymaster for the railroad.

Since land in the Texas panhandle was once plentiful and practically worthless, the state legislature in 1882 appropriated three million acres and offered it to whoever would build a state capitol building. The structure had to be more attractive than the U.S. Capitol in Washington and at least one foot taller.

A group of Chicago investors, none of whom had ever been to Texas or knew anything about operating a ranch, accepted the offer. They obligated themselves to build a state house to someone else's extravagant specifications in exchange for land they had never seen and that lay far from any railroad or market. Texans Mathias Schnell and A. R. Birck thereupon sold a contract to Chicagoans Abner Taylor, A. C. Babcock, and John V. and Charles Farwell, all of whom formed the Capitol Syndicate.

Babcock inspected the land during a thirty-six-day tour that covered 950 miles. Although he felt satisfied with what he saw, he discovered that the New Mexico-Texas survey line illegally provided New Mexico with a strip of land one-half mile wide and 350 miles long. Texas recovered it.

John Farwell visited England and talked the Capitol Freehold Land and Investment Company into helping develop the new ranch. An enormous outlay of money was needed for fences, headquarters, corrals, barns, water, cattle, and labor. The British contributed $5 million with the understanding that eventually the land would be subdivided and sold off as small farms and ranches. Incidentally, although the land swap totaled three million acres, the successful bidders received an extra 50,000 acres for surveying it.

Ab Blocker of Fort Concho delivered 2,500 longhorns to the ranch in July 1885. Oddly, the new ranchers were so distracted by their various liabilities that they completely overlooked considering a brand, so Blocker reputedly scratched XIT with his bootheel in the corral dust, and the owners accepted it. By some accounts, XIT stands for "Ten in Texas," with the Roman numeral X representing the ten counties—Dallam, Hartley, Oldham, Deaf Smith, Parmer, Bailey, Hockley, Lamb, Cochran, and Castro—that made up the ranch.

Modern-day communities located within the original ranch boundaries include Dalhart, Channing, Vega, Bovina, Amherst, Olton, Muleshoe, Farwell, and Littlefield. The ranch ran 200 miles north to south along the Texas-New Mexico border and averaged thirty miles in width. Two major differences distinguished the XIT from other panhandle ranches: The XIT grazed its cattle entirely within its boundaries while cattle on smaller ranches grazed on open range; and the XIT was never intended to survive in its original form. The owners knew from the beginning that the XIT eventually would be split up and sold off.

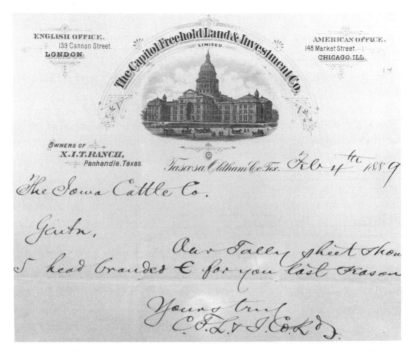

ENGLISH OFFICE.
139 Cannon Street.
LONDON.

The Capitol Freehold Land & Investment Co.
LIMITED

AMERICAN OFFICE.
148 Market Street.
CHICAGO, ILL.

OWNERS OF
X.I.T. RANCH,
Panhandle, Texas.

Tascosa, Oldham Co. Tex. Feb 14th 1889

The Iowa Cattle Co.

Gentn,

Our Tally sheet shows
5 head Branded € for you last Season

Yours truly
C.F.L. & I. Co. Ld.

Letterhead of the Capitol Freehold Land and Investment Co., Ltd. The firm was organized to raise money to stock the XIT Ranch. —Southwest Collection, Texas Tech University

Meanwhile, the greatest fence-building project in American history commenced. One fence ran 150 miles without a turn. In all, the owners used 6,000 miles of single-strand barbed wire to section off pastures, homes, and mark the limits of the vast ranch.

The Texas state capitol building cost the Capitol Syndicate over $3.2 million, which meant it paid about $1.07 per acre for the XIT. Land elsewhere in the panhandle at that time sold for about 25¢ an acre. The capitol was finished in 1888, and by then the ranch had 125,000 head of cattle. At its peak, the ranch employed 150 cowboys, each of whom earned $25 to $30 a month.

The Fort Worth & Denver City Railroad steamed through the XIT in 1887, creating the town of Channing on its way. The XIT built a twenty-two-room headquarters there, and Channing became the XIT town.

Cordia Sloan married ranch foreman Robert L. Duke in 1907, becoming practically a lone female among 150 cowhands. She carried a note pad in her apron pocket and jotted down events and recollections whenever she could. She encouraged scores of cowhands to do the same, and in 1961, at the age of eighty-four, she persuaded the University of Texas Press to publish *6,000 Miles of Fence,* a compilation of everybody's experiences. The book is still in print, and likely will be for as long as people read.

During its life of twenty-seven years, the XIT never made a profit. The owners finally realized their panhandle grassland was far more valuable when planted with sorghum, cotton, and wheat than it had been as forage for cattle. The big "sell off" started during the 1890s at $2.50 an acre. By 1912 the mighty ranch had sold 90 percent of its acreage, leaving only 350,000 for leasing until they, too, were sold. The glory days of the XIT became only memories, but they are kept alive still by the annual XIT Reunion in Dalhart.

Boys Ranch

"Cal Farley's Boys Ranch" was founded in 1939 by the ex-world welterweight wrestling champion and Amarillo businessman. The project started when rancher Julia Bivins donated the old Tascosa courthouse to Farley.

During the Great Depression, Farley salvaged six under-privileged boys and quartered them in the courthouse with substitute parents. Most of Farley's kids were roughnecks heading for the reformatory. Yet, by 1975, the ranch had 400 boys plus staff, with everybody living on 120 shady, spring-fed acres also donated by Bivins.

That space has now expanded to over 4,000 acres for farming and ranching plus fifty modern buildings. Education at the facility goes through high school and teaches academic subjects as well as fourteen vocations. The ranch accepts boys as young as three and has less than a hundred vacancies each year. The boys represent a cross-section of religions and races from practically every state. The ranch is a home first, a school second, and a job third. There are no fences, guards, locked doors, and gates. As Farley used to say, "each youngster needs a shirttail to hang on to."

Although Cal Farley died at the ranch of a cerebral hemorrhage on February 19, 1967, life, education, and work continue on the ranch.

Tascosa

Mexican buffalo hunters, *ciboleros*, came here before the Indian-trading Comancheros. They were attracted by Atascosa (Boggy) Creek, which flows into the Canadian River. In the 1870s, these immigrants along with Mexican sheepmen and freighters led by a Mexican colonist named Casimero Romero built small villages and homes called plazas. One of the best was Plaza Atascosa, an easy ford across the creek for cattle and freight moving north and south through the panhandle.

Large cattle ranches started springing up in this region in 1875, and Plaza Atascosa became simply Tascosa. It was the second town founded in the Texas panhandle and served as a shipping and supply point for the LIT, LX, XIT, Frying Pan, and LS ranches. As blacksmith shops, general stores, and saloons took root, Tascosa became the seat of legal business for at least nine unorganized counties in 1880. The town attracted gunmen like Billy the Kid, Pat Garrett, Dave Rudabaugh, Wyatt Earp, Bat Masterson, and Charles

Siringo. They felt right at home in this place known as the "Cowboy Capital of the Plains."

Headquarters for the LX Ranch lay twenty miles downriver from Tascosa, while that of the LS Ranch was fifteen miles to the southeast and the Frying Pan Ranch was about five miles farther in the same direction.

But all wasn't happy in this cowboy kingdom. The big outfits formed the Panhandle Cattlemen's Association, and agreements among its members allowed ranch foremen to treat their hired hands as they saw fit. They could regulate wages (usually $25 to $30 a month), for instance, and cowboys would have no recourse because all the cattlemen in the region paid the same. To improve their economic conditions, cowboys started gathering mavericks (unbranded, ownerless cattle) from the open range and placing their own brands on them. A hard-working cowboy could accumulate a small herd either to sell or to start his own spread. But the big ranchers forbade this, so in 1883 the cowboys submitted this ultimatum, the original of which is in the Panhandle Plains Historical Museum at Canyon, Texas:

> We, the undersigned cowboys of Canadian River, do these presents agree to bind ourselves into the following obligations, viz:
> First: That we will not work for less than $50 per mo. and we further more agree no one shall work for less than $50 per mo. after the 31st of Mch.
> Second: Good cooks shall also receive $50 per mo.
> Third: Any one running an outfit [foreman, wagon boss, or manager] shall not work for less than $75 per mo.
> Any one violating the above obligations shall suffer the consequences. Those not having funds to pay board after March 31 will be provided for 30 days at Tascosa.

The conditions were signed by twenty-four cowboys, none of whom used an X.

For the first and only time in history, a 200-member association of cowboys went on strike. Despite the underfunding, poor communication, and weak leadership in their organization, the cowboys refused to use force.

W. M. D. Lee, owner of the LS Ranch, talked with cowboy strike leader Tom Harris. Lee offered each LS cowboy $40 a month. Although Harris turned him down, he admitted that some of the men were not worth $50 a month. Lee then offered to pay $50 a month to every man Harris recommended as a top hand if they'd stay on the job, and $100 a month to Harris, $25 more than the going wage for wagon bosses. Harris decided to stick with his men, so Lee fired him.

And that's the way it went across the panhandle. The cowboys had to submit to the usual wages or lose their jobs, and the ranchers had little trouble replacing them. After thirty days the striking cowboys were blacklisted, meaning none of them worked in the panhandle again.

Tascosa had lasted through its first four years without a single death due to a gunfight. But in June 1881, that silence crumbled. Cowboy Frank Leigh tried to shoot the sheriff, and missed. The sheriff did not. Leigh was buried on a rocky hill overlooking Tascosa. Soon after, local merchant Jules Howard shot and killed Bob Russell in a dispute over Russell's wife. Tascosa Boot Hill started taking on a population. Eventually about fifty people were buried there, but only a dozen or so are identified.

In the spring of 1886, the cattlemen formed a squad of Texas Rangers, home rangers in a sense, sanctioned by the state government but retained by the Panhandle Cattlemen's Association and supported and defended primarily by the LS outfit. Former Lincoln County, New Mexico, sheriff Pat Garrett, the tall slayer of Billy the Kid, became captain and leader of the group generally known as the LS-Pat Garrett Rangers.

Garrett's rangers tried to enforce three edicts: first, civilians could not wear six-shooters; second, small ranch owners could not participate in the huge annual roundups of the large outfits; and third, mavericks could not be branded by just anyone who found them, especially since many of the brands were illegal.

After a brief time, even Garrett couldn't abide the regulations he had been hired to enforce. He quit, and whatever legitimacy the rangers might have had went with him.

On the night of March 20, 1886, several LS cowboys rode into Tascosa to attend a Mexican dance. At two in the morning, cowboy Ed King was shot while walking with a lady friend. Other shots started ringing out, too, and by the time Sheriff Jim East and his deputy restored the peace, four men lay dead and two were wounded. Texas historians call it "The Big Fight." No lasting arrests were made.

Soft-spoken editor Charles Rudolph of the *Tascosa Pioneer* relentlessly campaigned for a railroad to lay tracks to the town, and just as relentlessly he believed the panhandle's salvation lay in farming, not ranching. W. M. D. Lee, owner of the LS Ranch, complained that higher taxes only made life more comfortable "for the little men of Tascosa." He donated land for a new town site called Cheyenne (later changed to Magenta), three miles west of Tascosa. Even though the Fort Worth & Denver Railroad laid tracks to it, the new town lasted only a year.

Tascosa's last hurrah was when editor Rudolph struggled and failed to bring in the Rock Island Railroad. By then the big ranchers had strung barbed wire that kept them in and Tascosa out. The Rock Island went to Vega, which means "meadow" in Spanish, and so did the county seat in 1911. The "Cowboy Capital of the Plains" became a ghost town that was only slightly revived by Cal Farley's Boys Ranch after 1939.

Amarillo—Childress

115 miles

Claude

Railroad engineer Claude Ayes brought the first Fort Worth & Denver train through here in 1887. The old Armstrong County jail had such little use that the local Methodist minister turned it into a parsonage. Today, Claude is an agricultural center. The nearby Texas 207 is a marvelously scenic drive.

Goodnight

When Charles Goodnight built his home here in 1876, only thirty people lived in the county, and all of them worked on the Goodnight Ranch. The JA Ranch was also called the Goodnight Ranch, since it was owned jointly by Goodnight and John George Adair, an Irish nobleman and financier. In 1887

Charles Goodnight poses with author and researcher J. Evetts Haley. Haley wrote the classic biography Charles Goodnight: Cattleman and Plainsman *(U. of Oklahoma Press).*
—Nita Stewart Haley Memorial Library

the ranch was divided. Goodnight sold his portion in 1890 and continued living at his ranch in Goodnight until his death in 1929.

Goodnight started a junior college in the town, but it failed and became part of an orphanage before it was absorbed into the public school system. In an effort to keep buffalo from going extinct, the cattleman raised a private herd on his ranch in Goodnight.

Clarendon

Lewis Henry Carhart, a minister interested in bringing more people to the Texas panhandle, started Clarendon in 1878 and named it after his wife, Clara. Carhart wanted material gain in the panhandle, but he wanted God, education, and temperance even more. He received enough support that settlers weren't allowed to consume liquor or operate saloons or gambling houses. Cowboys and buffalo hunters checked their weapons at the general store. The town was so peaceful that outlying homesteaders and ranchers referred to it as "Saints' Roost." During the late 1880s, though, the Fort Worth & Denver City Railroad laid its tracks six miles to the north, so the town moved there and the atmosphere that created Saints' Roost faded from existence.

But Clarendon thrived in its new location. Clarendon College grew out of the old Allentown Academy, thanks in part to the ten acres of ground and the two-story brick building the community donated to the Methodist Episcopal Church for Clarendon College. In 1927 it evolved into the Clarendon Junior College. Like most other panhandle towns, Clarendon has grown into an agricultural community.

Memphis

An 1890 founder of this town noticed a letter addressed to Memphis, Texas, rather than Memphis, Tennessee, so he suggested a village name of Memphis on the assumption that the town might receive at least one letter. The village may look larger than it really is because early settlers constructed multistory buildings instead of the single-story structures more typical to early development. Agriculture remains the primary industry.

Famed country music singer Ernest Tubb gave his last performance here before his death in 1984. The residents still celebrate Ernest Tubb Day in September.

Estelline

When the local post office was established in 1892, this village two miles south of the Red River was named for Estelle de Shields. Two years earlier it had been the largest cattle shipping point on the Fort Worth & Denver City Railroad. Large ranches adjacent to Estelline were the 62 Wells, the Mill Iron, the Diamond Trail, and the Shoe Nail.

Thirty miles west of Estelline on Texas 36 is Turkey, named for Turkey Creek, which took its name from a flock of wild turkeys that lived here in 1893. But the town didn't grow much until 1928, when the Fort Worth & Denver City Railroad finally decided to come through. The Hotel Turkey, built in 1927, still operates and serves meals.

Turkey is famous primarily as the hometown of James Robert Wills, better known as "Bob Wills, the King of Western Swing." He was born in 1906, and in 1940 he recorded the country classic "San Antonio Rose." Wills was admitted to the Country Music Hall of Fame and the National Cowboy Hall of Fame. A series of heart attacks and strokes brought his amazing career to an end on May 13, 1975. The town thought so much of Wills that it built an eight-foot red granite monument etched with the figure of Bob with his fiddle and cigar, his war record, his movie credits, and a list of musical hits. "Ahhh-ha, take it away, Leon."

I-27
Amarillo—Lubbock
119 miles

Canyon

In 1878 Canyon City was named for Palo Duro Canyon, just a few miles distant. The village site was originally chosen by Jot Gunter and William B. Munson as headquarters for the T Anchor Ranch, even though the first settler was L. G. Conner, who built a dugout here in 1889. Al Hammon, a T Anchor cowboy, constructed a blacksmith shop in Canyon City before it had a courthouse and saloon. The Pecos & Northern Railroad made Canyon a shipping point in 1898.

Today Canyon is many things. It is a shipping point for crops and cattle as well as a financial hub for the panhandle. It is an intellectual center due to the 130-acre campus of West Texas State University. Located on campus is the massive Panhandle-Plains Museum—without question the pre-eminent museum in the Southwest and one of the top fifty tourist attractions in Texas. The museum exhibits range from archaeology, prehistoric animals, and Indians to cowboys, ranching, petroleum, and art. Canyon is also a principal gateway to Palo Duro Canyon.

Palo Duro Canyon

A huge cleft in the earth twelve miles east of Canyon City on Texas 217 ranks as one of the top ten tourist attractions in Texas. (Palo Duro is Spanish for "hard wood," referring to the junipers that grow along the canyon rim.) Some 230 million years ago this was a land of shallow seas and swamps inhabited by dinosaurs and toothy amphibians. That era ended 70 million years ago, when continental shift caused the Rocky Mountains to rise and subsequently created the Llano and the Balcones escarpments.

Palo Duro Canyon was cut from the plains by the once-active Tierra Blanca and Palo Duro creeks, both of which are now so insignificant that they rarely appear on maps. Over many centuries they cut through sedimentary layers of four geological periods and merged into a single stream now known as Prairie Dog Town Fork of the Red River. Behind them lay a gorge 120 miles long and ranging from one-half mile to twenty miles wide.

Coronado visited this area in 1541, more than three hundred years before Capt. R. B. Marcy explored and mapped the canyon. The Indians of the southern plains made a last stand in Palo Duro Canyon. Gen. Ranald Mackenzie dealt them a catastrophic blow when he attacked a Comanche, Kiowa, and Cheyenne village in Palo Duro Canyon on September 28, 1874. The soldiers found a trail and descended to the canyon floor, 700 feet below the rim. After the fighting started, most of the Indians escaped, but Mackenzie destroyed their lodges, their winter food supply, and 1,480 ponies. The fleeing Comanches were left destitute, with no horses to help them hunt or move and no food to get them through the coming winter. Those who survived that harsh season surrendered at Fort Sill on June 2, 1875. The Red River War terminated with relatively few casualties on either side, all things considered.

With the fighting over and the Indians gone, Americans started entering the canyon. In 1876 Charles Goodnight drove 1,800 head of cattle into the canyon and founded the JA Ranch with John Adair. Adair funded the operation while Goodnight supplied the herd and expertise. Eventually the JA had 100,000 cattle. The partnership ended in 1887, although the JA Ranch is still in operation.

When attempts failed to make the canyon a national park in 1930, Fred Emery, who had an interest in 16,000 acres of canyon land, opened his portion to visitors. Over 25,000 people came in 1931. Two years later the Civilian Conservation Corps built a canyon road, cabins, lodges, and an entrance building.

Over 15,000 acres of the canyon became a state park in 1934. The eight-mile drive to it approximates the route followed by Goodnight when he entered the area. Today the Sad Monkey train hauls visitors to significant areas of the canyon.

The musical drama "TEXAS" is the most famous outdoor pageant in the state. Horsemen carrying flags ride atop the 600-foot canyon wall. Colorful singers and dancers sweep across the stage. A professional cast of eighty portrays the struggles, strengths, celebrations, burials, and politics of the early settlers, the cowboys, and the Indians. From mid-June to late August the pageant runs nightly except on Sunday.

Tulia

This town arose the same year the county was organized, 1880. Its name was supposed to be Tullie, derived from nearby Tule Creek, but a postal clerk made an error and the town became Tulia.

Near Tule Creek, Gen. Ranald Mackenzie ordered the 1874 slaughter of nearly 1,500 ponies to keep the Indians from recovering them. The animals were slain on the caprock of the canyon's mouth, and their bones remained there bleaching in the weather for years. Old-timers refer to this location as "bone ford," and tales still circulate of riderless, phantom herds galloping wildly in the moonlight.

Plainview

Plainview got its name from its location on high ground that offers a magnificent view of the plains. German Americans moved into this area in 1878, and the community flourished within a decade. Soon small wooden homes replaced the original dugouts and sod houses. Supplies came in by wagon from Colorado City, 250 miles distant, until 1888 when Amarillo was organized just 90 miles away.

The Panhandle & Santa Fe Railroad reached Plainview in late 1906. Although the countryside had been ranching oriented, it slowly switched to farming because of the fertile and productive land.

In 1945 archaeologists discovered a distinctive piece of ancient flint work here and dubbed it the Plainview Point. The Llano Estacado Museum is excellent.

Lubbock

The term Lubbock Site Lake is misleading. There is no lake and there hasn't been one for a half-century. It dried up. In the old lake bed, though, archaeologists found everything from the bones of elephants and prehistoric horses to the dire wolf and Clovis and Folsom points. The lake site was at North Indiana and Loop 289, two miles northwest of present-day College Avenue. Springs seeping from Yellow House Canyon fed the lake.

Yellow House and Blackwater draws twisted through present-day Lubbock. The cliffs were a yellowish hue, and when seen from certain positions they resembled the walls of a great city, hence the "Yellow House."

Yellow House Canyon was a popular Indian and Hispanic trading ground; it is now a portion of Mackenzie State Park. The Spanish called it Cañon de

Rescate, the "Canyon of Ransoms," and one can only wonder at the human sufferings that must have inspired that name.

Buffalo hunters were common in this region. And one of the last Indian battles fought around here took place during the winter of 1874-75 inside of what is now the city limits of Lubbock. It began in 1873 when buffalo hunters decided to ignore the Medicine Lodge Treaty, which forbade whites from entering the southern buffalo range.

The hunters established Rath City at the Double Mountain Fork of the Brazos, thirty miles east of Post, and used it as a supply base for the Lubbock area, although nothing remains at the site today. A band of Comanches who had a legal right to be hunting on the plains killed a buffalo hunter named Marshal Sewell. At first, 500 men from Rath City decided to take vengeance, but only 125 showed up. Even then, only 46 decided to fight, and of these, just 26 were mounted while the rest rode in wagons. One of the wagons carried nothing but whiskey. After a series of misadventures and marching off in wrong directions, the hunters caught up with the Comanche leader at what is now Mackenzie State Park. The white men opened fire, but after the Indians wounded three, the rest began to retreat. Twenty-three days after leaving Rath City, the bedraggled Indian fighters returned. Meanwhile, by the end of the 1870s, the buffalo had disappeared from the south plains, although a few remained in the Yellow House area.

The IOA Ranch started in the 1880s, and its pastures cut across several counties. The ranch survived the droughts and the 1887 blizzard. It even justified the killing of troublesome mustangs. The ranch never made a profit, but it operated seventeen years before creditors took control and sold the property. Out of that ranch arose Lubbock.

Modern Lubbock is the story of two rival town builders. In 1890, W. E. Rayner started a town site called Monterey, which was south of Yellow House Canyon and north of the present campus of Texas Technological University. F. E. Wheelock and Rollie Burns began a development north of the canyon and east of the Plainview highway. It was called "Old Lubbock." Neither community made much progress, so in 1891 the two developers consolidated, moved to a third area, and called it Lubbock. Both the town and the county were named for Tom S. Lubbock, a former Texas Ranger, Confederate officer, and brother of Francis R. Lubbock, the Civil War governor of the state. Although settlers complained of prairie fires, sandstorms, droughts, and bugs, the town grew modestly and was incorporated in 1909.

Lubbock was "dry" except for one saloon during the early days, and the citizens petitioned its owner to close. He complied and accepted a job with one of the signers.

Lubbock is the home of Texas Tech University and its School of Medicine. The Texas Tech Museum is housed in a $7 million complex that includes a twelve-acre ranching heritage center of blacksmith shops, barns, windmills, dugouts, sod huts, wooden buildings, and much more. It is unique in the land.

There is the Lubbock County Museum, the Lubbock Fine Arts Center, and Mackenzie State Park, one of the most visited in the state. Lubbock is the chrysanthemum capital of the world. Residents are encouraged to plant them.

US 60
Canyon—Farwell
79 miles

Umbarger

Umbarger began as a two-teacher schoolhouse in 1902. It grew slightly in 1915, when the Panhandle & Santa Fe Railroad steamed in. The German-rooted farming community built the barnlike St. Mary's Catholic Church. Little happened there until the Second World War, when 7,000 Italian prisoners of war arrived in Hereford. The prisoners remained from 1942 until 1945.

In early 1945, nine Italians were loaded into trucks and deposited at the Umbarger church to install rows of ornate painted-glass windows. They carved an incredible wood reproduction of Leonardo da Vinci's "The Last Supper." Behind the altar went a ten-foot canvas depicting the Assumption. The work of love and art was dedicated as a memorial to five POWs who died at the camp.

Inside the chapel is a marker that reads:

> On the first of May 1988, Italian soldiers imprisoned in this county of Texas during World War II and visiting the USA 42 years after their repatriation, laid this mark in memory of their brothers, dead in captivity, and as a token of the new friendship between the Italian and the American peoples.

Hereford

Herds of Hereford cattle grazed near here, so in 1890 that's what the town founders decided to name their community. The town has always encouraged irrigated farming, and because of fluorine and iodides in the soil, the community has been known as the "town without a toothache."

One of the first barbed-wire fences in Texas was erected here in 1881. It kept T Anchor Ranch cattle from drifting south. Three million cattle currently move through community feedlots.

County Courthouse, Hereford, Texas.

Sites worth seeing include the Deaf Smith County Historical Museum and the National Cowgirl Hall of Fame & Western Heritage Center. The latter honors the western spirit and women who have excelled in rodeos. Cowgirl memorabilia occupies 6,000 square feet of museum space.

Friona

The Capitol Syndicate, formed to build the Texas state capitol in exchange for the three-million-acre XIT Ranch, named this shipping point on the Pecos & Northern Texas Railroad Frio in 1898. When the post office was established in 1905, the town became Friona. Today it is primarily a tourist and agricultural center.

Farwell

Texico, New Mexico, and Farwell, Texas, are twin cities. The latter was established in 1905 and named for John V. Farwell and the Farwell family, executives of the Capitol Syndicate (see Friona and Channing). The Pecos & Northern Texas Railroad made the town a shipping center in 1913. It remains a marketing complex for a strong agricultural region.

419

Muleshoe

The nearby Muleshoe Ranch, which broke up into farms about 1910, provided this town a name in 1926. Ranching and farming are the two main industries. The nearby Muleshoe National Wildlife Refuge, the oldest in Texas, was founded in 1935.

The National Mule Memorial is in Muleshoe. It stands near the intersection of US 70/84, and was unveiled on July 4, 1965. The mule is one of the most photographed statues in Texas.

Littlefield

George Washington Littlefield was born in Mississippi, fought with Terry's Texas Rangers during the Civil War, and organized the LFD and LIT ranches in the Texas panhandle. The Panhandle & Santa Fe Railroad arrived in 1913,

George Washington Littlefield, cattleman, Confederate officer, banker, and member of the University of Texas Board of Regents. His Panhandle interests included the LFD and LIT ranches. —Archives Division, Texas State Library

but Littlefield's niece had already surveyed a town site in 1912 and named it for her uncle.

Intensive cotton production arrived by the 1920s, and cotton, grain, and feedlots still play chief economic roles. The world's tallest windmill—132 feet—used to be at Littlefield, but it blew down on Thanksgiving Day, 1926. The replica is 114 feet.

Isaac L. Ellwood once owned the great Spade Ranch between Littlefield and Lubbock. Ellwood, along with J. F. Glidden, who manufactured barbed wire, introduced the new fencing material into Texas. One of Ellwood and Glidden's top salesmen was John W. (later "Bet-a-million") Gates.

Post

Illinois-born Charles William Post suffered nervous disorders that caused him to experiment with treatments. He invented a cereal drink called Postum, and in 1894 he built a small factory near Battle Creek, Michigan, that soon started creating other cereals such as Post Toasties and Post Bran. In 1906 he moved to Texas and purchased a quarter-million-acre ranch, and on it he built Post City. The surrounding land was subdivided into 160-acre homesteads, each with a five- or six-room farmhouse. In this manner, Post colonized about 1,200 families.

The town of Post took care of the families' material needs by importing goods on mule trains from Big Spring until a railroad arrived at Post in 1910. Charles Post ran the community though a group of managers and a firm he created called the Double U Company. It enforced sanitary regulations, forbade the sale of liquor in town, and refused to sell town lots to speculators.

Between 1911 and 1914, Charles Post spent $50,000 on elaborate experiments to make rain by blasting dynamite along fifteen stations sitting on the edge of the caprock. Not even a heavy dew fell.

His farming experiments were more successful as he helped develop the plains into an agricultural region. These challenges couldn't buy him health or peace of mind, however, and in 1914 he committed suicide in California. But Post, the town he created, endures as an agricultural center. The restored Algerita Hotel is now an art center. The Garza County Museum is delightful, and the Garza Theatre was one of the first movie houses in Texas. There is a Llano Estacado tourist marker.

Snyder

Snyder is forty-five miles south of Post and a couple miles off US 84 at the crossroads of Texas 208, Texas 350, and US 180.

W. H. "Pete" Snyder opened a trading post here in 1877. When buffalo-hide dwellings and dugouts sprang up, the site was dubbed "Robbers Roost." It attracted many desperados and fugitives.

C. W. Post. —The Institute of Texan Cultures

J. Wright Mooar, from Vermont, was perhaps the greatest buffalo hunter who ever lived. After working as a streetcar conductor in Chicago, he moved to Kansas and began making his reputation as a buffalo hunter. When the buffalo thinned, he drifted to the south plains. He claimed to have killed 20,000 buffalo, including a white buffalo less than ten miles from Snyder. A white buffalo statue stands in the town square. Mooar died at Snyder on May 1, 1940.

Cattlemen arrived in the 1880s, and fence-cutting wars broke out. The Roscoe, Snyder & Pacific Railroad reached town in 1908.

After the Canyon Reef Oil Field was discovered in 1950, the population boomed as the town became a leading petroleum processor. The Towie Memorial Park is a recreation site, while the Scurry County Museum specializes in the Old West.

Roscoe

This town was originally called Vista, but the name was changed to Roscoe for an engineer on the Texas & Pacific Railroad.

US 70

Matador—Muleshoe

117 miles

Matador

A buffalo hunter named Ballard built and briefly lived in a dugout at Ballard Springs in the mid-1870s. Joe Browning came along with a small herd in 1878 and took over the abandoned dugout. Then Henry H. "Hank" Campbell purchased the cattle and range rights from Browning and went into partnership with A. M. Briton. The Matador Ranch was thus born in 1878. Capitalist S. W. Lomax added financing, and the firm was reorganized as the Matador Cattle Company. In 1882 the company sold out to the Matador Land and Cattle Company of Dundee, Scotland. Soon it amassed about 300,000 acres and 60,000 cattle, and by 1885 it started fencing one of the largest ranches in Texas. It also dug water wells and built windmills.

Motley County was organized in 1891, and Hank Campbell picked out a town site. The law required at least twenty businesses in operation, so cowboys from the Matador Ranch set up firms that lasted one day in the town designated as "Matador."

By 1910, the Matador Land and Cattle Company was operating ranches in Texas, South Dakota, and Wyoming. Back in the panhandle, the company began selling land to small settlers. The Quanah, Acme & Pacific Railroad built through the Matador Ranch and on into the town of Matador in 1914. By the mid-1920s, the company had almost completely withdrawn from its northern ranches and focused on conducting agricultural experiments in the panhandle. The ranch was sold in July 1951, but it is still called the Matador. The town of Matador remains an agricultural and range center.

Floydada, Springlake, Earth

James and Ada Price donated 640 acres of land for Floyd City in 1890. The U.S. Postal Service rejected the name, so the residents combined Floyd with Mrs. Price's first name and got Floydada. This area produces lots of wheat, and the town is home to the Floyd County Museum.

Springlake incorporated in 1915 with a population of fifteen. For the previous sixteen years, the place served as the headquarters for William Electius Halsell's Mashed O. Ranch on a site he selected because of the nearby natural spring-fed lake.

Earth began as Fairleen in the early 1900s and was founded by W. E. Halsell. When C. H. Reeves became postmaster in 1925, he rejected Fairleen as the town's name. He considered Tulsa, but Earth won out reportedly because of a sandstorm in progress.

US 82

Guthrie—Lubbock

96 miles

Dickens

The Spur, Pitchfork, and Matador ranches often used this area for cowboy line camps. Other settlers started moving in by the late 1880s, and the county was organized in 1891.

South of Dickens about eleven miles on Texas 70 is Spur, founded in 1909 as the famous Spur Ranch. Major portions of the ranch were owned by several syndicates that became more interested in colonization than in ranching, so they built a railroad line from Stamford, just north of Abilene, to the ranch. The fertile land, reasonable prices, and lack of middlemen in acquiring property made the area attractive. Many well-known American writers visited here—Emerson Hough, B. M. Bowers, George Patullo, and John A. Lomax, to mention a few. The town was named for Alamo defender J. Dickens.

Lubbock—Whiteface
45 miles

Levelland, Whiteface

C. W. Post (see Post) bought the Oxsheer Ranch and in 1912 surveyed and plotted Hockley City for the site. But no buildings went up until 1921, and a year later the name was changed to Levelland because of regional topography. The town is now known as the "City of Mosaics" because so many public buildings are adorned with colorful outdoor mosaics. The South Plains College Art Museum has a nice collection of old masters' art.

Whiteface, fourteen miles west of Levelland on the same highway, is so named for the whitefaced cattle in the region.

Roscoe—Midland
98 miles

Colorado City

The first Texas legislature selected Colorado City as the republic's capital, but President Sam Houston vetoed it. Nevertheless, great plans were laid out for this city on the west bank of the Colorado River at the La Bahía Crossing. It was directly across from LaGrange, and the Colorado City promoters of the 1830s hoped to make their village the greatest city on the Llano, with eleven streets running east and west and twelve running north and south. They hoped it would become the "Mother City of West Texas," the oldest town between Weatherford and El Paso, but the legislature doomed that dream. Still, the place survived on a lesser scale.

A Texas Ranger camp arrived in 1877. Business houses started in 1880 and the first train reached town in 1881, quickly turning the place into a shipping and supply center. Today it is a popular recreation spot as well.

In the early days, saloons were everywhere, but so were droughts, hard times, and bad luck. Cattleman W. P. Patterson ran into some of the latter when he apparently started shooting near the Nip and Tuck Saloon. Texas

Rangers Jeff Milton, J. M. Sedberry, and L. B. Wells came quickly and demanded that Patterson give up his pistol. Patterson fired at Sedberry, inflicting a powder burn on his face. Within an instant Milton shot Patterson down and Wells put a bullet into him as he hit the ground. The cattleman died on the spot.

Although floods had wrecked the town early in this century, the oil strikes of the 1920s gave it new life. Today the community is an agriculture and petroleum center. Don't miss its Colorado City Historical Museum.

Big Spring

The Cap Rock escarpment has a rocky gorge between two high foothills, and inside these foothills is Sulphur Draw, reputedly the longest dry draw in Texas. Despite that reputation, it had a spring-fed watering hole significant enough to attract buffalo, wild mustangs, and other animals. Comanches used to stop at it and regarded it as both a place of peace and of war. The spring became a campsite for forty-niners, stagecoach passengers, and military surveyors such as Capt. Randolph B. Marcy. Finally, this big spring gave its name to a remarkable town.

Big Spring started as a settlement of hide huts, tents, dugouts, wagon yards, and more than a few saloons in 1882. Lumber for building came from Colorado City piled high in long wagons pulled by oxen. The first general store opened in 1882, and the town soon became a shipping point for cotton, livestock, and grain. Oil was discovered in 1927, and the military showed up in 1942 to train cadets in precision, high-altitude bombing at the Big Spring Army Air Force Bombardier School. It closed in December 1945.

Titled Englishmen purchased ranches in this vicinity, but most outfits gave up during the drought of 1894. The Earl of Aylesford moved to town, bought the Cosmopolitan Hotel, and died there. As the open range went out of business, cowboys from large nearby ranches did all they could through the turn of the century to keep from turning the place over to farmers. But in the end, the plow won.

The Big Spring State Park has many recreational sites, while the city park has the original Big Spring.

The Potton House, a restored Victorian home, showcases turn-of-the-century furnishings. The Heritage Museum is strong on pioneer and Indian artifacts, and features a display of longhorn cattle horns, with some sets up to ten and one-half feet wide.

Stanton

The Texas & Pacific Railroad brought in German Catholic settlers, many of them monks, to a station they called Grelton in 1881. Adam Konz and his family organized the colony, surveyed much of the land, and petitioned the railroad to change the town's name to Mariensfield.

Heneage Finch, the 7th Earl of Aylesford, left England and came to Texas because of a divorce scandal. —The Institute of Texan Cultures

A store and church were built during that first year of the settlement, and Carmelite Monastery opened the following year. The monks left in 1894, and the Sisters of Mercy converted the structure to a convent-boarding school; about 2,000 students graduated before a tornado destroyed the building in 1938.

The severe drought in 1886 staggered the ranchers and almost destroyed the area farmers, but a few survived. The town had to fence itself in to keep C. C. Slaughter's cowboys and cattle from trampling the crops. In place of those who left to search for greener pastures came Protestant settlers in 1890, and they petitioned to change the name of the village. They chose Stanton to honor Abraham Lincoln's secretary of war, Edwin M. Stanton.

The old 1908 jail displays many artifacts in restored condition, and the Marlin County Historical Museum takes a broad view of the past.

Midland

The "Queen City of the South Plains" was settled by thrifty, law-abiding people from the Ohio River Valley and Great Lakes regions. By 1880, about 300 people lived on established farms and ranches, while those who lived in town built substantial homes around the public square.

When oil was discovered in the Permian Basin in 1923, Midland quickly evolved from its farming and ranching origins into a twentieth-century oil and finance center. The town became headquarters for 150 oil companies, even though the county had no oil wells. Machine and oil-tool assembly shops went up, and Midland soon had chemical plants and oil refineries.

Sloan Field opened halfway between Odessa and Midland in 1931, and in 1942 the site became the Midland Army Flying School to train bombardiers. The base closed in 1947, and the facility is now the Midland-Odessa Air Terminal.

An ancient skull identified by archaeologists as Midland Man (actually a female) was discovered on the nearby Scharbauer Ranch. It is 22,000 years old.

Midland is the "tall city" of West Texas and the southern plains. It creates a startling impression as skyscrapers seem to rise out of the flat horizon. Midland got its name because it is halfway between Fort Worth and El Paso, and its remoteness tends to confound visitors. But the city is a sophisticated, intellectual center, even if its skyline is straight. Wealth and sophistication have combined with breezy western characteristics to create an enjoyable atmosphere to the place.

Midland is home to a branch of the University of Texas. Its Midland County Museum and Museum of the Southwest are excellent. There is a Fredda Turner Durham Children's Museum and a Permian Basin Petroleum Museum, Library, and Hall of Fame. Last but not least is the Nita Stewart Haley Memorial Library/J. Evetts Haley History Center, a must for anyone researching southwestern history.

428

Christopher Columbus Slaughter, cattleman, early 1900s. —The Institute of Texan Cultures

US 87
Lubbock—Big Spring
103 miles

Tahoka

Near this town is a body of water called Lake Tahoka, which the Indians named for its depth or clarity. Buffalo hunters and Indians stopped here to refresh themselves, as did Gens. William Rufus Shafter and Ranald Mackenzie when they were pursuing Comanches and Kiowas. Cattle drives and immigrants passed this way, and C. C. Slaughter built his ranch headquarters alongside the lake. The town became a county seat in 1906.

During the 1920s and 1930s, when black and Mexican itinerant workers picked cotton, it seemed nobody went to bed at night. Groceries stayed open constantly, and the sweet sound of picking guitars and spiritual lyrics wafted through the air. The first all-black rodeo took place in Tahoka on Juneteenth

(June 19) 1939, the Texas Emancipation Day. The Pioneer Museum is worth visiting. Cotton remains the economic mainstay of the community.

About six miles west of Tahoka on US 380, then two miles north, are two lakes known as the Double Lakes or the Twin Lakes. The T Bar Ranch, established in 1883, had its headquarters on the north shore of the upper lake. A company of the 10th U.S. Cavalry and some buffalo hunters lost their way while trailing Indians; they wandered ninety-six hours without water before finding these lakes, but by then five of their party had died of thirst.

Lamesa

Believe it or not, this town was called Chicago when it was established as the county seat in 1905. That same year the name was changed to Lamesa, an English corruption of the Spanish term meaning "tableland." Cotton and oil dominate the local economy. The Lamesa-Dawson County Museum & Art Center is very worthwhile.

Thirty-two miles east of Lamesa on US 180 is Gail. In 1891 it was named for Gail Borden, a Texas pioneer as well as the inventor of condensed milk and founder of Borden Foods. For years Gail had no hotel, theater, railroad, doctor, bank, preacher, or lawyer, and it doesn't have all of them yet. Visitors sometimes used to sleep in the jail. The owner of the town's only cafe kept the key. Even today, if you want to visit the Borden County Historical Museum, you must first see someone in the courthouse for access. During the land rush of 1902, claimants had to file with the county clerk. But the cowboys didn't want to see the area turn to farming, so they walked back and forth through the line of settlers, forcibly removing them from their place in line. Fights broke out, but in the end Gail remained cow country.

US 385
Lubbock—Odessa
142 miles

Brownfield

The Santa Fe Railroad reached this area in 1917, but Brownfield had been laid out and named for a prominent ranching family for fourteen years by then. Hill's Hotel was the first building. For a while Brownfield had the largest individual enterprise of its kind in the state: Bibricora feeding pens capable of holding 10,000 head of feeder stock shipped in from Mexico. The Terry County Historical Museum is in the restored A. M. Brownfield home.

Thirty-two miles west of Brownfield on US 380 is Plains. It got started when a man named Miller settled there in a dugout during the 1890s. Although it sounds primitive, he had a piano. The town became county seat in 1907. The Wassom Oil Field blew in during 1935.

Seagraves

The Spearman Land Company, a spin-off of the Santa Fe Railroad, founded this town in the northern part of Gaines County in 1915. The community was originally known as Blythe for the Blythe Ranch, but it became Seagraves for an official with the Santa Fe Railroad. A fire in 1928 destroyed everything on Main Street. The single surviving building is now the Gaines County Museum & Art Center. Quanah Parker was born twenty miles east of here at Cedar Lake, the largest salt lake on the plains.

Denver City lies fifteen miles west of Seagraves on Texas 83 and 214 (north). This was rangeland until the Wassom Oil Field arrived in 1935. That same year, Denver City popped up in the center of the oil field.

Seminole

There are some Indian watering holes south and west of here called Seminole Wells. So in 1905 Seminole took the same name as the wells. The town was primarily a trading post until the Midland & Northwestern Railroad arrived in 1918. Today the town balances its economy between oil and agriculture.

Andrews

When the county seat was organized in 1910, Andrews was chosen. The town serves as a retail and banking center primarily for oil and livestock interests. It was named for Richard "Big Dick" Andrews, a man of immense size and strength. He was also an Indian fighter and Texas revolutionary killed in the battle of Concepcion in 1835. A Permian Basin oil discovery called Deep Rock Pool came in during 1930, and for a while at least Andrews had one of the wealthiest school districts in the nation.

BIBLIOGRAPHY

The Best of Texas

Serious students of Texas history should read the monthly magazine *Texas Highways* and join the Texas State Historical Association, which is open to buffs and professionals alike. And those interested in learning about ethnic origins of Texans should keep in mind that the Institute of Texas Cultures in San Antonio is not only a marvelous museum, but it also publishes pamphlets on Afro-American Texans, Greek Texans, Chinese Texans, and German Texans, to mention but a few.

The following is a list of some of my favorite Texas books. There are hundreds more.

Abernethy, Francis E., ed. *The Bounty of Texas*. Texas Folklore Society, 1990.

Adams, Ramon F. *The Old-Time Cowhand*. University of Nebraska Press, 1961.

Anders, Evan. *Boss Rule in South Texas*. University of Texas Press, 1982.

Baker, T. Lindsay. *Lighthouses of Texas*. Texas A&M, 1991.

———. *Building the Lone Star: An Illustrated Guide to Historic Sites*. Texas A&M, 1986.

———. *Ghost Towns of Texas*. University of Oklahoma Press, 1986.

Barr, Alwyn. *Black Texans: A History of Negroes in Texas, 1528-1971*. Jenkins, 1973.

Blodgett, Jan. *Land of Bright Promise: Advertising the Texas Panhandle and South Plains, 1870-1917*. University of Texas Press, 1988.

Bode, Elroy. *This Favored Place*. Shearer Publications, 1983.

Bones, Jim, Jr. *Texas West of the Pecos*. Texas A&M, 1981.

Brice, Donaly E. *The Great Comanche Raid: Boldest Indian Attack of the Texas Republic*. Eakin, 1987.

Burka, Paul. *Texas, Our Texas*. Texas Monthly, 1986.

Chariton, Wallace O. *Unsolved Texas Mysteries*. Wordware Publishing, 1991.

Cisneros, José. *Riders Across the Centuries: Horsemen of the Spanish Borderlands*. Texas Western Press, 1984.

Davis, John L. *Exploration in Texas, Ancient & Otherwise*. University of Texas Press, 1984.

Dearen, Patrick. *Castle Gap on the Pecos Frontier*. Texas Christian University Press, 1988.

Dooley, Claude W., comp. *Why Stop?* Lone Star Legends Company, 1978.

Driskill, Frank A., and Noel Grisham. *Historic Churches of Texas*. Eakin, 1980.

Faulk, Odie B. *The Last Years of Spanish Texas, 1778-1821*. Mouton, 1964.

Fehrenbach, T. R. *Texas: A Salute from Above*. Portland House, 1990.

———. *Comanches: The Destruction of a People*. Knopf, 1974.

———. *Lone Star: A History of Texas and the Texans*. Macmillan, 1968.

Fox, Daniel E. *Traces of Texas History: Archaeological Evidence of the Past 450 Years*. Corona, 1983.

Gomez, Arthur R. *A Most Singular Country: A History of Occupation in the Big Bend*. Brigham Young University, 1990.

Guthrie, Keith. *Texas Forgotten Ports*. Eakin, 1988.

Haley, James L. *Texas: An Album of History*. Doubleday, 1985.

Hardin, John Wesley. *The Life of John Wesley Hardin as written by himself*. University of Oklahoma Press, 1961.

History of the Cattlemen of Texas. Texas State Historical Assn., 1991.

Hogan, William Ransom. *The Texas Republic: A Social and Economic History*. University of Texas Press, 1990.

Hunter, J. Marvin, ed. and comp. *The Trail Drivers of Texas*. University of Texas Press, 1985.

Jordan, Terry G. *Texas Graveyards*. University of Texas, 1982.

———. *Texas Log Buildings: A Folk Architecture*. University of Texas Press, 1978.

———. *German Seed in Texas Soil*. University of Texas Press, 1966.

Jameson, W. C. *Buried Treasures of Texas*. August House, 1991.

Jonathan, Eisen, and Harold Straughn. *Unknown Texas*. Collier, 1988.

Lamar, Howard R. *Texas Crossings: The Lone Star State and the American Far West, 1836-1986.* University of Texas Press, 1991.

Loughmiller, Campbell and Lynn, comps. *Big Thicket Legacy.* University of Texas Press, 1977.

Lynch, Gerald. *Roughnecks, Drillers, and Tool Pushers.* University of Texas Press, 1987.

Marks, Paula Mitchell. *Turn Your Eyes Toward Texas: Pioneers Sam and Mary Maverick.* Texas A&M, 1989.

Martin, Howard. *Myths & Folktales of the Alabama-Coushatta Indians of Texas.* Encino Press, 1977.

Mayhall, Mildred P. *Indian Wars of Texas.* Texian Press, 1965.

McComb, David G. *Texas: A Modern History.* University of Texas Press, 1989.

———. *Galveston: A History.* University of Texas Press, 1986.

———. *Houston: A History.* University of Texas Press, 1981.

Merk, Frederick. *Slavery and the Annexation of Texas.* Knopf, 1972.

Metz, Leon C. *Border: The U.S-Mexico Line.* Mangan Books, 1989.

Myres, Samuel D. *The Permian Basin: Petroleum Empire of the Southwest.* 2 vols. Permian Press, 1973.

Nance, Joseph M. *Attack and Counter-Attack: The Texas-Mexican Frontier, 1842.* University of Texas Press, 1964.

———. *After San Jacinto: The Texas-Mexican Frontier, 1836-1841.* University of Texas Press, 1963.

Neighbours, Kenneth F. *Robert Simpson Neighbors and the Texas Frontier, 1836-1859.* Texian Press, 1975.

Ornish, Natalie. *Pioneer Jewish Texans.* Texas Heritage, 1989.

Peña, José Enrique de la. *With Santa Anna in Texas: A Personal Narrative of the Revolution.* Texas A&M, 1975.

Ramsdell, Charles W. *Reconstruction in Texas.* University of Texas Press, 1970.

Rathjen, Frederick W. *The Texas Panhandle Frontier.* University of Texas Press, 1973.

Richter, William L. *The Army in Texas During Reconstruction, 1865-1870.* Texas A&M, 1987.

Robertson, Pauline and R.L. *Panhandle Pilgrimage.* Paramount Publishing, 1989.

———. *Cowman's Country: Fifty Frontier Ranches in the Texas Panhandle.* Paramount Publishing, 1981.

Robinson, Charles M. *Frontier Forts of Texas.* Gulf Publishing, 1986.

———. *Gone From Texas: Our Lost Architectural History.* Texas A&M, 1981.

Selcer, Richard F. *Hell's Half Acre.* Texas Christian University Press, 1991.

Silverthorne, Elizabeth. *Plantation Life in Texas.* Texas A&M, 1986.

Simpson, Harold B., coord. *Frontier Forts of Texas.* Texian Press, 1966.

Sonnichsen, C. L. *Pass of the North: Four Centuries on the Rio Grande.* Texas Western Press, 1968.

———. *I'll Die Before I'll Run: The Story of the Great Feuds of Texas.* Devin-Adair, 1962.

———. *Ten Texas Feuds.* University of New Mexico Press, 1957.

Spearing, Darwin. *Roadside Geology of Texas.* Mountain Press, 1991.

St. Clair, Kathleen and Clifton. *Little Towns of Texas.* Jayroe, 1982.

Stephens, A. Ray, and William M. Holmes. *Historical Atlas of Texas.* University of Oklahoma Press, 1989.

Syers, Ed. *Backroads of History.* Gulf, 1979.

Thompson, Jerry D. *Warm Weather & Bad Whiskey.* Texas Western Press, 1991.

———. *Sabers on the Rio Grande.* Presidial, 1974.

Timmons, W. H. *El Paso: A Borderlands History.* Texas Western Press, 1990.

Truett, Joe C., and Daniel W. Lay. *Land of Bears and Honey: A Natural History of East Texas.* University of Texas Press, 1984.

Wallace, Ernest. *The Howling of Coyotes: Reconstruction Efforts to Divide Texas.* Texas A&M, 1979.

Webb, Walter Prescott. *The Texas Rangers: A Century of Frontier Defense.* Houghton Mifflin, 1935.

Webb, Walter P., and H. Bailey Carroll, eds. *Handbook of Texas.* Texas State Historical Association, 1952.

Weddle, Robert S. *The San Saba Mission: Spanish Pivot in Texas.* University of Texas Press, 1964.

Welch, June Rayfield. *Historic Sites of Texas.* G.L.A., 1972.

Whisenhunt, Donald W. *Chronology of Texas History.* Eakin, 1986.

Williams, Clayton W. *Texas' Last Frontier: Fort Stockton and the Trans-Pecos.* Texas A&M, 1982.

Williams, J. W. *Old Texas Trails.* Eakin, 1979.

Wooster, Robert. *Soldiers, Sutlers, and Settlers: Garrison Life on the Texas Frontier.* Texas A&M, 1987.

ACKNOWLEDGMENTS

First, I thank all the libraries and librarians in Texas. I am also grateful to the Institute of Texan Cultures in San Antonio, where I obtained many photos.

The *Roadside History of Texas* became such an involved, complex project that several people died before the book was released. One was David Flaccus, founder of Mountain Press. As two strangers in San Diego, David and I sat down beside one another at a hotel breakfast counter. I was looking for a writing project, and David needed someone to research Texas. The result was a friendship and partnership.

Francis and Roberta Fugate, who wrote Roadside Histories of New Mexico and Oklahoma for Mountain Press, were invaluable in providing advice and counsel regarding Texas. They were longtime treasured friends who also didn't lived to see the final result.

Dan Greer, the editor at Mountain Press, has been patient, understanding, and helpful.

Special friends Frank Mangan, Myrna Zanetell, and Martha Peterson read the manuscript and saved me from numerous fumbles. William Schilling, my father-in-law, was also invaluable in rooting out mistakes and typos.

Finally, I thank my wife, Cheryl. She made our house a pleasant place to write.

INDEX

448